ACL-PASCAL Workshop on Textual Entailment and Paraphrasing 2007

Held in conjunction with ACL 2007

Prague, Czech Republic
28-29 June 2007

ISBN: 978-1-61738-523-0

Printed from e-media with permission by:

Curran Associates, Inc.
57 Morehouse Lane
Red Hook, NY 12571
www.proceedings.com

Some format issues inherent in the e-media version may also appear in this print version.

Printed by Curran Associates, Inc. (2010)

Association for Computational Linguistics
209 N. Eighth Street
Stroudsburg, Pennsylvania 18360

Phone: 1-570-476-8006
Fax: 1-570-476-0860

acl@aclweb.org

PREFACE

Recognizing and generating textual entailment and paraphrases are regarded as important technologies in a broad range of NLP applications, including, information extraction, summarization, question answering, information retrieval, machine translation and text generation. Both textual entailment and paraphrasing address relevant aspects of natural language semantics. Entailment is a directional relation between two expressions in which one of them implies the other, whereas paraphrase is a relation in which two expressions convey essentially the same meaning. Indeed, paraphrase can be defined as bi-directional entailment. While it may be debatable how such semantic definitions can be made well-founded, in practice we have already seen evidence that such knowledge is essential for many applications.

There have been two lines of workshops in this field. One is a series of three workshops on paraphrasing -- in Tokyo 2001, in Sapporo at ACL-2003 and in Jeju at IJCNLP-2005. The other is the Workshop on Empirical Modeling of Semantic Equivalence and Entailment (at ACL-2005), and two workshops of the previous PASCAL Recognizing Textual Entailment (RTE) Challenges (2005 and 2006). We combine those two lines of similar effort together at this workshop in order to see the convergence of the field and exchange ideas among a wider audience.

The workshop has two parts. The first is the general session where submission was open, which covers a wide variety of topics including knowledge formalisms and resources and techniques for acquiring and utilizing knowledge. The second part is the concluding workshop of the 3rd PASCAL RTE Challenge, the primary benchmark for textual entailment recognition systems (see the RTE-3 organizers paper). The workshop program includes the general session papers and selected presentations and a poster session of participating RTE-3 systems.

We appreciate the contributions of all presenters and participants.

Workshop Chairs,

General Session:
Satoshi Sekine (New York University)
Kentaro Inui (Nara Institute of Science and Technology)

PASCAL RTE-3 Challenge:
Ido Dagan (Bar Ilan University)
Bill Dolan (Microsoft Research)
Danilo Giampiccolo (CELCT)
Bernardo Magnini (ITC-irst)

Organizers

Chairs:

General Session:

Satoshi Sekine, New York University
Kentaro Inui, Nara Institute of Science and Technology

PASCAL RTE-3 Challenge:

Ido Dagan, Bar Ilan University
Bill Dolan, Microsoft Research
Danilo Giampiccolo, CELCT
Bernardo Magnini, ITC-irst

Program Committee:

Caroline Brun, Xerox Research Centre Europe, France
Johan Bos, University of Rome "La Sapienza"
Robert Dale, Macquarie University
Mark Dras, Macquarie University
Anette Frank, University of Heidelberg
Ralph Grishman, New York University
Sanda Harabagiu, University of Texas at Dallas
Graeme Hirst, University of Toronto
Yves Lepage, Universite de Caen
Dekang Lin, Google
Katja Markert, University of Leeds
Chris Manning, Stanford University
Rada Mihalcea, University of North Texas
Dan Moldovan, University of Texas at Dallas
Patrick Pantel, ISI
Kiyonori Ohtake, ATR
Ellen Riloff, University of Utah
Dan Roth, University of Illinois at Urbana-Champaign
Satoshi Sato, Nagoya University
Hinrich Schuetze, University of Stuttgart
Donia Scott, Open University
Kentaro Torisawa, JAIST
Lucy Vanderwende, Microsoft Research
Kazuhide Yamamoto, Nagaoka University of Technology
Fabio Zanzotto, University of Rome "Tor Vergata"

Invited Speaker:

Oren Etzioni, University of Washington

Website:

http://nlp.cs.nyu.edu/WTEP

Table of Contents

Conference Program

Thursday, June 28, 2007

2:00–2:05 Introduction

RTE SESSION

2:05–2:30 *The Third PASCAL Recognizing Textual Entailment Challenge*
Danilo Giampiccolo, Bernardo Magnini, Ido Dagan and Bill Dolan

Linguistic-Semantic Systems

2:30–2:55 *A Semantic Approach To Textual Entailment: System Evaluation and Task Analysis*
Aljoscha Burchardt, Nils Reiter, Stefan Thater and Anette Frank

2:55–3:20 *Precision-focused Textual Inference*
Daniel Bobrow, Dick Crouch, Tracy Halloway King, Cleo Condoravdi, Lauri Karttunen, Rowan Nairn, Valeria de Paiva and Annie Zaenen

3:20–3:45 *COGEX at RTE 3*
Marta Tatu and Dan Moldovan

COFFEE BREAK

GENERAL SESSION–Resources for Entailment

4:15–4:40 *A Corpus of Fine-Grained Entailment Relations*
Rodney D. Nielsen and Wayne Ward

4:40–5:10 RTE Poster Booster (2 min presentation each)

5:10–6:15 RTE Poster Session

Recognizing Textual Entailment Using Sentence Similarity based on Dependency Tree Skeletons
Rui Wang and Günter Neumann

Learning Textual Entailment using SVMs and String Similarity Measures
Prodromos Malakasiotis and Ion Androutsopoulos

Thursday, June 28, 2007 (continued)

Textual Entailment Through Extended Lexical Overlap and Lexico-Semantic Matching
Rod Adams, Gabriel Nicolae, Cristina Nicolae and Sanda Harabagiu

Friday, June 29, 2007

RTE–Transfromation-based systems

9:00–9:25 *Hypothesis Transformation and Semantic Variability Rules Used in Recognizing Textual Entailment*
Adrian Iftene and Alexandra Balahur-Dobrescu

9:25–9:50 *Semantic Inference at the Lexical-Syntactic Level for Textual Entailment Recognition*
Roy Bar-Haim, Ido Dagan, Iddo Greental, Idan Szpektor and Moshe Friedman

9:50–10:15 *An Extensible Probabilistic Transformation-based Approach to the Third Recognizing Textual Entailment Challenge*
Stefan Harmeling

10:15–10:45 Hoa Trang Dang, Ellen Voorhees, Christopher Manning, Dan Moldovan: Pilot Task Overview

COFFEE BREAK

GENERAL SESSION–Paraphrase Generation

11:15–11:40 *Mutaphrase: Paraphrasing with FrameNet*
Michael Ellsworth and Adam Janin

11:40–12:05 *A Compositional Approach toward Dynamic Phrasal Thesaurus*
Atsushi Fujita, Shuhei Kato, Naoki Kato and Satoshi Sato

12:05–1:00 Invited Talk–Oren Etzioni: Machine Reading and Open Information Extraction

Friday, June 29, 2007 (continued)

LUNCH BREAK

RTE-Other Approaches

2:30–2:55 *Machine Learning Based Semantic Inference: Experiments and Observations at RTE-3*
Baoli Li, Joseph Irwin, Ernest V. Garcia and Ashwin Ram

2:55–3:20 *Learning Alignments and Leveraging Natural Logic*
Nathanael Chambers, Daniel Cer, Trond Grenager, David Hall, Chloe Kiddon, Bill MacCartney, Marie-Catherine de Marneffe, Daniel Ramage, Eric Yeh and Christopher D. Manning

3:20-3:45 *A Discourse Commitment-Based Framework for Recognizing Textual Entailment*
Andrew Hickl and Jeremy Bensley

COFFEE BREAK

GENERAL SESSION–Entailment and Paraphrase Acquisition

4:15–4:40 *Biology Based Alignments of Paraphrases for Sentence Compression*
João Cordeiro, Gaël Dias and Guillaume Cleuziou

4:40–5:05 *A first order semantic approach to adjectival inference*
Marilisa Amoia and Claire Gardent

5:05–5:30 *Natural Logic for Textual Inference*
Bill MacCartney and Christopher D. Manning

5:30–6:15 Open discussion–what next?

The Third PASCAL Recognizing Textual Entailment Challenge

Danilo Giampiccolo
CELCT
Via alla Cascata 56/c
38100 POVO TN
giampiccolo@celct.it

Bernardo Magnini
FBK-ITC
Via Sommarive 18,
38100 Povo TN
magnini@itc.it

Ido Dagan
Computer Science Department
Bar-Ilan University
Ramat Gan 52900, Israel
dagan@macs.biu.ac.il

Bill Dolan
Microsoft Research
Redmond, WA, 98052, USA
billdol@microsoft.com

Abstract

This paper presents the Third PASCAL Recognising Textual Entailment Challenge (RTE-3), providing an overview of the dataset creating methodology and the submitted systems. In creating this year's dataset, a number of longer texts were introduced to make the challenge more oriented to realistic scenarios. Additionally, a pool of resources was offered so that the participants could share common tools. A pilot task was also set up, aimed at differentiating unknown entailments from identified contradictions and providing justifications for overall system decisions. 26 participants submitted 44 runs, using different approaches and generally presenting new entailment models and achieving higher scores than in the previous challenges.

1.1 The RTE challenges

The goal of the RTE challenges has been to create a benchmark task dedicated to textual entailment – recognizing that the meaning of one text is entailed, i.e. can be inferred, by another[1]. In the recent years, this task has raised great interest since applied semantic inference concerns many practical Natural Language Processing (NLP) applications, such as Question Answering (QA), Information Extraction (IE), Summarization, Machine Translation and Paraphrasing, and certain types of queries in Information Retrieval (IR). More specifically, the RTE challenges have aimed to focus research and evaluation on this common underlying semantic inference task and separate it from other problems that different NLP applications need to handle. For example, in addition to textual entailment, QA systems need to handle issues such as answer retrieval and question type recognition.

By separating out the general problem of textual entailment from these task-specific problems, progress on semantic inference for many application areas can be promoted. Hopefully, research on textual entailment will finally lead to the development of entailment "engines", which can be used as a standard module in many applications (similar to the role of part-of-speech taggers and syntactic parsers in current NLP applications).

In the following sections, a detailed description of RTE-3 is presented. After a quick review

[1] The task was first defined by Dagan and Glickman (2004).

Proceedings of the Workshop on Textual Entailment and Paraphrasing, pages 1–9,
Prague, June 2007.

of the previous challenges (1.2), section 2 describes the preparation of the dataset. In section 3 the evaluation process and the results are presented, together with an analysis of the performance of the participating systems.

1.2 The First and Second RTE Challenges

The first RTE challenge[2] aimed to provide the NLP community with a new benchmark to test progress in recognizing textual entailment, and to compare the achievements of different groups. This goal proved to be of great interest, and the community's response encouraged the gradual expansion of the scope of the original task.

The Second RTE challenge[3] built on the success of the first, with 23 groups from around the world (as compared to 17 for the first challenge) submitting the results of their systems. Representatives of participating groups presented their work at the PASCAL Challenges Workshop in April 2006 in Venice, Italy. The event was successful and the number of participants and their contributions to the discussion demonstrated that Textual Entailment is a quickly growing field of NLP research. In addition, the workshops spawned an impressive number of publications in major conferences, with more work in progress. Another encouraging sign of the growing interest in the RTE challenge was represented by the increase in the number of downloads of the challenge datasets, with about 150 registered downloads for the RTE-2 development set.

1.3 The Third Challenge

RTE-3 followed the same basic structure of the previous campaigns, in order to facilitate the participation of newcomers and to allow "veterans" to assess the improvements of their systems in a comparable test exercise. Nevertheless, some innovations were introduced, on the one hand to make the challenge more stimulating and, on the other, to encourage collaboration between system developers. In particular, a limited number of longer texts, i.e. up to a paragraph in length, were incorporated in order to move toward more comprehensive scenarios, which incorporate the need for discourse analysis. However, the majority of examples remained similar to those in the previous challenges, providing pairs with relatively short texts.

Another innovation was represented by a resource pool[4], where contributors had the possibility to share the resources they used. In fact, one of the key conclusions at the second RTE Challenge Workshop was that entailment modeling requires vast knowledge resources that correspond to different types of entailment reasoning. Moreover, entailment systems also utilize general NLP tools such as POS taggers, parsers and named-entity recognizers, sometimes posing specialized requirements to such tools. In response to these demands, the RTE Resource Pool was built, which may serve as a portal and forum for publicizing and tracking resources, and reporting on their use.

In addition, an optional pilot task, called "*Extending the Evaluation of Inferences from Texts*" was set up by the US National Institute of Standards and Technology (NIST), in order to explore two other sub-tasks closely related to textual entailment: differentiating unknown entailments from identified contradictions and providing justifications for system decisions. In the first sub-task, the idea was to drive systems to make more precise informational distinctions, taking a three-way decision between "YES", "NO" and "UNKNOWN", so that a hypothesis being unknown on the basis of a text would be distinguished from a hypothesis being shown false/contradicted by a text. As for the other subtask, the goal for providing justifications for decisions was to explore how eventual users of tools incorporating entailment can be made to understand how decisions were reached by a system, as users are unlikely to trust a system that gives no explanation for its decisions. The pilot task exploited the existing RTE-3 Challenge infrastructure and evaluation process by using the same test set, while utilizing human assessments for the new sub-tasks.

---

[2] http://www.pascal-network.org/Challenges/RTE/.

[3] http://www.pascal-network.org/Challenges/RTE2./

4 http://aclweb.org/aclwiki/index.php?title=Textual_Entailment_Resource_Pool.

TASK	TEXT	HYPOTHESIS	ENTAILMENT
IE	At the same time the Italian digital rights group, Electronic Frontiers Italy, has asked the nation's government to investigate Sony over its use of anti-piracy software.	Italy's government investigates Sony.	NO
IE	Parviz Davudi was representing Iran at a meeting of the Shanghai Co-operation Organisation (SCO), the fledgling association that binds Russia, China and four former Soviet republics of central Asia together to fight terrorism	China is a member of SCO.	YES
IR	Between March and June, scientific observers say, up to 300,000 seals are killed. In Canada, seal-hunting means jobs, but opponents say it is vicious and endangers the species, also threatened by global warming	Hunting endangers seal species.	YES
IR	The Italian parliament may approve a draft law allowing descendants of the exiled royal family to return home. The family was banished after the Second World War because of the King's collusion with the fascist regime, but moves were introduced this year to allow their return.	Italian royal family returns home.	NO
QA	Aeschylus is often called the father of Greek tragedy; he wrote the earliest complete plays which survive from ancient Greece. He is known to have written more than 90 plays, though only seven survive. The most famous of these are the trilogy known as Orestia. Also well-known are The Persians and Prometheus Bound.	"The Persians" was written by Aeschylus.	YES
SUM	A Pentagon committee and the congressionally chartered Iraq Study Group have been preparing reports for Bush, and Iran has asked the presidents of Iraq and Syria to meet in Tehran.	Bush will meet the presidents of Iraq and Syria in Tehran.	NO

Table 1: Some examples taken from the Development Set.

2 The RTE-3 Dataset

2.1 Overview

The textual entailment recognition task required the participating systems to decide, given two text snippets *t* and *h*, whether *t* entails *h*. Textual entailment is defined as a directional relation between two text fragments, called *text* (*t*, the entailing text), and hypothesis (*h*, the entailed text), so that a human being, with common understanding of language and common background knowledge, can infer that *h* is most likely true on the basis of the content of *t*.

As in the previous challenges, the RTE-3 dataset consisted of 1600 text-hypothesis pairs, equally divided into a development set and a test set. While the length of the hypotheses (*h*) was the same as in the past datasets, a certain number of texts (*t*) were longer than in previous datasets, up to a paragraph. The longer texts were marked as L, after being selected automatically when exceeding 270 bytes. In the test set they were about 17% of the total.

As in RTE-2, four applications – namely IE, IR, QA and SUM – were considered as settings or contexts for the pairs generation (see 2.2 for a detailed description). 200 pairs were selected for each application in each dataset. Although the datasets were supposed to be perfectly balanced, the number of negative examples were slightly higher in both development and test sets (51.50% and 51.25% respectively; this was unintentional). Positive entailment examples, where *t* entailed *h*, were annotated *YES*; the negative ones, where entailment did not hold, *NO*. Each pair was annotated with its related task (IE/IR/QA/SUM) and entailment judgment (YES/NO, obviously released only in the development set). Table 1 shows some examples taken from the development set.

The examples in the dataset were based mostly on outputs (both correct and incorrect) of Web-based systems. In order to avoid copyright problems, input data was limited to either what had already been publicly released by official competitions or else was drawn from freely available sources such as WikiNews and Wikipedia.

In choosing the pairs, the following judgment criteria and guidelines were considered:

§ As entailment is a directional relation, the hypothesis must be entailed by the given text, but the text need not be entailed by the hypothesis.
§ The hypothesis must be fully entailed by the text. Judgment must be NO if the hypothesis includes parts that cannot be inferred from the text.
§ Cases in which inference is very probable (but not completely certain) were judged as YES.
§ Common world knowledge was assumed, e.g. the capital of a country is situated in that country, the prime minister of a state is also a citizen of that state, and so on.

2.2 Pair Collection

As in RTE-2, human annotators generated *t-h* pairs within 4 application settings.

The IE task was inspired by the Information Extraction (and Relation Extraction) application, where texts and structured templates were replaced by *t-h* pairs. As in the 2006 campaign, the pairs were generated using four different approaches:

1) Hypotheses were taken from the relations tested in the ACE-2004 RDR task, while texts were extracted from the outputs of actual IE systems, which were provided with relevant news articles. Correctly extracted instances were used to generate positive examples and incorrect instances to generate negative examples.
2) The same procedure was followed using output of IE systems on the dataset of the MUC-4 TST3 task, in which the events are acts of terrorism.
3) The annotated MUC-4 dataset and the news articles were also used to manually generate entailment pairs based on ACE relations.
4) Hypotheses corresponding to relations not found in the ACE and MUC datasets were used both to be given to IE systems and to manually generate *t-h* pairs from collected news articles. Examples of these relations, taken from various semantic fields, were "X beat Y", "X invented Y", "X steal Y" etc.

The common aim of all these processes was to simulate the need of IE systems to recognize that the given text indeed entails the semantic relation that is expected to hold between the candidate template slot fillers.

In the IR (Information Retrieval) application setting, the hypotheses were propositional IR queries, which specify some statement, e.g. "*robots are used to find avalanche victims*". The hypotheses were adapted and simplified from standard IR evaluation datasets (TREC and CLEF). Texts (*t*) that did or did not entail the hypotheses were selected from documents retrieved by different search engines (e.g. Google, Yahoo and MSN) for each hypothesis. In this application setting it was assumed that relevant documents (from an IR perspective) should entail the given propositional hypothesis.

For the QA (Question Answering) task, annotators used questions taken from the datasets of official QA competitions, such as TREC QA and QA@CLEF datasets, and the corresponding answers extracted from the Web by actual QA systems. Then they transformed the question-answer pairs into *t-h* pairs as follows:

§ An answer term of the expected answer type was picked from the answer passage - either a correct or an incorrect one.
§ The question was turned into an affirmative sentence plugging in the answer term.
§ *t-h* pairs were generate, using the affirmative sentences as hypotheses (*h's*) and the original answer passages as texts (*t*'s).

For example, given the question *"How high is Mount Everest?"* and a text (*t*) *"The above mentioned expedition team comprising of 10 members was permitted to climb 8848m. high Mt. Everest from Normal Route for the period of 75 days from 15 April, 2007 under the leadership of Mr. Wolf Herbert of Austria"*, the annotator, extracting the piece of information "8848m." from the text, would turn the question into an the affirmative sentence *"Mount Everest is 8848m high"*, generating a positive entailment pair. This process simulated the need of a QA system to verify that the retrieved passage text actually entailed the provided answer.

In the SUM (Summarization) setting, the entailment pairs were generated using two procedures.

In the first one, *t's* and *h's* were sentences taken from a news document cluster, a collection of news articles that describe the same news item. Annotators were given the output of multi-document summarization systems -including the document clusters and the summary generated for each cluster. Then they picked sentence pairs with high lexical overlap, preferably where at least one of the sentences was taken from the summary (this sentence usually played the role of *t*). For positive examples, the hypothesis was simplified by removing sentence parts, until it was fully entailed by *t*. Negative examples were simplified in a similar manner. In alternative, *"pyramids"* produced for the experimental evaluation mehod in DUC 2005 (Passonneau et al. 2005) were exploited. In this new evaluation method, humans select subsentential content units (SCUs) in several manually produced summaries on a subject, and collocate them in a "pyramid", which has at the top the SCUs with the higher frequency, i.e. those which are present in most summaries. Each SCU is identified by a label, a sentence in natural language which expresses the content. Afterwards, the annotators individuate the SCUs present in summaries generated automatically (called *peers*), and link them to the ones present in the pyramid, in order to assign each peer a weight. In this way, the SCUs in the automatic summaries linked to the SCUs in the higher tiers of the pyramid are assigned a heavier weight than those at the bottom. For the SUM setting, the RTE-3 annotators selected relevant passages from the peers and used them as T's, meanwhile the labels of the corresponding SCUs were used as H's. Small adjustments were allowed, whenever the texts were not grammatically acceptable. This process simulated the need of a summarization system to identify information redundancy, which should be avoided in the summary.

2.3 Final dataset

Each pair of the dataset was judged by three annotators. As in previous challenges, pairs on which the annotators disagreed were filtered-out.

On the test set, the average agreement between each pair of annotators who shared at least 100 examples was 87.8%, with an average Kappa level of 0.75, regarded as substantial agreement according to Landis and Koch (1997).

19.2 % of the pairs in the dataset were removed from the test set due to disagreement. The disagreement was generally due to the fact that the *h* was more specific than the *t*, for example because it contained more information, or made an absolute assertion where *t* proposed only a personal opinion. In addition, 9.4 % of the remaining pairs were discarded, as they seemed controversial, too difficult, or too similar when compared to other pairs.

As far as the *texts* extracted from the web are concerned, spelling and punctuation errors were sometimes fixed by the annotators, but no major change was allowed, so that the language could be grammatically and stylistically imperfect. The hypotheses were finally double-checked by a native English speaker.

3 The RTE-3 Challenge

3.1 Evaluation measures

The evaluation of all runs submitted in RTE-3 was automatic. The judgments (classifications) returned by the system were compared to the Gold Standard compiled by the human assessors. The main evaluation measure was *accuracy,* i.e. the percentage of matching judgments.

For systems that provided a confidence-ranked list of the pairs, in addition to the YES/NO judgment, an Average Precision measure was also computed. This measure evaluates the ability of systems to rank all the T-H pairs in the test set according to their entailment confidence (in decreasing order from the most certain entailment to the least certain). Average precision is computed as the average of the system's precision values at all points in the ranked list in which recall increases, that is at all points in the ranked list for which the gold standard annotation is YES, or, more formally:

$$\frac{1}{R}\sum_{i=1}^{n}\frac{E(i)\times\#\,EntailmentUpToPair(i)}{i} \quad (1)$$

where n is the number of the pairs in the test set, R is the total number of positive pairs in the test set, $E(i)$ is 1 if the i-th pair is positive and 0 otherwise, and i ranges over the pairs, ordered by their ranking.

In other words, the more the system was confident that t entails h, the higher was the ranking of the pair. A perfect ranking would have placed all the positive pairs (for which the entailment holds) before all the negative ones, yielding an average precision value of 1.

3.2 Submitted systems

Twenty-six teams participated in the third challenge, three more than in previous year. Table 2 presents the list of the results of each submitted runs and the components used by the systems. Overall, we noticed a move toward deep approaches, with a general consolidation of approaches based on the syntactic structure of Text and Hypothesis. There is an evident increase of systems using some form of logical inferences (at least seven systems). However, these approaches, with few notably exceptions, do not seem to be consolidated enough, as several systems show results not still at the state of art (e.g. Natural Logic introduced by Chambers et al.). For many systems an open issue is the availability and integration of different and complex semantic resources-

A more extensive and fine grained use of specific semantic phenomena is also emerging. As an example, Tatu and Moldovan carry on a sophisticated analysis of named entities, in particular Person names, distinguishing first names from last names. Some form of relation extraction, either through manually built patterns (Chambers et al.) or through the use of an information extraction system (Hickl and Bensley) have been introduced this year, even if still on a small scale (i.e. few relations).

On the other hand, RTE-3 confirmed that both machine learning using lexical-syntactic features and transformation-based approaches on dependency representations are well consolidated techniques to address textual entailment. The extension of transformation-based approaches toward probabilistic settings is an interesting direction investigated by some systems (e.g. Harmeling). On the side of "light" approaches to textual entailment, Malakasiotis and Androutpoulos provide a useful baseline for the task (0.61%) using only POS tagging and then applying string-based measures to estimate the similarity between Text and Hypothesis.

As far as resources are concerned, lexical databases (mostly WordNet and DIRT) are still widely used. Extended WordNet is also a common resource (for instance in Iftene and Balahur-Dobrescu) and the Extended Wordnet Knowledge Base has been successfully used in (Tatu and Moldovan). Verb-oriented resources are also largely present in several systems, including Framenet (e.g. Burchardt et al.), Verbnet (Bobrow et al.) and Propbank (e.g. Adams et al.). It seems that the use of the Web as a resource is more limited when compared to the previous RTE workshop. However, as in RTE-2, the use of large semantic resources is still a crucial factor affecting the performance of systems (see, for instance, the use of a large corpus of entailment examples in Hickl and Bensley).

Finally, an interesting aspect is that, stimulated by the percentage of longer texts included this year, a number of participating systems addressed anaphora resolution (e.g. Delmonte, Bar-Haim et al., Iftene and Balahur-Dobrescu).

3.3 Results

The accuracy achieved by the participating systems ranges from 49% to 80% (considering the best run of each group), while most of the systems obtained a score in between 59% and 66%. One submission, Hickl and Bensley achieved 80% accuracy, scoring 8% higher than the second system (Tatu and Moldovan, 72%), and obtaining the best absolute result achieved in the three RTE challenges.

First Author	Accuracy	Average precision	System Components								
			Lexical Relation, WordNet	n-gram\word similarity	Syntactic Match-ing\Aligning	Semantic Role Labeling\ Framenet\Probank, Verbnet	Logical Inference	Corpus/ Web-based Statistics, LSA	ML Classification	Anaphora resolution	Entailment Corpora – DIRT Background Knowledge
Adams	0.6700		X	X				X	X		
Bar-Haim	0.6112	0.6118	X		X			X		X	X
	0.5837	0.6093	X		X			X		X	
Baral	0.4963	0.5364	X				X				X
Blake	0.6050	0.5897	X		X				X		
	0.6587	0.6096	X		X				X		
Bobrow	0.5112	0.5720	X			X	X				
	0.5150	0.5807	X			X	X				
Burchardt	0.6250		X		X	X					
	0.6262										
Burek	0.5500			X				X			
	0.5500	0.5514									
Chambers	0.6050	0.6341	X		X		X		X	X	
	0.6362	0.6527	X		X		X		X	X	
Clark	0.5088	0.4961	X				X				X
	0.4725	0.4961	X				X				X
Delmonte	0.5875	0.5830	X		X	X	X			X	
Ferrandez	0.6563		X	X	X						
	0.6375										
Ferrés	0.6062		X	X					X		
	0.6150		X	X					X		
Harmling	0.5600	0.5813	X		X				X		
	0.5775	0.5952	X		X				X		
Hickl	0.8000	0.8815	X	X			X		X	X	X
Iftene	0.6913		X		X						X
	0.6913		X		X						X
Li	0.6400		X	X					X		
	0.6488										
Litkowski	0.6125										
Malakasiotis	0.6175	0.6808		X					X		
Marsi	0.5913				X						X
Montejo-Ràez	0.5888		X	X	X				X		
	0.6038		X	X	X				X		
Rodrigo	0.6238		X	X	X				X		
	0.6312		X	X	X				X		
Roth	0.6262		X	X							X
	0.5975				X					X	
Settembre	0.6100	0.6195	X	X					X		
	0.6262	0.6274	X	X					X		
Tatu	0.7225	0.6942	X				X			X	X
	0.7175	0.6797	X				X			X	
Wang	0.6650				X				X		
	0.6687										
Zanzotto	0.6675	0.6674	X		X				X		
	0.6575	0.6732	X		X				X		

Table 2: Submission results and components of the systems.

As far as the per-task results are concerned, the trend registered in RTE-2 was confirmed, in that there was a marked difference in the performances obtained in different task settings.

In fact, the average accuracy achieved in the QA setting (0.71) was 20 points higher than that achieved in the IE setting (0.52); the average accuracy in the IR and Sum settings was 0.66 and 0.58 respectively. In RTE-2 the best results were achieved in SUM, while the lower score was always recorded in IE. As already pointed out by Bar-Haim (2006), these differences should be further investigated, as they could lead to a sensible improvement of the performance.

As for the LONG pairs, which represented a new element of this year's challenge, no substantial difference was noted in the systems' performances: the average accuracy over the long pairs was 58.72%, compared to 61.93% over the short ones.

4 Conclusions and future work

At its third round, the Recognizing Textual Entailment task has reached a noticeable level of maturity, as the very high interest in the NLP community and the continuously increasing number of participants in the challenges demonstrate. The relevance of Textual Entailment Recognition to different applications, such as the AVE[5] track at QA at CLEF[6], has also been acknowledged. Furthermore, the debates and the numerous publications about the Textual Entailment have contributed to the better understanding the task and its nature.

To keep a good balance between the consolidated main task and the need for moving forward, longer texts were introduced in the dataset, in order to make the task more challenging, and a pilot task was proposed. The Third RTE Challenge have also confirmed that the methodology for the creation of the datasets, developed in the first two campaigns, is robust. Overall, the transition of the challenge coordination from Bar-Ilan –which organized the first two challenges- to CELCT was successful, though some problems were encountered, especially in the preparation of the data set. The systems which took part in RTE-3 showed that the technology applied to Entailment Recognition has made significant progress, confirmed by the results, which were generally better than last year. In particular, visible progress in defining several new principled scenarios for RTE was represented, such as Hickl's commitment-based approach, Bar Haim's proof system, Harmeling's probabilistic model, and Standford's use of Natural Logic.

If, on the one hand, the success that RTE has had so far is very encouraging, on the other, it incites to overcome certain current limitations, and to set realistic and, at the same time, stimulating goals for the future. First at all, theoretical refinements both of the task and the models applied to it need to be developed. In particular, more efforts are required to improve knowledge acquisition, as little progress has been made on this front so far. Also the data set generation and the evaluation methodology need to be refined and extended. A major problem in the current setting of the data collection is that the distribution of the examples is arbitrary to a large extent, being determined by manual selection. Therefore new evaluation methodologies, which can reflect realistic distributions should be investigated, as well as the possibility of evaluating Textual Entailment Recognition within additional concrete application scenarios, following the spirit of the QA Answer Validation Exercise.

Acknowledgments

The following sources were used in the preparation of the data:

• PowerAnswer question answering system, from Language Computer Corporation, provided by Dan Moldovan and Marta Tatu.
http://www.languagecomputer.com/solutions/question answering/power answer/

• Cicero Custom and Cicero Relation information extraction systems, from Language Computer Corporation, provided by Sanda M. Harabagiu, Andrew Hickl, John Lehmann and and Paul Aarseth.
http://www.languagecomputer.com/solutions/information_ext action/cicero/index.html

• Columbia NewsBlaster multi-document summarization system, from the Natural Language Proc-

[5] http://nlp.uned.es/QA/ave/.
[6] http://clef-qa.itc.it/.

essing group at Columbia University's Departmentof Computer Science.
http://newsblaster.cs.columbia.edu/

• NewsInEssence multi-document summarization system provided by Dragomir R. Radev and Jahna Otterbacher from the Computational Linguistics and Information Retrieval research group, University of Michigan.
http://www.newsinessence.com

• New York University's information extraction system, provided by Ralph Grishman, Department of Computer Science, Courant Institute of Mathematical Sciences, New York University.

• MUC-4 information extraction dataset, from the National Institute of Standards and Technology (NIST).
http://www.itl.nist.gov/iaui/894.02/related projects/muc/

• ACE 2004 information extraction templates, from the National Institute of Standards and Technology (NIST).
http://www.nist.gov/speech/tests/ace/

• TREC IR queries and TREC-QA question collections, from the National Institute of Standards and Technology (NIST).
http://trec.nist.gov/

• CLEF IR queries and CLEF-QA question collections, from DELOS Network of Excellence for Digital Libraries.
http://www.clef-campaign.org/, http://clef-qa.itc.it/

• DUC 2005 annotated peers, from Columbia University, NY, provided by Ani Nenkova.
http://www1.cs.columbia.edu/~ani/DUC2005/

We would like to thank the people and organizations that made these sources available for the challenge. In addition, we thank Idan Szpektor and Roy Bar Haim from Bar-Ilan University for their assistance and advice, and Valentina Bruseghini from CELCT for managing the RTE-3 website.

We would also like to acknowledge the people and organizations involved in creating and annotating the data: Pamela Forner, Errol Hayman, Cameron Fordyce from CELCT and Courtenay Hendricks, Adam Savel and Annika Hamalainen from the Butler Hill Group, which was funded by Microsoft Research.

This work was supported in part by the IST Programme of the European Community, under the *PASCAL Network of Excellence*, IST-2002-506778. We wish to thank the managers of the PASCAL challenges program, Michele Sebag and Florence d'Alche-Buc, for their efforts and support, which made this challenge possible. We also thank David Askey, who helped manage the RTE 3 website.

References

Roy Bar-Haim, Ido Dagan, Bill Dolan, Lisa Ferro, Danilo Giampiccolo, Bernardo Magnini and Idan Szpektor. 2006. The Second PASCAL Recognizing Textual Entailment Challenge. In Proceedings of the Second PASCAL Challenges Workshop on Recognizing Textual Entailment, Venice, Italy.

Ido Dagan, Oren Glickman, and Bernardo Magnini. 2006. The PASCAL Recognizing Textual Entailment Challenge. In Quiñonero-Candela et al., editors, MLCW 2005, LNAI Volume 3944, pages 177-190. Springer-Verlag.

J. R. Landis and G. G. Koch. 1997. The measurements of observer agreement for categorical data. *Biometrics*, 33:159–174.

Rebecca Passonneau, Ani Nenkova., Kathleen McKeown, and Sergey Sigleman. 2005. Applying the pyramid method in DUC 2005. In Proceedings of the Document Understanding Conference (DUC 05), Vancouver, B.C., Canada.

Ellen M. Voorhees and Donna Harman. 1999. Overview of the seventh text retrieval conference. In Proceedings of the Seventh Text Retrieval Conference (TREC-7). NIST Special Publication.

A Semantic Approach To Textual Entailment: System Evaluation and Task Analysis

Aljoscha Burchardt, Nils Reiter, Stefan Thater
Dept. of Computational Linguistics
Saarland University
Saarbrücken, Germany
{albu,reiter,stth}@coli.uni-sb.de

Anette Frank*
Dept. of Computational Linguistics
University of Heidelberg
Germany
frank@cl.uni-heidelberg.de

Abstract

This paper discusses our contribution to the third RTE Challenge – the SALSA RTE system. It builds on an earlier system based on a relatively deep linguistic analysis, which we complement with a shallow component based on word overlap. We evaluate their (combined) performance on various data sets. However, earlier observations that the combination of features improves the overall accuracy could be replicated only partly.

1 Introduction

This paper reports on the system we used in the third PASCAL challenge on Recognizing Textual Entailment. The system is based to a large extent on Burchardt and Frank's system (2006) used in the second RTE challenge (Bar-Haim et al., 2006); it relies on a relatively deep linguistic analysis, which we complement with a shallow component based on word overlap. As the system has been described earlier, we concentrate on a more systematic discussion of the system behaviour, aiming at spotting promising anchors for future extensions and improvements.

It has been observed for related systems that a combination of separately trained features in the machine learning component can lead to an overall improvement in system performance, in particular if features from a more "informed" component and shallow ones are combined (Hickl et al., 2006; Bos and Markert, 2006). We provide a detailed analysis of our system's behaviour on different training and test sets. However, we could not replicate the effects observed by others on all corpora – often, the accuracy of the combined features is not higher than the best individual features or feature sets. For the RTE 3 test set, the combined features actually lead to a slightly lower accuracy.

One candidate future enhancement of our system is to refine the relatively unrestricted graph matching that compares the analyses of text and hypothesis and underlies the definition of the deep features. But a more controlled, "rule based" definition of an adequate graph matching seems to rely on a deeper understanding of the notion of textual entailment.

In Section 2, we review the basic architecture of our system, and report on improvements and extensions. In Section 3, we provide a detailed evaluation of the system on different data sets. In Section 4, we report on some findings we made in a small annotation experiment we conducted at our department. In Section 5, we conclude and give a short outlook.

2 The SALSA RTE System

In this Section, we review the basic architecture of the SALSA RTE system, and report on some improvements and extensions. More details can be found in (Burchardt and Frank, 2006).

2.1 Architecture

The SALSA RTE system is based on three main components: (i) a linguistic analysis of text and hypothesis based primarily on LFG and Frame Semantics (Baker et al., 1998), (ii) the computation of a *match graph* that encodes the "semantic overlap" between text and hypothesis, and (iii) a statistical entailment decision.

*By the time of writing, Anette Frank was affiliated at Saarland University and DFKI Saarbrücken.

Proceedings of the Workshop on Textual Entailment and Paraphrasing, pages 10–15,
Prague, June 2007.

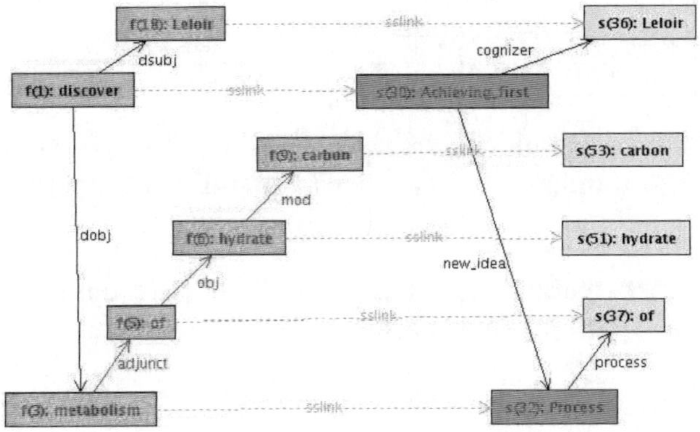

Figure 1: Linguistic Analysis of *Leloir discovered the metabolism of carbon hydrates.* (RTE3-test).

Linguistic analysis. The primary linguistic analysis components are the probabilistic LFG grammar for English developed at PARC (Riezler et al., 2002), and a combination of systems for frame semantic annotation: the probabilistic *Shalmaneser* system for frame and role annotation (Erk and Pado, 2006), and the rule-based *Detour* system for frame assignment (Burchardt et al., 2005).

Frame semantic analysis is especially interesting for the task of recognising textual entailment as it offers a robust yet relatively precise measure for semantic overlap. The lexical meaning of predicates and their arguments are modelled in terms of *frames* and *roles*. A frame describes a prototypical situation and roles identify participants involved in the situation. Frames provide normalisations over divers surface realisations, including variations in argument structure realisations. For instance, *buy*, *sell*, and *purchase* are all associated with the same frame.

The linguistic analysis combines LFG f-structures and FrameNet frames computed by the Shalmaneser and Detour systems, resulting in a projection from f-structures to a semantic layer of frames and "pseudo predicates" for f-structure predicates that do not project frames. Figure 1 shows the most important parts of the analysis of hypothesis 109 from the RTE 3 test set as an example. The LFG f-structure is shown on the left, and the dotted lines indicate the projection to semantic nodes on the right. The predicate *discover* is associated with the frame ACHIEVING_FIRST, the semantic role COGNIZER points to the pseudo-predicate *Leloir* and NEW_IDEA points to the PROCESS frame evoked by *metabolism*.

Semantic nodes are further projected into an ontological analysis layer containing WordNet (Fellbaum, 1997) senses and SUMO (Niles and Pease, 2001) classes. Semantic phenomena not treated by FrameNet like anaphora, negation or modality are (approximately) encoded with special operators. The resulting, layered graph structures for text and hypothesis thus provide access to the different types of information in a principled way.

Semantic overlap and match graphs. The system approximates textual entailment in terms of the "semantic overlap" between text and hypothesis. It compares their LFG f-structures with semantic and ontological projection by determining compatible, *matching* nodes and edges. The result is stored in a *match graph*, which contains all (pairs of) matched nodes and edges. Nodes can match if they are labelled with identical frames or predicates, or if the nodes are semantically related on the basis of WordNet or FrameNet frame relations. One node from the hypothesis may match multiple nodes from the text and vice versa. The matching of edges is restricted to edges that connect matching nodes, or nodes taking identical atomic values.

The match graph primarily encodes the "similarity" of text and hypothesis. In order to capture also a certain degree of "dissimilarity," nodes are deleted from the match graph if they occur in incompatible modality contexts.

Statistical entailment decision. Given a match graph and the graphs for text and hypothesis, we extract various features to train a machine learning model for textual entailment. In total, we extract 47 distinct features, which can be grouped according to their (i) level of representation (lexical, syntactic, semantic), (ii) degree of connectedness in the match graph, (iii) source (text, hypothesis or match graph), and (iv) proportional relation (hypothesis/text, match/hypothesis ratio).

2.2 Improvements

Sentence splitter. To cope with longer texts, we integrated the sentence splitter of the JTok tokeniser (Schäfer, 2005) into the system.

WordNet interface. The WordNet interface now treats particle verbs like *throw out* correctly. Moreover, we tested the usability of WordNet's verb entailment information as well as antonymy on nouns, verbs, and adjectives as basis for heuristic inferences in the graph matching process. However, for the given data, the number of text-hypothesis pairs where the relations are instantiated at all is marginal.

Frame semantic projection. The interface between the LFG and the Detour and Shalmaneser systems has been improved: by now 97% (+7%) of the frames and 74% (+10%) of the roles can be projected (on the RTE3 test set), resulting in an average of 6.6 frames and 5.5 roles per sentence.

2.3 Extensions

In addition to the above improvements, the system has been extended in two respects. We added a shallow component based on lexical overlap and a "meta learner" to study the combinatorics of machine learners' results.

Lexical overlap. In order to evaluate the performance of our system, we implemented a simple baseline system that approximates textual entailment in terms of lexical overlap between text and hypothesis. This shallow system is also used as a component to complement our full system in one of the two runs submitted to the RTE3 challenge.

The shallow system measures the relative number of words in the hypothesis that also occur in the text. Both text and hypothesis are tagged and lemmatised using Tree Tagger (Schmid, 1994), taking only nouns, non-auxiliary verbs, adjectives and adverbs into account. Training a decision tree on the relative word-overlap as single feature yields a system which performs comparable to earlier word-overlap based systems, achieving an accuracy of 60.6 % if trained and tested on the RTE 2 development and test set, respectively (using Weka's J48 classifier), or 57.5 % if we use Weka's LogitBoost classifier.

Weka Interface. Finally, we improved the machine learning back-end which feeds our extracted features into the Weka toolkit (Witten and Frank, 2005). This allows to train features in arbitrary combinations, with different machine learners.[1] Moreover, it supports testing the effect of using voting or a "meta learner" after training individual features or feature groups separately.

[1]The figures we present in the following are all computed with the LogitBoost classifier.

		IE	IR	QA	SUM
Run 1 (III)	62.25%	51%	68%	74%	57%
Run 2 (II)	62.62%	50%	69%	72.5%	59%

Table 1: Results of the SALSA RTE system (combined training set: RTE2-dev/-test and RTE3-dev).

3 Results

3.1 RTE3 Results

In the RTE3 task, we submitted two runs, one with (run 1) and one without (run 2) the lexical overlap component. Both achieved almost the same results, as can be seen in Table 1. The feature combinations (II, III) are explained below in detail.

3.2 Feature Combination

We investigated the behaviour of our systems on various combinations of three different sets of 800 text hypothesis pairs (RTE2-dev/-test and RTE3-dev). We tested four different feature configurations:

(I) All 47 features generated in our system (excluding the lexical overlap component)

(II) Three selected features of our system (run 2):

- Overlap of LFG predicates
- Matching of grammatical functions (deep subject/object, modifier, ...)
- Average size of connected parts ("clusters") of the match graph, comprising syntactic and semantic information

(III) The features from II plus lexical overlap (run 1)

(IV) Lexical overlap alone

In every configuration (except IV), the features were trained separately first, then a "meta classifier" was used to make the final entailment decision. We will use `Featureset-Training_set-Test_set` as notation for the configurations, e.g., `I-D2T2-D3` means all 47 features trained on the development and test set of RTE2, tested on the development set of RTE3. The results are shown in Table 2.

test → ↓ train	D2				T2				D3			
	I	II	III	IV	I	II	III	IV	I	II	III	IV
D2					56.25	57.25	58.625	57.5	57.875	61.125	66.375	66.625
T2	56.375	58.75	60.625	61.625					57.5	60.875	63.75	64.625
D3	53.875	61.25	61.75	61.75	56.625	58.75	57.25	57.25				
D2T2									58.5	64.25	65.875	66.375
D2D3					58	58.625	60	58.5				
T2D3	56.75	61.25	60.875	60.875								

Table 2: Performance of the different feature combinations on different training and test sets.

3.3 Corpus Variance

A general observation is, that almost all features behave quite differently on different training and test sets, as do feature combinations. Testing on T2 (RTE2-test) seems to be the hardest task. Not a single feature combination achieved an accuracy of more than 60%. In contrast, the best performance was 66.625% accuracy (IV-D2-D3). [2]

Usually, using a larger training set (the bottom part of table 2) should lead to a better performance.[3] However, this effect could not be observed here for all configurations. For most feature sets the performance gain is very small, e.g. from 56.375 (I-T2-D2) and 53.875 (I-D3-D2) to 56.75 (I-T2D3-D2). On some feature sets, the performance even drops, e.g. from 61.625 (IV-T2-D2) and 61.75 (IV-D3-D2) to 60.875 (IV-T2D3-D2). The largest boost occurred for feature set II. It's performance increased from 61.125 (II-D2-D3) and 60.875 (II-T2-D3) to 64.25 (II-D2T2-D3). It would be very interesting to see how the performance would develop on a much larger training set.

3.4 Feature Variance

The variance among individual features and feature sets is also large. Feature set II contains the most reliable and stable features. We tested how this "more informed" feature set (II) compares to the shallow word overlap feature (IV) and whether their combination (III) increases accuracy.

As can be seen from Table 2, in most of the cases, IV performs best, e.g. in the D2-D3 configuration, where feature set II alone achieves 61.125, while the combination with IV boosts the performance by 5% (III). On the other hand, there are cases, where the inclusion of the word overlap feature lowers the performance, e.g. from 61.25 (II-T2D3-D2) to 60.875 (III-T2D3-D2).

It is also interesting that combinations of features often perform lower than the best individual feature in the set. For instance, in D2T2-D3 III achieves 65.875, compared to 66.375 for IV alone. We generally could not observe a positive effect for the combination of features in a meta feature. In almost all configurations, the meta feature performed worse or equally well as the best individual feature. Apart from the size of the training data, feature dependence might be an explanation for this.

3.5 Task Variance

Figure 2 shows a per task analysis for the feature sets II, III and IV (D2T2-D3). The system performs best on the Question Answering task, where it achieves almost 80% accuracy. This differs from last year's experience, where the system performed best in the Summarization task. Given the general variance discussed above, this observation does not seem to allow general conclusions.

Again, there is a large variability of the overlap feature as well, which ranges between 52.5% (IE) and 79% (QA). This variability can partly be explained if we compare the average word overlap measures for positive and negative pairs among the individual tasks (Table 3). Note however, that the difference (Δ) between positive and negative examples in IE and IR is identical while the accuracy of the word overlap feature differs drastically.

[2] One indicator for the "difficulty" of a test set is the average lexical overlap of text and hypothesis. The difference of the proportion between the entailed and not entailed pairs – the discriminative power of the overlap feature – differs among different sets: e.g. 0.05 on T2 and 0.13 on D3.

[3] In terms of machine learning, extending a training set by factor 2 (from 800 to 1.600 items) does not make a qualitative difference. The improvement observed by (Hickl et al., 2006) was achieved by going to 10.000 items.

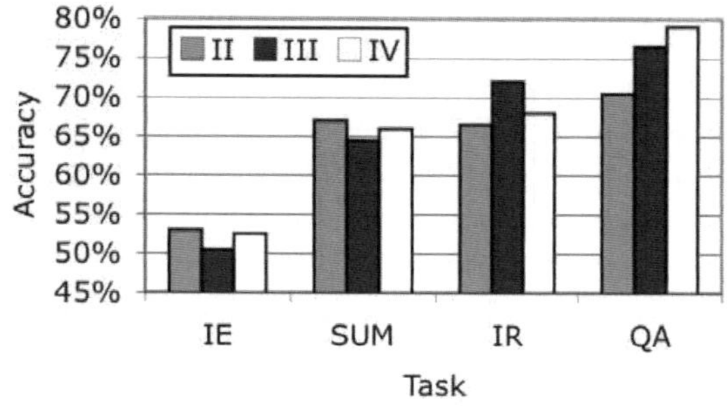

Figure 2: Per task accuracy (D2T2-D3).

Task	Entailed	Not Entailed	Δ
IE	0.41	0.35	0.06
SUM	0.39	0.22	0.17
IR	0.29	0.23	0.06
QA	0.44	0.20	0.24

Table 3: Average word overlap per task for D3

The per task analysis also confirms the observation that the combination of (deep and shallow) features behaves heterogeneously in terms of accuracy.

A somewhat unexpected result is that the more "informed" feature II performs better in SUM as the shallow feature IV while it is the other way round in QA (see Figure 2).

4 Discussion

It is a bit surprising that a shallow feature like word overlap performs comparable to, or even better than, more informed features obtained from a relatively deep linguistic analysis, and that the combination of both types of features does not always increase the overall accuracy.

One possible explanation is the limited size of the training data, which seems to be too small for the machine learner to exploit the full potential of the deep features. One way to compensate for the limited training size would be to make the implicit linguistic information encoded in the features more explicit, for instance by making the graph matching linguistically more informed. Options are to compute a proper embedding of the hypothesis graph into the text graph, or interlinking of the various layers of analysis (syntax, semantics, ontology) in some other more controlled way.

However, to come up with a more explicit model of textual entailment, a deeper understanding of the principles involved in establishing textual entailment relations is necessary. An idea which is derived from the traditional notion of logical entailment is that the information encoded in the hypothesis must (somehow) be subsumed by the text for the entailemt to hold. Although most approaches to textual entailment seem to rely on this assumption in one way or another, it is easy to find pairs in the RTE corpora where the relation between text and hypothesis cannot be modelled so straightforwardly. In (1), for instance, textual entailment holds although *was born in* is more specific than *be from*.

(1a) As a real native Detroiter, I want to remind everyone that Madonna **is from** Bay City, Mich., [. . .].

(1b) Madonna **was born** in Bay City, Mich.

Interestingly, textual entailment sometimes does not hold even if the information expressed by the hypothesis is subsumed by the text:

(2a) [. . .] Nizar Hamdoun, announced today, Sunday, that thousands of people **were killed** or injured during the four days of air bombardment against Iraq.

(2b) Nizar HAMDOON, Iraqi ambassador to the United Nations, announced that thousands of people **could be killed** or wounded due to the aerial bombardment of Iraq.

Although the hypothesis is logically entailed by the text (if we ignore the report context) – 'kill' implies 'possibly kill' – pragmatic principles seem to block entailment here.

The observation that standard logical entailment and textual entailment deviate in certain respects is not surprising and has also been addressed in a discussion initiated by (Zaenen et al., 2005). Still, there is no consensus regarding the precise mechanisms involved in the latter such as "general principles of plausibility" or pragmatic principles.

We conducted a short annotation experiment during a reading circle at our department on a randomly chosen subset of 10 pairs from the RTE 1 (including (1) and (2) from above). A central result was that it is relatively easy to decide *whether* textual entailment holds while it often remained controversial *why* this is the case. In particular, it seems difficult to tell whether an inference is strict or just plausible, and whether it relies on lexical knowledge only or whether "world knowledge" is involved. Currently, a larger subset of the RTE datasets is annotated as part of a Master's thesis project, and we hope to learn more about the principles that underly the notion of textual entailment from the analysis of this data.

5 Conclusion and Outlook

In this paper, we have compared two approximations to textual entailment – a shallow one based on word overlap, and a more informed one based on a relatively deep linguistic analysis. The evaluation on various data sets shows that both perform (by and large) comparable; sometimes the shallow component even outperforms the deeper one. A modest improvement in accuracy can be achieved by combining both components, but this effect cannot be observed invariably on all data sets.

One reason why the deep system does not perform better seems to be the limited size of the training data available for the machine learning component. As we cannot expect the necessary amount of training data to be available in the near future, we currently investigate the data more closely in order to arrive at a more controlled model of textual entailment. In another current effort, we work on an interface to upper-level ontologies (Reiter, 2007) in order to access more "world-knowledge" which is a desideratum in natural language processing in general, as in many approaches to textual entailment.

Acknowledgements

This work has partly been funded by the German Research Foundation DFG (grant PI 154/9-2). We also acknowledge Katrin Erk's support of the Shalmaneser system.

References

Collin F. Baker, Charles J. Fillmore, and John B. Lowe. 1998. The Berkeley FrameNet project. In *Proceedings of COLING-ACL*, Montreal, Canada.

Roy Bar-Haim, Ido Dagan, Bill Dolan, Lisa Ferro, Danilo Giampiccolo, Bernardo Magnini, and Idan Szpektor, editors. 2006. *Proceedings of the Second PASCAL Challenges Workshop on Recognising Textual Entailment*, Venice, Italy.

Johan Bos and Katja Markert. 2006. When logical inference helps determining textual entailment (and when it doesn't). In *Proceedings of PASCAL RTE2 Workshop*.

Aljoscha Burchardt and Anette Frank. 2006. Approximating Textual Entailment with LFG and FrameNet Frames. In *Proceedings of PASCAL RTE2 Workshop*.

Aljoscha Burchardt, Katrin Erk, and Anette Frank. 2005. A WordNet Detour to FrameNet. In B. Fisseni, H.-C. Schmitz, B. Schröder, and P. Wagner, editors, *Sprachtechnologie, mobile Kommunikation und linguistische Resourcen*, volume 8 of *Computer Studies in Language and Speech*. Peter Lang, Frankfurt/Main.

Katrin Erk and Sebastian Pado. 2006. Shalmaneser - a flexible toolbox for semantic role assignment. In *Proceedings of LREC 2006*, Genoa, Italy.

Christiane Fellbaum. 1997. English verbs as semantic net. In *WordNet: an electronic lexical database*. MIT.

Andrew Hickl, Jeremy Bensley, John Williams, Kirk Roberts, Bryan Rink, and Ying Shi. 2006. Recognizing Textual Entailment with LCC's Groundhog System. In *Proceedings of PASCAL RTE2 Workshop*.

Ian Niles and Adam Pease. 2001. Towards a standard upper ontology. In *Proceedings of the International Conference on Formal Ontology in Information Systems (FOIS)*, pages 2–9. ACM Press.

Nils Reiter. 2007. Towards linking FrameNet and SUMO. Diploma Thesis (in preparation).

Stefan Riezler, Tracy H. King, Ronald M. Kaplan, Richard Crouch, John T. III Maxwell, and Mark Johnson. 2002. Parsing the Wall Street Journal using a Lexical-Functional Grammar and Discriminative Estimation Techniques. In *Proceedings of ACL'02*, Philadelphia, PA.

Ulrich Schäfer, 2005. *Heart of Gold, User and Developer Documentation*. DFKI Language Technology Lab, Saarbrücken, Germany.

Helmut Schmid. 1994. Probabilistic part-of-speech tagging using decision trees. In *Proceedings of International Conference on New Methods in Language Processing*, Manchester, UK.

Ian H. Witten and Eibe Frank. 2005. *Data Mining: Practical Machine Learning Tools and Techniques*. Morgan Kaufmann, San Francisco, 2 edition.

Annie Zaenen, Lauri Karttunen, and Richard Crouch. 2005. Local textual inference: Can it be defined or circumscribed? In *Proceedings of the ACL Workshop on Empirical Modeling of Semantic Equivalence and Entailment*, Ann Arbor, Michigan, June.

Precision-focused Textual Inference

D. G. Bobrow, C. Condoravdi, R. Crouch, V. de Paiva, L. Karttunen, T. H. King, R. Nairn, L. Price, A. Zaenen
Palo Alto Research Center

Abstract

This paper describes our system as used in the RTE3 task. The system maps premise and hypothesis pairs into an abstract knowledge representation (AKR) and then performs entailment and contradiction detection (ECD) on the resulting AKRs. Two versions of ECD were used in RTE3, one with strict ECD and one with looser ECD.

1 Introduction

In the RTE textual entailment challenge, one is given a source text T and a hypothesis H, and the task is to decide whether H can be inferred from T. Our system interprets inference in a strict way. Given the knowledge of the language embedded in the system, does the hypothesis logically follow from the information embedded in the text? Thus we are emphasizing precision, particularly in question-answering. This was reflected in our results in the RTE3 challenge. We responded correctly with YES to relatively few of the examples, but on the QA-type examples, we achieved 90-95% average precision.

The methodology employed is to use the linguistic information to map T and H onto a logical form in AKR, our Abstract Knowledge Representation. The AKR is designed to capture the propositions the author of a statement is committed to. For the sake of ECD, the representation of T may include elements that are not directly expressed in the text. For example, in the AKR of *John bought a car* includes the fact that the car was sold. The AKR of *John forgot to buy milk* includes the fact that John did not buy milk. Our reasoning algorithm tries to determine whether the AKR of H is subsumed by the AKR of T and detect cases when they are in conflict.

The Entailment and Contradiction Detection (ECD) algorithm makes a distinction that is not part of the basic RTE challenge. If T entails the negation of H, we answer NO (Contradiction). On the other hand, if there is no direct entailment we answer UNKNOWN. We do not try to construct a likely scenario that would link T and H. Nor have we tried to collect data on phrases that would tend to indicate such likely associations between T and H. That approach is clearly very useful (e.g. (Hickl et al., 2006)), and could be used as a backup strategy with our more formal entailment approach. We have chosen to focus on strict structural and lexical entailments.

Process	Output
Text-Breaking	Delimited sentences
Named-entity recognition	Type-marked Entities
Morphological Analysis	Word stems plus features
LFG Parsing	Functional Structure
Semantic processing	Scope, Predicate-argument structure
AKR rules	Conceptual, Contextual, Temporal Structure

Figure 1: The processing pipeline: processes with their ambiguity-enabled packed outputs

This paper describes the processing pipeline for mapping to AKR, the ECD algorithm, the challenges we faced in processing the RTE data and a summary of our results on RTE3.

2 Process Pipeline

Figure 1 shows the processing pipeline for mapping texts to AKR. The input is a text of one or more sentences.

All components of the system are "ambiguity enabled" (Maxwell and Kaplan, 1991). This allows each component to accept ambiguous input in a "packed" format, process it without unpacking the ambiguities, and then pass packed input to the next stage. The syntactic component, LFG Parsing, also has a stochastic disambiguation system which allows us to pass the n-best on to the semantics (Riezler et al., 2002); for the RTE3 challenge, we used

Proceedings of the Workshop on Textual Entailment and Paraphrasing, pages 16–21,
Prague, June 2007.

n=50.

The parser takes the output of the morphology (i.e. a series of lemmata with their tags) and produces a tree (constituent-structure) and a dependency structure (functional-structure) represented as an attribute-value matrix. The functional-structure is of primary importance for the semantics and AKR. In particular, it encodes predicate-argument relations, including long-distance dependencies, and provides other syntactic features (e.g. number, tense, noun type).

The output of the syntax is input for the semantics that is produced by an ambiguity enabled packed rewriting system. The semantics is described in detail in (Crouch and King, 2006). Semantic processing assigns scope to scope-bearing elements such as negation and normalizes the output of the syntax. This normalization includes reformulating syntactic passives as actives (e.g. *The cake was eaten by Mary. / Mary ate the cake.*), resolving many null pronouns (e.g. *Laughing, John entered the room / $John_i$ laughing, $John_i$ entered the room.*), and canonicalizing measure phrases, comparatives, and dates. More complex normalizations involve converting nominal deverbals into the equivalent verbal form, identifying arguments of the verb from the arguments of the nominal (Gurevich et al., 2006). For example, the semantic representation of *Iraq's destruction of its* WMD is similar to the representation of *Iraq destroyed its* WMD.

The final main task of the semantics rules is to convert words into concepts and syntactic grammatical functions into roles. The mapping onto concepts uses WordNet (Fellbaum, 1998) to map words into lists of synsets. The named entity types provided by the morphology and syntax are used to create more accurate mapping of proper nouns since these are not systematically represented in WordNet. The semantic rules use the grammatical function subcategorization information from the verb and the role information found in extended VerbNet (Kipper et al., 2000) to map syntactic subjects, objects, and obliques into more abstract thematic roles such as Agent, Theme, and Goal (Crouch and King, 2005). This mapping into thematic-style roles allows the system to correctly align the arguments in pairs like (1) and (2), something which is impossible using just syntactic functions. In the first, the object and subject have a common thematic role in the alternation between transitive and intransitive; while in the second, the common role is shared by the subjects.

(1) John broke the $\text{vase}_{syn:object,sem:patient}$.
The $\text{vase}_{syn:subject,sem:patient}$ broke.

(2) $\text{John}_{syn:subject,sem:agent}$ ate the cake.
$\text{John}_{syn:subject,sem:agent}$ ate.

The goal of these semantic normalizations is to abstract away from the syntactic representation so that sentences with similar meaning have similar semantic representations. However, the semantics is still fundamentally a linguistic level of representation; further abstraction towards the meaning is done in the mapping from semantics to AKR. The AKR is the level of representation that is used to determine entailment and contradiction in our RTE3 system. A preliminary description of its logic was provided in (Bobrow et al., 2005). The AKR mapping converts grammatical tense and temporal modifiers into temporal relations, identifies anaphoric referents and makes explicit the implied relation between complement clauses and the main verb (e.g. for *manage*, *fail*) (Nairn et al., 2006). AKR also deals with standard phrases that are equivalent to simple vocabulary terms. For example, *take a flight to New York* is equivalent to *fly to New York*. These uses of "light" verbs (e.g. *take*, *give*) are not included in synonyms found in WordNet. Another class of phrasal synonyms involve inchoatives (e.g. *take a turn for the worse/worsen*). We included a special set of transformation rules for phrasal synonyms: some of the rules are part of the mapping from semantics to AKR while others are part of the ECD module. The mapping to AKR is done using the same ambiguity-enabled ordered rewriting system that the semantics uses, allowing the AKR mapping system to efficiently process the packed output of the semantics.

The AKR for a sentence like *Bush claimed that Iraq possessed* WMDs in Figure 2 introduces two contexts: a top level context t, representing the commitments of the speaker of sentence, and an embedded context claim_cx:37 representing the state of affairs according to Bush's claim. The two contexts are related via the Topic role of the claim event. The representation contains terms like claim:37 or

Conceptual Structure

```
subconcept(claim:37,[claim-1,. . .,claim-5])
role(Topic,claim:37,claim_cx:37)
role(Agent,claim:37,Bush:1)
subconcept(Bush:1,[person-1])
alias(Bush:1,[Bush])
role(cardinality_restriction,Bush:1,sg)
subconcept(possess:24,[possess-1,own-1,possess-3])
role(Destination,possess:24,wmd:34)
role(Agent,possess:24,Iraq:19)
subconcept(Iraq:19,[location-1,location-4])
alias(Iraq:19,[Iraq])
role(cardinality_restriction,Iraq:19,sg)
subconcept(wmd:34,
  [weapon_of_mass_destruction-1])
role(cardinality_restriction,wmd:34,pl)
```

Contextual Structure

```
context(t)
context(claim_cx:37)
context_relation(t,claim_cx:37,crel(Topic,claim:37))
instantiable(Bush:1,t)
instantiable(Iraq:19,t)
instantiable(claim:37,t)
instantiable(Iraq:19,claim_cx:37)
instantiable(possess:24,claim_cx:37)
instantiable(wmd:34,claim_cx:37)
```

Temporal Structure

```
temporalRel(After,Now,claim:37)
temporalRel(After,claim:37,possess:24)
```

Figure 2: AKR for *Bush claimed that Iraq possessed* WMD*s.*

Bush:1 which refer to the kinds of object that the sentence is talking about. The subconcept facts explicitly link these terms to their concepts in WordNet. Thus claim:37 is stated to be some subkind of the type claim-1, etc., and wmd:34 to be some subkind of the type weapon_of_mass_destruction-1. Terms like claim:37 and wmd:34 do not refer to individuals, but to concepts (or types or kinds). Saying that there is some subconcept of the kind weapon_of_mass_destruction-1, where this subconcept is further restricted to be a kind of WMD possessed by Iraq, does not commit you to saying that there are any instances of this subconcept.

The instantiable assertions capture the commitments about the existence of the kinds of object described. In the top-level context t, there is a commitment to an instance of Bush and of a claim:37 event made by him. However, there is no top-level commitment to any instances of wmd:34 possessed by Iraq:19. These commitments are only made in the embedded claim_cx:37 context. It is left open whether these embedded commitments correspond, or not, to the beliefs of the speaker. Two distinct levels of structure can thus be discerned in AKR: a conceptual structure and a contextual structure. The conceptual structure, through use of subconcept and role assertions, indicates the subject matter. The contextual structure indicates commitments as to the existence of the subject matter via instantiability assertions linking concepts to contexts, and via context relations linking contexts to contexts. In addition, there is a temporal structure that situates the events described with respect to the time of utterance and temporally relates them to one another.

3 Entailment and Contradiction Detection

ECD is implemented as another set of rewrite rules, running on the same packed rewrite system used to generate the AKR representations. The rules (i) align concept and context terms in text (T) and hypothesis (H) AKRs, (ii) calculate concept subsumption orderings between aligned T and H terms, and (iii) check instantiability and uninstantiability claims in the light of subsumption orderings to determine whether T entails H, T contradicts H, or T neither entails not contradicts H. For the purposes of RTE3, both contradiction and neither contradiction nor entailment are collapsed into a NO (does not follow) judgment.

One of the novel features of this approach is that T and H representations do not need to be disambiguated before checking for entailment or contradiction. The approach is able to detect if there is one reading of T that entails (or contradicts) one reading of H. The T and H passages can in effect mutually disambiguate one another through the ECD. For example, although *plane* and *level* both have multiple readings, they can both refer to a horizontal surface, and in that sense *The plane is dry* entails *The level is dry*, and vice versa.

The first phase of ECD aligns concepts and context terms in the T and H AKRs. Concepts are represented as lists of WordNet hypernym lists, in WordNet sense order. Two concept terms can be aligned if a sense synset of one term (i.e. the first element of one of the term's hypernym lists) is contained in a hypernym list of the other term. The alignment can be weighted according to word sense; so a concept overlap on the first senses of a T and H term counts for more than a concept overlap on the *n* and *m*th senses. However, no weightings were used in RTE3. For named entities, alignment demands not only a concept overlap, but also an intersection in the "alias" forms of the proper nouns. For example,"George Bush" may be aligned with "George" or with "Bush". Context alignment relies on associating each context with an indexing concept, usually the concept for the main verb in the clause heading the context. Contexts are then aligned on the basis of these concept indices.

Typically, an H term can align with more than one T term. In such cases all possible alignments are proposed, but the alignment rules put the alternative alignments in different parts of the choice space.

Having aligned T and H terms, rules are applied to determine concept specificity and subsumption relations between aligned terms. Preliminary judgments of specificity are made by looking for hypernym inclusion. For example, an H term denoting the concept "person" is less specific than a T term denoting "woman". These preliminary judgments need to be revised in the light of role restrictions modifying the terms: a "tall person" is neither more nor less specific than a "woman". Revisions to specificity judgments also take into account cardinality modifiers: while "person" is less specific than "woman", "all persons" is judged to be more specific than "all women".

With judgments of concept specificity in place, it is possible to determine entailment relations on the basis of (un)instantiability claims in the T and H AKRs. For example, suppose the T and H AKRs contain the facts in (3).

(3) T: instantiable(C_T, Ctx_T)
H: instantiable(C_H, Ctx_H)

where concept C_T is aligned with C_H, C_T is judged to be more specific than C_H, and context Ctx_T is aligned with context Ctx_H. In this case, the hypothesis instantiability claim is entailed by the text instantiability claim (existence of something more specific entails existence of something more general). This being so, the H instantiability claim can be deleted without loss of information.

If instead we had the (un)instantiability claims in (4) for the same alignments and specificity relations,

(4) T: instantiable(C_T, Ctx_T)
H: uninstantiable(C_H, Ctx_H)

we would have a contradiction: the text says that there is something of the more specific type C_T, whereas the hypothesis says there are no things of the more general type C_H. In this case, the rules explicitly flag a contradiction.

Once all (un)instantiability claims have been compared, it is possible to judge whether the text entails or contradicts the hypothesis. Entailed hypothesis (un)instantiability assertions are deleted from the representation. Consequently, if there is one T and H AKR readings and one set of alignments under which all the H (un)instantiability assertions have been removed, then there is an entailment of H by T. If there is a pair of readings and a set of alignments under which a contradiction is flagged, then there is a contradiction. If there is no pair of readings or set of alignments under which there is either an entailment or a contradiction, then T and H are merely consistent with one another. There are exceptional cases such as (5) where one reading of T entails H and another reading contradicts it.

(5) T: John did not wait to call for help.
H: John called for help.

Our ECD rules detect such cases.

WordNet often misses synonyms needed for the alignment in the ECD. In particular, the hierarchy and synsets for verbs are one of WordNet's least developed parts. To test the impact of the missing synonyms, we developed a variation on the ECD algorithm that allows loose matching.

First, in concept alignment, if a verb concept in H does not align with any verb concept in T, then we permit it to (separately) align with all the text verb concepts. We do not permit the same loose alignment for noun concepts, since we judge WordNet information to be more reliable for nouns. This free alignment of verbs might sound risky, but in general these alignments will not lead to useful concept specificity judgments unless the T and H verbs have very similar arguments / role restrictions.

When such a loose verb alignment is made, we explicitly record this fact in a justification term included in the alignment fact. Similarly, when judging concept specificity, each rule that applies adds a term to a list of justifications recorded as part of the fact indicating the specificity relation. This means that when the final specificity judgments are determined, each judgment has a record of the sequence of decisions made to reach it.

(Un)instantiability comparisons are made as in strict matching. However, the criteria for detecting an entailment are selectively loosened. If no contradiction is flagged, and there is a pairing of readings and alignments under which just a single H instantiability assertion is left standing, then this is allowed through as a loose entailment. However, further rules are applied to block those loose entailments that are deemed inappropriate. These blocking rules look at the form of the justification terms gathered based on specificity judgments.

These blocking rules are manually selected. First, a loose matching run is made without any blocking rules. Results are dumped for each T-H pair, recording the expected logical relation and the justifications collected. Blocking rules are created by detecting patterns of justification that are associated with labeled non-entailments. One such blocking rule says that if you have just a single H instantiability left, but the specificity justifications leading to this have been shown to be reliable on training data, then the instantiability should not be eliminated as a loose entailment.

4 Challenges in Processing the RTE Data

The RTE3 data set contains inconsistencies in spelling and punctuation between the text and the hypothesis. To handle these, we did an automatic prepass where we compared the strings in the passage text to those in the hypothesis. Some of the special cases that we handled include:

- Normalize capitalization and spacing
- Identify acronyms and shorten names
- Title identification
- Spelling correction

Role names in VerbNet are in part intended to capture the relation of the argument to the event being described by the verb. For example, an object playing an Agent role is causally involved in the event, while an object playing a Theme or Patient role is only supposed to be affected. This allows participants in an action to be identified regardless of the syntactic frame chosen to represent the verb; this was seen in (1) and (2). Sometimes the roles from VerbNet are not assigned in such a way as to allow such transparent identification across frames or related verbs. Consider an example. In *Ed travels/goes to Boston* VerbNet identifies Ed as playing a Theme role. However, in *Ed flies to Boston* VerbNet assigns Ed an Agent role; this difference can make determining contradiction and entailment between T and H difficult. We have tried to compensate in our ECD, by using a backoff strategy where fewer role names are used (by projecting down role names to the smaller set). As we develop the system further, we continue to experiment with which set of roles works best for which tasks.

Another open issue involves identifying alternative ways vague relations among objects appear in text. We do not match the expression *the Boston team* with *the team from Boston*. To improve our recall, we are considering loose matching techniques.

5 Summary of our results on RTE3

We participated in the RTE challenge as a way to understand what our particular techniques could do with respect to a more general version of textual entailment. The overall experiment was quite enlightening. Tables 1 and 2 summarize how we did on the RTE3 challenge. System 1 is our standard system with strict ECD. System 2 used the looser set of ECD rules.

	Gold YES	Sys YES	Correct	R	P	F
IE	105	6	5	0.048	0.83	0.20
IR	87	4	4	0.046	1.00	0.21
QA	106	10	9	0.085	0.90	0.28
SUM	112	11	7	0.063	0.64	0.20
Total	410	31	25	0.060	0.84	0.22

Table 1: **System 1 with Strict** ECD

	Gold YES	Sys YES	Correct	R	P	F
IE	105	15	10	0.095	0.67	0.25
IR	87	6	4	0.046	0.67	0.18
QA	106	14	13	0.12	0.93	0.34
SUM	112	17	10	0.089	0.59	0.23
Total	410	52	37	0.088	0.71	0.25

Table 2: **System 2 with Loose** ECD

As can be seen, we answered very few of the questions; only 31 of the possible 410 with a YES answer. However, for those we did answer (requiring only linguistic, and not world knowledge), we achieved high precision: up to 90% on QA. However, we were not perfect even from this perspective. Here are simplified versions of the errors where our system answered YES, and the answer should be NO with an analysis of what is needed in the system to correct the error.

The wrong result in (6) is due to our incomplete coverage of intensional verbs (*seek*, *want*, *look for*, *need*, etc.).

(6) T: The US sought the release of hostages.
H: Hostages were released.

The object of an intensional verb cannot be assumed to exist or to occur. Intensional verbs need to be marked systematically in our lexicon.

The problem with (7) lies in the lack of treatment for generic sentences.

(7) T: Girls and boys are segregated in high school during sex education class.
H: Girls and boys are segregated in high school.

The natural interpretation of H is that girls and boys are segregated in high school ALL THE TIME. Because we do not yet handle generic sentences properly, our algorithm for calculating specificity produces the wrong result here. It judges segregation in H to be less specific than in T whereas the opposite is in fact the case. Adding the word "sometimes" to H would make our YES the correct answer.

The distinction between generic and episodic readings is difficult to make but crucial for the interpretation of bare plural noun phrases such as *girls* and *boys*. For example, the most likely interpretation of *Counselors are available* is episodic: SOME counselors are available. But *Experts are highly paid* is weighted towards a generic reading: MOST IF NOT ALL experts get a good salary.

These examples are indicative of the subtlety of analysis necessary for high precision textual inference.

References

Danny Bobrow, Cleo Condoravdi, Richard Crouch, Ronald Kaplan, Lauri Karttunen, Tracy Holloway King, Valeria de Paiva, and Annie Zaenen. 2005. A basic logic for textual inference. In *Proceedings of the AAAI Workshop on Inference for Textual Question Answering*.

Dick Crouch and Tracy Holloway King. 2005. Unifying lexical resources. In *Proceedings of the Interdisciplinary Workshop on the Identification and Representation of Verb Features and Verb Classes*.

Dick Crouch and Tracy Holloway King. 2006. Semantics via F-structure rewriting. In *Proceedings of LFG06*. CSLI On-line Publications.

Dick Crouch, Mary Dalrymple, Ron Kaplan, Tracy King, John Maxwell, and Paula Newman. 2007. XLE documentation. Available on-line.

Christiane Fellbaum, editor. 1998. *WordNet: An Electronic Lexical Database*. The MIT Press.

Olga Gurevich, Richard Crouch, Tracy Holloway King, and Valeria de Paiva. 2006. Deverbal nouns in knowledge representation. In *Proceedings of FLAIRS 2006*.

Andres Hickl, John Williams, Jeremy Bensley, Kirk Roberts, Bryan Rink, and Ying Shi. 2006. Recognizing textual entailment with LCC's GROUNDHOG system. In *The Second PASCAL Recognising Textual Entailment Challenge*.

Karin Kipper, Hoa Trang Dang, and Martha Palmer. 2000. Class-based construction of a verb lexicon. In *AAAI-2000 17th National Conference on Artificial Intelligence*.

John Maxwell and Ron Kaplan. 1991. A method for disjunctive constraint satisfaction. *Current Issues in Parsing Technologies*.

Rowan Nairn, Cleo Condoravdi, and Lauri Karttunen. 2006. Computing relative polarity for textual inference. In *Proceedings of ICoS-5*.

Stefan Riezler, Tracy Holloway King, Ron Kaplan, Dick Crouch, John Maxwell, and Mark Johnson. 2002. Parsing the Wall Street Journal using a Lexical-Functional Grammar and discriminative estimation techniques. In *Proceedings of the Annual Meeting of the Association for Computational Linguistics*.

COGEX at RTE3

Marta Tatu and **Dan Moldovan**
Language Computer Corporation
Richardson, Texas, 75080
United States
marta,moldovan@languagecomputer.com

Abstract

This paper reports on LCC's participation at the Third PASCAL Recognizing Textual Entailment Challenge. First, we summarize our semantic logical-based approach which proved successful in the previous two challenges. Then we highlight this year's innovations which contributed to an overall accuracy of 72.25% for the RTE 3 test data. The novelties include new resources, such as eXtended WordNet KB which provides a large number of world knowledge axioms, event and temporal information provided by the TARSQI toolkit, logic form representations of events, negation, coreference and context, and new improvements of lexical chain axiom generation. Finally, the system's performance and error analysis are discussed.

1 Introduction

Continuing a two-year tradition, the PASCAL Network organized the Third Recognizing Textual Entailment Challenge[1] (RTE 3) to further the research on reasoning systems able to decide whether the meaning of one text (the entailed hypothesis, H) can be inferred from another text (the entailing text, T). Among this year's challenges, approximately 15% of the (T, H) pairs contained long texts (more details in Section 5.1).

We approach the *textual entailment* problem as a *logical implication between meanings* (Fowler et al., 2005; Tatu et al., 2006). Our system transforms the two text snippets into three-layered semantically-rich logic form representations, generates an abundant set of lexical, syntactic, semantic, and world knowledge axioms and, iteratively, searches for a proof for the entailment between the text T and a possibly relaxed version of the hypothesis H. A pair is labeled as positive if the score of the found proof (reflecting H's degree of relaxation) is above a threshold learned on the training data. Figure 1 summarizes our approach to RTE.

2 Cogex's Innovations for RTE 3

2.1 EXtended WordNet Knowledge Base

eXtended WordNet Knowledge Base (XWN-KB) is the result of our ongoing research which captures and stores the rich world knowledge encoded in WordNet's glosses into a knowledge base. In XWN-KB, the glosses have been transformed into a set of semantic relations using a semantic parser whose output has been verified by human annotators. Fig. 2 displays the semantic relations derived for *Nobel laureate*'s definition. Our system used this representation for QA Dev pair 579 and QA Test pair 582 [2].

2.2 TARSQI Toolkit

The TARSQI project (Temporal Awareness and Reasoning Systems for Question Interpretation)[3] (Verhagen et al., 2005) builds a modular system which detects, resolves and normalizes time expressions (both absolute and relative times) - GUTime tagger; marks events and their grammatical features -

[1] www.pascal-network.org/Challenges/RTE3

[2] Table 6 lists the pairs referenced throughout the paper.

[3] http://www.timeml.org/site/tarsqi

Proceedings of the Workshop on Textual Entailment and Paraphrasing, pages 22–27,
Prague, June 2007.

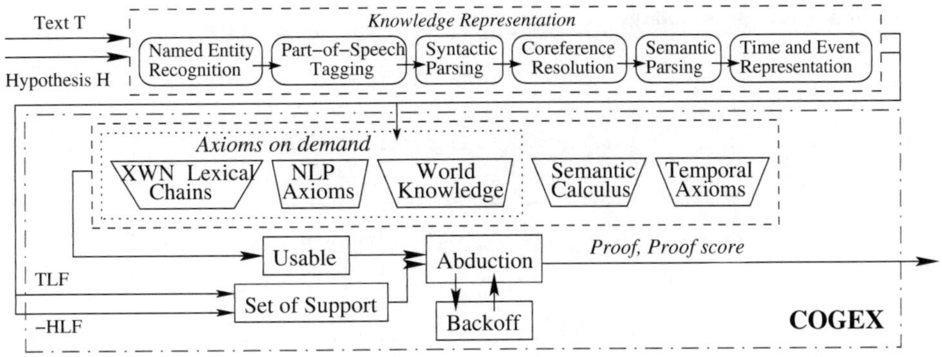

Figure 1: Cogex's Architecture

The Pet passport alone can be [used]$_{e_1:occurrence}$ to [enter]$_{e_2:occurrence}$ the UK, but it will not [suffice]$_{e_3:occurrence}$ to [enter]$_{e_4:occurrence}$ many countries. For instance Guatemala, like almost every country, [demands]$_{e_5:occurrence}$ that all imported pets have a rabies vaccination, but will not [accept]$_{e_6:i\_action}$ the Pet passport as proof of [said]$_{e_7:reporting}$ vaccination.
modality: (e_1:*can*); **tense**: (e_2:infinitive), (e_3:future), (e_4:infinitive), (e_5:present), (e_6:future), (e_7:past); **polarity**: (e_3:negative), (e_6:negative); **slink**: modal(e_1, e_2), modal(e_5, e_6), factive(e_6, e_7); **tlink**: before(e_1, e_2), before(e_5, e_6), before(e_4, e_5), before(e_6, e_7), before(e_2, e_3), before(e_2, e_4)

Table 1: TARSQI's Treatment of IE Dev pair 63's T

Nobelist, Nobel_laureate; synsetId: 06822770
gloss: *winner of a Nobel_prize*
ISA(Nobel_laureate,winner)
THEME(Nobel_prize,winner)

Figure 2: XWN-KB Treatment of *Nobel_laureate*

Evita; identifies subordination constructions introducing modality information - Slinket; adds temporal relations between events and temporal expressions - GUTenLINK; and computes temporal closures - SputLink. We used the information provided by the TARSQI toolkit (*Run #1*) as an alternative to our event detection and temporal expression identification and normalization modules (*Run #2*). Table 1 shows TARSQI's output for IE Dev pair 63's T.

The following sections present innovations related to the logic form knowledge representation.

2.3 Logic Representation of Events

For events, the logic representation of their describing concept was augmented with a special predicate (`event_EV(e1)`). When we made use of TARSQI's output (Run #1), the event predicate was replaced by the class of the event (`occurrence_EV(e1)`, `state_EV(e1)`, `reporting_EV(e1)`, etc.).

2.4 Negation

Recently, the logic representation of sentences with negated concepts was altered to mark as negated the entire scope of the negation. For example, the logic form of IE Dev pair 90's H: *Kennon did not participate in the WWII*, formerly equal to `Kennon_NN(x1) & -participate_VB(e1,x1,x4) & in_IN(e1,x2) & WWII_NN(x2) & _conflict_NE(x2) & AGT_SR(x1,e1)`, became `Kennon_NN(x1) & WWII_NN(x2) & _conflict_NE(x2) & -(exists e1 (participate_VB(e1,x1,x3) & in_IN(e1,x2) & AGT_SR(x1,e1)))` which is closer to the meaning of the English text snippet. For Run #1 (with TARSQI output), we only used the *polarity* information attached to the identified events and negated the event's predicate.

2.5 Coreference Resolution

In order to cope with the long text pairs, we added in our processing pipeline a dedicated pronominal coreference resolution module which replaced the inter-sentential resolution processing we used until now. The new tool combines Hobbs algorithm (Hobbs, 1978) and the Resolution of Anaphora Procedure (RAP) algorithm (Lappin and Leass, 1994). For the RTE task, it is very important to have tight connections between the predicates of

Semantic Relation	Axiom Templates
ISA	`n1(x1) -> n2(x1);v1(e1,x1,x2) -> v2(e1,x1,x2)`
DERIVATION	`n(x1) -> v(e1,x1,x2) & AGENT_SR(x1,e1);n(e1) -> v(e1,x1,x2)` `v(e1,x1,x2) -> n(x1);v(e1,x1,x2) -> n(e1)`
CAUSE	`v1(e1,x1,x2) -> v2(e2,x2,x3) & CAUSE_SR(e1,e2)`
AGENT	`n1(x1) -> n2(x2) & AGENT_SR(x1,x2)`
PERTAIN	`a(x1,x2) -> n(x1)`

Table 2: Semantic Relation - Axiom Template mapping

long texts. For example, for QA Dev pair 409, resolving the pronoun *he* to *George H.W. Bush* is a step needed to correctly label the pair. But IE Dev pair 92 requires more advanced anaphora resolution which corefers *the team* and *the Kinston Indians*.

3 Natural Language Axiom Improvements

3.1 XWN Lexical Chains

In order to take advantage of XWN-KB, we implemented few changes in our lexical chain axioms generation module. The most significant refinement is the one axiom-per-chain relation approach. Previously, the system was generating one axiom for the entire lexical chain, but, given the diversity of semantic relations which link the WordNet concepts and the difficulty to reduce an entire semantically rich chain to one implication which captures its meaning, a remodeling of our axiom generation module was required. Therefore, for each relation in the best lexical chain found between one of T's constituents and one of H's constituents, an axiom is created. For each semantic relation, we created a set of axiom templates to be used during the axiom generation process. Several examples of axiom templates are shown in Table 2. Therefore, a lexical chain is broken down into several axioms whose relations are combined by the logic prover as it sees fit. For instance, the chain *oil_company#n#1* $\xrightarrow{agent}$ *sell#v#1* $\xleftarrow{entailment}$ *trade#v#1* is translated into the axioms `oil_company_NN(x1) -> sell_VB(e1,x1,x2) & AGENT_SR(x1,e1)` and `sell_VB(e1,x1,x2) -> trade_VB(e1,x1,x2)` used to prove the entailment for IE Dev pair 196.

We also changed the subset of senses considered when lexical chains are built. Previously, this subset contained the first k ($k = 3$) senses for each content word. For this year's challenge, we changed the sense selection mechanism and we used the cluster of WordNet senses to which the fine-grained sense assigned by the Word Sense Disambiguation system corresponds. We used the coarse-grained sense inventory for WordNet 2.1 released for Task #7 in SemEval-2007[4]. This clustering was created automatically with the aid of a methodology described in (Navigli, 2006). For example, the 10 WordNet senses for the noun *bank* are mapped into 3 clusters.

3.2 NLP Axioms

In addition to the syntactic re-writing rules which break down complex syntactic structures, including complex nominals and coordinating conjunctions, we added a new type of NLP axioms which links a named entity to its set of aliases. For IE Dev pair 35, the link between the *Central Intelligence Agency* mentioned in T and H's *CIA* is very important.

We also added a deeper analysis of multi-word human named entities which marks *last names* (*Hawking*), *first (male/female) names* (*Stephen*), *titles* (*Prime Minister*) and *names* for human entities found in WordNet (*Tony Blair*). This fine classification has three goals: (1) to mark human entities with the gender information (used by the pronominal coreference module); (2) to prevent lexical chains to use first names of human entities as their source or target (*Elizabeth* as part of *Elizabeth Alexandra Mary* should not be mapped to {*Elizabeth#1, Elizabeth_II#1*} or {*Elizabeth#2, Elizabeth_I#1*} - QA Dev pair 407); (3) to create more precise NLP axioms for human entities denoting noun compounds. These axioms follow rules such as `title(x1) & last_name(x2) & nn_NNC(x3,x1,x2) -> last_name(x3) & title(x3)`, `title(x1) & first_name(x2) & last_name(x3) & nn_NNC(x4,x1,x2,x3) -> nn_NNC(x4,x2,x3)`, etc. For IR Dev pair 287, the

[4] `nlp.cs.swarthmore.edu/semeval`

axiom `Prime_Minister_NN(x6) & Giulio_NN(x7) & Andreotti_NN(x8) & nn_NNC(x9,x6,x7,x8) & _human_NE(x9) -> Andreotti_NN(x9)` expresses the equivalence between *Prime Minister Giulio Andreotti* and *Andreotti*. During the processing of the development set, the prover used 75 axioms of this type. During testing, 112 axioms proved to be useful in finding proofs.

4 Named Entity Check

Based on the guidelines for judging whether T entails or not H, hypotheses that introduce entities which cannot be derived from T are not entailed by the text (the pair is labeled as *NO*). Therefore, we created a proof's score adjustment module which deducts points for each pair whose H contains at least one *named entity* not-derivable from T. Once the prover used the loaded axioms to derive all the possible information from the text, this named entity check is performed. We note that the named entity heuristic is not equivalent with the removal of a named entity predicate from the hypothesis in the relaxation stage which can also occur if the syntactic constraints in which the named entity participates are not satisfied. For instance, for IR Dev pair 387, *Puncheon Lama* is a new entity introduced by the hypothesis without any connection to the text.

5 Experiments and Results

5.1 Experimental Data

The RTE 3 data set was derived with four NLP applications in mind: Information Extraction (IE), Information Retrieval (IR), Question Answering (QA), and Multi-document Summarization (SUM). Statistics for this year's dataset are shown in Table 3. On average, the *long* texts contain twice the number of words found in texts from pairs marked as *short*.

5.2 Cogex's Performance

Table 4 details our submission results for Run #1 (TARSQI's events, temporal expressions and event-event and event-time relations) and Run #2 (LCC's event, temporal expressions and event-time relations)[5]. The two runs do not differ significantly. The

Dataset	True	False	Overall
IE	105 (8)	95 (11)	200 (19)
IR	87 (23)	113 (31)	200 (54)
QA	106 (22)	94 (13)	200 (35)
SUM	112 (5)	88 (4)	200 (9)
Test	410 (58)	390 (59)	800 (117)
Development	412 (78)	388 (57)	800 (135)

Table 3: Data split between *true* and *false* classes. The number of pairs with *long* text is shown in parenthesis.

Task	A	AvgP	P	R	F
Run #1					
IE	63.50	61.44	59.20	98.10	73.84
IR	78.00	78.83	76.54	71.26	73.81
QA	87.50	87.81	87.85	88.68	88.26
SUM	60.00	61.54	58.99	93.75	72.41
Test	**72.25**	69.42	67.41	88.78	76.63
Dev	76.37	72.12	75.17	80.82	77.89
Run #2					
IE	64.50	56.26	60.12	96.19	73.99
IR	75.50	77.65	75.00	65.52	69.94
QA	85.00	87.40	81.67	92.45	86.73
SUM	62.00	58.16	60.47	92.86	73.12
Test	**71.75**	67.97	67.16	87.80	76.11
Dev	74.12	71.28	71.95	81.55	76.45

Table 4: Results for Run #1 and Run #2

extra information captured in the logic representations used in Run #1 (as compared with Run #2) was not the focus of the entailment; the understanding it brings was not exercised during the entailment recognition process. For the IR and QA tasks, Run #1 results are better when compared to Run #2's. For these tasks, the performance of the system is much higher when compared with the results obtained for IE and SUM. Even tough the thresholds learned for these two tasks best separate the positive from the negative pairs on the development set, they prove to be fairly low for the test set. Almost all positive IE and SUM pairs are identified as such (very high recall for both tasks), but a lot of negatives are also labeled as positives (low precision, smaller accuracy).

5.3 Named Entity Heuristic Impact

Table 5 details the interaction between the prover (Run #1) and the named entity heuristic[6]. The

[5] **A**, **AvgP**, **P**, **R** and **F** stand for accuracy, average precision, precision, recall, and f-measure, respectively.

[6] **Coverage** shows the number of pairs for which the heuristic fired, **H's A**, **C's A** and **C+H's A** indicate, respectively, the named entity heuristic accuracy, Cogex's and the prover's when

heuristic fires for 167 pairs, while only 154 of them are true negative entailments (92.21% accuracy). The prover's accuracy for the same subset of pairs is 65.86%. The maximum overall improvement in accuracy that the heuristic can bring is 5.5%, but, because of the way the heuristic penalizes the proof scores, its overall improvement is 4.12%.

Task	Coverage	H's A	C's A	C+H's A
IE	19	100.00	42.10	100.00
IR	56	94.64	73.21	94.64
QA	59	94.91	77.96	94.91
SUM	33	78.78	45.45	45.45
Test	167	92.21	65.86	85.63

Table 5: NE heuristic's performance for Run #1

In theory, the named entity check should not fail. But, in practice, its performance is influenced by the knowledge that the prover collects and, if this information is not complete, then the heuristic fails. For example, for QA Dev pair 419, H mentions number *three* and because the prover cannot infer it as the cardinality of the elementary particles mentioned in T, the heuristic fires incorrectly.

5.4 Error Analysis

Some of the sources of errors are:

Lexical chains For IR Test pair 377, *black_plague* can be derived from T's *plague* only if we allow lexical chains with more than 2 HYPONYMY relations (*plague#n#1* $\xrightarrow{hyponymy}$ *bubonic_plague#n#1* $\xrightarrow{hyponymy}$ *black_plague#n#1*). This restriction on lexical chains was added last year. However, in this year's data this restriction was detrimental as shown in the above example.

Named entity heuristic Some of the errors introduced by the named entity heuristic are debatable. For example, IR Test pair 355's hypothesis introduces the named entity *German* which cannot be derived from the text. Similarly, for QA Test pairs 495 and 496, the name *Christian Democratic Union* cannot be inferred from the text's mention of *Christian Democrat party*. On the other hand, pairs for which the score adjustment introduced by the named entity heuristic did not change the label assigned by the prover include SUM Test pair 656 whose hypothesis mentions *US* without it being derivable from the text (unless we consider the adjective *domestic*).

the scores it computes are adjusted according to the heuristic.

World Knowledge For SUM Test pair 744, the system fails to infer *nearly half a million dollars* from $480,350. Similarly, the system failed to entail *died in 1970* from the biographical markings "(1890-1970)" for QA Test pair 486.

High word overlap SUM pairs have a high degree of word-overlap between T and H and detection of the non-entailment requires careful processing. SUM Test pair 666's text contains an extra adverbial phrase which changes the label of the pair.

Reports and Modality Even though reporting verbs (*X said that Y*) and modalities (*X may Y*, *X tried to Y*) should influence the validity of the statement they modify, most Y clauses are considered true in the RTE data (SUM Dev pair 756, IR Dev pair 295, IE Dev pair 148 are just few examples). Therefore, our solutions for representing[7] or checking these modifiers[8] failed to bring any improvement on the development set and were not included in the processing of the test set.

But, for IE Test pair 172, T's main verb is qualified by *threatened* which is not present in H. For SUM Test pair 672, *cited strong volume gains* does not entail *makes strong profits*.

6 Conclusion

The XWN-KB is an invaluable resource for recognizing textual entailment. Its impact in RTE 3 was significant. However, we are still exploring ways of fully exploiting this resource. The use of the TARSQI toolkit did not impact the performance because the temporal knowledge was not exercised in this year's task. Contrary to our expectations, the representation of modality had a negative impact on the performance. This is perhaps due to incorrect representation. For our system, the introduction of long texts did not cause significant problems. The system is robust enough to handle longer texts.

[7]Our representation for *X said Y* which prevents the entailment that *Y* is `(X(x1) & _report_CTXT(c1,x1)) -> (Y(e1))`

[8]We attempted to penalize proofs which infer the second argument of an MODAL slink without entailing the first. Pairs IE Dev 191 and IR Dev 203 fall in this category, but have different gold annotation labels.

Id	Tag	Pair Text and Hypothesis
D35	YES	T: A leading human rights group on Wednesday identified Poland and Romania as the likely locations in eastern Europe of secret prisons where al-Qaeda suspects are interrogated by the Central Intelligence Agency. H: CIA secret prisons were located in Eastern Europe.
D92	YES	T: The Kinston Indians are a minor league baseball team in Kinston, North Carolina. The team, a Class A affiliate of the Cleveland Indians, plays in the Carolina League. H: Kinston Indians participate in the Carolina League.
D191	YES	T: Though Wilkins and his family settled quickly in Italy, it wasn't a successful era for Milan, and Wilkins was allowed to leave in 1987 to join French outfit Paris Saint-Germain. H: Wilkins departed Milan in 1987.
D196	YES	T: Some large Russian oil companies, including Lukoil, Zarubezhneft, the state-owned oil company, and Alpha Eco, the trader, were implicated by the report. H: Zarubezhneft trades in oil.
D203	NO	T: A decision to allow the exiled Italian royal family to return to Italy may be granted amid the discovery that the head of the family, Prince Vittorio Emmanuele, addressed the president of Italy properly. He has called President Ciampi "our president, the president of all Italians". H: Italian royal family returns home.
D287	YES	T: Italy's highest court has upheld a court verdict that partially cleared former Prime Minister Giulio Andreotti of having colluded with the Mafia. H: Andreotti is accused of Mafia collusion.
D387	NO	T: Thus, China's President repeatedly sent letters and envoys to the Dalai Lama and to the Tibetan Government asking that Tibet "join" the Republic of China. H: Dalai Lama and the government of the People's Republic of China are in dispute over Panchen Lama's reincarnation.
D409	YES	T: George H.W. Bush served this country not only as President but also as Vice President, Member of Congress, United Nations Ambassador, chief of the U.S. Liaison Office to the People's Republic of China, Director of the Central Intelligence Agency and also, as a naval aviator in World War II. Coming back from the war, he married his sweetheart, Barbara Pierce of Rye, New York, and later that year made his first civilian adult decision when he made the appropriate choice of moving to Texas, where he lived the rest of his life. H: The name of George H.W. Bush's wife is Barbara.
D419	YES	T: Discovery of the top quark, if confirmed, completes one set of subatomic building blocks whose existence is predicted by the prevailing theory, called the Standard Model, of the particles and forces that determine the fundamental nature of matter and energy. In the whimsical lexicon of modern physics, the elementary particles are called quarks, leptons and bosons. H: Quarks, leptons, and bosons are the three elementary particles of physics according to the Standard Model.
D579	YES	T: Salma Hayek drew a crowd in Veracruz, Mexico, at the July 8 premiere of 'Nobody Writes to the Colonel', a movie based on a short novel by Nobel laureate Gabriel Garcia Marquez. H: Gabriel Garcia Marquez is a Nobel prize winner.
D756	YES	T: The contaminated pills included metal fragments ranging in size from "microdots" to portions of wire one-third of an inch long, the FDA said. H: The contaminated pills contained metal fragments.
T172	NO	T: This year thousands of Hindu Holy Men, also known as sadhus, threatened to boycott festivals during their pilgrimage to the Ganges, where their rituals involve washing away their sins by bathing in the water. H: Hindu Holy Men boycotted festivals during their pilgrimage to the Ganges.
T355	YES	T: Before reconstruction began, the Reichstag was wrapped by the Bulgarian artist Christo and his wife Jeanne-Claude in 1995, attracting millions of visitors. H: Christo wraps German Reichstag.
T377	YES	T: The U.S. enjoyed miraculously long immunity from the dreaded plague that used to sweep Europe. H: Black plague swept Europe.
T495	YES	T: Former German Chancellor Helmut Kohl said Thursday he will not break pledges he made to campaign contributors by publicly disclosing their names even though his Christian Democrat party has directed him to reveal their identities. H: The name of Helmut Kohl's political party is the Christian Democratic Union.
T561	YES	T: Pope John Paul II arrived Saturday in the birthplace of the Solidarity movement that he sparked with his first papal visit 20 years ago, offering Poles "the greeting of a fellow Pole who comes among you to fulfill the needs of his own heart." H: Pope John Paul II was born in Poland.
T565	NO	T: On the domestic tobacco front, operating income rose by 12 per cent to Dollars 914m, with "slightly higher unit volume". H: US tobacco income has risen.
T666	NO	T: Boys and girls will be segregated during sex education in junior high school. H: Boys and girls will be segregated in junior high school.
T672	NO	T: Philip Morris cited strong volume gains in Germany, Italy, France, Spain, central and eastern Europe, the Far East, Japan, Korea, Argentina and Brazil. H: Philip Morris makes strong profits also in Europe.
T725	YES	T: After years of battling between oil companies, the Ecuadorian government decided to collaborate with indigenous groups. H: The Ecuadorian government collaborated with indigenous groups.

Table 6: Examples of RTE 3 pairs. D# and T# refer to the # pair from the dev and the test set, respectively

Acknowledgments

We would like to thank Iulia Nica for her helpful suggestions (including the named entity check) and Marc Verhagen and James Pustejovsky for presenting us with TARSQI's output for the RTE datasets.

References

A. Fowler, B. Hauser, D. Hodges, I. Niles, A. Novischi, and J. Stephan. 2005. Applying COGEX to Recognize Textual Entailment. In *Proceedings of the PASCAL Challenges Workshop*.

J. Hobbs. 1978. Resolving Pronoun References. *Lingua*, 44:311–338.

S. Lappin and H. Leass. 1994. An Algorithm for Pronominal Anaphora Resolution. *Computational Linguistics*, 20(4):535–561.

R. Navigli. 2006. Meaningful Clustering of Senses Helps Boost Word Sense Disambiguation Performance. In *Proceedings of COLING-ACL 2006*.

M. Tatu, B. Iles, J. Slavick, A. Novischi, and D. Moldovan. 2006. COGEX at the Second Recognizing Textual Entailment Challenge. In *Proceedings of the Second PASCAL Challenges Workshop on Recognising Textual Entailment*, Venice, Italy.

M. Verhagen, I. Mani, R. Sauri, R. Knippen, J .Littman, and J. Pustejovsky. 2005. Automating Temporal Annotation with TARSQI. In *Proceedings of ACL 2005. Demo Session*.

A Corpus of Fine-Grained Entailment Relations

Rodney D. Nielsen and Wayne Ward
Center for Spoken Language Research
Institute of Cognitive Science
Department of Computer Science
University of Colorado, Boulder
Rodney.Nielsen, Wayne.Ward@Colorado.edu

Abstract

This paper describes on-going efforts to annotate a corpus of almost 16000 answer pairs with an estimated 69000 fine-grained entailment relationships. We illustrate the need for more detailed classification than currently exists and describe our corpus and annotation scheme. We discuss early statistical analysis showing substantial inter-annotator agreement even at the fine-grained level. The corpus described here, which is the only one providing such detailed annotations, will be made available as a public resource later this year (2007). This is expected to enable application development that is currently not practical.

1 Introduction

Determining whether the propositions in one text fragment are entailed by those in another fragment is important to numerous NLP applications. Consider an intelligent tutoring system (ITS), where it is critical for the tutor to assess which specific facets of the desired or reference answer are entailed by the student's answer. Truly effective interaction and pedagogy is only possible if the automated tutor can assess this entailment at a relatively fine level of detail (c.f. Jordan et al., 2004).

The PASCAL Recognizing Textual Entailment (RTE) challenge (Dagan et al., 2005) has brought the issue of textual entailment before a broad community of researchers in a task independent fashion. This task requires systems to make simple yes-no judgments as to whether a human reading a text *t* of one or more full sentences would typically consider a second, hypothesis, text *h* (usually one full sentence) to most likely be true. This paper discusses some of the extensions necessary to this scheme in order to satisfy the requirements of an ITS and provides a preliminary report on our efforts to produce an annotated corpus applying some of these additions to children's answers to science questions.

We first provide a brief overview of the RTE challenge task and a synopsis of answer assessment technology within existing ITSs and large scale assessment applications. We then detail some of the types of changes required in order to facilitate more effective pedagogy. We provide a report on our work in this direction and describe a corpus we are annotating with fine-grained entailment information. Finally, we discuss future direction and the relevance of this annotation scheme to other applications such as question answering.

2 Prior Work

2.1 RTE Challenge Task

Example 1 shows a typical *t-h* pair from the RTE challenge. The task is to determine whether typically a reader would say that *h* is most likely true having read *t*. The system output is a simple yes or no decision about this entailment – in this example, the decision is *no* – and that is similarly the extent to which training data is annotated. There is no indication of whether some facets of, the potentially quite long, *h* are addressed (as they are in this case) in *t* or conversely, which facets are not discussed or are explicitly contradicted.

```
(1)    <t>At an international disas-
ter conference in Kobe, Japan, the
```


Proceedings of the Workshop on Textual Entailment and Paraphrasing, pages 28–35,
Prague, June 2007.

```
U.N. humanitarian chief said the
United Nations should take the lead
in creating a tsunami early-warning
system in the Indian Ocean.</t>
<h>Nations affected by the Asian
tsunami disaster have agreed the UN
should begin work on an early warning
system in the Indian Ocean.</h>
```

However, in the third RTE challenge, there is an optional pilot task[1] that begins to address some of these issues. Specifically, they have extended the task by including an unknown label, where *h* is neither entailed nor contradicted, and have requested justification for decisions. The form that these justifications will take has been left up to the groups participating, but could conceivably provide some of the information about which specific facets of the hypothesis are entailed, contradicted and unaddressed.

2.2 Existing Answer Assessment Technology

Effective ITSs exist in the laboratory producing learning gains in high-school, college, and adult subjects through text-based dialog interaction (e.g., Graesser et al., 2001; Koedinger et al., 1997; Peters et al., 2004, VanLehn et al., 2005). However, most ITSs today provide only a shallow assessment of the learner's comprehension (e.g., a correct versus incorrect decision). Many ITS researchers are striving to provide more refined learner feedback (Aleven et al., 2001; Graesser et al., 2001; Jordan et al., 2004; Peters et al., 2004; Roll et al., 2005; Rosé et al., 2003). However, they are developing very domain-dependent approaches, requiring a significant investment in hand-crafted logic representations, parsers, knowledge-based ontologies, and or dialog control mechanisms. Simply put, these domain-dependent techniques will not scale to the task of developing general purpose ITSs and will never enable the long-term goal of effective unconstrained interaction with learners or the pedagogy that requires it.

There is also a small, but growing, body of research in the area of scoring free-text responses to short answer questions (e.g., Callear et al., 2001; Leacock, 2004; Mitchell et al., 2003; Pullman, 2005; Sukkarieh, 2005). Shaw (2004) and Whittington (1999) provide reviews of some of these approaches. Most of the systems that have been implemented and tested are based on Information Extraction (IE) techniques (Cowie & Lehnert, 1996). They hand-craft a large number of pattern rules, directed at detecting the propositions in common correct and incorrect answers. In general, short-answer free-text response scoring systems are designed for large scale assessment tasks, such as those associated with the tests administered by ETS. Therefore, they are not designed with the goal of accommodating dynamically generated, previously unseen questions. Similarly, these systems do not provide feedback regarding the specific aspects of answers that are correct or incorrect; they merely provide a raw score for each question. As with the related work directed specifically at ITSs, these approaches all require in the range of 100-500 example student answers for each planned test question to assist in the creation of IE patterns or to train a machine learning algorithm used within some component of their solution.

3 The Necessity of Finer-grained Analysis

Imagine that you are an elementary school science tutor and that rather than having access to the student's full response to your questions, you are simply given the information that their answer was correct or incorrect, a yes or no entailment decision. Assuming the student's answer was not correct, what question do you ask next? What follow up question or action is most likely to lead to better understanding on the part of the child? Clearly, this is a far from ideal scenario, but it is roughly the situation within which many ITSs exist today.

In order to optimize learning gains in the tutoring environment, there are myriad issues the tutor must understand regarding the semantics of the student's response. Here, we focus strictly on drawing inferences regarding the student's understanding of the low-level concepts and relationships or facets of the reference answer. I use the word facet throughout this paper to generically refer to some part of a text's meaning. The most common type of answer facet discussed is the meaning associated with a pair of related words and the relation that connects them.

Rather than have a single yes or no entailment decision for the reference answer as a whole, (i.e., does the student understand the reference answer in its entirety or is there some unspecified part of it that we are unsure whether the student understands), we instead break the reference answer

[1] http://nlp.stanford.edu/RTE3-pilot/

down into what we consider to be its lowest level compositional facets. This roughly translates to the set of triples composed of labeled dependencies in a dependency parse of the reference answer.[2] The following illustrates how a simple reference answer (2) is decomposed into the answer facets (2a-d) derived from its dependency parse and (2a'-d') provide a gloss of each facet's meaning. As can be seen in 2b and 2c, the dependencies are augmented by thematic roles (Kipper et al., 2000) (e.g., Agent, Theme, Cause, Instrument…) produced by a semantic role labeling system (c.f., Gildea and Jurafsky, 2002). The facets also include those semantic role relations that are not derivable from a typical dependency tree. For example, in the sentence *"As it freezes the water will expand and crack the glass"*, *water* is not a modifier of *crack* in the dependency tree, but it does play the role of Agent in a shallow semantic parse.

```
(2) A long string produces a low pitch.

(2a) NMod(string, long)
(2b) Agent(produces, string)
(2c) Product(produces, pitch)
(2d) NMod(pitch, low)

(2a') There is a long string.
(2b') The string is producing something.
(2c') A pitch is being produced.
(2d') The pitch is low.
```

Breaking the reference answer down into low-level facets provides the tutor's dialog manager with a much finer-grained assessment of the student's response, but a simple yes or no entailment at the facet level still lacks semantic expressiveness with regard to the relation between the student's answer and the facet in question. Did the student contradict the facet? Did they express a related concept that indicates a misconception? Did they leave the facet unaddressed? Can you assume that they understand the facet even though they did not express it, since it was part of the information given in the question? It is clear that, in addition to breaking the reference answer into fine-grained facets, it is also necessary to break the annotation into finer levels in order to specify more clearly the relationship between the student's answer and the reference answer aspect.

There are many other issues that the system must know to achieve near optimal tutoring, some of which are mentioned later in the discussion section, but these two – breaking the reference answer into fine-grained facets and utilizing more expressive annotation labels – are the emphasis of this effort.

4 Current Annotation Efforts

This section describes our current efforts in annotating a corpus of answers to science questions from elementary school students.

4.1 Corpus

Lacking data from a real tutoring situation, we acquired data gathered from 3rd-6th grade students in schools utilizing the Full Option Science System (FOSS). Assessment is a major FOSS research focus, of which the Assessing Science Knowledge project is a key component.[3] The FOSS project has developed sixteen science teaching and learning modules targeted at grades 3-6, as shown in Table 1. The ASK project created assessments for each of these modules, including multiple choice, fill in the blank, free response, and somewhat lengthy experimental design questions. We reviewed these questions and selected about 290 free response questions that were in line with the objectives of this research project, specifically we selected questions whose expected responses ranged in length from moderately short verb phrases to a few sentences, that could be assessed objectively, and that were not too open ended. Table 2 shows a

[2] The goal of most English dependency parsers is to produce a single projective tree structure for each sentence, where each node represents a word in the sentence, each link represents a functional category relation, usually labeled, between a governor (head) and a subordinate (modifier), and each node has a single governor (c.f., Nivre and Scholz, 2004).

[3] "FOSS is a research-based science program for grades K–8 developed at the Lawrence Hall of Science, University of California at Berkeley with support from the National Science Foundation and published by Delta Education. FOSS is also an ongoing research project dedicated to improving the learning and teaching of science."
Assessing Science Knowledge (ASK) is "designed to define, field test, and validate effective assessment tools and techniques to be used by grade 3–6 classroom teachers to assess, guide, and confirm student learning in science."
http://www.lawrencehallofscience.org/foss/

Grade	Life Science	Physical Science and Technology	Earth and Space Science	Scientific Reasoning and Technology
3-4	HB: Human Body ST: Structure of Life	ME: Magnetism & Electricity PS: Physics of Sound	WA: Water EM: Earth Materials	II: Ideas & Inventions MS: Measurement
5-6	FN: Food & Nutrition EV: Environments	LP: Levers & Pulleys MX: Mixtures & Solutions	SE: Solar Energy LF: Landforms	MD: Models & Designs VB: Variables

Table 1 FOSS / ASK Learning and Assessment Modules by Area and Grade

HB	Q:	Dancers need to be able to point their feet. The tibialis is the major muscle on the front of the leg and the gastrocnemius is the major muscle on the back of the leg. Describe how the muscles in the front and back of the leg work together to make the dancer's foot point.
	R:	The muscle in the back of the leg (the gastrocnemius) contracts and the muscle in the front of the leg (the tibialis) relaxes to make the foot point.
	A:	The back muscle and the front muscle stretch to help each other pull up the foot.
ST	Q:	Why is it important to have more than one shelter in a crayfish habitat with several crayfish?
	R:	Crayfish are territorial and will protect their territory. The shelters give them places to hide from other crayfish. [Crayfish prefer the dark and the shelters provide darkness.]
	A:	So all the crayfish have room to hide and so they do not fight over them.
ME	Q:	Lee has an object he wants to test to see if it is an insulator or a conductor. He is going to use the circuit you see in the picture. Explain how he can use the circuit to test the object.
	R:	He should put one of the loose wires on one part of the object and the other loose wire on another part of the object (and see if it completes the circuit).
	A:	You can touch one wire on one end and the other on the other side to see if it will run or not.
PS	Q:	Kate said: "An object has to move to produce sound." Do you agree with her? Why or why not?
	R:	Agree. Vibrations are movements and vibrations produce sound.
	A:	I agree with Kate because if you talk in a tube it produce sound in a long tone. And it vibrations and make sound.
WA	Q:	Anna spilled half of her cup of water on the kitchen floor. The other half was still in the cup. When she came back hours later, all of the water on the floor had evaporated but most of the water in the cup was still there. (Anna knew that no one had wiped up the water on the floor.) Explain to Anna why the water on the floor had all evaporated but most of the water in the cup had not.
	R:	The water on the floor had a much larger surface area than the water in the cup.
	A:	Well Anna, in science, I learned that when water is in a more open are, then water evaporates faster. So, since tile and floor don't have any boundaries or wall covering the outside, the water on the floor evaporated faster, but since the water in the cup has boundaries, the water in the cup didn't evaporate as fast.
EM	Q:	You can tell if a rock contains calcite by putting it into a cold acid (like vinegar). Describe what you would observe if you did the acid test on a rock that contains this substance.
	R:	Many tiny bubbles will rise from the calcite when it comes into contact with cold acid.
	A:	You would observe if it was fizzing because calcite has a strong reaction to vinegar.

Table 2 Sample Qs from FOSS-ASK with their reference (R) and an example student answer (A).

few questions that are representative of those selected for inclusion in the corpus, along with their reference answers and an example student answer for each. Questions without at least one verb phrase were rejected because they were assumed to be more trivial and less interesting from the research perspective. Examples of such questions along with their reference answers and an example student response include: Q: *Besides air, what (if anything) can sound travel through?* Reference Answer: *Sound can also travel through liquids and solids. (Also other gases.)* Student Answer: *A screen door.* Q: *Name a property of the sound of a fire engine's siren.* Reference Answer: *The sound is very loud. OR The sound changes in pitch.* Student Answer: *Annoying.* An example of a free response item that was dropped because it was too open ended is: *Design an investigation to find out a plant's range of tolerance for number of hours of sunlight per day. You can use drawings to help explain your design.*

We generated a corpus from a random sample of the kids' handwritten responses to these questions. The only special transcription instructions were to fix spelling errors (since these would be irrelevant in a spoken dialog environment), but not grammatical errors (which would still be relevant), and to skip blank answers and non-answers similar in nature to *I don't know* (since these are not particularly interesting from the research perspective).

Three modules were designated as the test set (Environments, Human Body, and Water) and the remaining 13 modules will be used for development and training of classification systems. We judged the three test set modules to be representative of the entire corpus in terms of difficulty and appropriateness for the types of questions that met our research interests. We transcribed the responses of approximately 40 randomly selected students for each question in the training set and 100 randomly selected students for each question in the test set. In order to maximize the diversity of language and knowledge represented by the training and test datasets, random selection of students was performed at the question level rather than using the same students' answers for all of the questions in a given module. However, in total there were only about 200 children that participated in any individual science module assessment, so there is still moderate overlap in the students from one question to another within a given module. On the other hand, each assessment module was given to a different group of kids, so there is no overlap in students between modules. There are almost 60 questions and 5700 student answers in the test set, comprising approximately 20% of all of the questions utilized and 36% of the total number of transcribed student responses. In total, including test and training datasets, there are nearly 16000 student responses.

4.2 Annotation

The answer assessment annotation described in this paper is intended to be a step toward specifying the detailed semantic understanding of a student's answer that is required for an ITS to interact effectively with a learner. With that goal in mind, annotators were asked to consider and annotate according to what they would want to know about the student's answer if they were the tutor (but a tutor that for some reason could not understand the unstructured text of the student's answer). The key exception here is that we are only annotating a student's answer in terms of whether or not it accurately and completely addresses the facets of the reference (desired or correct) answer. So, if the student also discusses concepts not addressed in the reference answer, we will not annotate those points regardless of their quality or accuracy.

Each reference answer in the corpus is decomposed into its constituent facets. Then each student answer is annotated relative to the facets in the corresponding reference answer. As described earlier, the reference answer facets are roughly extracted from the relations in a syntactic dependency parse (c.f., Nivre and Scholz, 2004) and a shallow semantic parse (Gildea and Jurafsky, 2002). These are modified slightly to either eliminate most function words or incorporate them into the relation labels (c.f., Lin and Pantel, 2001). Example 3 illustrates the decomposition of one of the reference answers into its constituent parts along with their glosses.

```
(3) The string is tighter, so the
pitch is higher.

(3a)  Is(string, tighter)
(3a') The string is tighter.
(3b)  Is(pitch, higher)
(3b') The pitch is higher.
(3c)  Cause(3b, 3a)
(3c') 3b is caused by 3a
```

The annotation tool lists the reference answer facets that students are expected to address. Both a formal relational representation and an English-like gloss of the facet are displayed in a table, one row per facet. The annotator's job is to label each of those facets to indicate the extent to which the student addressed it. We settled on the eight annotation labels noted in Table 3. Descriptions of where each annotation label applies and some of the most common annotation issues were detailed with several examples in the guidelines and are only very briefly summarized in the remainder of this subsection.

Example 4 shows a student answer corresponding to the reference answer in example 3, along with its initial annotation in 4a-c and its final annotation in 4a'-c'. It is assumed that the student understands that the pitch is higher (facet 4b), since this is given in the question (... *Write a note to David to tell him why the pitch gets higher rather than lower*) and similarly it is assumed that the student will be explaining what has the causal effect of producing this higher pitch (facet 4c). Therefore, these facets are initialized to `Assumed` by the system. Since the student does not contradict the fact that the string is tighter (the string can be both longer and tighter), we do not label this facet as `Contradicted`. If the student's response did not mention anything about either the string or tightness, we would annotate facet 4a as `Unaddressed`. However, the student did discuss a property of the string, *the string is long*, producing the facet `Is(string, long)`. This parallels the reference answer facet `Is(string, tighter)` with the exception of a different argument to the `Is` relation, resulting in the annotation `Diff-Arg`. This indicates to the tutor that the student expressed a related concept, but one which neither implies that they understand the reference answer facet nor that they explicitly hold a contradictory belief. Often, this indicates that the student has a misconception. For example, when asked about an effect on pitch, many students say things like *the pitch gets louder*, rather than higher or lower, which implies a misconception involving their understanding of pitch and volume. In this case, the `Diff-Arg` label can help focus the tutor on correcting this misconception. Facet 4c expressing the causal relation between 4a and 4b is labeled `Expressed`, since the student did express a causal relation between the concepts aligned with 4a and 4c. The tutor then knows that the student was on track in regard to attempting to express the desired causal relation and the tutor need only deal with the fact that the cause given was incorrect.

Expressed: Any facet directly expressed or inferred by simple reasoning	
Inferred: Facets inferred by pragmatics or nontrivial logical reasoning	
Contra-Expr: Facets directly contradicted by negation, antonymous expressions and their paraphrases	
Contra-Infr: Facets contradicted by pragmatics or complex reasoning	
Self-Contra: Facets that are both contradicted and implied (self contradictions)	
Diff-Arg: The core relation is expressed, but it has a different modifier or argument	
Assumed: The system assigns this label, which is changed if any of the above labels apply	
Unaddressed: Facets that are not addressed at all by the student's answer	

Table 3 Facet Annotation Labels

```
(4) David this is why because you
don't listen to your teacher. If the
string is long, the pitch will be
high.
```

```
(4a) Is(string, tighter), ---
(4b) Is(pitch, higher), Assumed
(4c) Cause(4b, 4a), Assumed
```

```
(4a') Is(string, tighter), Diff-Arg
(4b') Is(pitch, higher), Expressed
(4c') Cause(4b, 4a), Expressed
```

The `Self-Contra` annotation is used in cases like the response in example 5, where the student simultaneously expresses the contradictory notions that the string is tighter and that there is less tension.

```
(5) The string is tighter, so there is
less tension so the pitch gets higher.
```

```
(5a) Is(string, tighter), Self-Contra
```

There is no compelling reason from the perspective of the automated tutoring system to differentiate between `Expressed` and `Inferred` facets, since in either case the tutor can assume that the student understands the concepts involved. However, from the systems development perspective there are three primary reasons for differentiating between these facets and similarly between facets that are contradicted by inference versus more explicit expression. The first reason is that most statistical machine learning systems today cannot hope to detect very many pragmatic inferences and including these in the training data is likely to confuse the algorithm resulting in worse performance. Having separate labels allows one to remove the more difficult inferences from the training data, thus eliminating this problem. The second rationale is that systems hoping to handle both types of inference might more easily learn to discriminate between these opposing classifications if the classes are distinguished (for algorithms where this is not the case, the classes can easily be combined automatically). Similarly, this allows the possibility of training separate classifiers to handle the different forms of inference. The third reason for separate labels is that it facilitates system evaluation, including the comparison of various techniques and the effect of individual features.

Example 6 illustrates an example of a student answer with the label `Inferred`. In this case, the decision requires pragmatic inferences, applying the Gricean maxims of Relation, be relevant – why would the student mention vibrations if they did not know they were a form of movement – and Quantity, do not make your contribution more informative than is required (Grice, 1975).

```
(6) Q: Kate said: "An object has to
move to produce sound." Do you agree
with her? Why or why not?
Ref Ans: "Agree. Vibrations are move-
ments and vibrations produce sound."
Student Answer: Yes because it has to
vibrate to make sounds.

(6b) Is(vibration, movement), Inferred
```

Annotators are primarily students of Education and Linguistics and require moderate training on the annotation task. The annotated reference answers are stored in a stand-off markup in xml files, including an annotated element for each reference answer facet.

4.3 Inter-Annotator Agreement Results

The results reported here are preliminary, based on the first two annotators, and must be viewed under the light that we have not yet completed annotator training. We report results under three label groupings: (1) `All-Labels`, where all labels are left separate, (2) `Tutor-Labels`, where `Expressed`, `Inferred` and `Assumed` are combined as are `Contra-Expr` and `Contra-Infr`, and (3) `Yes-No`, which is a two-way division, `Expressed`, `Inferred` and `Assumed` versus all other labels.

Agreement on `Tutor-Labels` indicates the benefit to the tutor, since it is relatively unimportant to differentiate between the types of inference required in determining that the student understands a reference answer facet (or has contradicted it). We evaluated ***mid-training*** inter-annotator agreement on a random selection of 15 answers from each of 14 Physics of Sound questions, totaling 210 answers and 915 total facet annotations. Mid-training agreement on the `Tutor-Labels` is 87.4%, with a Kappa statistic of 0.717 corresponding with substantial agreement (Cohen, 1960). Inter-annotator agreement at mid-training is 81.1% on `All-Labels` and 90.1% on the binary `Yes-No` decision. These also have Kappa statistics in the range of substantial agreement.

The distribution of the 915 annotations is shown in Table 4. It is somewhat surprising that this science module had so few contradictions, just 2.7% of all annotations, particularly given that many of the questions seem more likely to draw contradictions than unaddressed facets (e.g., many ask about the effect on pitch and volume, typically eliciting one of two possible responses). An analysis of the inter-annotator confusion matrix indicates that the most probable disagreement is between `Inferred` and `Unaddressed`. The second most likely disagreement is between `Assumed` and `Expressed`. In discussing disagreements, the annotators almost always agree quickly, reinforcing our belief that we will increase agreement significantly with additional training.

Label	Count	%	Count	%
`Expressed`	348	38.0	657	71.8
`Inferred`	51	5.6		
`Assumed`	258	28.2		
`Contra-Expr`	21	2.3	25	2.7
`Contra-Infr`	4	0.4		
`Self-Contra`	1	0.1	1	0.1
`Diff-Arg`	33	3.6	33	3.6
`Unaddressed`	199	21.7	199	21.7

Table 4 Distribution of classifications (915 facets)

5 Discussion and Future Work

The goal of our fine-grained classification is to enable more effective tutoring dialog management. The additional labels facilitate understanding the type of mismatch between the reference answer and the student's answer. Breaking the reference answer down into low-level facets enables the tutor to provide feedback relevant specifically to the appropriate facet of the reference answer. In the question answering domain, this facet-based classification would allow systems to accumulate entailing evidence from a variety of corroborating sources and incorporate answer details that might not be found in any single sentence. In other applications outside of the tutoring domain, this fine-grained classification can also facilitate more directed user feedback. For example, both the additional classifications and the break down of facets can be used to justify system decisions, which is the stated goal of the pilot task at the third RTE challenge.

The corpus described in this paper, which will be released later this year (2007), represents a substantial contribution to the entailment community, including an estimated 69000 facet entailment annotations. By contrast, three years of RTE challenge data comprise fewer than 4600 entailment annotations. More importantly, this is the only corpus that provides entailment information at the fine-grained level described in this paper. This will enable application development that was not practical previously.

Future work includes training machine learning algorithms to perform the classifications described in this paper. We also plan to annotate other aspects of the students' understanding that are not direct inferences of reference answer knowledge. Consider example (4), in addition to the issues already annotated, the student contradicts a law of physics that they have surely encountered elsewhere in the text, specifically that longer strings produce lower, not higher, pitches. Under the current annotation scheme this is not annotated, since it does not pertain directly to the reference answer which has to do with the effect of string tension. In other annotation plans, it would be very useful for training learning algorithms if we provide an indication of which student answer facets played a role in making the inferences classified.

Initial inter-annotator agreement results look promising, obtaining substantial agreement according to the Kappa statistic. We will continue to refine our annotation guidelines and provide further training in order to push the agreement higher on all classifications.

Acknowledgement

We would like to thank Martha Palmer for valuable advice on this annotation effort.

References

Aleven V, Popescu O, & Koedinger K. (2001) A tutorial dialogue system with knowledge-based understanding and classification of student explanations. *IJCAI WS knowledge & reasoning in practical dialogue systems*

Callear, D., Jerrams-Smith, J., and Soh, V. (2001). CAA of short non-MCQ answers. In *5th Intl CAA*.

Cohen J. (1960). A coefficient of agreement for nominal scales. *Educational & Psych Measurement*. 20:37-46.

Cowie, J., Lehnert, W.G. (1996). Information Extraction. In *Communications of the ACM, 39*(1), 80-91.

Dagan, Ido, Glickman, Oren, and Magnini, Bernardo. (2005). The PASCAL Recognizing Textual Entailment Challenge. In *1st RTE Challenge Workshop*.

Gildea, D. & Jurafsky, D. (2002). Automatic labeling of semantic roles. *Computational Linguistics, 28*:3, 245–288.

Graesser, A.C., Hu, X., Susarla, S., Harter, D., Person, N.K., Louwerse, M., and Olde, B. (2001). AutoTutor: An Intelligent Tutor and Conversational Tutoring Scaffold. In *10th ICAI in Education*, 47-49.

Grice, H. Paul. (1975). Logic and conversation. In P Cole and J Morgan, editors, *Syntax and Semantics, Vol 3, Speech Acts*, 43–58. Academic Press.

Jordan, P. W., Makatchev, M., & VanLehn, K. (2004). Combining competing language understanding approaches in an intelligent tutoring system. In *7th ITS*.

Kipper, K, Dang, H, & Palmer, M. (2000). Class-Based Construction of a Verb Lexicon. *AAAI 17th NCAI*

Koedinger, K.R., Anderson, J.R., Hadley, W.H. & Mark, M.A. (1997). Intelligent tutoring goes to school in the big city. *Intl Jrnl of AI in Ed, 8*, 30-43.

Leacock, Claudia. (2004). Scoring free-response automatically: A case study of a large-scale Assessment. *Examens, 1*(3).

Lin, Dekang and Pantel, Patrick. (2001). Discovery of inference rules for Question Answering. In *Natural Language Engineering, 7*(4):343-360.

Mitchell, T. Aldridge, N., and Broomhead, P. (2003). Computerized marking of short-answer free-text responses. In *29th IAEA*.

Nivre, J. and Scholz, M. (2004). Deterministic Dependency Parsing of English Text. In *Proc COLING*.

Peters, S, Bratt, E.O., Clark, B., Pon-Barry, H. and Schultz, K. (2004). Intelligent Systems for Training Damage Control Assistants. In *Proc. of ITSE*.

Pulman S.G. & Sukkarieh J.Z. (2005). Automatic Short Answer Marking. *ACL WS Bldg Ed Apps using NLP*.

Roll, I, Baker, R, Aleven, V, McLaren, B, & Koedinger, K. (2005). Modeling Students' Metacognitive Errors in Two Intelligent Tutoring Systems. In *UM* 379–388

Rosé, P. Roque, A., Bhembe, D. & VanLehn, K. (2003). A hybrid text classification approach for analysis of student essays. In *Bldg Ed Apps using NLP*

Shaw, Stuart. (2004). Automated writing assessment: a review of four conceptual models. In *Research Notes, Cambridge ESOL*. Downloaded Aug 10, 2005 from http://www.cambridgeesol.org/rs_notes/rs_nts17.pdf

Sukkarieh, J. & Pulman, S. (2005). Information extraction and machine learning: Auto-marking short free text responses to science questions. In *Proc of AIED*.

VanLehn, K., Lynch, C., Schulze, K. Shapiro, J. A., Shelby, R., Taylor, L., Treacy, D., Weinstein, A., & Wintersgill, M. (2005). The Andes physics tutoring system: Five years of evaluations. In *12th ICAI in Ed*

Whittington, D., Hunt, H. (1999). Approaches to the Computerised Assessment of Free-Text Responses. *Third ICAA*.

Recognizing Textual Entailment Using Sentence Similarity based on Dependency Tree Skeletons

Rui Wang and Günter Neumann
LT-lab, DFKI
Stuhlsatzenhausweg 3, 66123 Saarbrücken, Germany
{wang.rui,Neumann}@dfki.de

Abstract

We present a novel approach to RTE that exploits a structure-oriented sentence representation followed by a similarity function. The structural features are automatically acquired from tree skeletons that are extracted and generalized from dependency trees. Our method makes use of a limited size of training data without any external knowledge bases (e.g. WordNet) or handcrafted inference rules. We have achieved an accuracy of 71.1% on the RTE-3 development set performing a 10-fold cross validation and 66.9% on the RTE-3 test data.

1 Introduction

Textual entailment has been introduced as a relation between text expressions, capturing the fact that the meaning of one expression can be inferred from the other (Dagan and Glickman, 2004). More precisely, textual entailment is defined as "... *a relationship between a coherent text **T** and a language expression, which is considered as a hypothesis, **H**. We say that **T** entails **H** (**H** is a consequent of **T**), denoted by **T** $\Rightarrow$ **H**, if the meaning of **H**, as interpreted in the context of **T**, can be inferred from the meaning of **T**.*"

Table 1 displays several examples from the RTE-3 development set. For the third pair (id=410) the key knowledge needed to decide whether the entailment relation holds is that "[PN1]*'s wife*, [PN2]" entails "The name of [PN1]*'s wife is* [PN2]", although **T** contains much more (irrelevant) information. On the other hand, the first pair (id=1) requires an understanding of concepts with opposite meanings (i.e. "*buy*" and "*sell*"), which is a case of semantic entailment.

The different sources of possible entailments motivated us to consider the development of specialized entailment strategies for different NLP tasks. In particular, we want to find out the potential connections between entailment relations belonging to different linguistic layers for different applications.

In this paper, we propose a novel approach towards structure-oriented entailment based on our empirical discoveries from the RTE corpora: 1) **H** is usually textually shorter than **T**; 2) not all information in **T** is relevant to make decisions for the entailment; 3) the dissimilarity of relations among the same topics between **T** and **H** are of great importance.

Based on the observations, our primary method starts from **H** to **T** (i.e. in the opposite direction of the entailment relation) so as to exclude irrelevant information from **T**. Then corresponding key topics and predicates of both elements are extracted. We then represent the structural differences between **T** and **H** by means of a set of Closed-Class Symbols. Finally, these acquired representations (named Entailment Patterns - EPs) are classified by means of a subsequence kernel.

The Structure Similarity Function is combined with two robust backup strategies, which are responsible for cases that are not handled by the EPs. One is a Triple Similarity Function applied on top of the local dependency relations of **T** and **H**; the other is a simple Bag-of-Words (BoW) approach that calculates the overlapping ratio of **H** and **T**. Together, these three methods deal with different entailment cases in practice.

Proceedings of the Workshop on Textual Entailment and Paraphrasing, pages 36–41,
Prague, June 2007. ©2007 Association for Computational Linguistics

Id	Task	Text	Hypothesis	Entails?
1	IE	*The sale was made to pay Yukos' US$ 27.5 billion tax bill, Yuganskneftegaz was originally sold for US$ 9.4 billion to a little known company Baikalfinansgroup which was later* ***bought*** *by the Russian state-owned oil*	*Baikalfinansgroup was* ***sold*** *to Rosneft.*	YES
390	IR	***Typhoon*** *Xangsane* ***lashed*** *the* ***Philippine*** *capital on Thursday, grounding flights, halting vessels and closing schools and markets after triggering fatal flash floods in the centre of the country.*	*A* ***typhoon batters*** *the* ***Philippines***.	YES
410	QA	*(Sentence 1 ...). Along with the first lady's mother, Jenna Welch, the weekend gathering includes the president's parents, former President* ***George H.W. Bush and his wife, Barbara*** *; his sister Doro Koch and her husband, Bobby; and his brother, Marvin, and his wife, Margaret.*	*The name of George H.W. Bush's wife is Barbara.*	YES
739	SUM	*The* ***FDA*** *would not say in which* ***states*** *the* ***pills*** *had been sold, but instead recommended that customers determine whether products they bought are being recalled by checking the store* ***list*** *on the* ***FDA*** *Web site, and the batch* ***list***. *The batch numbers appear on the container's label.*	*The* ***FDA*** *provided a* ***list*** *of* ***states*** *in which the* ***pills*** *have been*	NO

Table 1 Examples from RTE-3

2 Related Work

Conventional methods for RTE define measures for the similarity between **T** and **H** either by assuming an independence between words (Corley and Mihalcea, 2005) in a BoW fashion or by exploiting syntactic interpretations. (Kouylekov and Magnini, 2006) explore a syntactic tree editing distance to detect entailment relations. Since they calculate the similarity between the two dependency trees of **T** and **H** directly, the noisy information may decrease accuracy. This observation actually motivated us to start from **H** towards the most relevant information in **T**.

Logic rules (as proposed by (Bos and Markert, 2005)) or sequences of allowed rewrite rules (as in (de Salvo Braz et al., 2005)) are another fashion of tackling RTE. One the best two teams in RTE-2 (Tatu et al., 2006) proposed a knowledge representation model which achieved about 10% better performance than the third (Zanzotto and Moschitti, 2006) based on their logic prover. The other best team in RTE-2 (Hickl et al., 2006) automatically acquired extra training data, enabling them to achieve about 10% better accuracy than the third as well. Consequently, obtaining more training data and embedding deeper knowledge were expected

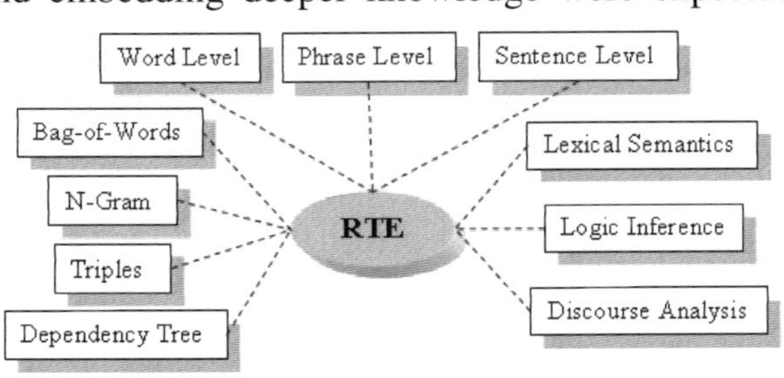

Figure 1 Overview of RTE

to be the two main directions pointed out for future research in the RTE-2 summary statement. However, except for the positive cases of SUM, **T-H** pairs are normally not very easy to collect automatically. Multi-annotator agreement is difficult to reach on most of the cases as well. The knowledge-based approach also has its caveats since logical rules are usually implemented manually and therefore require a high amount of specialized human expertise in different NLP areas.

Another group (Zanzotto and Moschitti, 2006) utilized a tree kernel method for cross-pair similarity, which showed an improvement, and this has motivated us to investigate kernel-based methods. The main difference in our method is that we apply subsequence kernels on patterns extracted from the dependency trees of **T** and **H**, instead of applying tree kernels on complete parsing trees. On the one hand, this allows us to discover essential parts indicating an entailment relationship, and on the other hand, computational complexity is reduced.

3 An Overview of RTE

Figure 1 shows the different processing techniques and depths applied to the RTE task. Our work focuses on constructing a similarity function operating between sentences. In detail, it consists of several similarity scores with different domains of locality on top of the dependency structure. Figure 2 gives out the workflow of our system. The main part of the sentence similarity function is the Structure Similarity Function; two other similarity scores are calculated by our backup strategies. The first backup strategy is a straightforward BoW method that we will not present in this paper (see more details in (Corley and Mihalcea, 2005));

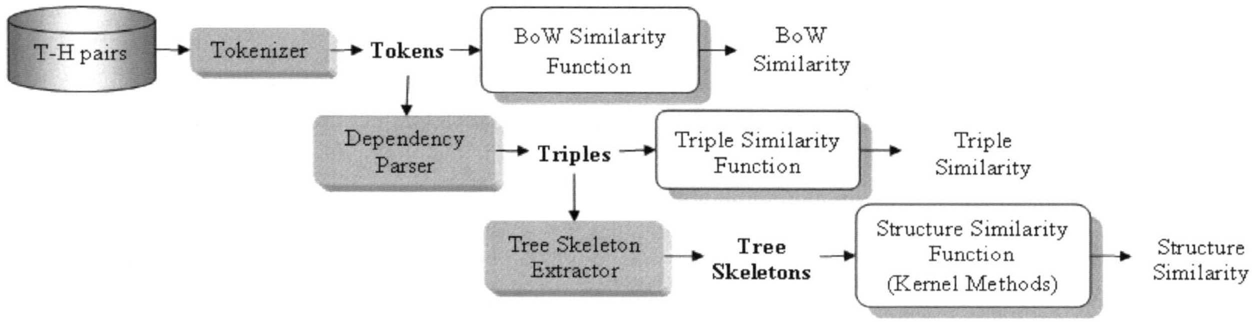

Figure 2 Workflow of the System

while the second one is based on a triple set representation of sentences that expresses the local dependency relations found by a parser[1].

A dependency structure consists of a set of triple relations (TRs). A TR is of the form <*node1, relation, node2*>, where *node1* represents the head, *node2* the modifier and *relation* the dependency relation. Chief requirements for the backup system are robustness and simplicity. Accordingly, we construct a similarity function, the Triple Similarity Function (TSF), which operates on two triple sets and determines how many triples of **H**[2] are contained in **T**. The core assumption here is that *the higher the number of matching triple elements, the more similar both sets are, and the more likely it is that* **T** *entails* **H**.

TSF uses an approximate matching function. Different cases (i.e. ignoring either the parent node or the child node, or the relation between nodes) might provide different indications for the similarity of **T** and **H**. In all cases, a successful match between two nodes means that they have the same lemma and POS. We then sum them up using different weights and divide the result by the cardinality of **H** for normalization. The different weights learned from the corpus indicate that the "amount of missing linguistic information" affect entailment decisions differently.

4 Workflow of the Main Approach

Our Structure Similarity Function is based on the hypothesis that *some particular differences between **T** and **H** will block or change the entailment relationship*. Initially we assume when judging the entailment relation that it holds for each **T-H** pair (using the default value "YES"). The major steps are as follows (see also Figure 2):

4.1 Tree Skeleton Extractor

Since we assume that **H** indicates how to extract relevant parts in **T** for the entailment relation, we start from the Tree Skeleton of **H** (TS_H). First, we construct a set of keyword pairs using all the nouns that appear in both **T** and **H**. In order to increase the hits of keyword pairs, we have applied a partial search using stemming and some word variation techniques on the substring level. For instance, the pair (id=390) in Table 1 has the following list of keyword pairs,

```
<Typhoon_Xangsane ## typhoon,
Philippine ## Philippines>
```

Then we mark the keywords in the dependency trees of **T** and **H** and extract the sub-trees by ignoring the inner yields. Usually, the Root Node of **H** (RN_H) is the main verb; all the keywords are contained in the two spines of TS_H (see Figure 3). Note that in the Tree Skeleton of **T** (TS_T), 1) the Root Node (RN_T) can either be a verb, a noun or even a dependency relation, and 2) if the two Foot Nodes (FNs) belong to two sentences, a dummy node is created that connects the two spines.

Thus, the prerequisite for this algorithm is that TS_H has two spines containing all keywords in **H**, and **T** satisfies this as well. For the RTE-3 development set, we successfully extracted tree skele-

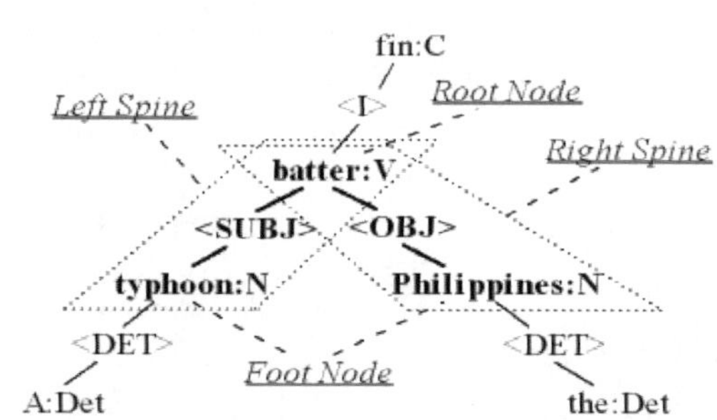

Figure 3 Example of a Tree Skeleton

[1] We are using Minipar (Lin, 1998) and Stanford Parser (Klein and Manning, 2003) as preprocessors, see also sec. 5.2.

[2] Note that henceforth T and H will represent either the original texts or the dependency structures.

tons from 254 pairs, i.e., 32% of the data is covered by this step, see also sec. 5.2.

Next, we collapse some of the dependency relation names from the parsers to more generalized tag names, e.g., collapsing <OBJ2> and <DESC> to <OBJ>. We group together all nodes that have relation labels like <CONJ> or <NN>, since they are assumed to refer to the same entity or belong to one class of entities sharing some common characteristics. Lemmas are removed except for the keywords. Finally, we add all the tags to the CCS set.

Since a tree skeleton TS consists of spines connected via the same root node, TS can be transformed into a sequence. Figure 4 displays an example corresponding to the second pair (id=390) of Table 1. Thus, the general form of a sequential representation of a tree skeleton is:

```
LSP #RN# RSP
```

where LSP represents the Left Spine, RSP represents the Right Spine, and RN is the Root Node. On basis of this representation, a comparison of the two tree skeletons is straightforward: 1) merge the two LSPs by excluding the longest common prefix, and 2) merge the two RSPs by excluding the longest common suffix. Then the Spine Difference (SD) is defined as the remaining infixes, which consists of two parts, SD_T and SD_H. Each part can be either empty (i.e. ε) or a CCS sequence. For instance, the two SDs of the example in Figure 4 (id=390) are (LSD – Left SD; RSD – Right SD; ## is a separator sign):

$LSD_T(N)$ ## $LSD_H(\varepsilon)$

$RSD_T(\varepsilon)$ ## $RSD_H(\varepsilon)$

We have observed that two neighboring dependency relations of the root node of a tree skeleton (<SUBJ> or <OBJ>) can play important roles in predicting the entailment relation as well. Therefore, we assign them two extra features named Verb Consistence (VC) and Verb Relation Consistence (VRC). The former indicates whether two root nodes have a similar meaning, and the latter

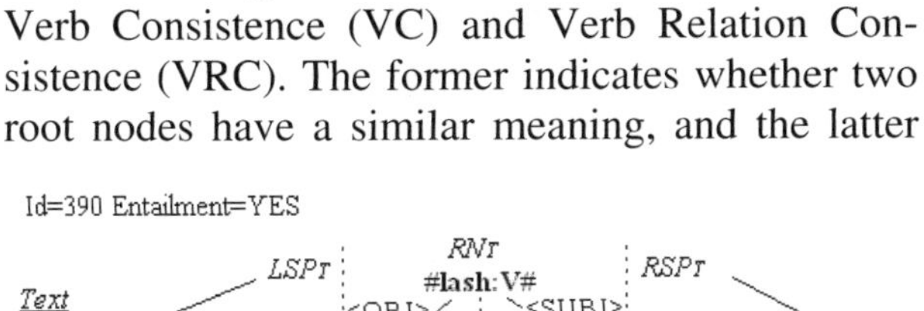

Figure 4 Spine Merging

indicates whether the relations are contradictive (e.g. <SUBJ> and <OBJ> are contradictive).

We represent the differences between TS_T and TS_H by means of an Entailment Pattern (EP), which is a quadruple <LSD, RSD, VC, VRC>. VC is either true or false, meaning that the two RNs are either consistent or not. VRC has ternary value, whereby 1 means that both relations are consistent, -1 means at least one pair of corresponding relations is inconsistent, and 0 means RN_T is not a verb.[3] The set of EPs defines the feature space for the subsequence kernels in our Structure Similarity Function.

4.2 Structure Similarity Function

We define the function by constructing two basic kernels to process the LSD and RSD part of an EP, and two trivial kernels for VC and VRC. The four kernels are combined linearly by a composite kernel that performs binary classification on them.

Since all spine differences SDs are either empty or CCS sequences, we can utilize subsequence kernel methods to represent features implicitly, cf. (Bunescu and Mooney, 2006). Our subsequence kernel function is:

$$K_{subsequence}(<T,H>,<T',H'>) = \sum_{i=1}^{|T|}\sum_{i'=1}^{|T'|} K_{CCS}(CCS_i, CCS_{i'}) + \sum_{j=1}^{|H|}\sum_{j'=1}^{|H'|} K_{CCS}(CCS_j, CCS_{j'})$$

whereby T and H refers to all spine differences SDs from **T** and **H**, and $|T|$ and $|H|$ represent the cardinalities of SDs. The function $K_{CCS}(CCS, CCS')$ checks whether its arguments are equal.

Since the RTE task checks the relationship between **T** and **H**, we need to consider collocations of some CCS subsequences between T and H as well. Essentially, this kernel evaluates the similarity of **T** and **H** by means of those CCS subsequences appearing in both elements. The kernel function is as follows:

$$K_{collocation}(<T,H>,<T',H'>) = \sum_{i=1}^{|T|}\sum_{i'=1}^{|T'|}\sum_{j=1}^{|H|}\sum_{j'=1}^{|H'|} K_{CCS}(CCS_i, CCS_{i'}) \cdot K_{CCS}(CCS_j, CCS_{j'})$$

On top of the two simple kernels, K_{VC}, and K_{VRC}, we use a composite kernel to combine them linearly with different weights: $K_{composite} = \alpha K_{subsequence} + \beta K_{collocation} + \gamma K_{VC} + \delta K_{VRC}$,

[3] Note that RN_H is guaranteed to be a verb, because otherwise the pair would have been delegated to the backup strategies.

where γ and δ are learned from the training corpus; $\alpha=\beta=1$.

5 Evaluation

We have evaluated four methods: the two backup systems as baselines (BoW and TSM, the Triple Set Matcher) and the kernel method combined with the backup strategies using different parsers, Minipar (Mi+SK+BS) and the Stanford Parser (SP+SK+BS). The experiments are based on RTE-3 Data[4]. For the kernel-based classification, we used the classifier SMO from the WEKA toolkit (Witten and Frank, 1999).

5.1 Experiment Results

RTE-3 data include the Dev Data (800 T-H pairs, each task has 200 pairs) and the Test Data (same size). Experiment A performs a 10-fold cross-validation on Dev Data; Experiment B uses Dev Data for training and Test Data for testing cf. Table 2 (the numbers denote accuracies):

Systems\Tasks	**IE**	**IR**	**QA**	**SUM**	**All**
Exp A: 10-fold Cross Validation on RTE-3 Dev Data					
BoW	54.5	70	76.5	**68.5**	67.4
TSM	53.5	60	68	62.5	61.0
Mi+SK+BS	**63**	74	79	68.5	**71.1**
SP+SK+BS	**60.5**	70	81.5	68.5	**70.1**
Exp B: Train: Dev Data; Test: Test Data					
BoW	54.5	66.5	76.5	56	63.4
TSM	54.5	62.5	66	54.5	59.4
Mi+SP+SK+BS	58.5	70.5	79.5	59	**66.9**

Table 2 Results on RTE-3 Data

For the IE task, Mi+SK+BS obtained the highest improvement over the baseline systems, suggesting that the kernel method seems to be more appropriate if the underlying task conveys a more "relational nature." Improvements in the other tasks are less convincing as compared to the baselines. Nevertheless, the overall result obtained in experiment B would have been among the top 3 of the RTE-2 challenge. We utilize the system description table of (Bar-Haim et al., 2006) to compare our system with the best two systems of RTE-2 in Table 3[5]:

Systems	Lx	Ng	Sy	Se	**LI**	C	M	B	**L**
Hickl et al.	X	X	X	X		X	X		**X**
Tatu et al.	X				**X**			X	
Ours		X	X				X		

Table 3 Comparison with the top 2 systems in RTE-2.

Note that the best system (Hickl et al., 2006) applies both shallow and deep techniques, especially in acquiring extra entailment corpora. The second best system (Tatu et al., 2006) contains many manually designed logical inference rules and background knowledge. On the contrary, we exploit no additional knowledge sources besides the dependency trees computed by the parsers, nor any extra training corpora.

5.2 Discussions

Table 4 shows how our method performs for the task-specific pairs matched by our patterns:

Tasks	IE	IR	QA	SUM	ALL
ExpA:Matched	**53**	19	23.5	31.5	**31.8**
ExpA:Accuracy	67.9	78.9	91.5	71.4	**74.8**
ExpB:Matched	**58.5**	16	27.5	42	**36**
ExpB:Accuracy	57.2	81.5	90.9	65.5	**68.8**

Table 4 Performances of our method

For IE pairs, we find good coverage, whereas for IR and QA pairs the coverage is low, though it achieves good accuracy. According to the experiments, BoW has already achieved the best performance for SUM pairs cf. Table 2.

As a whole, developing task specific entailment operators is a promising direction. As we mentioned in the first section, the RTE task is neither a one-level nor a one-case task. The experimental results uncovered differences among pairs of different tasks with respect to accuracy and coverage.

On the one hand, our method works successfully on structure-oriented **T-H** pairs, most of which are from IE. If both TS_T and TS_H can be transformed into CCS sequences, the comparison performs well, as in the case of the last example (id=410) in Table 1. Here, the relation between "*wife*", "*name*", and "*Barbara*" is conveyed by the punctuation ",", the verb "*is*", and the preposition "*of*". Other cases like the "*work for*" relation of a person and a company or the "*is located in*" relation between two location names are normally conveyed by the preposition "*of*". Based on these findings, taking into account more carefully the lexical semantics based on inference rules of functional words might be helpful in improving RTE.

[4] See (Wang and Neumann, 2007) for details concerning the experiments of our method on RTE-2 data.

[5] Following the notation in (Bar-Haim et al., 2006): Lx: Lexical Relation DB; Ng: N-Gram / Subsequence overlap; Sy: Syntactic Matching / Alignment; Se: Semantic Role Labeling; LI: Logical Inference; C: Corpus/Web; M: ML Classification; B: Paraphrase Technology / Background Knowledge; L: Acquisition of Entailment Corpora.

On the other hand, accuracy varies with **T-H** pairs from different tasks. Since our method is mainly structure-oriented, differences in modifiers may change the results and would not be caught under the current version of our tree skeleton. For instance, "*a commercial company*" will not entail "*a military company*", even though they are structurally equivalent.

Most IE pairs are constructed from a binary relation, and so meet the prerequisite of our algorithm (see sec. 4.1). However, our method still has rather low coverage. **T-H** pairs from other tasks, for example like IR and SUM, usually contain more information, i.e. more nouns, the dependency trees of which are more complex. For instance, the pair (id=739) in Table 1 contains four keyword pairs which we cannot handle by our current method. This is one reason why we have constructed extra **T-H** pairs from MUC, TREC, and news articles following the methods of (Bar-Haim et al., 2006). Still, the overall performance does not improve. All extra training data only serves to improve the matched pairs (about 32% of the data set) for which we already have high accuracy (see Table 4). Thus, extending coverage by machine learning methods for lexical semantics will be the main focus of our future work.

6 Conclusions and Future Work

Applying different RTE strategies for different NLP tasks is a reasonable solution. We have utilized a structure similarity function to deal with the structure-oriented pairs, and applied backup strategies for the rest. The results show the advantage of our method and direct our future work as well. In particular, we will extend the tree skeleton extraction by integrating lexical semantics based on inference rules for functional words in order to get larger domains of locality.

Acknowledgements

The work presented here was partially supported by a research grant from BMBF to the DFKI project HyLaP (FKZ: 01 IW F02) and the EC-funded project QALL-ME.

References

Bar-Haim, R., Dagan, I., Dolan, B., Ferro, L., Giampiccolo, D., Magnini, B. and Szpektor, I. 2006. *The Second PASCAL Recognising Textual Entailment Challenge*. In Proc. of the PASCAL RTE-2 Challenge.

Bos, J. and Markert, K. 2005. *Combining Shallow and Deep NLP Methods for Recognizing Textual Entailment*. In Proc. of the PASCAL RTE Challenge.

Bunescu, R. and Mooney, R. 2006. *Subsequence Kernels for Relation Extraction*. In Advances in Neural Information Processing Systems 18. MIT Press.

Corley, C. and Mihalcea, R. 2005. *Measuring the Semantic Similarity of Texts*. In Proc. of the ACL Workshop on Empirical Modeling of Semantic Equivalence and Entailment.

Dagan, R., Glickman, O. 2004. *Probabilistic textual entailment: Generic applied modelling of language variability*. In PASCAL Workshop on Text Understanding and Mining.

de Salvo Braz, R., Girju, R., Punyaka-nok, V., Roth, D., and Sammons, M. 2005. *An Inference Model for Semantic Entailment in Natural Language*. In Proc. of the PASCAL RTE Challenge.

Hickl, A., Williams, J., Bensley, J., Roberts, K., Rink, B. and Shi, Y. 2006. *Recognizing Textual Entailment with LCC's GROUNDHOG System*. In Proc. of the PASCAL RTE-2 Challenge.

Klein, D. and Manning, C. 2003. *Accurate Unlexicalized Parsing*. In Proc. of ACL 2003.

Kouylekov, M. and Magnini, B. 2006. *Tree Edit Distance for Recognizing Textual Entailment: Estimating the Cost of Insertion*. In Proc. of the PASCAL RTE-2 Challenge.

Lin, D. 1998. *Dependency-based Evaluation of MINIPAR*. In Workshop on the Evaluation of Parsing Systems.

Tatu, M., Iles, B., Slavik, J., Novischi, A. and Moldovan, D. 2006. *COGEX at the Second Recognizing Textual Entailment Challenge*. In Proc. of the PASCAL RTE-2 Challenge.

Wang, R. and Neumann, G. 2007. *Recognizing Textual Entailment Using a Subsequence Kernel Method*. In Proc. of AAAI 2007.

Witten, I. H. and Frank, E. *Weka: Practical Machine Learning Tools and Techniques with Java Implementations*. Morgan Kaufmann, 1999.

Zanzotto, F.M. and Moschitti, A. 2006. Automatic Learning of Textual Entailments with Cross-pair Similarities. In Proc. of ACL 2006.

Learning Textual Entailment using SVMs and String Similarity Measures

Prodromos Malakasiotis and **Ion Androutsopoulos**
Department of Informatics
Athens University of Economics and Business
Patision 76, GR-104 34 Athens, Greece

Abstract

We present the system that we submitted to the 3rd Pascal Recognizing Textual Entailment Challenge. It uses four Support Vector Machines, one for each subtask of the challenge, with features that correspond to string similarity measures operating at the lexical and shallow syntactic level.

1 Introduction

Textual Entailment is desirable in many natural language processing areas, such as question answering, information extraction, information retrieval, and multi-document summarization. In the Pascal Recognizing Textual Entailment Challenge (RTE), it is defined as the task of deciding whether or not the meaning of a *hypothesis* text (H) can be inferred from the meaning of another text (T).[1] For instance:

> T: The drugs that slow down or halt Alzheimer's disease work best the earlier you administer them.
>
> H: Alzheimer's disease is treated using drugs.

is a correct entailment pair, but the following is not:

> T: Drew Walker, NHS Tayside's public health director, said: "It is important to stress that this is not a confirmed case of rabies."
>
> H: A case of rabies was confirmed.

In previous RTE challenges (Dagan et al., 2006; Bar-Haim et al., 2006), several machine-learning approaches appeared, but their results showed that significant improvements were still necessary. In this paper, we present the system we used in the third RTE challenge. The latter had four different development and test sets (QA, IR, IE, SUM), intended to evaluate textual entailment recognition in the four natural language processing areas mentioned above.

[1] See `http://www.pascal-network.org/`.

2 System overview

Our system uses SVMs (Vapnik, 1998) to determine whether each T–H pair constitutes a correct textual entailment or not. In particular, it employs four SVMs, each trained on the development dataset of the corresponding RTE subtask (QA, IR, IE, SUM) and used on the corresponding test dataset. Preliminary experiments indicated that training a single SVM on all four subsets leads to worse results, despite the increased size of the training set, presumably because of differences in how the pairs were constructed in each subtask, which do not allow a single SVM to generalize well over all four.

The system is based on the assumption that string similarity at the lexical and shallow syntactic level can be used to identify textual entailment reasonably well, at least in question answering, the main area we are interested in. We, therefore, try to capture different kinds of similarity by employing 10 different string similarity measures, to be discussed below. In each T–H case, every measure is applied to the following 8 pairs of strings, producing a total of 80 measurements:

pair 1: two strings with the *original words* of T and H, respectively; although we refer to 'words', this and the following string pairs also contain non-word tokens, such as punctuation.[2]

[2] We use OPENNLP's tokenizer, POS-tagger, and chunker (see `http://opennlp.sourceforge.net/`), and our own implementation of Porter's stemmer.

Proceedings of the Workshop on Textual Entailment and Paraphrasing, pages 42–47,
Prague, June 2007.

pair 2: two strings containing the corresponding *stems* of the words of T and H, respectively;

pair 3: two strings containing the *part-of-speech* (POS) tags of the words of T and H;

pair 4: two strings containing the *chunk* tags (see below) of the words of T and H;

pair 5: two strings containing only the *nouns* of T and H, as identified by a POS-tagger;

pair 6: two strings containing only the *stems of the nouns* of T and H;

pair 7: two strings containing only the *verbs* of T and H, as identified by a POS-tagger;

pair 8: two strings containing only the *stems of the verbs* of T and H.

Chunk tags are of the form B-x, I-x or O, were B and I indicate the initial and other words of the chunks, respectively, whereas O indicates words outside all chunks; x can be NP, VP, or PP, for noun phrase, verb phrase, and prepositional phrase chunks.

Partial matches: When applying the string similarity measures, one problem is that T may be much longer than H, or vice versa. Consider, for example, the following T–H pair. The difference in the lengths of T and H may mislead many similarity measures to indicate that the two texts are very dissimilar, even though H is included verbatim in T.

T: Charles de Gaulle died in 1970 at the age of eighty. He was thus fifty years old when, as an unknown officer recently promoted to the (temporary) rank of brigadier general, he made his famous broadcast from London rejecting the capitulation of France to the Nazis after the debacle of May-June 1940.

H: Charles de Gaulle died in 1970.

To address this problem, when we consider a pair of strings (s_1, s_2), if s_1 is longer than s_2, we also compute the ten values $f_i(s'_1, s_2)$, where f_i $(1 \leq i \leq 10)$ are the string similarity measures, for every s'_1 that is a substring of s_1 of the same length as s_2. We then locate the s'_1 with the best average similarity to s_2, shown below as s'^*_1:

$$s'^*_1 = \arg\max_{s'_1} \sum_{i=1}^{10} f_i(s'_1, s_2)$$

and we keep the ten $f_i(s'^*_1, s_2)$ values and their average as 11 additional measurements. Similarly, if s_2 is longer than s_1, we keep the ten $f_i(s_1, s'^*_2)$ values and their average. This process could be applied to all pairs 1–8 above, but the system we submitted applied it only to pairs 1–4; hence, there is a total of 44 additional measurements in each T–H case.

The 124 measurements discussed above provide 124 candidate numeric features that can be used by the SVMs.[3] To those, we add the following four:

Negation: Two Boolean features, showing if T or H, respectively, contain negation, identified by looking for words like "not", "won't", etc.

Length ratio: This is $\frac{\min(L_T, L_H)}{\max(L_T, L_H)}$, were L_T and L_H are the lengths, in words, of T and H.

Text length: Binary feature showing if the markup of the dataset flags T as 'long' or 'short'.

Hence, there are 128 candidate features in total. From those, we select a different subset for the SVM of each subtask, as will be discussed in following sections. Note that similarity measures have also been used in previous RTE systems as features in machine learning algorithms; see, for example, Kozareva and Montoyo (2006), Newman et al. (2006). However, the results of those systems indicate that improvements are still necessary, and we believe that one possible improvement is the use of more and different similarity measures.

We did not use similarity measures that operate on parse trees or semantic representations, as we are interested in RTE methods that can also be applied to less spoken languages, where reliable parsers, fact extractors, etc. are often difficult to obtain.

2.1 String similarity measures

We now describe the ten string similarity measures that we use.[4] The reader is reminded that the measures are applied to string pairs (s_1, s_2), where s_1 and s_2 derive from T and H, respectively.

Levenshtein distance: This is the minimum number of operations (edit distance) needed to transform one string (in our case, s_1) into the other one (s_2),

[3] All feature values are normalized in $[-1, 1]$.

[4] We use the SIMMETRICS library; see `http://www.dcs.shef.ac.uk/~sam/simmetrics.html`.

where an operation is an insertion, deletion, or substitution of a single character. In pairs of strings that contain POS or chunk tags, it would be better to consider operations that insert, delete, or substitute entire tags, instead of characters, but the system we submitted did not do this; we addressed this issue in subsequent work, as will be discussed below.

Jaro-Winkler distance: The Jaro-Winkler distance (Winkler, 1999) is a variation of the Jaro distance (Jaro, 1995), which we describe first. The Jaro distance d_j of s_1 and s_2 is defined as:

$$d_j(s_1, s_2) = \frac{m}{3 \cdot l_1} + \frac{m}{3 \cdot l_2} + \frac{m - t}{3 \cdot m},$$

where l_1 and l_2 are the lengths (in characters) of s_1 and s_2, respectively. The value m is the number of characters of s_1 that match characters of s_2. Two characters from s_1 and s_2, respectively, are taken to match if they are identical and the difference in their positions does not exceed $\frac{\max(l_1, l_2)}{2} - 1$. Finally, to compute t ('transpositions'), we remove from s_1 and s_2 all characters that do not have matching characters in the other string, and we count the number of positions in the resulting two strings that do not contain the same character; t is half that number.

The Jaro-Winkler distance d_w emphasizes prefix similarity between the two strings. It is defined as:

$$d_w(s_1, s_2) = d_j(s_1, s_2) + l \cdot p \cdot [1 - d_j(s_1, s_2)],$$

where l is the length of the longest common prefix of s_1 and s_2, and p is a constant scaling factor that also controls the emphasis placed on prefix similarity. The implementation we used considers prefixes up to 6 characters long, and sets $p = 0.1$.

Again, in pairs of strings (s_1, s_2) that contain POS tags or chunk tags, it would be better to apply this measure to the corresponding lists of tags in s_1 and s_2, instead of treating s_1 and s_2 as strings of characters, but the system we submitted did not do this; this issue was also addressed in subsequent work.

Soundex: Soundex is an algorithm intended to map each English name to an alphanumeric code, so that names whose pronunciations are the same are mapped to the same code, despite spelling differences.[5] Although Soundex is intended to be used on names, and in effect considers only the first letter and the first few consonants of each name, we applied it to s_1 and s_2, in an attempt to capture similarity at the beginnings of the two strings; the strings were first stripped of all white spaces and non-letter characters. We then computed similarity between the two resulting codes using the Jaro-Winkler distance. A better approach would be to apply Soundex to all words in T and H, forming a 9th pair (s_1, s_2), on which other distance measures would then be applied; we did this in subsequent work.

Manhattan distance: Also known as City Block distance or L_1, this is defined for any two vectors $\vec{x} = \langle x_1, \ldots, x_n \rangle$ and $\vec{y} = \langle y_1, \ldots, y_n \rangle$ in an n-dimensional vector space as:

$$L_1(\vec{x}, \vec{y}) = \sum_{i=1}^{n} |x_i - y_i|.$$

In our case, n is the number of distinct words (or tags) that occur in s_1 and s_2 (in any of the two); and x_i, y_i show how many times each one of these distinct words occurs in s_1 and s_2, respectively.

Euclidean distance: This is defined as follows:

$$L_2(\vec{x}, \vec{y}) = \sqrt{\sum_{i=1}^{n} (x_i - y_i)^2}.$$

In our case, $\vec{x}$ and $\vec{y}$ correspond to s_1 and s_2, respectively, as in the previous measure.

Cosine similarity: The definition follows:

$$\cos(\vec{x}, \vec{y}) = \frac{\vec{x} \cdot \vec{y}}{\|\vec{x}\| \cdot \|\vec{y}\|}.$$

In our system $\vec{x}$ and $\vec{y}$ are as above, except that they are binary, i.e., x_i and y_i are 1 or 0, depending on whether or not the corresponding word (or tag) occurs in s_1 or s_2, respectively.

N-gram distance: This is the same as L_1, but instead of words we use all the (distinct) character n-grams in s_1 and s_2; we used $n = 3$.

Matching coefficient: This is $|X \cap Y|$, where X and Y are the sets of (unique) words (or tags) of s_1 and s_2, respectively; i.e., it counts how many common words s_1 and s_2 have.

[5]See `http://en.wikipedia.org/wiki/Soundex`.

Dice coefficient: This is the following quantity; in our case, X and Y are as in the previous measure.

$$\frac{2 \cdot |X \cap Y|}{|X| + |Y|}$$

Jaccard coefficient: This is defined as $\frac{|X \cap Y|}{|X \cup Y|}$; again X and Y are as in the matching coefficient.

2.2 SVM tuning and feature selection

As already noted, we employed four SVMs, one for each subtask of the challenge (IR, IE, QA, SUM).[6] In each subtask, feature selection was performed as follows. We started with a set of 20 features, which correspond to the ten similarity measures applied to both words and stems (string pairs 1 and 2 of section 1); see table 1. We then added the 10 features that correspond to the ten similarity measures applied to POS tags (string pair 3). In IE and IR, this addition led to improved leave-one-out cross-validation results on the corresponding development sets, and we kept the additional features (denoted by 'X' in table 1). In contrast, in QA and SUM the additional 10 features were discarded, because they led to no improvement in the cross-validation. We then added the 10 features that corresponded to the ten similarity measures applied to chunk tags (string pair 4), which were retained only in the IE SVM, and so on.

The order in which we considered the various extensions of the feature sets is the same as the order of the rows of table 1, and it reflects the order in which it occurred to us to consider the corresponding additional features while preparing for the challenge. We hope to investigate additional feature selection schemes in further work; for instance, start with all 128 features and explore if pruning any groups of features improves the cross-validation results.

With each feature set that we considered, we actually performed multiple leave-one-out cross-validations on the development dataset, for different values of the parameters of the SVM and kernel, using a grid-search utility. Each feature set was evaluated by considering its best cross-validation result. The best cross-validation results for the final feature sets of the four SVMs are shown in table 2.

[6]We use LIBSVM (Chang and Lin, 2001), with a Radial Basis Function kernel, including LIBSVM's grid search tuning utility.

Subtask	*Accuracy (%)*
QA	86.50 (90.00)
IR	80.00 (75.50)
SUM	73.00 (72.50)
IE	62.00 (61.50)
all	75.38 (74.88)

Table 2: Best cross-validation results of our system on the *development datasets*. Results with subsequent improvements are shown in brackets.

Subtask	*Accuracy (%)*	*Average Precision (%)*
QA	73.50 (76.00)	81.03 (81.08)
IR	64.50 (63.50)	63.61 (67.28)
SUM	57.00 (60.50)	60.88 (61.58)
IE	52.00 (49.50)	58.16 (51.57)
all	61.75 (62.38)	68.08 (68.28)

Table 3: *Official results* of our system. Results with subsequent improvements are shown in brackets.

3 Official results and discussion

We submitted only one run to the third RTE challenge. The official results of our system are shown in table 3.[7] They are worse than the best results we had obtained in the cross-validations on the development datasets (cf. table 2), but this was expected to a large extent, since the SVMs were tuned on the development datasets; to some extent, the lower official results may also be due to different types of entailment being present in the test datasets, which had not been encountered in the training sets.

As in the cross-validation results, our system performed best in the QA subtask; the second and third best results of our system were obtained in IR and SUM, while the worst results were obtained in IE. Although a more thorough investigation is necessary to account fully for these results, it appears that they support our initial assumption that string similarity at the lexical and shallow syntactic level can be used to identify textual entailment reasonably well in question answering systems. Some further reflections on the results of our system follow.

In the QA subtask of the challenge, it appears that each T was a snippet returned by a question answering system for a particular question.[8] We are not aware of exactly how the Ts were selected by the

[7]See the RTE Web site for a definition of 'average precision'.

[8]Consult http://www.pascal-network.org/Challenges/RTE3/Introduction/.

Feature sets	*features*	IE	IR	QA	SUM
similarity measures on **words**	10	X	X	X	X
similarity measures on **stems**	10	X	X	X	X
+ similarity measures on **POS tags**	+10	X	X		
+ similarity measures on **chunk tags**	+10	X			X
+ **average** of sim. measures on **words** of best **partial** match	+1				X
+ **average** of sim. measures on **stems** of best **partial** match	+1			X	X
+ **average** of sim. measures on **POS tags** of best **partial** match	+1			X	X
+ **average** of sim. measures on **chunk tags** of best **partial** match	+1		X		X
+ similarity measures on **words** of best **partial** match	+10				
+ similarity measures on **stems** of best **partial** match	+10				X
+ similarity measures on **POS tags** of best **partial** match	+10	X			
+ similarity measures on **chunk tags** of best **partial** match	+10				
+ **negation**	+2	X			
+ **length ratio**	+1	X			
+ similarity measures on **nouns**	+10	X			
+ similarity measures on **noun stems**	+10				
+ similarity measures on **verbs**	+10				X
+ similarity measures on **verb stems**	+10				
+ **short/long** T	+1	X		X	
Total	128	64	31	23	54

Table 1: Feature sets considered and chosen in each subtask.

systems used, but QA systems typically return Ts that contain the expected answer type of the input question; for instance, if the question is "When did Charles de Gaulle die?", T will typically contain a temporal expression. Furthermore, QA systems typically prefer Ts that contain many words of the question, preferably in the same order, etc. (Radev et al., 2000; Ng et al., 2001; Harabagiu et al., 2003). Hence, if the answers are sought in a document collection with high redundancy (e.g., the Web), i.e., a collection where each answer can be found with many different phrasings, the Ts (or parts of them) that most QA systems return are often very similar, in terms of phrasings, to the questions, provided that the required answers exist in the collection.

In the QA datasets of the challenge, for each T, which was a snippet returned by a QA system for a question (e.g., "When did Charle de Gaulle die?"), an H was formed by "plugging into" the question an expression of the expected answer type from T. In effect, this converted all questions to propositions (e.g., "Charle de Gaulle died in 1970.") that require a "yes" or "no" answer. Note that this plugging in does not always produce a true proposition; T may contain multiple expressions of the expected answer type (e.g., "Charle de Gaulle died in 1970. In 1990, a monument was erected…") and the wrong one may be plugged into the question (H = "Charle de Gaulle died in 1990.").

Let us first consider the case where the proposition (H) is true. Assuming that the document collection is redundant and that the answer to the question exists in the collection, T (or part of it) will often be very similar to H, since it will be very similar to the question that H was derived from. In fact, the similarity between T and H may be greater than between T and the question, since an expression from T has been plugged into the question to form H. Being very similar, T will very often entail H, and, hence, the (affirmative) responses of our system, which are based on similarity, will be correct.

Let us now consider the case where H is false. Although the same arguments apply, and, hence, one might again expect T to be very similar to H, this is actually less likely now, because H is false and, hence, it is more difficult to find a very similarly phrased T in the presumed trustful document collection. The reduced similarity between T and H will lead the similarity measures to suggest that the T–H entailment does not hold; and in most cases, this is a correct decision, because H is false and, thus, it cannot be entailed by a (true) T that has been extracted from a trustful document collection.

Similar arguments apply to the IR subtask, where our system achieved its second best results. Our results in this subtask were lower than in the QA subtask, presumably because the Ts were no longer filtered by the additional requirement that they must contain an expression of the expected answer type.

We attribute the further deterioration of our results in the SUM subtask to the fact that, according to the challenge's documentation, all the T–H pairs of that subtask, both true and false entailments, were chosen to have high lexical similarity, which does not allow the similarity measures of our system to distinguish well between the two cases. Finally, the lower results obtained in the IE subtask may be due to the fact that the T–H pairs of that subtask were intended to reflect entailments identified by information extraction systems, which specialize on identifying particular semantic relations by employing more complicated machinery (e.g., named entity recognizers and matchers, fact extractors, etc.) than simple string similarity measures; the results may also be partly due to the four different ways that were used to construct the T–H pairs of that subtask. It is interesting to note (see table 1) that the feature sets were larger in the subtasks where our system scored worse, which may be an indication of the difficulties the corresponding SVMs encountered.

4 Conclusions and further work

We presented a textual entailment recognition system that relies on SVMs whose features correspond to string similarity measures applied to the lexical and shallow syntactic level. Experimental results indicate that the system performs reasonably well in question answering (QA), which was our main target, with results deteriorating as we move to information retrieval (IR), multi-document summarization (SUM), and information extraction (IE).

In work carried out after the official submission of our system, we incorporated two of the possible improvements that were mentioned in previous sections: we treated strings containing POS or chunk tags as lists of tags; and we applied Soundex to each word of T and H, forming a 9th pair of strings, on which all other similarity measures were applied; feature selection was then repeated anew. The corresponding results are shown in brackets in tables 2 and 3. There was an overall improvement in all tasks (QA, IR, SUM), except for IE, where textual entailment is more difficult to capture via textual similarity, as commented above. We have suggested two additional possible improvements: applying partial matching to all of the string pairs that we consider, and investigating other feature selection schemes. In future work, we also plan to exploit WordNet to capture synonyms, hypernyms, etc.

Acknowledgements

This work was funded by the Greek PENED 2003 programme, which is co-funded by the European Union (75%), and the Greek General Secretariat for Research and Technology (25%).

References

R. Bar-Haim, I. Dagan, B. Dolan, L. Ferro, D. Giampiccolo, B. Magnini, and I. Szpektor. 2006. The 2nd PASCAL recognising textual entailment challenge. In *Proceedings of the 2nd* PASCAL *Challenges Workshop on Recognising Textual Entailment*, Venice, Italy.

C.-C. Chang and C.-J. Lin, 2001. *LIBSVM: a library for Support Vector Machines.* Software available at http://www.csie.ntu.edu.tw/~cjlin/libsvm.

I. Dagan, O. Glickman, and B. Magnini. 2006. The PASCAL recognising textual entailment challenge. In Quiñonero-Candela et al., editor, *MLCW 2005, LNAI*, volume 3904, pages 177–190. Springer-Verlag.

S.M. Harabagiu, S.J. Maiorano, and M.A. Pasca. 2003. Open-domain textual question answering techniques. *Natural Language Engineering*, 9(3):231–267.

M.A. Jaro. 1995. Probabilistic linkage of large public health data file. *Statistics in Medicine*, 14:491–498.

Z. Kozareva and A. Montoyo. 2006. MLENT: The machine learning entailment system of the University of Alicante. In *Proc. of 2nd* PASCAL *Challenges Workshop on Recognising Textual Entailment*, Venice, Italy.

E. Newman, J. Dunnion, and J. Carthy. 2006. Constructing a decision tree classifier using lexical and syntactic features. In *Proc. of 2nd* PASCAL *Challenges Workshop on Recognising Textual Entailment*, Venice, Italy.

H.T. Ng, J.L.P. Kwan, and Y. Xia. 2001. Question answering using a large text database: A machine learning approach. In *Proc. of Empirical Methods in Natural Language Processing*, Carnegie Mellon Univ., PA.

D.R. Radev, J. Prager, and V. Samn. 2000. Ranking suspected answers to natural language questions using predictive annotation. In *Proc. of* NAACL-ANLP, pages 150–157, Seattle, WA.

V. Vapnik. 1998. *Statistical learning theory*. John Wiley.

W.E. Winkler. 1999. The state of record linkage and current research problems. Statistical Research Report RR99/04, US Bureau of the Census, Washington, DC.

Entailment and Anaphora Resolution in RTE3

Rodolfo Delmonte, Antonella Bristot, Marco Aldo Piccolino Boniforti, Sara Tonelli
Department of Language Sciences
Università Ca' Foscari – Ca' Bembo
30123, Venezia, Italy
delmont@unive.it

Abstract

We present VENSES, a linguistically-based approach for semantic inference which is built around a neat division of labour between two main components: a grammatically-driven subsystem which is responsible for the level of predicate-arguments well-formedness and works on the output of a deep parser that produces augmented head-dependency structures. A second subsystem fires allowed logical and lexical inferences on the basis of different types of structural transformations intended to produce a semantically valid meaning correspondence. In the current challenge, we produced a new version of the system, where we do away with grammatical relations and only use semantic roles to generate weighted scores. We also added a number of additional modules to cope with fine-grained inferential triggers which were not present in previous dataset. Different levels of argumenthood have been devised in order to cope with semantic uncertainty generated by nearly-inferrable Text-Hypothesis pairs where the interpretation needs reasoning. RTE3 has introduced texts of paragraph length: in turn this has prompted us to upgrade VENSES by the addition of a discourse level anaphora resolution module, which is paramount to allow entailment in pairs where the relevant portion of text contains pronominal expressions. We present the system, its relevance to the task at hand and an evaluation.

1 Introduction

The system for semantic evaluation VENSES (Venice Semantic Evaluation System) is organized as a pipeline of two subsystems: the first is a reduced version of GETARUN, our system for Text Understanding; the second is the semantic evaluator which was previously created for Summary and Question evaluation and has now been thoroughly revised for the new more comprehensive RTE task.

The reduced GETARUN is composed of the usual sequence of sub-modules common in Information Extraction systems, i.e. a tokenizer, a multiword and NE recognition module, a PoS tagger based on finite state automata; then a multilayered cascaded RTN-based parser which produces c-structures and has an additional module to map them into tentative grammatical functions in LFG terms. The functionally labeled constituents are then passed to an interpretation module that uses subcategorization information to choose final grammatical relations and assign semantic roles. Eventually, the system has a pronominal binding module that works at clause level for lexical personal, possessive and reflexive pronouns, which are substituted by the heads of their antecedents - if available. The output of the binding module can contain one or more "external" pronouns, which need to be bound in the discourse. This output is passed to the Anaphora Resolution module presented in detail in Delmonte (2006) and outlined below. This module works on the so-called History List of entities present in the text so far. In order to make the output of this module usable by the Semantic Evaluator, we decided to produce a flat list of semantic vectors which contain all semantic related items of the current sentence. Inside these vectors, pronominal expressions are substituted by the heads of their antecedents.

Basically, the output of the system is elaborated on top of the output of the parser, which produces a flat list of fully indexed augmented head-dependent structures (AHDS) with Grammatical Relations (GRs) and Semantic Roles (SRs) labels. Notable additions to the usual formalism is the presence of a distinguished Negation relation; we

Proceedings of the Workshop on Textual Entailment and Paraphrasing, pages 48–53,
Prague, June 2007.

also mark modals and progressive mood, tense and voice (for similar approaches see Bos et al., Raina et al.).

The evaluation system uses a cost model with rewards/penalties for T/H pairs where text entailment is interpreted in terms of semantic similarity: the closest the T/H pairs are in semantic terms the more probable is their entailment. Rewards in terms of scores are assigned for each "similar" semantic element; penalties on the contrary can be expressed in terms of scores or they can determine a local failure and a consequent FALSE decision – more on scoring below.

The evaluation system is made up of two main Modules: the first takes care of paraphrases and idiomatic expressions; the second is a sequence of linguistic rule-based sub-modules. Their work is basically a count of how much similar are linguistic elements in the H/T pair. Similarity may range from identical linguistic descriptions, to synonymous or just morphologically derivable ones. As to GRs and SRs, they are scored higher according to whether they belong to the subset of core relations and roles, i.e. obligatory arguments, or not, that is adjuncts. Both Modules go through General Consistency checks which are targeted to high level semantic attributes like presence of modality, negation, and opacity operators. The latter ones are expressed either by the presence of discourse markers of conditionality or by a secondary level relation intervening between the main predicate and a governing higher predicate belonging to the class of non factual verbs, but see below.

All rule-based sub-modules are organized into a sequence of syntactic-semantic transformation rules going from those containing axiomatic-like paraphrase HDSs which are ranked higher, to rules stating conditions for similarity according to a scale of argumentality (more below) and are ranked lower. All rules address HDSs and SRs. Propositional level ones have access to vectors of semantic features which encode propositional level information.

2 The Task of Semantic Inference Evaluation

As happened in the previous Challenge, this year's Challenge is also characterized by the presence of a relatively high number (we counted more than 100 True and another 100 False pairs, i.e. 25%) of T/H pairs which require two particularly hard NLP processes to set up:

- reasoning
- paraphrases (reformulation)

In addition to that, we found a significant number of pairs – about 150 in the development set and some 100 in the test set – in which pronominal binding and anaphora resolution are essential to the definition of entailment. In particular, in such cases it is only by virtue of the substitution of a pronominal expression with the linguistic description of its antecedent that the appropriate Predicate-Argument relations required in order to fire the inference is made available – but see below.

Setting up rules for Paraphrase evaluation, requires the system to actually use the lemmas – and in some cases the wordforms - to be matched together in axiomatic-like structures: in other words, in these cases the actual linguistic expressions play a determining role in the task to derive a semantic inference. In order for these rules to be applied by the SE, we surmise it is important to address a combination of Syntactic and Semantic structures, where Lexical Inference also may play a role: the parser in this case has a fundamental task of recovering the heads of antecedents of all possible pronominal and unexpressed Grammatical relations. It is important to remark that besides pronominal-antecedent relations, our system also recovers all those cases defined as Control in LFG theory, where basically the unexpressed subject of an untensed proposition (infinitival, participial, gerundive) either lexically, syntactically or structurally controlled is bound to some argument of the governing predicate.

2.1 Pronominal Binding and Anaphora Resolution

This year RTE introduces as a novelty a certain number (117 in the Test set – 135 in the Dev set) of long Texts, of paragraph length. This move is justified by the need to address more realistic data, and consequently to tune the whole process of semantic evaluation to the problems related to such data. Thus more relevance is given to empirical issues to be tackled, rather than to the theoretical ones, which however don't disappear but may assume less importance.

When a system has to cope with paragraph length texts, the basic difference with short texts regards the problem of anaphora resolution. In short texts, pronominal expressions constituted a minor problem and all referring expressions were specified fully. Not so in long texts, as can be seen from the Table below:

	He	Him	His	She	Her	It	Its	They	Their	Them	Total
Test	80	15	91	19	18	91	68	43	63	15	485
Dev.	113	16	136	27	35	123	76	44	64	18	652
Total	193	31	227	46	53	214	144	87	127	33	1137

Table 1. 3rd person pronominal expressions contained in RTE3 data sets

As can be seen from this table, the problem a system is faced with is not just to cope with an ad hoc solution for single cases where the pronoun is placed, for instance, in sentence first position and it might be easy to recover its antecedent by some empirical ad hoc procedure. The problem needs to be addressed fully and this requires a full-fledged system for anaphora resolution. One such system is shown in Fig. 2 below, where we highlight the architecture and main processes undergoing at the anaphora level. First of all, the subdivision of the system into two levels: Clause level – intrasentential pronominal phenomena – where all pronominal expressions contained in modifiers, adjuncts or complement clauses receive their antecedent locally. Possessive pronouns, pronouns contained in relative clauses and complement clauses choose preferentially their antecedents from list of higher level referring expressions. Not so for those pronouns contained in matrix clauses. In particular the ones in subject position are to be coreferred in the discourse. This requires the system to be equipped with a History List of all referring expressions to be used when needed.
In the system, three levels are indicated: Clause level, i.e. simple sentences; Utterance level, i.e. complex sentences; Discourse level, i.e. intersententially. Our system computes semantic structures in a sentence by sentence fashion and any information useful to carry out anaphoric processes needs to be made available to the following portion of text, and eventually to the Semantic Evaluation that computes entailment. We will comment a number of significant examples to clarify the way in which our system operates.

3. Anaphora Resolution for RTE

Why is it important to implement an anaphora resolution algorithm for RTE? I think the reason is quite straightforward: pronominal expressions do not allow any inference to be drawn or any otherwise semantic similarity processes to be fired, being inherently referentially poor. In order to be able to use information made available by the verb in the sentence in which a pronoun is used, the antecedent must be recovered and the pronoun substituted by its head. So, very simply, RTE needs anaphora resolution in order to allow the system to use verb predicates where pronouns have been used to corefer to some antecedent in the previous text. In turn that verb predicate is just what is being searched for in the first place, and in our case it is the one contained in the Hypothesis.
The current algorithm for anaphora resolution works on the output of the complete deep robust parser which builds an indexed linear list of dependency structures where clause boundaries are clearly indicated. As said above, our system elaborates both grammatical relations and semantic roles information for arguments and adjuncts. Semantic roles are very important in the weighting procedures.
As to the anaphoric resolution algorithm, it is a distributed, local – clause-based - approach to anaphora resolution which we regard more efficient than monolithic, global ones. Linguistic theory has long since established without any doubt the existence in most languages of the world of at least two classes of pronouns: the class which must be bound locally in a given domain – roughly the clause, and the class which must be left free in the same domain.

In our approach, we proceed in a clause by clause fashion, weighting each candidate antecedent w.r.t. that domain, trying to resolve it locally. Weighting criteria are amenable on the one hand to linear precedence constraints, with scores assigned on a functional/semantic basis. On the other hand, these criteria may be overrun by a functional ranking of clauses which requires to treat main clauses differently from secondary clauses, and these two differently from complement clauses.

There are also two general referential policy assumption that we adopt in our approach: The first one is related to pronominal expressions, the second one to referring expressions or entities to be asserted in the History List, and are expressed as follows:

- no more than two pronominal expressions are allowed to refer back in the previous discourse portion;
- at discourse level, referring expressions are stored in a push-down stack according to Persistence principles.

Only "persistent" referring expressions are allowed to build up the History List, where persistence is established on the basis of the frequency of topicality for each referring expression which must be higher than 1. All referring expression asserted as Topic (Main, Secondary, Potential) only once are discarded in case they appeared at a distance measured in 5 previous utterances. Proximate referring expressions are allowed to be asserted in the History List. The first procedure is organized as follows.

A. For each clause,

1. we collect all referential expressions and weight them – this is followed by an automatic ranking;
2. then we subtract pronominal expressions;
3. at clause level, we try to bind personal and possessive pronouns obeying specific structural properties; we also bind reflexive pronouns and reciprocals if any, which must be bound obligatorily in this domain;
4. when binding a pronoun, we check for disjointness w.r.t. a previously bound pronoun if any;
5. all unbound pronouns and all remaining personal pronouns are asserted as "externals", and are passed up to the higher clause levels;

B. Then we turn at the higher level – if any -, and we proceed as in A., in addition we try to bind pronouns passed up by the lower clause levels

- o if successful, this will activate a retract of the "external" label and a label of "antecedenthood" for the current pronoun with a given antecedent;
- o the best antecedent is chosen by recursively trying to match features of the pronoun with the first available antecedent previously ranked by weighting;
- o here again whenever a pronoun is bound we check for disjointness at utterance level.

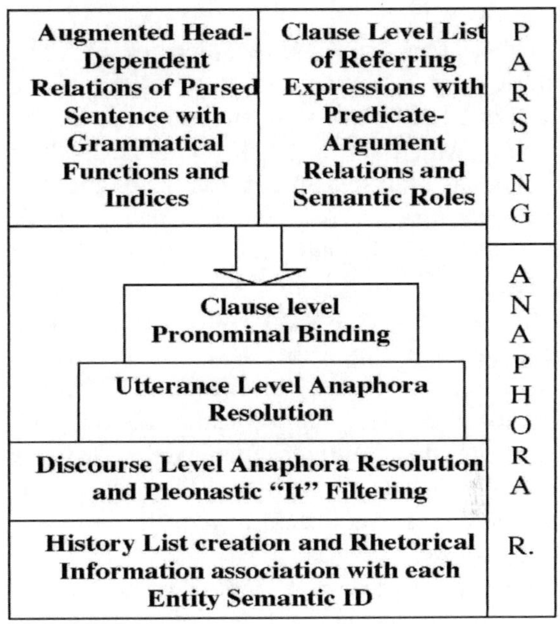

Fig. 1. Anaphoric Processes in VENSES

C. This is repeated until all clauses are examined and all pronouns are scrutinised and bound or left free.

D. Pronouns left free – those asserted as externals – will be matched tentatively with the best candidates provided this time by a "centering-like" algorithm. Step A. is identical and is recursively repeated until all clauses are processed.

3.1 Focussing Revisited

Our version of the focussing algorithm follows Sidner's proposal (Sidner C., 1983; Grosz B., Sidner C., 1986), to use a Focus Stack, a certain Focus Algorithm with Focus movements and data structures to allow for processing simple inferential relations between different linguistic descriptions co-specifying or coreferring to a given entity.

Our Focus Algorithm is organized as follows: for each utterance, we assert three hierarchically ordered "centers" that we call Main, Secondary and the first Potential Topic, which represent the best three referring expressions as they have been weighted in the candidate list used for pronominal binding; then we also keep a list of Potential Topics for the remaining best candidates. These three best candidates repositories are renovated at each new utterance, and are used both to resolve pronominal and nominal cospecification and coreference: this is done both in case of strict identity of linguistic description and of non-identity.

The Main Topic may be regarded the Forward Looking Center in the centering terminology or the Current Focus. All entities are stored in the History List (HL) which is a stack containing their morphological and semantic features. In the HL every new entity is assigned a semantic index which identifies it uniquely. To allow for Persistence evaluation, we also assert rhetorical properties associated to each entity, i.e. we store the information of topicality (i.e. whether it has been evaluated as Main, Secondary or Potential Topic), together with the semantic ID and the number of the current utterance. This is subsequently used to measure the degree of Persistence in the overall text of a given entity, as explained below.

In order to decide which entity has to become Main, Secondary or Potential Topic we proceed as follows:

- we collect all entities present in the History List with their semantic identifier and feature list and proceed to an additional weighting procedure;
- nominal expressions, they are divided up into four semantic types: definite, indefinite, bare NPs, quantified NPs. Both definite and indefinite NP may be computed as new or old entity according to contextual conditions as will be discussed below and are given a rewarding score;
- we enumerate for each entity its persistence in the previous text, and keep entities which have frequency higher than 1, we discard the others;
- we recover entities which have been asserted in the HL in proximity to the current utterance, up to four utterances back;
- we use this list to "resolve" referring expressions contained in the current utterance;
- if this succeeds, we use the "resolved" entities as new Main, Secondary, and Potential Topics and assert the rest in the Potential Topics stack;
- if this fails – also partially – we use the best candidates in the weighted list of referring expressions to assert the new Topics. It may be the case that both resolved and current best candidates are used, and this is by far the most common case.

In example n.3 below, the first possessive pronoun "his" is met at Utterance level – the first sentence has two clauses: clause 1, headed by the predicate DIVORCE, and clause 2, headed by MARRY. "His" will look for a masculine antecedent and Chabrol will be chosen, also for weights associated to it, being the higher subject. This will produce the following semantic structure, which is made of a Head, a Semantic Role and an Index,

- Chabrol-poss-sn2

which is the output of the substitution of "his" present in the same structure by means of information made available by the Anaphoric module. Note that the index of a modifier points to the governing head, in this case "wife", the apposition associated to "Agnes", which in turn is the OBJect of DIVORCE.

T/H pair n. 3
T: Claude Chabrol divorced Agnes, his first wife, to marry the actress Stèphane Audran. His third wife is Aurore Paquiss.
H: Aurore Paquiss married Chabrol.

When the first sentence is passed to the semantic interpreter, anaphoric processes have already been completed and the information is then transferred to semantic structure which will register the anaphoric relation by the substitution operation. However this specific relation is not the one that really matters in the current T/H pair. When the system passes to the analysis of the following sentence it has another possessive pronoun which is contained in a SUBJect NP. By definition, these pronouns take their antecedent from the discourse level. To have the system do that, the pronoun has to be left free at sentence level, i.e. it must be computed as "external" to the current sentence, and not bound locally. Discourse level processes will look for antecedents from the History list and from the socalled Topic Hierarchy, our way to compute centering (but see again Delmonte, 2006). This is shown schematically in the output of the Anaphora Resolution module shown here below, which reports the listing of pronouns, Topic Hierarchy, and Anaphora Resolution processes carried out. In this case, every referring expression will have a semantic index (SI) associated which is unique in the History List. In example n.31, here below, the pronominal expressions are two: an Utterance level possessive pronoun bound to the local SUBJect; and a Discourse level personal pronoun "He" which receives its antecedent from the History List. In both cases, substitution with their antecedents' head will take place in the semantic interpretation level.

T/H pair n. 31
T: Upon receiving his Ph.D., Wetherill became a staff member at Carnegie's Department of Terrestrial Magnetism (DTM) in Washington, D.C. He originated the concept of the Concordia Diagram for the uranium-lead isotopic system.
H: Wetherill was the inventor of the concept of the Concordia Diagram.

Clause No.	**Main Topic**	**Secondary Topic**	**Potential Topics**	**Pronouns + Features**	**Disjointness**	**Pronominal Binding**	**Anaphora Resolution**
id_3_1 Text	'Claude Chabrol'		Agnes				
id_3_2 Text	**Main resolved as** Claude Chabrol - SI=id1	wife	Aurore Paquiss	his-[sem:hum, cat:poss, gen:mas, num:sing, pers:3, pred:he, gov_pred:be]	disj=[sn1-wife]	**External pronoun** (be, his)	his **resolved as** 'Claude Chabrol'
id_3_3 Hypothesis	Aurore Paquiss - SI=id4	Claude Chabrol - SI=id1					

Table 2. Output of the Anaphora Resolution Module

4 Results and Discussion

Results for the Test set 485 total pronominal expressions amount to 69% accuracy, 92% recall – this includes computing It-expletives. The F-measure computed is thus 79%. Overall, we evaluated the contribution of the Anaphora Resolution Module as 15% additional correct results. Of course, the impact of using this module would have been different in case all T/H pairs were constituted by long texts.
The RTE task is a hard task: in our case 10-15% mistakes are ascribable to the parser or any other analysis tool; another 5-10% mistakes will certainly come from insufficient semantic information.

	ACCURACY	AVERAGE PRECISION
IE	**0.5850**	**0.5992**
IR	**0.6050**	**0.5296**
QA	**0.5900**	**0.6327**
SUMM	**0.5700**	**0.6132**
TOTAL	**0.5875**	**0.5830**

Table 3. Results for First Run

References

Bos, J., Clark, S., Steedman, M., Curran, J., Hockenmaier, J.: Wide-coverage semantic representations from a ccg parser. In: Proc. of the 20th International Conference on Computational Linguistics. Geneva, Switzerland (2004)

Delmonte, R.: Text Understanding with GETARUNS for Q/A and Summarization, Proc. ACL 2004 - 2nd Workshop on Text Meaning & Interpretation, Barcelona, Columbia University (2004) 97-104

Delmonte R., et al. Another Evaluation of Anaphora Resolution Algorithms and a Comparison with GETARUNS' Knowledge Rich Approach. In: ROMAND 2006 - 11th EACL. Geneva, (2006) 3-10

Grosz B. and C. Sidner 1986. Attention, Intentions, and the Structure of Discourse, *Computational Linguistics* 12 (3), 175-204.

Raina, R., et al.: Robust Textual Inference using Diverse Knowledge Sources. In: Proc. of the 1st. PASCAL Recognision Textual Entailment Challenge Workshop, Southampton, U.K., (2005) 57-60

Sidner C. 1983. Focusing in the Comprehension of Definite Anaphora, in Brady M., Berwick R.(eds.), *Computational Models of Discourse*, MIT Press, Cambridge, MA, 267-330.

On the Role of Lexical and World Knowledge in RTE3

Peter Clark[1], William R. Murray[1], John Thompson[1], Phil Harrison[1], Jerry Hobbs[2], Christiane Fellbaum[3]
[1]Boeing Phantom Works, The Boeing Company, Seattle, WA 98124
[2]USC/ISI, 4676 Admiralty Way, Marina del Rey, CA 90292
[3]Princeton University, NJ 08544
{peter.e.clark,william.r.murray,john.a.thompson,philip.harrison}@boeing.com, hobbs@isi.edu, fellbaum@clarity.princeton.edu

Abstract

To score well in RTE3, and even more so to create good justifications for entailments, substantial lexical and world knowledge is needed. With this in mind, we present an analysis of a sample of the RTE3 positive entailment pairs, to identify where and what kinds of world knowledge are needed to fully identify and justify the entailment, and discuss several existing resources and their capacity for supplying that knowledge. We also briefly sketch the path we are following to build an RTE system (Our implementation is very preliminary, scoring 50.9% at the time of RTE). The contribution of this paper is thus a framework for discussing the knowledge requirements posed by RTE and some exploration of how these requirements can be met.

1 Introduction

The Pascal RTE site defines entailment between two texts T and H as holding "if, typically, a human reading T would infer that H is most likely true" assuming "common human understanding of language as well as common background knowledge." While a few RTE3 entailments can be recognized using simple syntactic matching, the majority rely on significant amounts of this "common human understanding" of lexical and world knowledge. Our goal in this paper is to analyze what that knowledge is, create a preliminary framework for it, and explore a few available sources for it. In the short term, such knowledge can be (and has been) used to drive semantic matching of the T and H dependency/parse trees and their semantic representations, as many prior RTE systems perform, e.g., (Hickl et al., 2006). In the long term, computers should be able to perform deep language understanding to build a computational model of the scenario being described in T, to reason about the entailment, answer further questions, and create meaningful justifications. With this longer term goal in mind, it is useful to explore the types of knowledge required. It also gives a snapshot of the kinds of challenges that RTE3 poses.

The scope of this paper is to examine the underlying lexical/world knowledge requirements of RTE, rather than the more syntactic/grammatical issues of parsing, coreference resolution, named entity recognition, punctuation, coordination, typographical errors, etc. Although there is a somewhat blurry line between the two, this separation is useful for bounding the analysis. It should be noted that the more syntactic issues are themselves vast in RTE, but here we will not delve into them. Instead, we will perform a thought experiment in which they have been handled correctly.

2 Analysis

Based on an analysis of 100 (25%) of the positive entailments in the RTE3 test set, we have divided the knowledge requirements into several rough categories, which we now present. We then summarize the frequency with which examples in this sample fell into these categories. The examples below are fragments of the original test questions, abbreviated and occasionally simplified.

2.1 Syntactic Matching

In a few cases, entailment can be identified by syntactic matching of T and H, for example:

Proceedings of the Workshop on Textual Entailment and Paraphrasing, pages 54–59,
Prague, June 2007.

489.T "The Gurkhas come from Nepal and…"
489.H "The Gurkhas come from Nepal."

Other examples include 299, 489, and 456. In some cases, the syntactic matching can be very complex, e.g., examples 152, 724.

2.2 Synonyms

Synonymy is often needed to recognize entailment,

648.T "…go through … licencing procedures..."
648.H "…go through the licencing processes."

Other examples include 286 ("dismiss"/"throw out"), 37 ("begin"/"start"), 236 ("wildfire"/"bush fire"), and, arguably, 462 ("revenue"/"proceeds").

2.3 Generalizations (Hypernyms)

Similarly, subsumption (generalization) relationships between word senses need to be recognized (whether or not a fixed set of senses are used), eg.

148.T "Beverly served...at WEDCOR"
148.H "Beverly worked for WEDCOR."

Others include 178 ("succumbed" as a kind of "killed"), and 453 ("take over" as a kind of "buy").

2.4 Noun Redundancy

Sometimes a noun in a compound can be dropped:

607.T "single-run production process..."
607.H "Single-run production..."

Other examples include 269 ("increasing prevalence of" → "increasing"), 604 ("mini-mill process" → "mini-mill"), and (at the phrase level) 668 ("all segments of the public" → "the public").

2.5 Noun-Verb Relations

Often derivationally related nouns and verbs occur in the pairs. To identify and justify the entailment, the relationship and its nature is needed, as in:

480 "Marquez is a winner..." →"Marquez won..."

Other examples include 286 ("pirated", "piracy"), and 75 ("invent", "invention"). In some cases, the deverbal noun denotes the verb's event, in other cases it denotes one of the verb's arguments (e.g., "winner" as the subject/agent of a "win" event).

2.6 Compound Nouns

Some examples require inferring the semantic relation between nouns in a compound, e.g.,

168 "Sirius CEO Karmazin" → "Karmazin is an executive of Sirius"
583 "physicist Hawking" → "Hawking is a physicist"
In some cases this is straightforward, others require more detailed knowledge of the entities involved.

2.7 Definitions

Although there is somewhat of a fuzzy boundary between word and world knowledge, we draw this distinction here. Some examples of RTE pairs which require knowing word meanings are:

667 "… found guilty..." → "…convicted..."
328 "sufferers of coeliac disease..." → "coeliacs..."

The second example is particularly interesting as many readers (and computers) will not have encountered the word "coeliacs" before, yet a person can reasonably infer its meaning on the fly from context and morphology - something challenging for a machine to do. Definitions of compound nouns are also sometimes needed, e.g., "family planning" (612) and "cough syrup" (80).

2.8 World Knowledge: General

A large number of RTE pairs require non-definitional knowledge about the way the world (usually) is, e.g.,:

273 "bears kill people" → "bears attack people"

People recognize this entailment as they know (have heard about) how people might be killed by a bear, and hence can justify why the entailment is valid. (They know that the first step in the bear killing a person is for the bear to attack that person.) Some other examples are:

499 "shot dead" → "murder"
705 "under a contract with" → "cooperates with"
721 "worked on the law" → "discussed the law"
731 "cut tracts of forest" → "cut trees in the forest"
732 "establishing tree farms"
→ "trees were planted"
639 "*X*'s plans for reorganizing"
→ "*X* intends to reorganize"
328 "the diets must be followed by *<person>*"
→ "the diets are for *<person>*"
722 *X* and *Y* vote for *Z* → *X* and *Y* agree to *Z*.

All these cases appeal to a person's world knowledge concerning the situation being described.

2.9 World Knowledge: Core Theories

In addition to this more specific knowledge of the world, some RTE examples appeal to more general, fundamental knowledge (e.g., space, time, plans, goals). For example

6.T "Yunupingu is one of the clan of..."
6.H "Yunupingu is a member of..."

appeals to a basic rule of set inclusion, and 10 (a negative entailment: "unsuccessfully sought election" → not elected) appeals to core notions of goals and achievement. Several examples appeal to core spatial knowledge, e.g.:

491.T "...come from the high mountains of Nepal."
491.H "...come from Nepal."

178.T "...3 people in Saskatchewan succumbed to the storm."
178.H "...a storm in Saskatchewan."

491 appeals to regional inclusion (if X location Y, and Y is in Z, then X location Z), and 178 appeals to colocation (if X is at Y, and X physically interacts with Z, then Z is at Y). Other spatial examples include 236 ("around Sydney" → "near Sydney"), and 129 ("invasion of" → "arrived in").

2.10 World Knowledge: Frames and Scripts

Although loosely delineated, another category of world knowledge concerns stereotypical places, situations and the events which occur in them, with various representational schemes proposed in the AI literature, e.g., Frames (Minsky 1985), Scripts (Schank 1983). Some RTE examples require recognizing the implicit scenario ("frame", "script", etc.) which T describes to confirm the new facts or relationships introduced in H are valid. A first example is:

358.T "Kiesbauer was target of a letter bomb..."
358.H "A letter bomb was sent to Kiesbauer."

A person recognizes H as entailed by T because he/she knows the "script" for letter bombing, which includes sending the bomb in the mail. Thus a person could also recognize alternative verbs in 358.H as valid (e.g., "mailed", "delivered") or invalid (e.g., "thrown at", "dropped on"), even though these verbs are all strongly associated with words in T. For a computer to fully explain the entailment, it would need similar knowledge.

As a second example, consider:

538.T "...the O. J. Simpson murder trial..."
538.H "O. J. Simpson was accused of murder."

Again, this requires knowing about trials: That they involve charges, a defendant, an accusation, etc., in order to validate H as an entailed expansion of T. In this example, there is also a second twist to it as the noun phrase in 538.T equally supports the hypothesis "O. J. Simpson was murdered." (e.g., consider replacing "O. J." with "Nicole"). It is only a reference elsewhere in the T sentence to "Simpson's attorneys" that suggests Simpson is still alive, and hence couldn't have been the victim, and hence must be the accused, that clarifies 538.H as being correct, a highly complex chain of reasoning.

As a third example, consider:
736.T "In a security fraud case, Milken was sentenced to 10 years in prison."
736.H "Milken was imprisoned for security fraud."

This example is particularly interesting, as one needs to recognize security fraud as Milken's crime, a connection which not stated in T. A human reader will recognize the notion of sentencing, and thus expect to see a convict and his/her crime, and hence can align these expectations with T, validating H. Thus again, deep knowledge of sentencing is needed to understand and justify the entailment.

Some other examples requiring world knowledge to validate their expansions, include 623 ("narcotics-sniffing dogs" → "dogs are used to sniff out narcotics"), and 11 ("the Nintendo release of the game" → "the game is produced by Nintendo").

2.11 Implicative Verbs

Some RTE3 examples contain complement-taking verbs that make an implication (either positive or negative) about the complement. For example:

668 "A survey shows that *X*..." → "*X*..."
657 "...*X* was seen..." → "...*X*..."
725 "...decided to *X*..." → "...*X*..."
716 "...have been unable to *X*..." → "...do not *X*"

In the first 3 the implication is positive, but in the last the implication is negative. (Nairn et al, 2006) provide a detailed analysis of this type of behavior. In fact, this notion of implicature (one part of a sentence making an implication about another part) extends beyond single verbs, and there are some more complex examples in RTE3, e.g.:

453 "...won the battle to *X*..." → "...*X*..."

784.T "X reassures Russia it has nothing to fear..."
784.H "Russia fears..."

In this last example the implication behavior is quite complex: (loosely) If X reassures Y of Z, then Y is concerned about not-Z.

2.12 Metonymy/Transfer

In some cases, language allows us to replace a word (sense) with a closely related word (sense):

708.T "Revenue from stores funded..."
708.H "stores fund..."

Rules for metonymic transfer, e.g., (Fass 2000), can be used to define which transfers are allowed. Another example is 723 "...pursue its drive towards *X*" → "...pursue *X*".

2.13 Idioms/Protocol/Slang

Finally, some RTE pairs rely on understanding idioms, slang, or special protocols used in language, for example:

12 "Drew served as Justice. Kennon returned to claim Drew's seat" → "Kennon served as Justice."
486 "*name*, 1890-1970" → "*name* died in 1970"
408 "takes the title of" → "is"
688 "art finds its way back" → "art gets returned"

The phrases in these examples all have special meaning which cannot be easily derived compositionally from their words, and thus require special handling within an entailment system.

2.14 Frequency Statistics

Table 1 shows the number of positive entailments in our sample of 100 that fell into the different categories (some fell into several). While there is a certain subjectivity in the boundaries of the categories, the most significant observation is that very few entailments depend purely on syntactic manipulation and simple lexical knowledge (synonyms, hypernyms), and that the vast majority of entailments require significant world knowledge, highlighting one of the biggest challenges of RTE. In addition, the category of general world knowledge -- small, non-definitional facts about the way the world (usually) is -- is the largest, suggesting that harvesting and using this kind of knowledge should continue to be a priority for improving performance on RTE-style tasks.

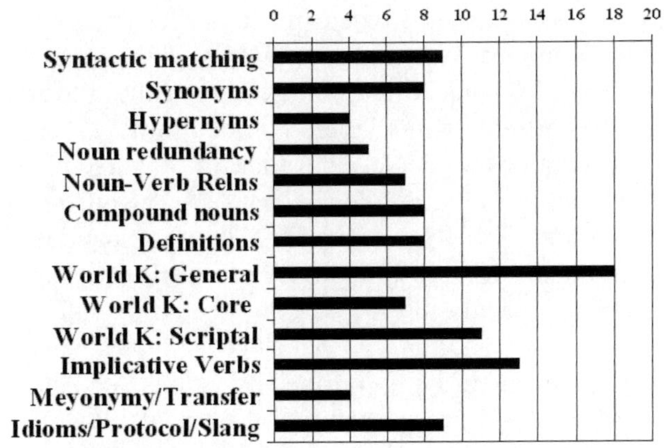

Table 1: Frequency of different entailment phenomena from a sample of 100 RTE3 pairs.

3 Sources of World Knowledge

While there are many potential sources of the knowledge that we have identified, we describe three in a bit more detail and how they relate to the earlier analysis.

3.1 WordNet

WordNet (Fellbaum, 1998) is one of the most extensively used resources in RTE already and in computational linguistics in general. Despite some well-known problems, it provides broad coverage of several key relationships between word senses (and words), in particular for synonyms, hypernyms (generalizations), meronyms (parts), and semantically ("morphosemantically") related forms. From the preceding analysis, WordNet does contain the synonyms {"procedure","process"}, {"dismiss","throw out"}, {"begin","start"}, but does not contain the compound "wild fire" and (strictly correctly) does not contain {"revenue","proceeds"} as synonyms. In addition, the three hypernyms mentioned in the earlier analysis are in WordNet. WordNet also links (via the "morphosemantic" link) the 3 noun-verb pairs mentioned earlier (win/winner, pirated/piracy, invent/invention) – however it does not currently distinguish the nature of that link (e.g., agent, result, event). WordNet is currently being expanded to include this information, as part of the AQUAINT program.

Two independently developed versions of the WordNet glosses expressed in logic are also available: Extended WordNet (Moldovan and Rus, 2001) and a version about to be released with WordNet3.0 (again developed under AQUAINT). These in principle can help with definitional knowledge. From our earlier analysis, it turns out "convicted" is conveniently defined in WordNet as "pronounced or proved guilty" potentially bridging the gap for pair 667, although there are problems with the logical interpretation of this particular gloss in both resources mentioned. WordNet does have "coeliac", but not in the sense of a person with coeliac disease[1].

In addition, several existing "core theories" (e.g., TimeML, IKRIS) that can supply some of the fundamental knowledge mentioned earlier (e.g., space, time, goals) are being connected to WordNet under the AQUAINT program.

3.2 The DIRT Paraphrase Database

Paraphrases have been used successfully by several RTE systems (e.g., Hickl et al., 2005). With respect to our earlier analysis, we examined Lin and Pantel's (2001) paraphrase database built with their system DIRT, containing 12 million entries. While there is of course noise in the database, it contains a remarkable amount of sensible world knowledge as well as syntactic rewrites, albeit encoded as shallow rules lacking word senses.

Looking at the examples from our earlier analysis of general world knowledge, we find that three are supported by paraphrase rules in the database:

273: X kills Y → X attacks Y
499: X shoots Y → X murders Y
721: X works on Y → X discusses Y

And one that could be is not, namely:

705: X is under a contract with Y → X cooperates with Y (not in the database)

Other examples are outside the scope of DIRT's approach (i.e., "X $pattern_1$ Y" → "X $pattern_2$ Y"), but nonetheless the coverage is encouraging.

3.3 FrameNet

In our earlier analysis, we identified knowledge about stereotypical situations and their events as important for RTE. FrameNet (Baker et al, 1998) attempts to encode this knowledge. FrameNet was used with some success in RTE2 by Burchardt and Frank (2005). FrameNet's basic unit - a Frame - is a script-like conceptual schema that refers to a situation, object, or event along with its participants (Frame Elements), identified independent of their syntactic configuration.

We earlier discussed how 538.T "...the O. J. Simpson murder trial..." might entail 538.H "O. J. Simpson was accused of murder." This case applies to FrameNet's Trial frame, which includes the Frame Elements Defendant and Charges, with Charges being defined as "The legal label for the crime that the Defendant is accused of.", thus stating the relationship between the defendant and the charges, unstated in T but made explicit in H, validating the entailment. However, the lexical units instantiating the Frame Elements are not yet disambiguated against a lexical database, limiting full semantic understanding. Moreover, FrameNet's world knowledge is stated informally in English descriptions, though it may be possible to convert these to a more machine-processable form either manually or automatically.

3.4 Other Resources

We have drawn attention to these three resources as they provide some answers to the requirements identified earlier. Several other publicly available resources could also be of use, including VerbNet (Univ Colorado at Boulder), the Component Library (Univ Texas at Austin), OpenCyc (Cycorp), SUMO, Stanford's additions to WordNet, and the Tuple Database (Boeing, following Schubert's 2002 approach), to name but a few.

[1] This seems to be an accidental gap; WordNet contains many interlinked disease-patient noun pairs, incl. "diabetes-diabetic," "epilepsy-eplileptic," etc.

4 Sketch of our RTE System

Although not the primary purpose of this paper, we briefly sketch the path we are following to build an RTE system able to exploit the above resources. Our implementation is very preliminary, scoring 50.9% at the time of RTE and 52.6% now (55.0% on the 525 examples it is able to analyze, guessing "no entailment" for the remainder). Nevertheless, the following shows the direction we are moving in

Like several other groups, our basic approach is to generate logic for the T and H sentences, and then explore the application of inference rules to elaborate T, or transform H, until H matches T. Parsing is done using a broad coverage chart parser. Subsequently, an abstracted form of the parse tree is converted into a logical form, for example:

299.H "Tropical storms cause severe damage."
subject(_Cause1, _Storm1)
sobject(_Cause1, _Damage1)
mod(_Storm1, _Tropical1)
mod(_Damage1, _Severe1)
input-word(_Storm1, "storm", noun)
[same for other words]

Entailment is determined if every clause in the semantic representation of H semantically matches (subsumes) some clause in T. Two variables in a clause match if their input words are the same, or some WordNet sense of one is the same as or a hypernym of the other. In addition, the system searches for DIRT paraphrase rules that can transform the sentences into a form which can then match. The explicit use of WordNet and DIRT results in comprehensible, machine-generated justifications when entailments are found, , e.g.,:

T: "The Salvation Army operates the shelter under a contract with the county."
H: "The Salvation Army collaborates with the county."
Yes! Justification: I have general knowledge that:
IF X works with Y THEN X collaborates with Y
Here: X = the Salvation Army, Y = the county
Thus, here:
I can see from T: the Salvation Army works with the county (because "operate" and "work" mean roughly the same thing)
Thus it follows that:
The Salvation Army collaborates with the county.

We are continuing to develop our system and expand the number of knowledge sources it uses.

5 Summary

To recognize and justify textual entailments, and ultimately understand language, considerable lexical and world knowledge is needed. We have presented an analysis of some of the knowledge requirements of RTE3, and commented on some available sources of that knowledge. The analysis serves to highlight the depth and variety of knowledge demanded by RTE3, and contributes a rough framework for organizing these requirements. Ultimately, to fully understand language, extensive knowledge of the world (either manually or automatically acquired) is needed. From this analysis, RTE3 is clearly providing a powerful driving force for research in this direction.

Acknowledgements

This work was performed under the DTO AQUAINT program, contract N61339-06-C-0160.

References

Collin Baker, Charles Fillmore, and John Lowe. 1998. "The Berkeley FrameNet Project". Proc 36th ACL

Aljoscha Burchardt and Anette Frank. 2005. Approaching Textual Entailment with LFG and FrameNet Frames. in 2nd PASCAL RTE Workshop, pp 92-97.

Dan Fass. 1991. "Met*: A Method for Discriminating Metonymy and Metaphor by Computer". In Computational Linguistics 17 (1), pp 49-90.

Christiane Fellbaum. 1998. "WordNet: An Electronic Lexical Database." The MIT Press.

Andrew Hickl, Jeremy Bensley, John Williams, Kirk Roberts, Bryan Rink, and Ying Shi. "Recognizing Textual Entailment with LCC's Groundhog System", in Proc 2nd PASCAL RTE Workshop, pp 80-85.

Dekang Lin and Patrick Pantel. 2001. "Discovery of Inference Rules for Question Answering". Natural Language Engineering 7 (4) pp 343-360.

Marvin Minsky. 1985. "A Framework for Representing Knowledge". In Readings in Knowledge Repn.

Dan Moldovan and Vasile Rus, 2001. Explaining Answers with Extended WordNet, ACL 2001.

Rowan Nairn, Cleo Condoravdi and Lauri Karttunen. 2006. Computing Relative Polarity for Textual Inference. In the Proceedings of ICoS-5.

Len Schubert. 2002. "Can we Derive General World Knowledge from Texts?", Proc. HLT'02, pp84-87.

Machine Learning with Semantic-Based Distances Between Sentences for Textual Entailment

Daniel Ferrés
TALP Research Center
Software Department
Universitat Politècnica de Catalunya
dferres@lsi.upc.edu

Horacio Rodríguez
TALP Research Center
Software Department
Universitat Politècnica de Catalunya
horacio@lsi.upc.edu

Abstract

This paper describes our experiments on Textual Entailment in the context of the Third Pascal Recognising Textual Entailment (RTE-3) Evaluation Challenge. Our system uses a Machine Learning approach with Support Vector Machines and AdaBoost to deal with the RTE challenge. We perform a lexical, syntactic, and semantic analysis of the entailment pairs . From this information we compute a set of semantic-based distances between sentences. The results look promising specially for the QA entailment task.

1 Introduction

This paper describes our participation in the RTE-3 challenge. It is our first attempt to RTE and we have taken profit of an analysis of the approaches followed in previous challenges (see (Dagan et al., 2005), and (Bar-Haim et al., 2006) for overviews of RTE-1 and RTE-2). Our approach, however, is based on a set of semantic-based distance measures between sentences used by our group in previous contests in Question Answering (TREC 2004, see (Ferrés et al., 2005), and CLEF 2004, see (Ferrés et al., 2004)) , and Automatic Summarization (DUC 2006, see (Fuentes et al., 2006)). Although the use of such measures (distance between question and sentences in passages candidates to contain the answer, distance between query and sentences candidates to be included in the summary, ...) is different for RTE task, our claim is that with some modifications the approach can be useful in this new scenario.

The organization of this paper is as follows. After this introduction we present in section 2 a description of the measures upon which our approach is built. Section 3 describes in detail our proposal. Results are discussed in section 4. Conclusions and further work is finally included in section 5.

2 System Description

Our approach for computing distance measures between sentences is based on the degree of overlapping between the semantic content of the two sentences. Obtaining the semantic content implies a depth Linguistic Processing. Upon this semantic representation of the sentences several distance measures are computed. We next describe such issues.

2.1 Linguistic Processing

Linguistic Processing (LP) consists of a pipe of general purpose Natural Language (NL) processors that performs tokenization, morphologic tagging, lemmatization, Named Entities Recognition and Classification (NERC) with 4 basic classes (PERSON, LOCATION, ORGANIZATION, and OTHERS), syntactic parsing and semantic labelling, with WordNet synsets, Magnini's domain markers and EuroWordNet Top Concept Ontology labels. The *Spear*[1] parser performs full parsing and robust detection of verbal predicate arguments. The syntactic constituent structure of each sentence (including the specification of the head of each constituent) and the relations among constituents (subject, direct and indirect object, modifiers) are obtained. As a result

[1] **Spear.** http://www.lsi.upc.edu/~surdeanu/spear.html

Proceedings of the Workshop on Textual Entailment and Paraphrasing, pages 60–65,
Prague, June 2007.

of the performance of these processors each sentence is enriched with a lexical and syntactic language dependent representations. A semantic language independent representation of the sentence (called *environment*) is obtained from these analyses (see (Ferrés et al., 2005) for details). The *environment* is a semantic network like representation built using a process to extract the semantic units (nodes) and the semantic relations (edges) that hold between the different tokens in the sentence. These units and relations belong to an ontology of about 100 semantic classes (as person, city, action, magnitude, etc.) and 25 relations (mostly binary) between them (e.g. *time_of_event*, *actor_of_action*, *location_of_event*, etc.). Both classes and relations are related by taxonomic links (see (Ferrés et al., 2005) for details) allowing inheritance. Consider, for instance, the sentence "Romano_Prodi 1 is 2 the 3 prime 4 minister 5 of 6 Italy 7". The following environment is built:

i_en_proper_person(1), *entity_has_quality(2)*, *entity(5)*, *i_en_country(7)*, *quality(4)*, *which_entity(2,1)*, *which_quality(2,5)*, *mod(5,7)*, *mod(5,4)*.

2.2 Semantic-Based Distance Measures

We transform each environment into a labelled directed graph representation with nodes assigned to positions in the sentence, labelled with the corresponding token, and edges to predicates (a dummy node, 0, is used for representing unary predicates). Only unary (e.g. *entity(5)* in Figure 1) and binary (e.g. in Figure 2 *which_quality(2,5)*) predicates are used. Over this representation a rich variety of lexico-semantic proximity measures between sentences have been built. Each measure combines two components:

- A lexical component that considers the set of common tokens occurring in both sentences. The size of this set and the strength of the compatibility links between its members are used for defining the measure. A flexible way of measuring token-level compatibility has been set ranging from word-form identity, lemma identity, overlapping of WordNet synsets, approximate string matching between Named Entities etc. For instance, "Romano Prodi" is lexically compatible with "R. Prodi" with a score of 0.5 and with "Prodi" with a score of 0.41. "Italy" and "Italian" are also compatible with score 0.7. This component defines a set of (partial) weighted mapping between the tokens of the two sentences that will be used as anchors in the next component.

- A semantic component computed over the subgraphs corresponding to the set of lexically compatible nodes (anchors). Four different measures have been defined:

  - Strict overlapping of unary predicates.
  - Strict overlapping of binary predicates.
  - Loose overlapping of unary predicates.
  - Loose overlapping of binary predicates.

The loose versions allow a relaxed matching of predicates by climbing up in the ontology of predicates (e.g. provided that A and B are lexically compatible, *i_en_city(A)* can match *i_en_proper_place(B)*, *i_en_proper_named_entity(B)*, *location(B)* or *entity(B)*) [2]. Obviously, loose overlapping implies a penalty on the score that depends on the length of the path between the two predicates and their informative content.

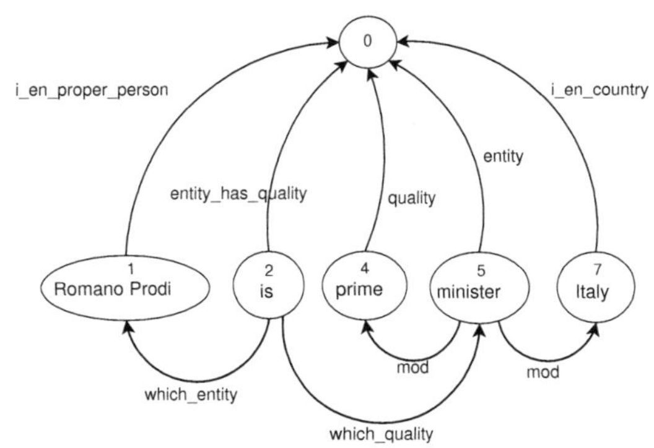

Figure 1: Example of an environment of a sentence.

[2]The ontology contains relations as *i_en_city* **isa** *i_en_proper_place*, *i_en_proper_place* **isa** *i_en_proper_named_entity*, *proper_place* **isa** *location*, *i_en_proper_named_entity* **isa** *entity*, *location* **isa** *entity*

3 System Architecture

We have adapted the set of measures described before for RTE in the following way:

1. We follow a Machine Learning (ML) approach for building a classifier to perform the RTE task. In previous applications the way of weighting and combining the different measures was based on a crude optimization using a development corpus.

2. We extract a more complex set of features for describing the semantic content of the Text (T) and the Hypothesis (H) as well as the set of semantic measures between them. Table 1 contains a brief summary of the features used.

3. We perform minor modifications on the token-level compatibility measures for dealing with the asymmetry of the entailment relation (basically using the hyponymy and the verbal entailment relations of WordNet)

4. We add three new task-specific features (see Table 1)

The overall architecture of the system is depicted in Figure 2. As usual in ML, the system proceeds in two phases, learning and classification. The left side of the figure shows the learning process and the right part the classification process. The set of examples (tuples H, T) is first processed, in both phases, by LP for obtaining a semantic representation of the tuple (H_{sem} and T_{sem}). From this representation a Feature Extraction component extracts a set of features. This set is used in the learning phase for getting a classifier that is applied to the set of features of the test, during the classification phase, in order to obtain the answer.

4 Experiments

Before the submission we have performed a set of experiments in order to choose the Machine Learning algorithms and the training sets to apply in the final submission.

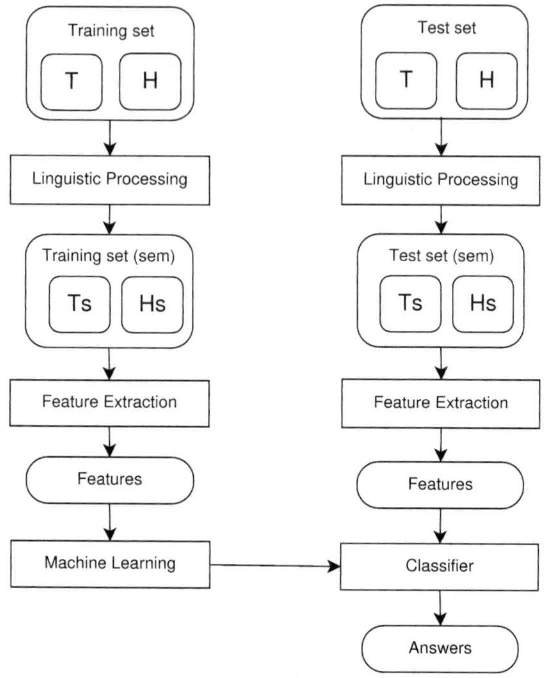

Figure 2: System Architecture.

4.1 Machine Learning Experiments

We used the WEKA[3] ML platform (Witten and Frank, 2005) to perform the experiments. We tested 9 different ML algorithms: *AdaBoostM1*, *Bayes Networks*, *Logistic Regression*, *MultiBoostAB*, *Naive Bayes*, *RBF Network*, *LogitBoost* (Simple Logistic in WEKA), *Support Vector Machines* (SMO in WEKA), and *Voted Perceptron*. We used the previous corpora of the RTE Challenge (RTE-1 and RTE-2) and the RTE-3 development test. A filtering process has been applied removing pairs with more than two sentences in the text or hypothesis, resulting a total of 3335 Textual Entailment (TE) pairs. The results over 10-fold-Cross-Validation using a data set composed by RTE-1, RTE-2, and RTE-3 development set are shown in Table 2.

The results shown that *AdaBoost*, *LogitBoost*, and *SVM* obtain the best results. Then we selected *AdaBoost* and *SVM* to perform the classification of the RTE-3 test set. The *SVM* algorithm tries to compute the hyperplane that best separates the set of training examples (the hyperplane with maximum margin) (Vapnik, 1995). On the other hand, *AdaBoost* com-

[3]**WEKA.** `http://www.cs.waikato.ac.nz/ml/weka/`

Features	#features	Description
semantic content of T	12	#locations, #persons, #dates, #actions, ...
semantic content of H	12	...
intersection of T and H	12	...
Strict overlapping of unary predicates	5	length of intersection score of intersection ratio of intersection related to shortest env ratio of intersection related to longest env ratio of intersection related to both (union of)
Strict overlapping of binary predicates	5	...
Loose overlapping of unary predicates	5	...
Loose overlapping of binary predicates	5	...
Verbal entailment (WordNet)	1	V1 ϵ T, V2 ϵ H, such that V1 verbal_entails V2
Antonymy	1	A1 ϵ T, A2 ϵ H, such that A1 and A2 are antonyms and no token compatible with A2
#occurs in H Negation	1	Difference between # negation tokens in H and T

Table 1: Features used for classification with Machine Learning algorithms.

Algorithm	#correct	Accuracy
AdaBoostM1	1989	59.6402
BayesNet	1895	56.8216
Logistic	1951	58.5007
MultiBoostAB	1959	58.7406
NaiveBayes	1911	57.3013
RBFNetwork	1853	55.5622
LogitBoost	1972	59.1304
SVM	1972	59.1304
VotedPerceptron	1969	59.0405

Table 2: Results over 10-fold-Cross-Validation using a filtered data set composed by RTE-1, RTE-2, and RTE-3 (a total of 3335 entailment pairs).

bines a set of weak classifiers into a strong one using lineal combination (Freund and Schapire, 1996). The idea is combining many moderately accurate rules into a highly accurate prediction rule. A weak learning algorithm is used to find the weak rules.

4.2 Training Set Experiments

We designed two experiments in order to decide the best training set to apply in the RTE-3 challenge. We performed an experiment using RTE-1 and RTE-2 data sets as a training set and the RTE-3 development set filtered (541 TE pairs) as a test set. In this experiment *AdaBoost* and *SVM* obtained accuracies of 0.6672 and 0.6396 respectively (see results in Table 3. We performed the same experiment joining the Answer Validation Exercise[4] (AVE) 2006 English data set (Peñas et al., 2006) and the Microsoft Research Paraphrase Corpus[5] (MSRPC) (Dolan et al., 2004) to the previous corpora (RTE-1 and RTE-2) resulting a total of 8585 entailment pairs filtering pairs with a text or a hypothesis with more than 1 sentence. In our approach we considered that paraphrases were bidirectional entailments. The paraphrases of the MSRPC have been used as textual entailments in only one direction: the first sentence in the paraphrase has been considered the hypothesis and the second one has been considered the text.

Using the second corpus for training and the RTE-3 development set as test set resulted in a notable degradation of accuracy (see Table 3).

	Accuracy	
Algorithm	Corpus A	Corpus B
AdaBoost	66.72%	53.78%
SVM	63.95%	59.88%

Table 3: Results over the RTE-3 development set filtered (541 TE pairs) using as training set corpus A (RTE-1 and RTE-2) and corpus B (RTE-1, RTE-2, MSRPC, and AVE2006 English)

Finally, we performed a set of experiments to detect the contribution of the different features used for Machine Learning. These experiments revealed that

[4]**AVE.** `http://nlp.uned.es/QA/AVE`
[5]**MSRPC.** `http://research.microsoft.com/nlp/msr_paraphrase.htm`

the three most relevant features were: Strict overlapping of unary predicates, Semantic content of Hypothesis, and Loose overlapping of unary predicates.

4.3 Official Results

Our official results at RTE-3 Challenge are shown in Table 4. We submitted two experiments: the first one with *AdaBoost* (run1) and the second one with *SVM* (run2). Training data set for final experiments were corpus: RTE-1 (development and test), RTE-2 (development and test), and RTE-3 development. The test set was the RTE-3 test set without filtering the entailments (text or hypothesis) with more than one sentence. In this case we joined multiple sentences in a unique sentence that has been processed by the LP component.

We obtained accuracies of 0.6062 and 0.6150. In the QA task we obtained the best per-task results with accuracies of 0.7450 and 0.7000 with *AdaBoost* and *SVM* respectively.

	Accuracy	
Task	run1 *AdaBoost*	run2 *SVM*
IE	0.4350	0.4950
IR	0.6950	0.6800
QA	0.7450	0.7000
SUM	0.5500	0.5850
Overall	0.6062	0.6150

Table 4: RTE-3 official results.

5 Conclusions and Further Work

This paper describes our experiments on Textual Entailment in the context of the Third Pascal Recognising Textual Entailment (RTE-3) Evaluation Challenge. Our approach uses Machine Learning algorithms (*SVM* and *AdaBoost*) with semantic-based distance measures between sentences. Although further analysis of the results is in process, we observed that our official per-task results at RTE-3 show a different distribution compared with the global results of all system at RTE-2 challenge. The RTE-2 per-task analysis showed that most of the systems scored higher in accuracy in the multidocument summarization (SUM) task while in our system this measure is low. Our system at RTE-3 challenge scored higher in the QA and IR tasks with accuracies of 0.7450 and 0.6950 respectively in the first run.

References

Roy Bar-Haim, Ido Dagan, Bill Dolan, Lisa Ferro, Danilo Giampiccolo, Bernardo Magnini, and Idan Szpektor. 2006. The second pascal recognising textual entailment challenge. In *Proceedings of the Second PASCAL Challenges Workshop on Recognising Textual Entailment.*

Ido Dagan, Oren Glickman, and Bernardo Magnini. 2005. The pascal recognising textual entailment challenge. In Joaquin Quiñonero Candela, Ido Dagan, Bernardo Magnini, and Florence d'Alché Buc, editors, *MLCW*, volume 3944 of *Lecture Notes in Computer Science*, pages 177–190. Springer.

Bill Dolan, Chris Quirk, and Chris Brockett. 2004. Unsupervised construction of large paraphrase corpora: exploiting massively parallel news sources. In *COLING '04: Proceedings of the 20th international conference on Computational Linguistics*, page 350, Morristown, NJ, USA. Association for Computational Linguistics.

Daniel Ferrés, Samir Kanaan, Alicia Ageno, Edgar González, Horacio Rodríguez, Mihai Surdeanu, and Jordi Turmo. 2004. The TALP-QA System for Spanish at CLEF 2004: Structural and Hierarchical Relaxing of Semantic Constraints. In Carol Peters, Paul Clough, Julio Gonzalo, Gareth J. F. Jones, Michael Kluck, and Bernardo Magnini, editors, *CLEF*, volume 3491 of *Lecture Notes in Computer Science*, pages 557–568. Springer.

Daniel Ferrés, Samir Kanaan, Edgar González, Alicia Ageno, Horacio Rodríguez, Mihai Surdeanu, and Jordi Turmo. 2005. TALP-QA System at TREC 2004: Structural and Hierarchical Relaxation Over Semantic Constraints. In *Proceedings of the Text Retrieval Conference (TREC-2004).*

Yoav Freund and Robert E. Schapire. 1996. Experiments with a new boosting algorithm. In *International Conference on Machine Learning*, pages 148–156.

Maria Fuentes, Horacio Rodríguez, Jordi Turmo, and Daniel Ferrés. 2006. Femsum at duc 2006: Semantic-based approach integrated in a flexible eclectic multitask summarizer architecture. In *Proceedings of the Document Understanding Conference 2006 (DUC 2006). HLT-NAACL 2006 Workshop.*, New York City, NY, USA, June.

Anselmo Peñas, Álvaro Rodrigo, Valentín Sama, and Felisa Verdejo. 2006. Overview of the answer validation exercise 2006. In *Working Notes for the*

CLEF 2006 Workshop. ISBN: 2-912335-23-x, Alicante, Spain, September.

Vladimir N. Vapnik. 1995. *The nature of statistical learning theory*. Springer-Verlag New York, Inc., New York, NY, USA.

Ian H. Witten and Eibe Frank. 2005. *Data Mining: Practical Machine Learning Tools and Techniques, Second Edition (Morgan Kaufmann Series in Data Management Systems)*. Morgan Kaufmann, June.

Acknowledgments

This work has been supported by the Spanish Research Dept. (TEXT-MESS, TIN2006-15265-C06-05). Daniel Ferrés is supported by a UPC-Recerca grant from Universitat Politècnica de Catalunya (UPC). TALP Research Center is recognized as a Quality Research Group (2001 SGR 00254) by DURSI, the Research Department of the Catalan Government.

A Perspective-Based Approach for Solving Textual Entailment Recognition

Óscar Ferrández, Daniel Micol, Rafael Muñoz, and Manuel Palomar
Natural Language Processing and Information Systems Group
Department of Computing Languages and Systems
University of Alicante
San Vicente del Raspeig, Alicante 03690, Spain
{ofe, dmicol, rafael, mpalomar}@dlsi.ua.es

Abstract

The textual entailment recognition system that we discuss in this paper represents a perspective-based approach composed of two modules that analyze text-hypothesis pairs from a strictly lexical and syntactic perspectives, respectively. We attempt to prove that the textual entailment recognition task can be overcome by performing individual analysis that acknowledges us of the maximum amount of information that each single perspective can provide. We compare this approach with the system we presented in the previous edition of *PASCAL Recognising Textual Entailment Challenge*, obtaining an accuracy rate 17.98% higher.

1 Introduction

Textual entailment recognition has become a popular Natural Language Processing task within the last few years. It consists in determining whether one text snippet (hypothesis) entails another one (text) (Glickman, 2005). To overcome this problem several approaches have been studied, being the *Recognising Textual Entailment Challenge* (RTE) (Bar-Haim et al., 2006; Dagan et al., 2006) the most referred source for determining which one is the most accurate.

Many of the participating groups in previous editions of RTE, including ourselves (Ferrández et al., 2006), designed systems that combined a variety of lexical, syntactic and semantic techniques. In our contribution to RTE-3 we attempt to solve the textual entailment recognition task by analyzing two different perspectives separately, in order to acknowledge the amount of information that an individual perspective can provide. Later on, we combine both modules to obtain the highest possible accuracy rate. For this purpose, we analyze the provided corpora by using a lexical module, namely *DLSITE-1*, and a syntactic one, namely *DLSITE-2*. Once all results have been obtained we perform a voting process in order to take into account all system's judgments.

The remainder of this paper is structured as follows. Section two describes the system we have built, providing details of the lexical and syntactic perspectives, and explains the difference with the one we presented in RTE-2. Third section presents the experimental results, and the fourth one provides our conclusions and describes possible future work.

2 System Specification

This section describes the system we have developed in order to participate in RTE-3. It is based on surface techniques of lexical and syntactic analysis. As the starting point we have used our previous system presented in the second edition of the RTE Challenge (Ferrández et al., 2006). We have enriched it with two independent modules that are intended to detect some misinterpretations performed by this system. Moreover, these new modules can also recognize entailment relations by themselves. The performance of each separate module and their combination with our previous system will be detailed in section three.

Next, Figure 1 represents a schematic view of the system we have developed.

Proceedings of the Workshop on Textual Entailment and Paraphrasing, pages 66–71,
Prague, June 2007.

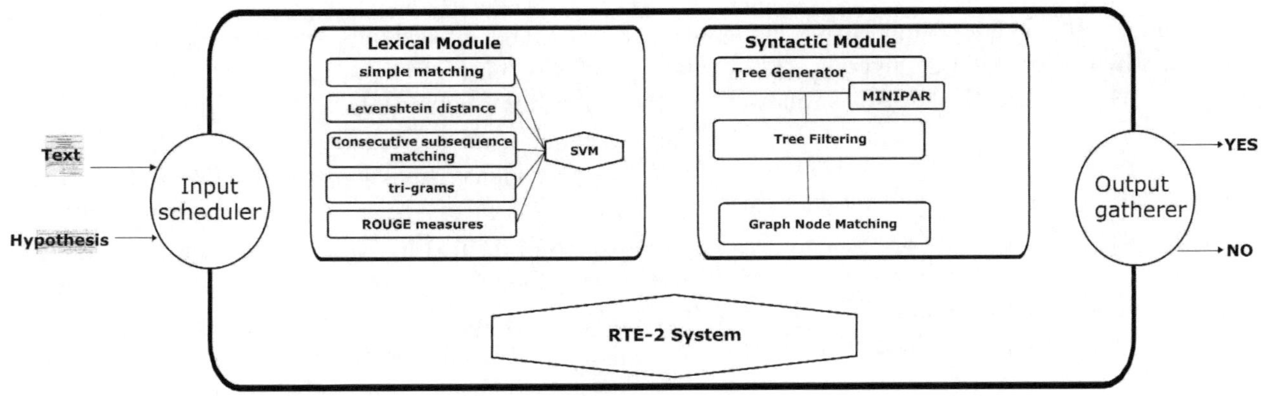

Figure 1: System architecture.

As we can see in the previous Figure, our system is composed of three modules that are coordinated by an input scheduler. Its commitment is to provide the text-hypothesis pairs to each module in order to extract their corresponding similarity rates. Once all rates for a given text-hypothesis pair have been calculated, they will be processed by an output gatherer that will provide the final judgment. The method used to calculate the final entailment decision consists in combining the outputs of both lexical and syntactic modules, and these outputs with our RTE-2 system's judgment. The output gatherer will be detailed later in this paper when we describe the experimental results.

2.1 RTE-2 System

The approach we presented in the previous edition of RTE attempts to recognize textual entailment by determining whether the text and the hypothesis are related using their respective derived logic forms, and by finding relations between their predicates using WordNet (Miller et al., 1990). These relations have a specific weight that provide us a score representing the similarity of the derived logic forms and determining whether they are related or not.

For our participation in RTE-3 we decided to apply our previous system because it allows us to handle some kinds of information that are not correctly managed by the new approaches developed for the current RTE edition.

2.2 Lexical Module

This method relies on the computation of a wide variety of lexical measures, which basically consists of overlap metrics. Although in other related work this kind of metrics have already been used (Nicholson et al., 2006), the main contribution of this module is the fact that it only deals with lexical features without taking into account any syntactic nor semantic information. The following paragraphs list the considered lexical measures.

Simple matching: initialized to zero. A boolean value is set to one if the hypothesis word appears in the text. The final weight is calculated as the sum of all boolean values and normalized dividing it by the length of the hypothesis.

Levenshtein distance: it is similar to simple matching. However, in this case we use the mentioned distance as the similarity measure between words. When the distance is zero, the increment value is one. On the other hand, if such value is equal to one, the increment is 0.9. Otherwise, it will be the inverse of the obtained distance.

Consecutive subsequence matching: this measure assigns the highest relevance to the appearance of consecutive subsequences. In order to perform this, we have generated all possible sets of consecutive subsequences, from length two until the length in words, from the text and the hypothesis. If we proceed as mentioned, the sets of length two extracted from the hypothesis will be compared to the sets of the same length from the text. If the same element is present in both the text and the hypothesis set, then a unit is added to the accumulated weight. This procedure is applied for all sets of different length extracted from the hypothesis. Finally, the sum of the weight obtained from each set of a specific length is normalized by the number of sets corresponding to this length, and the final accumulated weight is also normalized by the length of the hypothesis in words minus one. This measure is defined as follows:

$$CSmatch = \frac{\sum_{i=2}^{|H|} f(SH_i)}{|H| - 1} \tag{1}$$

where SH_i contains the hypothesis' subsequences of length i, and $f(SH_i)$ is defined as follows:

$$f(SH_i) = \frac{\sum_{j \in SH_i} match(j)}{|H| - i + 1} \tag{2}$$

being $match(j)$ equal to one if there exists an element k that belongs to the set that contains the text's subsequences of length i, such that $k = j$.

One should note that this measure does not consider non-consecutive subsequences. In addition, it assigns the same relevance to all consecutive subsequences with the same length. Furthermore, the longer the subsequence is, the more relevant it will be considered.

Tri-grams: two sets containing tri-grams of letters belonging to the text and the hypothesis were created. All the occurrences in the hypothesis' tri-grams set that also appear in the text's will increase the accumulated weight in a factor of one unit. The weight is normalized by the size of the hypothesis' tri-grams set.

ROUGE measures: considering the impact of n-gram overlap metrics in textual entailment, we believe that the idea of integrating these measures[1] into our system is very appealing. We have implemented them as defined in (Lin, 2004).

Each measure is applied to the words, lemmas and stems belonging to the text-hypothesis pair. Within the entire set of measures, each one of them is considered as a feature for the training and test stages of a machine learning algorithm. The selected one was a Support Vector Machine due to the fact that its properties are suitable for recognizing entailment.

2.3 Syntactic Module

The syntactic module we have built is composed of few submodules that operate collaboratively in order to obtain the highest possible accuracy by using only syntactic information.

The commitment of the first two submodules is to generate an internal representation of the syntactic dependency trees generated by *MINIPAR* (Lin, 1998). For this purpose we obtain the output of such parser for the text-hypothesis pairs, and then process it to generate an on-memory internal representation of the mentioned trees. In order to reduce our system's noise and increase its accuracy rate, we only keep the relevant words and discard the ones that we believe do not provide useful information, such as determinants and auxiliary verbs. After this step has been performed we can proceed to compare the generated syntactic dependency trees of the text and the hypothesis.

The graph node matching, termed alignment, between both the text and the hypothesis consists in finding pairs of words in both trees whose lemmas are identical, no matter whether they are in the same position within the tree. Some authors have already designed similar matching techniques, such as the one described in (Snow et al., 2006). However, these include semantic constraints that we have decided not to consider. The reason of this decision is that we desired to overcome the textual entailment recognition from an exclusively syntactic perspective. The formula that provides the similarity rate between the dependency trees of the text and the hypothesis in our system, denoted by the symbol ψ, is shown in Equation 3:

$$\psi(\tau, \lambda) = \sum_{\nu \in \xi} \phi(\nu) \tag{3}$$

where τ and λ represent the text's and hypothesis' syntactic dependency trees, respectively, and ξ is the set that contains all synsets present in both trees, being $\xi = \tau \cap \lambda \; \forall \alpha \in \tau, \beta \in \lambda$. As we can observe in Equation 3, ψ depends on another function, denoted by the symbol ϕ, which provides the relevance of a synset. Such a weight factor will depend on the grammatical category and relation of the synset. In addition, we believe that the most relevant words of a phrase occupy the highest positions in the dependency tree, so we desired to assign different weights depending on the depth of the synset. With all these factors we define the relevance of a word as shown

[1]The considered measures were ROUGE-N with n=2 and n=3, ROUGE-L, ROUGE-W and ROUGE-S with s=2 and s=3.

in Equation 4:

$$\phi(\beta) = \gamma \cdot \sigma \cdot \mu^{-\delta_\beta} \quad (4)$$

where β is a synset present in both τ and λ, γ represents the weight assigned to β's grammatical category (Table 1), σ the weight of β's grammatical relationship (Table 2), μ an empirically calculated value that represents the weight difference between tree levels, and δ_β the depth of the node that contains the synset β in λ. The performed experiments reveal that the optimal value for μ is 1.1.

Grammatical category	**Weight**
Verbs, verbs with one argument, verbs with two arguments, verbs taking clause as complement	1.0
Nouns, numbers	0.75
Be used as a linking verb	0.7
Adjectives, adverbs, noun-noun modifiers	0.5
Verbs *Have* and *Be*	0.3

Table 1: Weights assigned to the relevant grammatical categories.

Grammatical relationship	**Weight**
Subject of verbs, surface subject, object of verbs, second object of ditransitive verbs	1.0
The rest	0.5

Table 2: Weights assigned to the grammatical relationships.

We would like to point out that a requirement of our system's similarity measure is to be independent of the hypothesis length. Therefore, we must define the normalized similarity rate, as represented in Equation 5:

$$\overline{\psi(\tau, \lambda)} = \frac{\sum_{\nu \in \xi} \phi(\nu)}{\sum_{\beta \in \lambda} \phi(\beta)} \quad (5)$$

Once the similarity value has been calculated, it will be provided to the user together with the corresponding text-hypothesis pair identifier. It will be his responsibility to choose an appropriate threshold that will represent the minimum similarity rate to be considered as entailment between text and hypothesis. All values that are under such a threshold will be marked as not entailed.

3 System Evaluation

In order to evaluate our system we have generated several results using different combinations of all three mentioned modules. Since the lexical one uses a machine learning algorithm, it has to be run within a training environment. For this purpose we have trained our system with the corpora provided in the previous editions of RTE, and also with the development corpus from the current RTE-3 challenge. On the other hand, for the remainder modules the development corpora was used to set the thresholds that determine if the entailment holds.

The performed tests have been obtained by performing different combinations of the described modules. First, we have calculated the accuracy rates using only each single module separately. Later on we have combined those developed by our research group for this year's RTE challenge, which are *DLSITE-1* (the lexical one) and *DLSITE-2* (the syntactic one). Finally we have performed a voting process between these two systems and the one we presented in RTE-2.

The combination of *DLSITE-1* and *DLSITE-2* is described as follows. If both modules agree, then the judgement is straightforward, but if they do not, we then decide the judgment depending on the accuracy of each one for true and false entailment situations. In our case, *DLSITE-1* performs better while dealing with negative examples, so its decision will prevail over the rest. Regarding the combination of the three approaches, we have developed a voting strategy. The results obtained by our system are represented in Table 3. As it is reflected in such table, the highest accuracy rate obtained using the RTE-3 test corpus was achieved applying only the lexical module, namely *DLSITE-1*. On the other hand, the syntactic one had a significantly lower rate, and the same happened with the system we presented in RTE-2. Therefore, a combination of them will most likely produce less accurate results than the lexical module, as it is shown in Table 3. However, we would like to point out that these results depend heavily on the corpus idiosyncrasy. This can be proven with the results obtained for the RTE-2 test corpus, where the grouping of the three modules provided the highest accuracy rates of all possible combinations.

	RTE-2 test	RTE-3 dev	RTE-3 test				
	Overall	Overall	Overall	IE	IR	QA	SUM
RTE-2 system	0.5563	0.5523	0.5400	0.4900	0.6050	0.5100	0.5550
DLSITE-1	0.6188	0.7012	**0.6563**	**0.5150**	**0.7350**	**0.7950**	**0.5800**
DLSITE-2	0.6075	0.6450	0.5925	0.5050	0.6350	0.6300	0.6000
DLSITE-1&2	0.6212	0.6900	0.6375	0.5150	0.7150	0.7400	0.5800
Voting	0.6300	0.6900	0.6375	0.5250	0.7050	0.7200	0.6000

Table 3: Results obtained with the corpora from RTE-2 and RTE-3.

3.1 Results Analysis

We will now perform an analysis of the results shown in the previous section. First, we would like to mention the fact that our system does not behave correctly when it has to deal with long texts. Roughly 11% and 13% of the false positives of *DLSITE-1* and *DLSITE-2*, respectively, are caused by misinterpretations of long texts. The underlying reason of these failures is the fact that it is easier to find a lexical and syntactic match when a long text is present in the pair, even if there is not entailment.

In addition, we consider very appealing to show the accuracy rates corresponding to true and false entailment pairs individually. Figure 2 represents the mentioned rates for all system combinations that we displayed in Table 3.

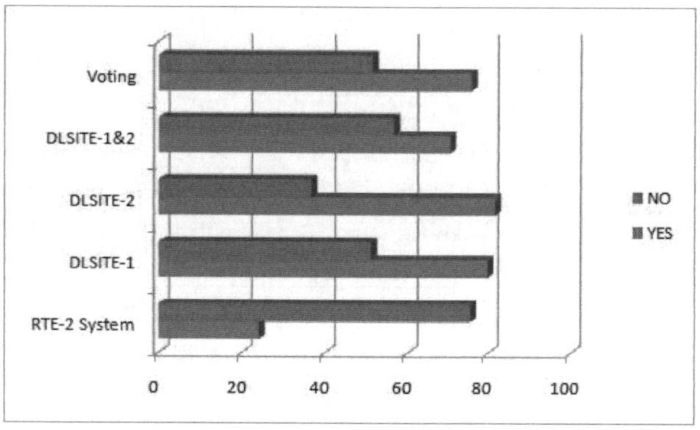

Figure 2: Accuracy rates obtained for true and false entailments using the RTE-3 test corpus.

As we can see in Figure 2, the accuracy rates for true and false entailment pairs vary significantly. The modules we built for our participation in RTE-3 obtained high accuracy rates for true entailment text-hypothesis pairs, but in contrast they behaved worse in detecting false entailment pairs. This is the opposite to the system we presented in RTE-2, since it has a much higher accuracy rate for false cases than true ones. When we combined *DLSITE-1* and *DLSITE-2*, their accuracy rate for true entailments diminished, although, on the other hand, the rate for false ones raised. The voting between all three modules provided a higher accuracy rate for false entailments because the system we presented at RTE-2 performed well in these cases.

Finally, we would like to discuss some examples that lead to failures and correct forecasts by our two new approaches.

Pair 246 entailment=YES task=IR

T: Overall the accident rate worldwide for commercial aviation has been falling fairly dramatically especially during the period between 1950 and 1970, largely due to the introduction of new technology during this period.

H: Airplane accidents are decreasing.

Pair 246 is incorrectly classified by *DLSITE-1* due to the fact that some words of the hypothesis do not appear in the same manner in the text, although they have similar meaning (e.g. airplane and aviation). However, *DLSITE-2* is able to establish a true entailment for this pair, since the hypothesis' syntactic dependency tree can be matched within the text's, and the similarity measure applied between lemmas obtains a high score. This fact produces that, in this case, the voting also achieves a correct prediction for pair 246.

Pair 736 entailment=YES task=SUM

T: In a security fraud case, Michael Milken was sentenced to 10 years in prison.

H: Milken was imprisoned for security fraud.

Pair 736 is correctly classified by *DLSITE-1* since there are matches for all hypothesis' words (except *imprisoned*) and some subsequences. In contrast, *DLSITE-2* does not behave correctly with this example because the main verbs do not match, being this fact a considerable handicap for the overall score.

4 Conclusions and Future Work

This research provides independent approaches considering mainly lexical and syntactic information. In order to achieve this, we expose and analyze a wide variety of lexical measures as well as syntactic structure comparisons that attempt to solve the textual entailment recognition task. In addition, we propose several combinations between these two approaches and integrate them with our previous RTE-2 system by using a voting strategy.

The results obtained reveal that, although the combined approach provided the highest accuracy rates for the RTE-2 corpora, it has not accomplished the expected reliability in the RTE-3 challenge. Nevertheless, in both cases the lexical-based module achieved better results than the rest of the individual approaches, being the optimal for our participation in RTE-3, and obtaining an accuracy rate of about 70% and 65% for the development and test corpus, respectively. One should note that these results depend on the idiosyncrasies of the RTE corpora. However, these corpora are the most reliable ones for evaluating textual entailment recognizers.

Future work can be related to the development of a semantic module. Our system achieves good lexical and syntactic comparisons between texts, but we believe that we should take advantage of the semantic resources in order to achieve higher accuracy rates. For this purpose we plan to build a module that constructs characterized representations based on the text using named entities and role labeling in order to extract semantic information from a text-hypothesis pair. Another future research line could consist in applying different recognition techniques depending on the type of entailment task. We have noticed that the accuracy of our approach differs when the entailment is produced mainly by lexical or syntactic implications. We intend to establish an entailment typology and tackle each type by means of different points of view or approaches.

Acknowledgments

This research has been partially funded by the QALL-ME consortium, which is a 6th Framework Research Programme of the European Union (EU), contract number FP6-IST-033860 and by the Spanish Government under the project CICyT number TIN2006-1526-C06-01. It has also been supported by the undergraduate research fellowships financed by the Spanish Ministry of Education and Science, and the project ACOM06/90 financed by the Spanish Generalitat Valenciana.

References

Roy Bar-Haim, Ido Dagan, Bill Dolan, Lisa Ferro, Danilo Giampiccolo, Bernardo Magnini, and Idan Szpektor. 2006. The Second PASCAL Recognising Textual Entailment Challenge. *Proceedings of the Second PASCAL Challenges Workshop on Recognising Textual Entailment*, pages 1–9.

Ido Dagan, Oren Glickman, and Bernardo Magnini. 2006. The PASCAL Recognising Textual Entailment Challenge. In *Quiñonero-Candela et al., editors, MLCW 2005, LNAI Volume 3944*, pages 177–190. Springer-Verlag.

Oscar Ferrández, Rafael M. Terol, Rafael Muñoz, Patricio Martínez-Barco, and Manuel Palomar. 2006. An approach based on Logic forms and wordnet relationships to textual entailment performance. In *Proceedings of the Second PASCAL Challenges Workshop on Recognising Textual Entailment*, pages 22–26, Venice, Italy.

Oren Glickman. 2005. *Applied Textual Entailment Challenge*. Ph.D. thesis, Bar Ilan University.

Dekang Lin. 1998. Dependency-based Evaluation of MINIPAR. In *Workshop on the Evaluation of Parsing Systems*, Granada, Spain.

Chin-Yew Lin. 2004. ROUGE: A Package for Automatic Evaluation of Summaries. In Stan Szpakowicz Marie-Francine Moens, editor, *Text Summarization Branches Out: Proceedings of the ACL-04 Workshop*, pages 74–81, Barcelona, Spain, July. Association for Computational Linguistics.

George A. Miller, Richard Beckwith, Christiane Fellbaum, Derek Gross, and Katherine J. Miller. 1990. Introduction to WordNet: An On-line Lexical Database. *International Journal of Lexicography*, 3(4):235–244.

Jeremy Nicholson, Nicola Stokes, and Timothy Baldwin. 2006. Detecting Entailment Using an Extended Implementation of the Basic Elements Overlap Metrics. In *Proceedings of the Second PASCAL Challenges Workshop on Recognising Textual Entailment*, pages 122–127, Venice, Italy.

Rion Snow, Lucy Vanderwende, and Arul Menezes. 2006. Effectively using syntax for recognizing false entailment. In *Proceedings of the North American Association of Computational Linguistics*, New York City, New York, United States of America.

Shallow Semantics in Fast Textual Entailment Rule Learners

Fabio Massimo Zanzotto
DISP
University of Rome "Tor Vergata"
Roma, Italy
zanzotto@info.uniroma2.it

Marco Pennacchiotti
Computerlinguistik
Universität des Saarlandes,
Saarbrücken, Germany
pennacchiotti@coli.uni-sb.de

Alessandro Moschitti
DIT
University of Trento
Povo di Trento, Italy
moschitti@dit.unitn.it

Abstract

In this paper, we briefly describe two enhancements of the *cross-pair similarity* model for learning textual entailment rules: 1) the typed anchors and 2) a faster computation of the similarity. We will report and comment on the preliminary experiments and on the submission results.

1 Introduction

Results of the second RTE challenge (Bar Haim et al., 2006) have suggested that both *deep semantic* models and *machine learning* approaches can successfully be applied to solve textual entailment. The only problem seems to be the size of the knowledge bases. The two best systems (Tatu et al., 2005; Hickl et al., 2005), which are significantly above all the others (more than +10% accuracy), use implicit or explicit knowledge bases larger than all the other systems. In (Tatu et al., 2005), a deep semantic representation is paired with a large amount of general and task specific semantic rules (*explicit knowledge*). In (Hickl et al., 2005), the machine learning model is trained over a large amounts of examples (*implicit knowledge*).

In contrast, Zanzotto&Moschitti (2006) proposed a machine-learning based approach which reaches a high accuracy by only using the available RTE data. The key idea is the *cross-pair similarity*, i.e. a similarity applied to two text and hypothesis pairs which considers the relations between the words in the two texts and between the words in the two hypotheses. This is obtained by using *placeholders* to link the related words. Results in (Bar Haim et al., 2006) are comparable with the best machine learning system when this latter is trained only on the RTE examples.

Given the high potential of the *cross-pair similarity* model, for the RTE3 challenge, we built on it by including some features of the two best systems: 1) we go towards a deeper semantic representation of learning pairs including shallow semantic information in the syntactic trees using *typed placeholders*; 2) we reduce the computational cost of the cross-pair similarity computation algorithm to allow the learning over larger training sets.

The paper is organized as follows: in Sec. 2 we review the cross-pair similarity model and its limits; in Sec. 3, we introduce our model for *typed anchors*; in Sec. 4 we describe how we limit the computational cost of the similarity; in Sec. 5 we present the two submission experiments, and in Sec. 6 we draw some conclusions.

2 Cross-pair similarity and its limits

2.1 Learning entailment rules with syntactic cross-pair similarity

The *cross-pair similarity* model (Zanzotto and Moschitti, 2006) proposes a similarity measure aiming at capturing *rewrite rules* from training examples, computing a *cross-pair similarity* $K_S((T',H'),(T'',H''))$. The rationale is that if two pairs are similar, it is extremely likely that they have the same entailment value. The key point is the use of *placeholders* to mark the relations between the sentence words. A *placeholder* co-indexes two substructures in the parse trees of text and hypothesis,

Proceedings of the Workshop on Textual Entailment and Paraphrasing, pages 72–77,
Prague, June 2007.

indicating that such substructures are related. For example, the sentence pair, "*All companies file annual reports*" implies "*All insurance companies file annual reports*", is represented as follows:

T_1	(S (NP:$\boxed{1}$ (DT All) (NNS:$\boxed{1}$ companies)) (VP:$\boxed{2}$ (VBP:$\boxed{2}$ file) (NP:$\boxed{3}$ (JJ:$\boxed{3}$ annual) (NNS:$\boxed{3}$ reports))))	
H_1	(S (NP:$\boxed{1}$ (DT All) (NNP Fortune) (CD 50) (NNS:$\boxed{1}$ companies)) (VP:$\boxed{2}$ (VBP:$\boxed{2}$ file) (NP:$\boxed{3}$ (JJ:$\boxed{3}$ annual) (NNS:$\boxed{3}$ reports))))	(E_1)

where the placeholders $\boxed{1}$, $\boxed{2}$, and $\boxed{3}$ indicate the relations between the structures of T and of H.

Placeholders help to determine if two pairs share the same *rewriting rule* by looking at the subtrees that they have in common. For example, suppose we have to determine if "*In autumn, all leaves fall*" implies "*In autumn, all maple leaves fall*". The related co-indexed representation is:

T_2	(S (PP (IN In) (NP (NN:$\boxed{a}$ automn))) (, ,) (NP:$\boxed{b}$ (DT all) (NNS:$\boxed{b}$ leaves)) (VP:$\boxed{c}$ (VBP:$\boxed{c}$ fall)))	
H_2	(S (PP (IN In) (NP:$\boxed{a}$ (NN:$\boxed{a}$ automn))) (, ,) (NP:$\boxed{b}$ (DT all) (NN maple) (NNS:$\boxed{a}$ leaves)) (VP:$\boxed{c}$ (VBP:$\boxed{c}$ fall)))	(E_2)

E_1 and E_2 share the following subtrees:

T_3	(S (NP:$\boxed{x}$ (DT all) (NNS:$\boxed{x}$)) (VP:$\boxed{y}$ (VBP:$\boxed{y}$)))	
H_3	(S (NP:$\boxed{x}$ (DT all) (NN) (NNS:$\boxed{x}$)) (VP:$\boxed{x}$ (VBP:$\boxed{x}$)))	(R_3)

This is the *rewrite rule* they have in common. Then, E_2 can be likely classified as a valid entailment, as it shares the rule with the valid entailment E_1.

The *cross-pair similarity* model uses: (1) a tree similarity measure $K_T(\tau_1, \tau_2)$ (Collins and Duffy, 2002) that counts the subtrees that τ_1 and τ_2 have in common; (2) a substitution function $t(\cdot, c)$ that changes names of the placeholders in a tree according to a set of correspondences between placeholders c. Given $\mathcal{C}$ as the collection of all correspondences between the placeholders of (T', H') and (T'', H''), the cross-pair similarity is computed as:

$$K_S((T', H'), (T'', H'')) = \max_{c \in \mathcal{C}}(K_T(t(T', c), t(T'', c)) + K_T(t(H', c), t(H'', c))) \quad (1)$$

The cross-pair similarity K_S, used in a kernel-based learning model as the support vector machines, allows the exploitation of implicit true and false entailment rewrite rules described in the examples.

2.2 Limits of the syntactic cross-pair similarity

Learning from examples using cross-pair similarity is an attractive and effective approach. However, the cross-pair strategy, as any machine learning approach, is highly sensitive on how the examples are represented in the feature space, as this can strongly bias the performance of the classifier.

Consider for example the following text-hypothesis pair, which can lead to an incorrect rule, if misused.

T_4	*"For my younger readers, Chapman killed John Lennon more than twenty years ago."*	
H_4	*"John Lennon died more than twenty years ago."*	(E_4)

In the basic cross-pair similarity model, the learnt rule would be the following:

T_5	(S (NP:$\boxed{x}$) (VP:$\boxed{y}$ (VBD:$\boxed{y}$) (NP:$\boxed{z}$) (ADVP:$\boxed{k}$)))	
H_5	(S (NP:$\boxed{z}$) (VP:$\boxed{y}$ (VBD:$\boxed{y}$) (ADVP:$\boxed{k}$)))	(R_5)

where the verbs *kill* and *die* are connected by the $\boxed{y}$ placeholder. This rule is useful to classify examples like:

T_6	*"Cows are vegetarian but, to save money on mass-production, farmers fed cows animal extracts."*	
H_6	*"Cows have eaten animal extracts."*	(E_6)

but it will clearly fail when used for:

T_7	*"FDA warns migraine medicine makers that they are illegally selling migraine medicines without federal approval."*	
H_7	*"Migraine medicine makers declared that their medicines have been approved."*	(E_7)

where *warn* and *declare* are connected as generically similar verbs.

The problem of the basic cross-pair similarity measure is that placeholders do not convey the semantic knowledge needed in cases such as the above, where the semantic relation between connected verbs is essential.

2.3 Computational cost of the cross-similarity measure

Let us go back to the computational cost of K_S (eq. 1). It heavily depends on the size of $\mathcal{C}$. We define p' and p'' as the placeholders of, respectively, (T', H') and (T'', H''). As $\mathcal{C}$ is combinatorial with respect to $|p'|$ and $|p''|$, $|\mathcal{C}|$ rapidly grows. Assigning placeholders only to chunks helps controlling their number. For example, in the RTE data the number of placeholders hardly goes beyond 7, as hypotheses are generally short sentences. But, even in these cases, the number of K_T computations grows. As the trees $t(\Gamma, c)$ are obtained from a single tree Γ (containing placeholder) applying different $c \in \mathcal{C}$, it is reasonable to think that they will share common subparts. Then, during the iterations of $c \in \mathcal{C}$, $K_T(t(\Gamma', c), t(\Gamma'', c))$ will compute the similarity between subtrees that have already been evaluated. The reformulation of the *cross-pair similarity* function we present takes advantage of this.

3 Adding semantic information to cross-pair similarity

The examples in the previous section show that the cross-pairs approach lacks the lexical-semantic knowledge connecting the words in a placeholder. In the examples, the missed knowledge is the type of semantic relation between the main verbs. The relation that links *kill* and *die* is not a generic similarity, as a WordNet based similarity measure can suggest, but a more specific causal relation. The learnt rewrite rule R_5 holds only for verbs in such relation. In facts, it is correctly applied in example E_6, as *feed* causes *eat*, but it gives a wrong suggestion in example E_7, since *warn* and *declare* are only related by a generic similarity relation.

We then need to encode this information in the syntactic trees in order to learn correct rules.

3.1 Defining anchor types

The idea of introducing anchor types should be in principle very simple and effective. Yet, this may be not the case: simpler attempts to introduce semantic information in RTE systems have often failed. To investigate the validity of our idea, we then need to focus on a small set of relevant relation types, and to carefully control ambiguity for each type.

A valuable source of relation types among words is WordNet. We choose to integrate in our system three important relation standing at the word level: *part-of*, *antinomy*, and *verb entailment*. We also define two more general anchor types: *similarity* and the *surface matching*. The first type links words which are similar according to some WordNet similarity measure. Specifically, this type is intended to capture the semantic relations of *synonymy* and *hyperonymy*. The second type is activated when words or lemmas match: then, it captures cases in which words are semantically equivalent. The complete set of relation types used in the experiments is given in Table 1.

Rank	***Relation Type***	***Symbol***
1.	*antinomy*	$\leftrightarrow$
2.	*part-of*	$\subset$
3.	*verb entailment*	$\leftarrow$
4.	*similarity*	$\approx$
5.	*surface matching*	$=$

Table 1: Ranked anchor types

3.2 Type anchors in the syntactic tree

To learn more correct *rewrite rules* by using the anchor types defined in the previous section, we need to add this information to syntactic trees. The best position would be in the same nodes of the anchors. Also, to be more effective, this information should be inserted in as many subtrees as possible. Thus we define the typed-anchor climbing-up rules. We then implement in our model the following climbing up rule:

> *if two typed anchors climb up to the same node, give precedence to that with the highest ranking in Tab. 1.*

This rule can be easily showed to be consistent with common sense intuitions. For an example like "*John is a tall boy*" that does not entail "*John is a short boy*", our strategy will produce these trees:

(E_8)

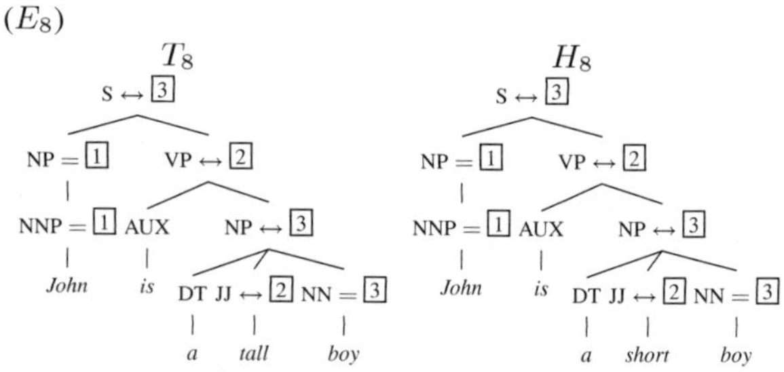

This representation can be used to derive a correct rewrite rule, such as:
if two fragments have the same syntactic structure $S(NP_1, VP(AUX, NP_2))$, and there is an antonym type ($\leftrightarrow$) on the S and NP_2 , then the

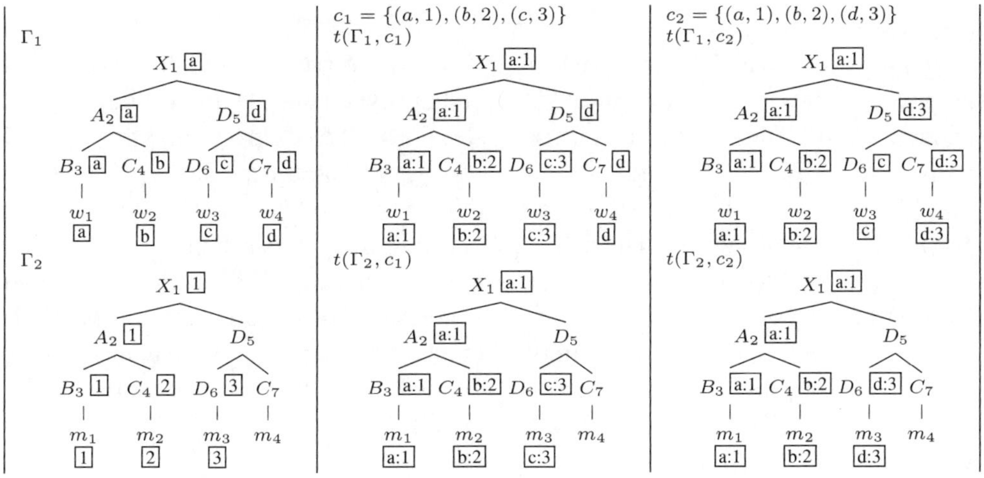

Figure 1: Tree pairs with placeholders and $t(T, c)$ transformation

entailment does not hold.

4 Reducing computational cost of the cross-pair similarity computation

4.1 The original kernel function

In this section, we describe more in detail the similarity function K_S (Eq. 1). To simplify, we focus on the computation of only one K_T of the kernel sum.

$$K_S(\Gamma', \Gamma'') = \max_{c \in \mathcal{C}} K_T(t(\Gamma', c), t(\Gamma'', c)), \qquad (2)$$

where the (Γ', Γ'') pair can be either (T', T'') or (H', H''). We apply this simplification since we are interested in optimizing the evaluation of the K_T with respect to different sets of correspondences $c \in \mathcal{C}$.

To better explain K_S, we need to analyze the role of the substitution function $t(\Gamma, c)$ and to review the tree kernel function K_T.

The aim of $t(\Gamma, c)$ is to coherently replace placeholders in two trees Γ' and Γ'' so that these two trees can be compared. The substitution is carried out according to the set of correspondences c. Let p' and p'' be placeholders of Γ' and Γ'', respectively, if $p'' \subseteq p'$ then c is a bijection between a subset $\widehat{p'} \subseteq p'$ and p''. For example (Fig. 1), the trees Γ_1 has $p_1 = \{\boxed{a}, \boxed{b}, \boxed{c}, \boxed{d}\}$ as placeholder set and Γ_2 has $p_2 = \{\boxed{1}, \boxed{2}, \boxed{3}\}$. In this case, a possible set of correspondence is $c_1 = \{(a, 1), (b, 2), (c, 3)\}$. In Fig. 1 the substitution function replaces each placeholder $\boxed{a}$ of the tree $\Gamma_1$with the new placeholder $\boxed{a{:}1}$ by $t(\cdot, c)$ obtaining the transformed tree $t(\Gamma_1, c_1)$, and each placeholder $\boxed{1}$ of Γ_2 with $\boxed{a{:}1}$. After these substitutions, the labels of the two trees can be matched and the similarity function K_T is applicable.

$K_T(\tau', \tau'')$, as defined in (Collins and Duffy, 2002), computes the number of common subtrees between τ' and τ''.

4.2 An observation to reduce the computational cost

The above section has shown that the similarity function K_S firstly applies the transformation $t(\cdot, c)$ and then computes the tree kernel K_T. The overall process can be optimized by factorizing redundant K_T computations.

Indeed, two trees, $t(\Gamma, c')$ and $t(\Gamma, c'')$, obtained by applying two sets of correspondences $c', c'' \in \mathcal{C}$, may partially overlap since c' and c'' can share a non-empty set of common elements. Let us consider the subtree set S shared by $t(\Gamma, c')$ and $t(\Gamma, c'')$ such that they contain placeholders in $c' \cap c'' = c$, then $t(\gamma, c) = t(\gamma, c') = t(\gamma, c'')\ \forall \gamma \in S$. Therefore if we apply a tree kernel function K_T to a pair (Γ', Γ''), we can find a c such that subtrees of Γ' and subtrees of Γ'' are invariant with respect to c' and c''. Therefore, $K_T(t(\gamma', c), t(\gamma'', c)) = K_T(t(\gamma', c'), t(\gamma'', c'))$ $= K_T(t(\gamma', c''), t(\gamma'', c''))$. This implies that it is possible to refine the dynamic programming algorithm used to compute the Δ matrices while computing the kernel $K_S(\Gamma', \Gamma'')$.

To better explain this idea let us consider Fig. 1 that represents two trees, Γ_1 and Γ_2, and the application of two different transformations $c_1 = \{(a,1),(b,2),(c,3)\}$ and $c_2 = \{(a,1),(b,2),(d,3)\}$. Nodes are generally in the form $X_i\boxed{z}$ where X is the original node label, $\boxed{z}$ is the placeholder, and i is used to index nodes of the tree. Two nodes are equal if they have the same node label and the same placeholder. The first column of the figure represents the original trees Γ_1 and Γ_2. The second and third columns contain respectively the transformed trees $t(\Gamma, c_1)$ and $t(\Gamma, c_2)$

Since the subtree of Γ_1 starting from $A_2\boxed{a}$ contains only placeholders that are in c, in the transformed trees, $t(\Gamma_1, c_1)$ and $t(\Gamma_1, c_2)$, the subtrees rooted in $A_2\boxed{a{:}1}$ are identical. The same happens for Γ_2 with the subtree rooted in $A_2\boxed{1}$. In the transformed trees, $t(\Gamma_2, c_1)$ and $t(\Gamma_2, c_2)$, subtrees rooted in $A_2\boxed{a{:}1}$ are identical. The computation of K_T applied to the above subtrees gives an identical result. Then, this computation can be avoided. If correctly used in a dynamic programming algorithm, the above observation can produce an interesting decrease in the time computational cost. More details on the algorithm and the decrease in computational cost may be found in (Moschitti and Zanzotto, 2007).

5 Experimental Results

5.1 Experimental Setup

We implemented the novel cross-similarity kernel in the SVM-light-TK (Moschitti, 2006) that encodes the basic syntactic kernel K_T in SVM-light (Joachims, 1999).

To assess the validity of the typed anchor model (**tap**), we evaluated two sets of systems: the *plain* and *lexical-boosted* systems. The *plain* systems are:
-**tap**: our tree-kernel approach using typed placeholders with climbing in the syntactic tree;
-**tree**: the cross-similarity model described in Sec.2. Its comparison with *tap* indicates the effectiveness of our approaches;
The *lexical-boosted* systems are:
-**lex**: a standard approach based on *lexical overlap*. The classifier uses as the only feature the lexical overlap similarity score described in (Corley and Mihalcea, 2005);
-**lex+tap**: these configurations mix lexical overlap and our typed anchor approaches;
-**lex+tree**: the comparison of this configuration with *lex+tap* should further support the validity of our intuition on typed anchors;

Preliminary experiments have been performed using two datasets: **RTE2** (the 1600 entailment pairs from the RTE-2 challenge) and **RTE3d** (the development dataset of this challenge). We randomly divided this latter in two halves: $RTE3d_0$ and $RTE3d_1$.

5.2 Investigatory Results Analysis and Submission Results

Table 2 reports the results of the experiments. The first column indicates the training set whereas the second one specifies the used test set. The third and the forth columns represent the accuracy of basic models: the original *tree* model and the enhanced *tap* model. The latter three columns report the basic *lex* model and the two combined models, *lex+tree* and *lex+tap*. The second and the third rows represent the accuracy of the models with respect to the first randomly selected half of $RTE3d$ whilst the last two rows are related to the second half.

The experimental results show some interesting facts. In the case of the **plain systems** (*tree* and *tap*), we have the following observations:
- The use of the *typed anchors* in the model seems to be effective. All the *tap* model results are higher than the corresponding *tree* model results. This suggests that the method used to integrate this kind of information in the syntactic tree is effective.
- The claim that *using more training material helps* seems not to be supported by these experiments. The gap between $tree$ and tap is higher when learning with $RTE2 + RTE3d_0$ than when learning with $RTE3_0$. This supports the claim. However, the result is not kept when learning with $RTE2 + RTE3d_1$ with respect to when learning with $RTE3_1$. This suggests that adding not very specific information, i.e. derived from corpora different from the target one (RTE3), may not help the learning of accurate rules.

On the other hand, in the case of the **lexical-boosted** systems (*lex*, *lex+tree*, and *lex+tap*), we see that:

Train	*Test*	**tree**	**tap**	**lex**	**lex+tree**	**lex+tap**
$RTE3d_0$	$RTE3d_1$	62.97	64.23	69.02	68.26	69.02
$RTE2 + RTE3d_0$	$RTE3d_1$	62.22	62.47	71.03	71.28	71.79
$RTE3d_1$	$RTE3d_0$	62.03	62.78	70.22	70.22	71.22
$RTE2 + RTE3d_0$	$RTE3d_0$	63.77	64.76	71.46	71.22	72.95

Table 2: Accuracy of the systems on two folds of RTE3 development

- There is an extremely high accuracy result for the pure *lex* model. This result is counterintuitive. A model like *lex* has been likely used by QA or IE systems to extract examples for the RTE3d set. If this is the case we may expect that positive and negative examples should have similar values for this *lex* distance indicator. It is then not clear why this model results in so high accuracy.
- Given the high results of the *lex* model, the model *lex+tree* does not increase the performances.
- On the contrary, the model *lex+tap* is always better (or equal) than the *lex* model. This suggests that for this particular set of examples the *typed anchors* are necessary to effectively use the *rewriting rules* implicitly encoded in the examples.
- When the *tap* model is used in combination with the *lex* model, it seems that the claim "*the more training examples the better*" is valid. The gaps between *lex* and *lex+tap* are higher when the $RTE2$ is used in combination with the $RTE3d$ related set.

Given this analysis we submitted two systems both based on the *lex+tap* model. We did two different training: one using $RTE3d$ and the other using $RTE2 + RTE3d$. Results are reported in the Table below:

Train	*Accuracy*
$RTE3d$	66.75%
$RTE2 + RTE3d$	65.75%

Such results seem too low to be statistically consistent with our development outcome. This suggests that there is a clear difference between the content of $RTE3d$ and the $RTE3$ test set. Moreover, in contrast with what expected, the system trained with only the $RTE3d$ data is more accurate than the others. Again, this suggests that the RTE corpora (from all the challenges) are most probably very different.

6 Conclusions and final remarks

This paper demonstrates that it is possible to effectively include shallow semantics in syntax-based learning approaches. Moreover, as it happened in RTE2, it is not always true that more learning examples increase the accuracy of RTE systems. This claim is still under investigation.

References

Roy Bar Haim, Ido Dagan, Bill Dolan, Lisa Ferro, Danilo Giampiccolo, Bernardo Magnini, and Idan Szpektor. 2006. The II PASCAL RTE challenge. In *PASCAL Challenges Workshop*, Venice, Italy.

Michael Collins and Nigel Duffy. 2002. New ranking algorithms for parsing and tagging: Kernels over discrete structures, and the voted perceptron. In *Proceedings of ACL02*.

Courtney Corley and Rada Mihalcea. 2005. Measuring the semantic similarity of texts. In *Proc. of the ACL Workshop on Empirical Modeling of Semantic Equivalence and Entailment*, pages 13–18, Ann Arbor, Michigan, June. Association for Computational Linguistics.

Andrew Hickl, John Williams, Jeremy Bensley, Kirk Roberts, Bryan Rink, and Ying Shi. 2005. Recognizing textual entailment with LCCs GROUNDHOG system. In *Proceedings of the Second PASCAL Challenges Workshop on Recognising Textual Entailment*, Venice, Italy.

Thorsten Joachims. 1999. Making large-scale svm learning practical. In B. Schlkopf, C. Burges, and A. Smola, editors, *Advances in Kernel Methods-Support Vector Learning*. MIT Press.

Alessandro Moschitti and Fabio Massimo Zanzotto. 2007. Fast and effective kernels for relational learning from texts. In *Proceedings of the International Conference of Machine Learning (ICML)*, Corvallis, Oregon.

Alessandro Moschitti. 2006. Making tree kernels practical for natural language learning. In *Proceedings of EACL'06*, Trento, Italy.

Marta Tatu, Brandon Iles, John Slavick, Adrian Novischi, and Dan Moldovan. 2005. COGEX at the second recognizing textual entailment challenge. In *Proceedings of the Second PASCAL Challenges Workshop on Recognising Textual Entailment*, Venice, Italy.

Fabio Massimo Zanzotto and Alessandro Moschitti. 2006. Automatic learning of textual entailments with cross-pair similarities. In *Proceedings of the 21st Coling and 44th ACL*, pages 401–408, Sydney, Australia, July.

Combining Lexical-Syntactic Information with Machine Learning for Recognizing Textual Entailment

Arturo Montejo-Ráez, Jose Manuel Perea, Fernando Martínez-Santiago, Miguel Ángel García-Cumbreras, Maite Martín-Valdivia, Alfonso Ureña-López
Dpto. de Informática, Universidad de Jaén
Campus de las Lagunillas s/n, 23071 - Jaén
{amontejo, jmperea, dofer, magc, maite, laurena}@ujaen.es

Abstract

This document contains the description of the experiments carried out by SINAI group. We have developed an approach based on several lexical and syntactic measures integrated by means of different machine learning models. More precisely, we have evaluated three features based on lexical similarity and 11 features based on syntactic tree comparison. In spite of the relatively straightforward approach we have obtained more than 60% for accuracy. Since this is our first participation we think we have reached a good result.

1 Approach description

We fill face the textual entailment recognition using Machine Learning methods, i.e. identifying features that characterize the relation between hypothesis and associated text and generating a model using existing entailment judgements that will allow us to provide a new entailment judgement agains unseen pairs text-hypothesis. This approach can be split into the two processes shown in Figures 1 and 2.

In a more formal way, given a text *t* and an hypothesis *h* we want to define a function *e* which takes these two elements as arguments and returns and answer to the entailment question:

$$e(t,h) = \begin{cases} YES & \text{if } h \text{ is entailed by } t \\ NO & \text{otherwise} \end{cases} \quad (1)$$

Now the question is to find that ideal function

Figure 1: Training processes

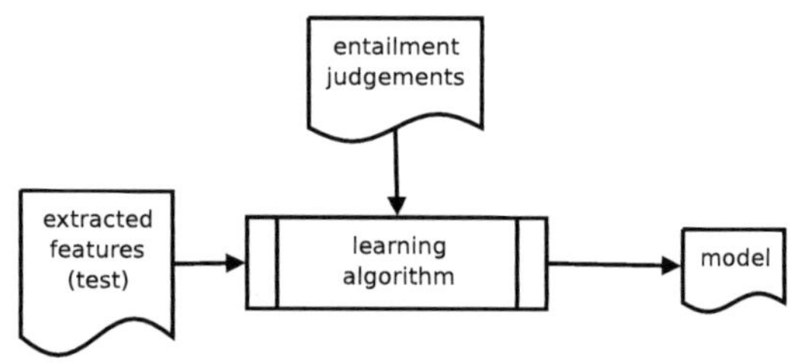

Figure 2: Classification processes

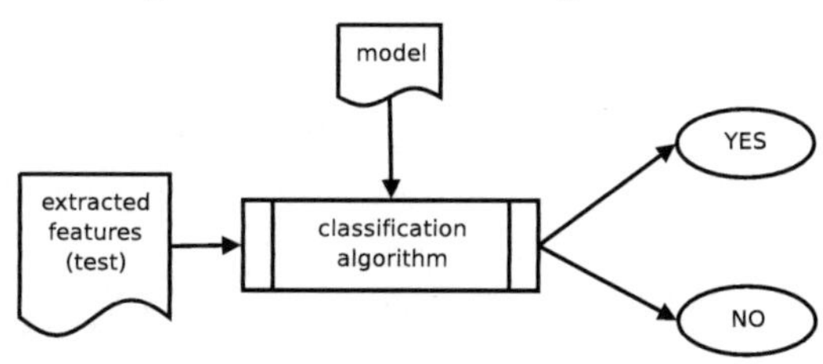

$e(t,h)$. We will approximate this function using a binary classifier:

$$\hat{e}(t,h) = bc(f,m) \quad (2)$$

where
bc is a binary classifier
f is a set of *features*
m is the learned model for the classifier

Therefore, it only remains to select a binary classifier and a feature extraction method. We have performed two experiments with different choices for both decisions. These two experiments are detailed below.

Proceedings of the Workshop on Textual Entailment and Paraphrasing, pages 78–82,
Prague, June 2007.

1.1 Lexical similarity

This experiment approaches the textual entailment task being based on the extraction of a set of lexical measures that show the existing similarity between the hypothesis-text pairs. Our approach is similar to (Ferrandez et al., 2007) but we make matching between similar words too while (Ferrandez et al., 2007) apply exact matching (see below).

The first step previous to the calculation of the different measures is to preprocess the pairs using the English *stopwords* list. Next we have used the GATE[1] architecture to obtain the stems of tokens. Once obtained stems, we have applied four different measures or techniques:

- **Simple Matching**: this technique consists of calculating the semantic distance between each stem of the hypothesis and text. If this distance exceeds a threshold, both stems are considered similar and the similarity weight value increases in one. The accumulated weight is normalized dividing it by the number of elements of the hypothesis. In this experiment we have considered the threshold 0.5. The values of semantic distance measure range from 0 to 1. In order to calculate the semantic distance between two tokens (stems), we have tried several measures based on WordNet (Alexander Budanitsky and Graeme Hirst, 2001). **Lin's similarity measure** (Lin, 1998) was shown to be best overall measures. It uses the notion of information content and the same elements as Jiang and Conrath's approach (Jiang and Conrath, 1997) but in a different fashion:

$$sim_L(c_1, c_2) = \frac{2 \times \log p(lso(c_1, c_2))}{\log p(c_1) + \log p(c_2)}$$

  where c_1 and c_2 are synsets, *lso*(c_1,c_2) is the information content of their lowest superordinate (most specific common subsumer) and *p(c)* is the probability of encountering an instance of a synset *c* in some specific corpus (Resnik, 1995). The Simple Matching technique is defined in the following equation:

$$SIM_{matching} = \frac{\sum_{i \in H} similarity(i)}{|H|}$$

  where *H* is the set that contains the elements of the hypothesis and *similarity(i)* is defined like:

$$similarity(i) = \begin{cases} 1 & \text{if } \exists j \in T sim_L(i,j) > 0.5 \\ 0 & \text{otherwise} \end{cases}$$

- **Binary Matching**: this measure is the same that the previous one but modifying the *similarity* function:

$$similarity(i) = \begin{cases} 1 & \text{if } \exists j \in T\ i = j \\ 0 & \text{otherwise} \end{cases}$$

- **Consecutive Subsequence Matching**: this technique relies on forming subsequences of consecutive stems in the hypothesis and matching them in the text. The minimal size of the consecutive subsequences is two and the maximum is the maximum size of the hypothesis. Every correct matching increases in one the final weight. The sum of the obtained weights of the matching between subsequences of a certain size or length is normalized by the number of sets of consecutive subsequences of the hypothesis created for this length. These weights are accumulated and normalized by the size of the hypothesis less one. The Consecutive Subsequence Matching technique is defined in the following equations:

$$CSS_{matching} = \frac{\sum_{i=2}^{|H|} f(SH_i)}{|H| - 1}$$

  where SH_i is the set that contains the subsequences of the hypothesis with *i* size or length and *f*(SH_i) is defined like:

$$f(SH_i) = \frac{\sum_{j \in SH_i} matching(j)}{|H| - i + 1}$$

  where

$$matching(i) = \begin{cases} 1 & \text{if } \exists k \in ST_i\ k = j \\ 0 & \text{otherwise} \end{cases}$$

  where ST_i represents the set that contains the subsequences with *i* size from text.

- **Trigrams**: this technique relies on forming trigrams of words in the hypothesis and matching them in the text. A trigram is a group of

[1] http://gate.ac.uk/

three words. If a hypothesis trigram matches in text, then the similarity weight value increases in one. The accumulated weight is normalized dividing it by the number of trigrams of the hypothesis.

1.2 Syntactic tree comparison

Some features have been extracted from pairs hypothesis-text related to the syntactic information that some parser can produce. The rationale behind it consists in measuring the similarity between the syntactic trees of both hypothesis and associated text. To do that, terms appearing in both trees are identified (we call this *alignment*) and then, graph distances (number of nodes) between those terms in both trees are compared, producing certain values as result.

In our experiments, we have applied the COLLINS (Collins, 1999) parser to generate the syntactic tree of both pieces of text. In Figure 3 the output of the syntactic parsing for a sample pair is shown. This data is the result of the syntactical analysis performed by the mentioned parser. A graph based view of the tree corresponding to the hypothesis is drawn in Figure 4. This graph will help us to understand how certain similarity measures are obtained.

Figure 3: Syntactic trees of sample hypothesis and its associated text

```
<t>
(TOP (S (LST (LS 0302) (. .)) (NP (JJ Next) (NN year))
(VP (VBZ is) (NP (NP (DT the) (JJ 50th) (NN anniversary))
(PP (IN of) (NP (NP (DT the) (NNP Normandy) (NN invasion)
(, ,)) (NP (NP (DT an)(NN event)) (SBAR (IN that) (S (VP
(MD would) (RB n't) (VP (VB have) (VP (VBN been) (ADJP
(JJ possible)) (PP (IN without) (NP (NP (DT the) (NNP
Liberty) (NN ships.)) (SBAR (S (NP (DT The) (NNS
volunteers)) (VP (VBP hope) (S (VP (TO to) (VP (VB raise)
(NP (JJ enough) (NN money)) (S (VP (TO to) (VP (VB sail)
(NP (DT the) (NNP O'Brien)) (PP (TO to) (NP (NNP France)))
(PP (IN for)(NP (DT the) (JJ big) (NNP D-Day) (NN celebration)
(. .)))))))))))))))))))))))))
</t>

<h>
(TOP (S (NP (NP (CD 50th) (NNP Anniversary)) (PP (IN of)
(NP (NNP Normandy) (NNP Landings)))) (VP (VBZ lasts) (NP
(DT a) (NN year) (. .)))))
</h>
```

From the sample above, the terms *normandy*, *year* and *anniversary* appear in both pieces of text. We say that these terms are "aligned". Therefore, for the three possible pairs of aligned terms we can compute the distance, in nodes, to go from one term to the other at each tree. Then, the difference of these

Figure 4: Syntact tree of sample hypothesis

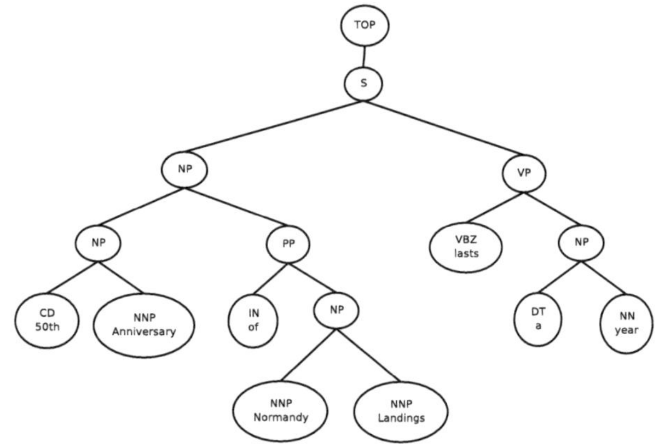

distances is computed and some statistics are generated. We can summarize the process of computing this differences in the algorithm detailed in Figure 6.

Figure 5: Tree comparison process

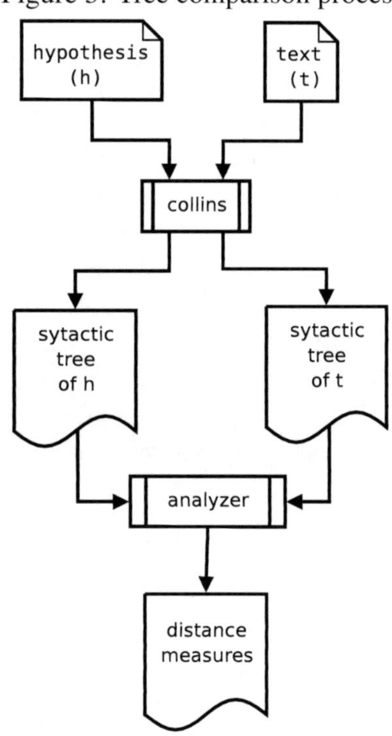

For instance, in the tree represented in Figure 4 we can see that we have to perform 5 steps to go from node *Anniversary* to node *Normandy*. Since there are no more possible occurrences of these two terms, then the minimal distance between them is 5. This value is also measured on the tree corresponding to the text, and the absolute difference between these two minimal distances is stored in order to compute final feature weights consisting in basic statistical values. The algorithm to obtain the distribution of distance differences is detailed in Figure 6.

Figure 6: Extraction of features based on syntactic distance

Input:
  a syntactic tree of the hypothesis S_h
  a syntactic tree of the text S_t
Output :
  the set of distance differences
  $Dd = \{dd_{ij} : t_i, t_j \in T\}$
Pseudo code:
  $T \leftarrow$ *aligned terms between* S_h *and* S_t
  $Dd \leftarrow \emptyset$
  for $i = 1..n$ do
    for $j = i + 1..n$ do
      $dist_h \leftarrow$ *minimal distance between nodes* t_i and t_j in S_h
      $dist_t \leftarrow$ *minimal distance between nodes* t_i and t_j in S_t
      $dd_{ij} \leftarrow |dist_h - dist_t|$
      $Dd \leftarrow \{dd_{ij}\} \cup Dd$
    end-for
  end-for

The statistics generated from the resulting list of distances differences Dd are the following:

1. The number of aligned terms (3 in the given example).

2. The number of matched POS values of aligned terms, that is, if the term appears with the same POS label in both texts (in the example *Anniversary* differs in the POS label assigned).

3. The number of unmatched POS labels of aligned terms.

4. The average distance in nodes through the syntactic tree to go from one aligned term to another.

5. The minimal distance difference found.

Table 1: Results with TiMBL and BBR classifiers (*Exp5* is the only official result reported in this paper).

Experiment	Classifier	Accuracy
Exp1	BBR	0.6475
Exp2	BBR	0.64625
Exp3	BBR	0.63875
Exp4	TiMBL	0.6062
Exp5	TiMBL	0.6037
Exp6	TiMBL	0.57

6. The maximal distance difference found.

7. The standard deviation of distance differences.

In a similar way, differences in the depth level of nodes for aligned terms are also calculated. From the example exposed the following values were computed:

```
* Aligned          3
* MatchedPOS       2
* UnmatchedPOS     1
* AvgDistDiff      0.0392156863
* MinDistDiff      0.0000000000
* MaxDistDiff      0.0588235294
* StdevDistDiff    0.0277296777
* AvgDepthDiff     2.0000000000
* MinDepthDiff     1.0000000000
* MaxDepthDiff     3.0000000000
* StdevDepthDiff   0.8164965809
```

2 Experiments and results

The algorithms used as binary classifiers are two: *Bayesian Logistic Regression* (BBR)[2] and TiMBL (Daelemans et al., 1998). Both algorithms have been trained with the *devel* data provided by the organization of the Pascal challange. As has been explained in previous sections, a model is generated via the supervised learning process. This model *m* is then feed into the classification variant of the algorithm, which will decide whether a new hypothesis sample is entailed by the given text or not.

The experiments and results are shown in Table 1: where:

- **Exp1** uses four features: three lexical similarities ($SIM_{matching} + CSS_{matching}$ + Trigrams) and Syntactic tree comparison.

[2]http://www.stat.rutgers.edu/~madigan/BBR/ [available at March 27, 2007]

- **Exp2** uses five features: four lexical similarities ($SIM_{matching}$ + $CSS_{matching}$ + Trigrams + $BIN_{matching}$) and Syntactic tree comparison.
- **Exp3** uses only three lexical similarities ($SIM_{matching}$ + $CSS_{matching}$ + Trigrams).
- **Exp4** uses the four lexical similarities ($SIM_{matching}$ + $CSS_{matching}$ + Trigrams + $BIN_{matching}$)
- **Exp5** uses only three lexical similarities ($SIM_{matching}$ + $CSS_{matching}$ + Trigrams).
- **Exp6** uses four features: three lexical similarities ($SIM_{matching}$ + $CSS_{matching}$ + Trigrams) and Syntactic tree comparison.

As we expected, the best result we have obtained is by means of the integration of the whole of the features available. More surprising is the good result obtained by using lexical features only, even better than experiments based on syntactical features only. On the other hand, we expected that the integration of both sort of features improve significatively the performance of the system, but the improvement respect of lexical features is poor (less than 2%). . Similar topics share similar vocabulary, but not similar syntax at all. Thus, we think we should to investigate semantic features better than the syntactical ones.

3 Conclusions and future work

In spite of the simplicity of the approach, we have obtained remarkable results: each set of features has reported to provide relevant information concerning to the entailment judgement determination. On the other hand, these two approaches can be merged into one single system by using different features all together and feeding with them several binary classifiers that could compose a voting system. We will do that combining TiMBL, SVM and BBR.We expect to improve the performance of the entailment recognizer by this integration.

Finally, we want to implement a hierarchical architecture based on constraint satisfaction networks. The constraints will be given by the set of available features and the maintenance of the integration across the semantic interpretation process.

4 Acknowledgements

This work has been partially financed by the TIMOM project (TIN2006-15265-C06-03) granted by the Spanish Government Ministry of Science and Technology and the RFC/PP2006/Id_514 granted by the University of Jaén.

References

Alexander Budanitsky and Graeme Hirst. 2001. Semantic distance in wordnet: An experimental, application-oriented evaluation of five measures.

Michael Collins. 1999. *Head-Driven Statistical Models for Natural Language Parsing*. Ph.D. thesis, University of Pennsylvania.

Walter Daelemans, Jakub Zavrel, Ko van der Sloot, and Antal van den Bosch. 1998. Timbl: Tilburg memory based learner, version 1.0, reference guide.

Oscar Ferrandez, Daniel Micolo, Rafael Mu noz, and Manuel Palomar. 2007. Técnicas léxico-sintácticas para reconocimiento de inmplicación textual. . *Tecnologías de la Informacón Multilingüe y Multimodal. In press.*

Jay J. Jiang and David W. Conrath. 1997. Semantic similarity based on corpus statistics and lexical taxonomy. In *Proceedings of International Conference on Research in Computational Linguistics*, Taiwan.

Dekang Lin. 1998. An information-theoretic definition of similarity. In *Proceedings of the 15th International Conference on Machine Learning*.

Philip Resnik. 1995. Using information content to evaluate semantic similarity. In *Proceedings of the 14th International Joint Conference on Artificial Intelligence*, Montreal.

Dependency-based paraphrasing for recognizing textual entailment

Erwin Marsi, Emiel Krahmer
Communication & Cognition
Tilburg University
The Netherlands
e.c.marsi@uvt.nl
e.j.krahmer@uvt.nl

Wauter Bosma
Human Media Interaction
University of Twente
The Netherlands
w.e.bosma@ewi.utwente.nl

Abstract

This paper addresses syntax-based paraphrasing methods for Recognizing Textual Entailment (RTE). In particular, we describe a dependency-based paraphrasing algorithm, using the DIRT data set, and its application in the context of a straightforward RTE system based on aligning dependency trees. We find a small positive effect of dependency-based paraphrasing on both the RTE3 development and test sets, but the added value of this type of paraphrasing deserves further analysis.

1 Introduction

Coping with paraphrases appears to be an essential subtask in Recognizing Textual Entailment (RTE). Most RTE systems incorporate some form of lexical paraphrasing, usually relying on WordNet to identify synonym, hypernym and hyponym relations among word pairs from text and hypothesis (Bar-Haim et al., 2006, Table 2). Many systems also address paraphrasing above the lexical level. This can take the form of identifying or substituting equivalent multi-word strings, e.g., (Bosma and Callison-Burch, 2006). A drawback of this approach is that it is hard to cope with discontinuous paraphrases containing one or more gaps. Other approaches exploit syntactic knowledge in the form of parse trees. Hand-crafted transformation rules can account for systematic syntactic alternation like active-passive form, e.g., (Marsi et al., 2006). Alternatively, such paraphrase rules may be automatically derived from huge text corpora (Lin and Pantel, 2001). There are at least two key advantages of syntax-based over string-based paraphrasing which are relevant for RTE: (1) it can cope with discontinuous paraphrases; (2) syntactic information such as dominance relations, phrasal syntactic labels and dependency relations, can be used to refine the coarse matching on words only.

Here we investigate paraphrasing on the basis of of syntactic dependency analyses. Our sole resource is the DIRT data set (Lin and Pantel, 2001), an extensive collection of automatically derived paraphrases. These have been used for RTE before (de Salvo Braz et al., 2005; Raina et al., 2005), and similar approaches to paraphrase mining have been applied as well (Nielsen et al., 2006; Hickl et al., 2006). However, in these approaches paraphrasing is always one factor in a complex system, and as a result little is known of the contribution of paraphrasing for the RTE task. In this paper, we focus entirely on dependency-based paraphrasing in order to get a better understanding of its usefulness for RTE. In the next Section, we describe the DIRT data and present an algorithm for dependency-based paraphrasing in order to bring a pair's text closer to its hypothesis. We present statistics on coverage as well as qualitative discussion of the results. Section 3 then describes our RTE system and results with and without dependency-based paraphrasing.

2 Dependency-based paraphrasing

2.1 Preprocessing RTE data

Starting from the text-hypothesis pairs in the RTE XML format, we first preprocess the data. As the text part may consist of more than one sentence, we first perform sentence splitting using Mxterminator (Reynar and Ratnaparkhi, 1997), a maximum

Proceedings of the Workshop on Textual Entailment and Paraphrasing, pages 83–88,
Prague, June 2007.

entropy-based end of sentence classifier trained on the Penn Treebank data. Next, each sentence is tokenized and syntactically parsed using the Minipar parser (Lin, 1998). From the parser's tabular output we extract the word forms, lemmas, part-of-speech tags and dependency relations. This information is then stored in an ad-hoc XML format which represents the trees as an hierarchy of node elements in order to facilitate tree matching.

2.2 DIRT data

The DIRT (Discovering Inference Rules from Text) method is based on extending Harris Distributional Hypothesis, which states that words that occurred in the same contexts tend to be similar, to dependency paths in parse trees (Lin and Pantel, 2001). Each dependency path consists of at least three nodes: a root node, and two non-root terminal nodes, which are nouns. The DIRT data set we used consists of over 182k paraphrase clusters derived from 1GB of newspaper text. Each cluster consists of a unique dependency path, which we will call the *paraphrase source*, and a list of equivalent dependency paths, which we will refer to as the *paraphrase translations*, ordered in decreasing value of point-wise mutual information. A small sample in the original format is

```
(N:by:V<buy>V:obj:N (sims
N:to:V<sell>V:obj:N      0.211704
N:subj:V<buy>V:obj:N     0.198728
...
))
```

The first two lines represent the inference rule: *X bought by Y* entails *X sold to Y*.

We preprocess the DIRT data by restoring prepositions, which were originally folded into a dependency relation, to individual nodes, as this eases alignment with the parsed RTE data. For the same reason, paths are converted to the same ad-hoc XML format as the parsed RTE data.

2.3 Paraphrase substitution

Conceptually, our paraphrase substitution algorithm takes a straightforward approach. For the purpose of explanation only, Figure 1 presents pseudo-code for a naive implementation. The main function takes two arguments (cf. line 1). The first is a preprocessed RTE data set in which all sentences from text and hypothesis are dependency parsed. The second is a collection of DIRT paraphrases, each one mapping a source path to one or more translation paths. For each text/hypothesis pair (cf. line 2), we look at all the subtrees of the text parses (cf. line 3-4) and attempt to find a suitable paraphrase of this subtree (cf. line 5). We search the DIRT paraphrases (cf. line 8) for a source path that matches the text subtree at hand (cf. line 9). If found, we check if any of the corresponding paraphrase translation paths (cf. line 10) matches a subtree of the hypothesis parse (cf. line 11-12). If so, we modify the text tree by substituting this translation path (cf. line 13). The intuition behind this is that we only accept paraphrases that bring the text closer to the hypothesis. The DIRT paraphrases are ordered in decreasing likelihood, so after a successful paraphrase substitution, we discard the remaining possibilities and continue with the next text subtree (cf. line 14).

The Match function, which is used for matching the source path to a text subtree and the translation path to an hypothesis subtree, requires the path to occur in the subtree. That is, all lemmas, part-of-speech tags and dependency relations from the path must have identical counterparts in the subtree; skipping nodes is not allowed. As the path's terminals specify no lemma, the only requirement is that their counterparts are nouns.

The Substitute function replaces the matched path in the text tree by the paraphrase's translation path. Intuitively, the path "overlays" a part of the subtree, changing lemmas and dependency relations, but leaving most of the daughter nodes unaffected. Note that the new path may be longer or shorter than the original one, thus introducing or removing nodes from the text tree.

As an example, we will trace our algorithm as applied to the first pair of the RTE3 dev set (id=1).

Text: *The sale was made to pay Yukos' US$ 27.5 billion tax bill, Yuganskneftegaz was originally sold for US$ 9.4 billion to a little known company Baikalfinansgroup which was later bought by the Russian state-owned oil company Rosneft.*
Hypothesis: *Baikalfinansgroup was sold to Rosneft.*
Entailment: *Yes*

While traversing the parse tree of the text, our algorithm encounters a node with POS tag V and lemma *buy*. The relevant part of the parse tree is shown at the right top of Figure 2. The logical arguments inferred by Minipar are shown between curly

```
def Paraphrase(parsed-rte-data, dirt-paraphrases):
    for pair in parsed-rte-data:
        for text-tree in pair.text-parses:
            for text-subtree in text-tree:
                Paraphrase-subtree(text-subtree, dirt-paraphrases, pair.hyp-parse)

def Paraphrase-subtree(text-subtree, dirt-paraphrases, hyp-tree):
    for (source-path, translations) in dirt-paraphrases:
        if Match(source-path, text-subtree):
            for trans-path in translations:
                for hyp-subtree in hyp-tree:
                    if Match(trans-path, hyp-subtree):
                        text-subtree = Substitute(trans-path, text-subtree)
                        return
```

Figure 1: *Pseudo-code for a naive implementation of the dependency-based paraphrase substitution algorithm*

brackets, e.g., *US$ 9.4 billion*. For this combination of verb and lemma, the DIRT data contains 340 paraphrase sets, with a total of 26950 paraphrases. The algorithm starts searching for a paraphrase source which matches the text. It finds the path shown at the left top of Figure 2: *buy* with a PP modifier headed by preposition *by*, and a nominal object. This paraphrase source has 108 alternative translations. It searches for paraphrase translations which match the hypothesis. The first, and therefore most likely (probability is 0.22) path it finds is rooted in *sell*, with a PP-modifier headed by *to* and a nominal object. This translation path, as well as its alignment to the hypothesis parse tree, is shown in the middle part of Figure 2. Finally, the source path in the text tree is substituted by the translation path. The bottom part of Figure 2 shows the updated text tree as well as its improved alignment to the hypothesis tree. The paraphrasing procedure can in effect be viewed as making the inference that Baikalfinansgroup was bought by Rosneft, therefore Baikalfinansgroup was sold to Rosneft.

The naive implementation of the algorithm is of course not very efficient. Our actual implementation uses a number of shortcuts to reduce processing time. For instance, the DIRT paraphrases are indexed on the lemma of their root in order to speed up retrieval. As another example, text nodes with less than two child nodes (i.e. terminal and unary-branching nodes) are immediately skipped, as they will never match a paraphrase path.

2.4 Paraphrasing results

We applied our paraphrasing algorithm to the RTE3 development set. Table 1 gives an impression of how many paraphrases were substituted. The first row lists the total number of nodes in the dependency trees of the text parts. The second row shows that for roughly 15% of these nodes, the DIRT data contains a paraphrase with the same lemma. The next two rows show in how many cases the source path matches the text and the translation path matches the hypothesis (i.e. giving rise to a paraphrase substitution). Clearly, the number of actual paraphrase substitutions is relatively small: on average about 0.5% of all text subtrees are subject to paraphrasing. Still, about one in six sentences is subject to paraphrasing, and close to half of all pairs is paraphrased at least once. Sentences triggering more than one paraphrase do occur. Also note that paraphrasing occurs more frequently in true entailment pairs than in false entailment pairs. This is to be expected, given that text and hypothesis are more similar when an entailment relation holds.

2.5 Discussion on paraphrasing

Type of paraphrases A substantial number of the paraphrases applied are single word synonyms or verb plus particle combinations which might as well be obtained from string-based substitution on the basis of a lexical resource like WordNet. Some randomly chosen examples include *X announces Y* entails *X supports Y*, *X makes Y* entails *X sells Y*, and *locates X at Y, discovers X at Y*. Nevertheless, more interesting paraphrases do occur. In the pair below (id=452), we find the paraphrase *X wins Y* entails *X*

Table 1: *Frequency of (partial) paraphrase matches on the RTE3 dev set*

	IE:	IR:	QA:	SUM:	Total:
Text nodes:	8899	10610	10502	8196	38207
Matching paraphrase lemma:	1439	1724	1581	1429	6173
Matching paraphrase source:	566	584	543	518	2211
Matching paraphrase translation:	71	55	23	79	228
Text sentences:	272	350	306	229	1157
Paraphrased text sentences:	63	51	20	66	200
Paraphrased true-entailment pairs:	32	25	12	39	108
Paraphrased false-entailment pairs:	26	21	5	23	75

(is) Y champion.

Text: *Boris Becker is a true legend in the sport of tennis. Aged just seventeen, he won Wimbledon for the first time and went on to become the most prolific tennis player.*
Hypothesis: *Boris Becker is a Wimbledon champion.*
Entailment: *True*

Another intriguing paraphrase, which appears to be false on first sight, is *X flies from Y* entails *X makes (a) flight to Y*. However, in the context of the next pair (id=777), it turns out to be correct.

Text: *The Hercules transporter plane which flew straight here from the first round of the trip in Pakistan, touched down and it was just a brisk 100m stroll to the handshakes.*
Hypothesis: *The Hercules transporter plane made a flight to Pakistan.*
Entailment: *True*

Coverage Although the DIRT data constitutes a relatively large collection of paraphrases, it is clear that many paraphrases required for the RTE3 data are missing. We tried to improve coverage to some extent by relaxing the Match function: instead of an exact match, we allowed for small mismatches in POS tag and dependency relation, reversing the order of a path's left and right side, and even for skipping nodes. However, subjective evaluation suggested that the results deteriorated. Alternatively, the coverage might be increased by deducing paraphrases on the fly using the web as a corpus, e.g., (Hickl et al., 2006).

Somewhat surprisingly, the vast majority of paraphrases concerns verbs. Even though the DIRT data contains paraphrases for nouns, adjectives and complementizers, the coverage of these word classes is apparently not nearly as extensive as that of verbs.

Another observation is that fewer paraphrases occur in pairs from the QA task. We have no explanation for this.

False paraphrases Since the DIRT data was automatically derived and was not manually checked, it contains noise in the form of questionable or even false paraphrases. While some of these surface in paraphrased RTE3 data (e.g. *X leaves for Y* entails *X departs Y*, and *X feeds Y* entails *Y feeds X*), their number appears to be limited. We conjecture this is because of the double constraint that a paraphrase must match both text and hypothesis.

Relevance Not all paraphrase substitutions are relevant for the purpose of recognizing textual entailment. Evidently, paraphrases in false entailment pairs are counterproductive. However, even in true entailment pairs paraphrases might occur in parts of the text that are irrelevant to the task at hand. Consider the following pair from the RTE3 dev set (id=417).

Text: *When comparing Michele Granger and Brian Goodell, Brian has to be the clear winner. In 1976, while still a student at Mission Viejo High, Brian won two Olympic gold medals at Montreal, breaking his own world records in both the 400 - and 1,500 - meter freestyle events. He went on to win three gold medals in he 1979 Pan American Games.*
Hypothesis: *Brian Goodell won three gold medals in the 1979 Pan American Games.*
Entailment: *True*

The second text sentence and hypothesis match the paraphrases: (1) *X medal at Y* entails *X medal in Y*, and (2) *X record in Y* entails *X medal in Y*. Even so, virtually all of the important information is in the third text sentence.

3 Results on RTE3 data

Since our contribution focuses on syntactic paraphrasing, our RTE3 system is a simplified version

Table 2: *Percent accuracy on RTE3 set without paraphrasing (−) and with paraphrasing (+)*

Task	Dev−	Dev+	Test−	Test+
IE	59.5	61.0	53.0	53.5
IR	67.0	68.0	58.5	61.5
QA	76.0	76.5	69.0	68.0
SUM	66.0	67.5	53.0	53.5
Overall	66.9	68.2	58.6	59.1

of our RTE2 system as described in **(ref supressed for blind reviewing)** The core of the system is still the tree alignment algorithm from (Meyers et al., 1996), but without normalization of node weights and applied to Minipar instead of Maltparser output. To keep things simple, we do not apply syntactic normalization, nor do we use WordNet or other resources to improve node matching. Instead, we simply align each text tree to the corresponding hypothesis tree and calculate the *coverage*, which is defined as the proportion of aligned content words in the hypothesis. If the coverage is above a task-specific threshold, we say entailment is true, otherwise it is false.

The results are summarized in Table 2. Overall results on the test set are considerably worse than on the development set, which is most likely due to overfitting task-specific parameters for node matching and coverage. Our main interest is to what extent dependency-based paraphrasing improves our baseline prediction. The improvement on the development set is more than 1%. This is reduced to 0.5% in the case of the test set.

Our preliminary results indicate a small positive effect of dependency-based paraphrasing on the results of our RTE system. Unlike most earlier work, we did not add resources other than Minipar dependency trees and DIRT paraphrase trees, in order to isolate the contribution of syntactic paraphrases to RTE. Nevertheless, our RTE3 system may be improved by using WordNet or other lexical resources to improve node matching, both in the paraphrasing step and in the tree-alignment step. In future work, we hope to improve both the paraphrasing method (along the lines discussed in Section 2.5) and the RTE system itself.

Acknowledgments We would like to thank Dekang Lin and Patrick Pantel for allowing us to use the DIRT data. This work was jointly conducted within the DAESO project funded by the Stevin program (De Nederlandse Taalunie) and the IMOGEN project funded by the Netherlands Organization for Scientific Research (NWO).

References

R. Bar-Haim, I. Dagan, B. Dolan, L. Ferro, D. Giampiccolo, B. Magnini, and I. Szpektor. 2006. The second pascal recognising textual entailment challenge. In *Proceedings of the Second PASCAL Challenges Workshop on Recognising Textual Entailment*, pages 1–9, Venice, Italy.

W. Bosma and C. Callison-Burch. 2006. Paraphrase substitution for recognizing textual entailment. In *Proceedings of CLEF*.

R. de Salvo Braz, R. Girju, V. Punyakanok, D. Roth, and M. Sammons. 2005. An inference model for semantic entailemnt in natural language. In *Proceedings of the First Pascal Challenge Workshop on Recognizing Textual Entailment*, pages 29–32.

A. Hickl, J. Williams, J. Bensley, K. Roberts, B. Rink, and Y. Shi. 2006. Recognizing textual entailment with lccs groundhog system. In *Proceedings of the Second PASCAL Challenges Workshop on Recognising Textual Entailment*, pages 80–85, Venice, Italy.

Dekang Lin and Patrick Pantel. 2001. Discovery of inference rules for question answering. *Natural Language Engineering*, 7(4):343–360.

Dekang Lin. 1998. Dependency-based evaluation of minipar. In *Proceedings of the Workshop on Evaluation of Parsing Systems at LREC 1998*, pages 317–330, Granada, Spain.

E. Marsi, E. Krahmer, W. Bosma, and M. Theune. 2006. Normalized alignment of dependency trees for detecting textual entailment. In *Proceedings of the Second PASCAL Challenges Workshop on Recognising Textual Entailment*, pages 56–61, venice, Italy.

Adam Meyers, Roman Yangarber, and Ralph Grisham. 1996. Alignment of shared forests for bilingual corpora. In *Proceedings of 16th International Conference on Computational Linguistics (COLING-96)*, pages 460–465, Copenhagen, Denmark.

R. Nielsen, W. Ward, and J.H. Martin. 2006. Toward dependency path based entailment. In *Proceedings of the Second PASCAL Challenges Workshop on Recognising Textual Entailment*, pages 44–49, Venice, Italy.

R. Raina, A. Haghighi, C. Cox, J. Finkel, J. Michels, K. Toutanova, B. MacCartney, M.C. de Marneffe, C.D. Manning, and A.Y. Ng. 2005. Robust textual inference using diverse knowledge sources. In *Proceedings of PASCAL Recognising Textual Entailment Workshop*.

J. C. Reynar and A. Ratnaparkhi. 1997. A maximum entropy approach to identifying sentence boundaries. In *Proceedings of the Fifth Conference on Applied Natural Language Processing*, Washington, D.C.

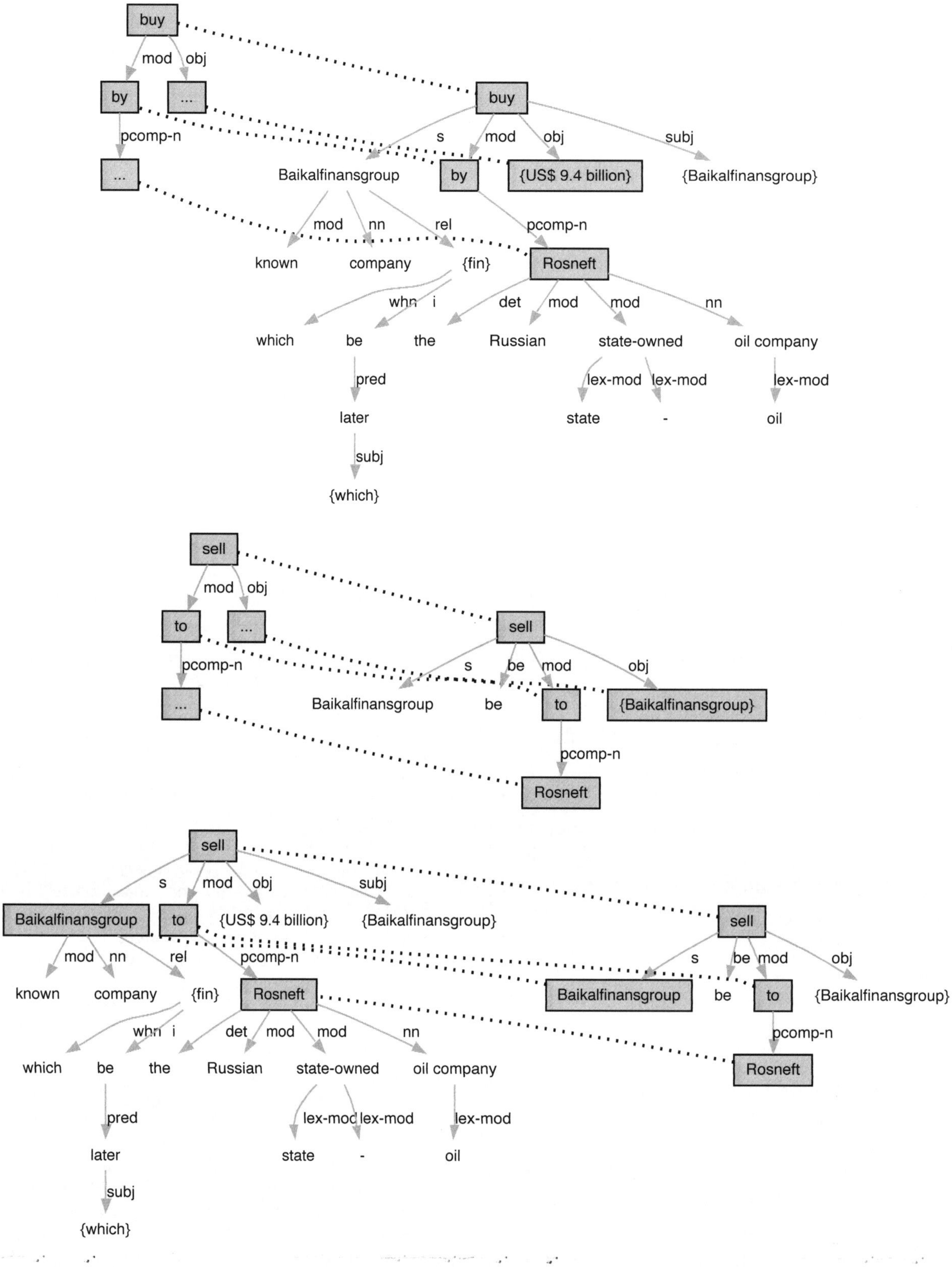

Figure 2: *Alignment of paraphrase source to text (top), alignment of paraphrase translation to hypothesis (mid), and alignment of hypothesis to paraphrased text (bottom) for pair 1 from RTE3 dev set*

Experiments of UNED at the Third Recognising Textual Entailment Challenge

Álvaro Rodrigo, Anselmo Peñas, Jesús Herrera, Felisa Verdejo
Departmento de Lenguajes y Sistemas Informáticos
Universidad Nacional de Educación a Distancia
Madrid, Spain
{alvarory, anselmo, jesus.herrera, felisa}@lsi.uned.es

Abstract

This paper describes the experiments developed and the results obtained in the participation of UNED in the Third Recognising Textual Entailment (RTE) Challenge. The experiments are focused on the study of the effect of named entities in the recognition of textual entailment. While Named Entity Recognition (NER) provides remarkable results (accuracy over 70%) for RTE on QA task, IE task requires more sophisticated treatment of named entities such as the identification of relations between them.

1 Introduction

The systems presented to the Third Recognizing Textual Entailment Challenge are based on the one presented to the Second RTE Challenge (Herrera et al., 2006b) and the ones presented to the Answer Validation Exercise (AVE) 2006 (Rodrigo et al., 2007).

Since a high quantity of pairs of RTE-3 collections contain named entities (82.6% of the hypotheses in the test collection contain at least one named entity), the objective of this work is to study the effect of named entity recognition on textual entailment in the framework of the Third RTE Challenge.

In short, the techniques involved in the experiments in order to reach these objectives are:

- Lexical overlapping between ngrams of text and hypothesis.
- Entailment between named entities.
- Branch overlapping between dependency trees of text and hypothesis.

In section 2, the main components of the systems are described in detail. Section 3 describes the information our systems use for the entailment decision. The description of the two runs submitted are given in Section 4. The results obtained and its analysis are described in Section 5. Section 6 shows a discussion of the results. Finally, some conclusions and future work are given.

2 Systems Description

The proposed systems are based on surface techniques of lexical and syntactic analysis considering each task (Information Extraction, Information Retrieval, Question Answering and Text Summarization) of the RTE Challenge independently.

The systems accept pairs of text snippets (text and hypothesis) at the input and give a boolean value at the output: YES if the text entails the hypothesis and NO otherwise. This value is obtained by the application of the learned model by a SVM classifier.

The main components of the systems are the following:

2.1 Linguistic processing

Firstly, each text-hypothesis pair is preprocessed in order to obtain the following information for the entailment decision:

- POS: a Part of Speech Tagging is performed in order to obtain lemmas for both text and hypothesis using the Freeling POS tagger (Carreras et al., 2004).

Proceedings of the Workshop on Textual Entailment and Paraphrasing, pages 89–94,
Prague, June 2007.

```
<t>...Iraq invaded Kuwait on <TIMEX>August_2_1990</TIMEX>...</t>
<h>Iraq invaded Kuwait in <NUMEX>1990</NUMEX></h>
```

Figure 1: Example of an error when disambiguating the named entity type.

```
<t>...Chernobyl accident began on
   <ENTITY>Saturday_April_26_1986</ENTITY>...</t>
<h>The Chernobyl disaster was in <ENTITY>1986</ENTITY></h>
```

Figure 2: Example of a pair that justifies the process of entailment.

```
<pair id=''5'' entailment=''NO'' task=''IE'' length=''short''>
   <t>The Communist Party USA was a small Maoist political party
   which was founded in 1965 by members of the Communist Party around
   Michael Laski who took the side of China in the Sino-Soviet split.
   </t>
   <h>Michael Laski was an opponent of China.</h>
</pair>

<pair id=''7'' entailment=''NO'' task=''IE'' length=''short''>
   <t>Sandra Goudie was first elected to Parliament in the 2002
   elections, narrowly winning the seat of Coromandel by defeating
   Labour candidate Max Purnell and pushing incumbent Green MP
   Jeanette Fitzsimons into third place.</t>
   <h>Sandra Goudie was defeated by Max Purnell.</h>
</pair>

<pair id=''8'' entailment=''NO'' task=''IE'' length=''short''>
   <t>Ms. Minton left Australia in 1961 to pursue her studies in
   London.</t>
   <h>Ms. Minton was born in Australia.</h>
</pair>
```

Figure 3: IE pairs with entailment between named entities but not between named entities relations.

- NER: the Freeling Named Entity Recogniser is also applied to recover the information needed by the named entity entailment module that is described in the following section. Numeric expressions, proper nouns and temporal expressions of each text and hypothesis are tagged.

- Dependency analysis: a dependency tree of each text and hypothesis is obtained using Lin's Minipar (Lin, 1998).

2.2 Entailment between named entities

Once the named entities of the hypothesis and the text are detected, the next step is to determine the entailment relations between the named entities in the text and the named entities in the hypothesis. In (Rodrigo et al., 2007) the following entailment relations between named entities were defined:

1. A Proper Noun E1 entails a Proper Noun E2 if the text string of E1 contains the text string of E2.

2. A Time Expression T1 entails a Time Expression T2 if the time range of T1 is included in the time range of T2.

3. A numeric expression N1 entails a numeric expression N2 if the range associated to N2 encloses the range of N1.

Some characters change in different expressions of the same named entity as, for example, in a proper noun with different wordings (e.g. *Yasser, Yaser, Yasir*). To detect the entailment in these situations, when the previous process fails, we implemented a modified entailment decision process taking into account the edit distance of Levenshtein (Levensthein, 1966). Thus, if two named entities differ in less than 20%, then we assume that exists an entailment relation between these named entities.

However, this definition of named entities entailment does not support errors due to wrong named entities classification as we can see in Figure 1. The expression 1990 represents a year but it is recognised as a numeric expression in the hypothesis. However the same expression is recognised as a temporal expression in the text and, therefore, the expression in the hypothesis cannot be entailed by it according to the named entities entailment definition above.

We quantified the effect of these errors in recognising textual entailment. For this purpose, we developed the following two settings:

1. A system based in dependency analysis and WordNet (Herrera et al., 2006b) that uses the categorization given by the NER tool, where the entailment relations between named entities are the previously ones defined.

2. The same system based on dependency analysis and WordNet but not using the categorization given by the NER tool. All named entities detected receive the same tag and a named entity E1 entails a named entity E2 if the text string of E1 contains the text string of E2 (see Figure 2).

We checked the performance of these two settings over the test corpus set of the Second RTE Challenge. The results obtained, using the accuracy measure that is the fraction of correct responses according to (Dagan et al., 2006), are shown in table 1. The table shows that with an easier and a more robust processing (NER without classification) the performance is not only maintained, but it is even slightly higher.

This fact led us to ignore the named entity categorization given by the tool and assume that text and hypothesis are related and close texts where same expressions must receive same categories, without the need of classification. Thus, all detected named entities receive the same tag and we consider that a named entity E1 entails a named entity E2 if the text string of E1 contains the text string of E2.

Table 1: Entailment between numeric expressions.

	Accuracy
Setting 1	0.610
Setting 2	0.614

2.3 Sentence level matching

A tree matching module, which searches for matching branches into the hypotheses' dependency trees, is used. There is a potential matching branch per leaf. A branch from the hypothesis is considered a "matching branch" only if all its nodes from the root to the leaf are involved in a lexical entailment (Herrera et al., 2006a). In this way, the subtree conformed by all the matching branches from a hypothesis' dependency tree is included in the respective text's dependency tree, giving an idea of tree inclusion.

We assumed that the larger is the included subtree of the hypothesis' dependency tree, the more semantically similar are the text and the hypothesis. Thus, the existence or absence of an entailment relation from a text to its respective hypothesis considers the portion of the hypothesis' tree that is included in the text's tree.

3 Entailment decision

A SVM classifier was applied in order to train a model from the development corpus. The model was trained with a set of features obtained from the processing described above. The features we have used and the training strategies were the following:

3.1 Features

We prepared the following features to feed the SVM model:

1. Percentage of nodes of the hypothesis' dependency tree pertaining to matching branches according to section 2.3 considering, respectively:
    - Lexical entailment between the words of the snippets involved.
    - Lexical entailment between the lemmas of the snippets involved.
2. Percentage of words of the hypothesis in the text (treated as bags of words).
3. Percentage of unigrams (lemmas) of the hypothesis in the text (treated as bags of lemmas).
4. Percentage of bigrams (lemmas) of the hypothesis in the text (treated as bags of lemmas).
5. Percentage of trigrams (lemmas) of the hypothesis in the text (treated as bags of lemmas).
6. A boolean value indicating if there is or not any named entity in the hypothesis that is not entailed by one or more named entities in the text according to the named entity entailment decision described in section 2.2.

Table 2: Experiments with separate training over the development corpus using cross validation.

	Accuracy with the same model for all tasks	Accuracy with a different model for each task
Setting 1	0.64	0.67
Setting 2	0.62	0.66

Table 3: Experiments with separate training over the test corpus.

	Accuracy with the same model for all tasks	Accuracy with a different model for each task
Setting 1	0.59	0.62
Setting 2	0.60	0.64

Table 4: Results for run 1 and run 2.

	Accuracy	
	run 1	run 2
IE	52.50%	53.50%
IR	67%	67%
QA	72%	72%
SUM	58%	60%
Overall	62.38%	63.12%

3.2 Training

About the decision of how to perform the training in our SVM models, we wanted to study the effect of training a unique model compared to training one different model per task.

For this purpose we used the following two settings:

1. A SVM model that uses features 2, 3, 4 and 5 from section 3.1.
2. A SVM model that uses features 2, 3, 4, 5 and 6 from section 3.1.

Each setting was training using cross validation over the development set of the Third RTE Challenge in two different ways:

1. Training a unique model for all pairs.

2. Training one model for each task. Each model is trained with only pairs from the same task that the model will predict.

The results obtained in the experiments are shown in table 2. As we can see in the table, with the training of one model for each task results are slightly better, increasing performance of both settings. Taking into account these results, we took the decision of using a different training for each task in the runs submitted.

Our decision was confirmed after the runs submission to RTE-3 Challenge with new experiments over the RTE-3 test corpus, using the RTE-3 development corpus as training (see table 3 for results).

4 Runs Submitted

Two different runs were submitted to the Third RTE Challenge. Each run was trained using the method described in section 3.2 with the following subset of the features described in section 3.1:

- Run 1 was obtained using the features 2, 3, 4 and 5 from section 3.1. These features obtained good results for pairs from the QA task, as we can see in (Rodrigo et al., 2007), and we wanted to check their performance in other tasks.

- Run 2 was obtained using the following features for each task:
  - IE: features 2, 3, 4, 5 and 6 from section 3.1. These ones were the features that obtained the best results for IE pairs in our experiments over the development set.
  - IR: features 2, 3, 4 and 5 from section 3.1. These ones were the features that obtained best results for IR pairs in our experiments over the development set.
  - QA: feature 6 from section 3.1. We chose this feature, which had obtained an accuracy over 70% in previous experiments over the development set in QA pairs, to study the effect of named entities in QA pairs.
  - SUM: features 1, 2 and 3 from section 3.1. We selected these features to show the importance of dependency analysis in SUM pairs as it is shown in section 6.

5 Results

Accuracy was applied as the main measure to the participating systems.

The results obtained over the test corpus for the two runs submitted are shown in table 4.

As we can see in both runs, different accuracy values are obtained depending on the task. The best result is obtained in pairs from QA with a 72% accuracy in the two runs, although two different systems are applied. This result pushes us to use this system for Answer Validation (Peñas et al., 2007). Results in run 2, which uses a different setting for each task, are slightly better than results in run 1, but only in IE and SUM. However, results are too close to accept a confirmation of our initial intuition that pairs from different tasks could need not only a different training, but also the use of different approaches for the entailment decision.

6 Discussion

In run 2 we used NER for IE and QA, the two tasks with the higher percentage of pairs with at least one named entity in the hypothesis (98.5% in IE and 97% in QA).

Our previous work about the use of named entities in textual entailment (Rodrigo et al., 2007) suggested that NER permitted to obtain good results. However, after the RTE-3 experience, we found that the use of NER does not improve results in all tasks, but only in QA in a solid way with the previous work.

We performed a qualitative study over the IE pairs showing that, as it can be expected, in pairs from IE the relations between named entities are more important that named entities themselves.

Figure 3 shows some examples where all named entities are entailed but not the relation between them. In pair 5 both *Michael Laski* and *China* are entailed but the relation between them is *took the side of* in the text, and *was an opponent of* in the hypothesis. The same problem appears in the other pairs with the relation *left* instead *was born in* (pair 8) or passive voice instead active voice (pair 7).

Comparing run 1 and run 2, dependency analysis shows its usefulness in SUM pairs, where texts and hypotheses have a higher syntactic parallelism than in pairs from other tasks. This statement is shown

Table 5: Percentage of hypothesis nodes in matching branches.

	Percentage
SUM	75,505%
IE	7,353%
IR	6,422%
QA	8,496%

in table 5 where the percentage of hypothesis nodes pertaining to matching branches in the dependency tree is much higher in SUM pairs than in the rest of tasks.

This syntactic parallelism seems to be the responsible for the 2% increasing between the first and the second run in SUM pairs.

7 Conclusions and future work

The experiments have been focused on the study of the importance of considering entailment between named entities in the recognition of textual entailment, and the use of a separate training for each task. As we have seen, both approaches increase slightly the accuracy of the proposed systems. As we have also shown, different approaches for each task could also increase the system performance.

Future work is focused on improving the performance in IE pairs taking into account relations between named entities.

Acknowledgments

This work has been partially supported by the Spanish Ministry of Science and Technology within the project R2D2-SyEMBRA (TIC-2003-07158-C04-02), the Regional Government of Madrid under the Research Network MAVIR (S-0505/TIC-0267), the Education Council of the Regional Government of Madrid and the European Social Fund.

References

X. Carreras, I. Chao, L. Padró, and M. Padró. 2004. *FreeLing: An Open-Source Suite of Language Analyzers..* In Proceedings of the 4th International Conference on Language Resources and Evaluation (LREC04). Lisbon, Portugal, 2004.

I. Dagan, O. Glickman and B. Magnini. 2006. *The PASCAL Recognising Textual Entailment Challenge.* In Quiñonero-Candela et al., editors, MLCW 2005, LNAI Volume 3944, Jan 2006, Pages 177 - 190.

J. Herrera, A. Peñas and F. Verdejo. 2006a. *Textual Entailment Recognition Based on Dependency Analysis and WordNet.* In Quiñonero-Candela et al., editors, MLCW 2005, LNAI Volume 3944, Jan 2006, Pages 231-239.

J. Herrera, A. Peñas, Á. Rodrigo and F. Verdejo. 2006b. *UNED at PASCAL RTE-2 Challenge.* In Proceedings of the Second PASCAL Challenges Workshop on Recognising Textual Entailment, Venice, Italy.

V. I. Levensthein. 1966. *Binary Codes Capable of Correcting Deletions, Insertions and Reversals.* In Soviet Physics - Doklady, volume 10, pages 707710, 1966.

D. Lin. 1998. *Dependency-based Evaluation of MINIPAR.* Workshop on the Evaluation of Parsing Systems, Granada, Spain, May, 1998.

A. Peñas, Á. Rodrigo, V. Sama and F. Verdejo. 2007. *Overview of the Answer Validation Exercise 2006.* In Lecture Notes in Computer Science. In press.

Á. Rodrigo, A. Peñas, J. Herrera and F. Verdejo. 2007. *The Effect of Entity Recognition on Answer Validation.* In Lecture Notes in Computer Science. In press.

Textual Entailment Using Univariate Density Model and Maximizing Discriminant Function

Scott Settembre
SNePS Research Group, Department of Computer Science and Engineering
University at Buffalo
Buffalo, NY 14214, USA
ss424@cse.buffalo.edu

Abstract

The primary focuses of this entry this year was firstly, to develop a framework to allow multiple researchers from our group to easily contribute metrics measuring textual entailment, and secondly, to provide a baseline which we could use in our tools to evaluate and compare new metrics. A development environment tool was created to quickly allow for testing of various metrics and to easily randomize the development and test sets. For each test, this RTE tool calculated two sets of results by applying the metrics to both a univariate Gaussian density and by maximizing a linear discriminant function. The metrics used for the submission were a lexical similarity metric and a lexical similarity metric using synonym and antonym replacement. The two submissions for RTE 2007 scored an accuracy of 61.00% and 62.62%.

1 Introduction

The task of textual entailment for the PASCAL Textual Entailment Challenge for 2007 was to create a system to determine if a given pair of sentences, called the Text-Hypothesis (T-H) pair, had the property of having the Text sentence entail the Hypothesis sentence. Each Text-Hypothesis pair is also assigned the type of entailment that should be applied to the pair when evaluating its entailment. There are four types of entailment, each of which may or may not need different techniques to determine entailment, and for the purposes of the RTE tool developed, are considered separate problems.

2 RTE Development Environment Tool

Our research group decided to begin focusing on the Recognizing Textual Entailment challenge this year in February and to continue our participation for years to come. It was decided to create a development environment from which our researchers could attempt different techniques of examining a Text-Hypothesis pair and yet all metrics resulting from those techniques could be used in calculating the final results. The RTE tool also randomly generates training and testing sets from the 800 Text-Hypothesis pairs provided for development by the competition to avoid over-fitting the data during the training stage.

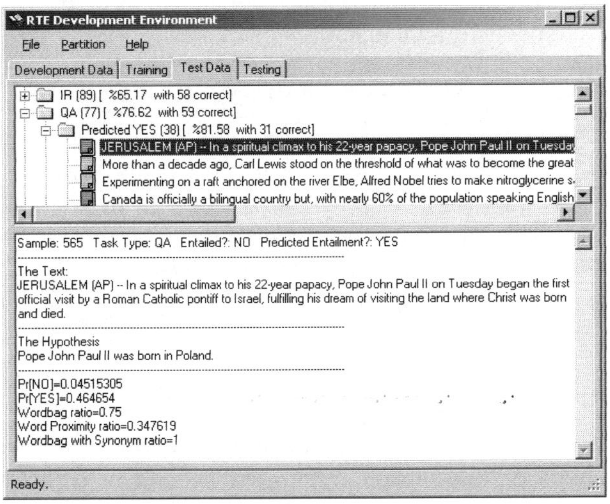

Figure 1. Screenshot of the RTE Development Environment.

Proceedings of the Workshop on Textual Entailment and Paraphrasing, pages 95–100,
Prague, June 2007.

The RTE Tool can generate a metric by calling a .NET object, COM object, web page, command line, or an internal function. These metrics are cached to speed testing, though a specific metric type can be cleared manually should the object or function generating the metric be changed.

In the image of the RTE tool above, we can see a typical results screen. We have a misclassified sample highlighted and all the relevant data for that sample displayed on the bottom. Each category is represented with a folder and displays the accuracy results of the last classification. In this way, we can easily compare and contrast different metrics and their effectiveness on the samples in a simple and intuitive way.

2.1 Defining Metrics

Each metric developed is required to produce a continuous variable that can measure a feature of the T-H pair. The metric value is required to be normalized between 0 and 1 inclusive so that we can use the same metrics for future expansion when possibly dealing with nearest-neighbor classification techniques and not be subject to scaling issues. This is also valuable if we intend to develop vague predicates [Brachman and Levesque, 2004] to use in Boolean rules, another potential classification implementation.

There is also currently a constraint that the metric value "0" means the least entailment (according to that particular metric) and the value "1" means the most entailment. This helped create an easy way to maximize our linear discriminant function (which will be described below). This constraint is unnecessary when classifying using the univariate density model.

2.2 Classification Methods

The tool classifies a T-H test pair using one of two classification methods. The first method uses the metrics of the training set to generate the parameters for eight Gaussian distributions, or two distributions for each type of textual entailment. Each distribution describes a *probability density function* (PDF) for a particular type of entailment. For example, there is one PDF for the entailment type of "Question Answering" (QA) whose entailment is "YES", and there is one PDF for the entailment type of QA whose entailment is "NO". This univariate normal model was chosen to simplify the calculations over the multivariate model we planned to use. Since the submissions would only consider one metric for each run, instead of using all the metrics we have defined, the univariate model was appropriate.

The second method of classification uses the metrics from the training set to develop a linear decision boundary to maximize the accuracy outcome in the test set. Once this boundary, or threshold, is determined for each of the four types of entailment, a simple comparison of the metric from a T-H pair can be classified based on what side of the boundary it is on. This linear discriminant function had a further constraint that required the metric values be described in a certain way to simplify the classification function. This requirement will be lifted for our next submission in order to deal with solution landscapes that may not adhere to our Gaussian distribution model.

3 Metric Set Used for Submission

Three different metrics were developed for use in our RTE tool this year. We decided to concentrate on producing simple measurements to create a baseline for which to judge the development of new metrics as well as to judge the performance of future training or classification methods.

Due to time constraints, we chose to employ simple metrics, which have been used before, in order to meet our primary goals. Despite the simplicity and the lack of semantic interpretation of the metrics, these metrics coupled with our pattern classification strategy yielded competitive results.

3.1 Lexical Similarity Ratio Metric

Our first metric is a simple lexical similarity ratio between the words in the Text and Hypothesis sentences in a T-H pair. The formula counts number of matches between the occurrences of a word in the Hypothesis and the words in the Text. The sum is then normalized by dividing it by the number of words in the Hypothesis itself. For baseline purposes, every word was considered and only punctuation was removed. This technique was also used by other teams in previous challenge submissions [Jijkoun and Rijke, 2005].

3.2 Average Matched Word Displacement

Our second metric was not used in the final results, but will be described for completeness. This metric was the average of the distances in the Text between matched words from the Hypothesis normalized by dividing that average by the maximum possible distance. In other words, if two words in the Hypothesis were found in the Text, the distance between them in the Text would be averaged with all the other combinations of matched word pair distances and then normalized by dividing the maximum possible distance value for that particular sentence. Preliminary results showed a less than significant correlation and so were not used in this submission.

3.3 Synonym and Antonym Replacement

The third metric is nearly identical to the lexical similarity metric defined above except that if a word in the Hypothesis sentence is not matched, then all its synonyms and antonyms are also searched for in the Text sentence. Any synonym matches raise the score and any antonym matches lower the score by a fixed amount, and in this case arbitrarily selected as ±1 (before normalization). A Microsoft Word 2003 COM object was used to search for the synonyms and antonyms from Microsoft Word's lexical database.

4 Classification used for Submission

Two different types of classification methods were used to classify entailment for a Text-Hypothesis pair. Both types are described below.

We chose to initially keep our classification models simple and easy to visualize so that both our experienced and inexperienced research group members could participate. The "No Free Lunch Theorem" [Duda, Hart, and Stork, 2001] shows that there is no inherent benefit to any specific classifier[1], and since the more important task of generating the metrics[2] crosses academic disciplines in our research group, we found communicating in terms of a Gaussian distribution was easily understood.

4.1 Univariate Normal Model

The continuous univariate normal model, or Gaussian density, allows us to calculate p(x), or the probability that feature x will appear in a dataset. The data points in the given dataset is assumed to be distributed in a Gaussian distribution, sometimes referred to as a bell curve. Of course if the data points in that data set turn out to be distributed in a non-Gaussian curve (i.e. exponential curve or even linear) or multimodal curve (more than one peak), then we may not be able to draw any conclusions. For the purposes of our metrics, we are assuming a Gaussian distribution, and encourage the developer of the metric function to attempt to fit the metric results into Gaussian curve.

The two parameters of interest are the mean μ and the variance σ^2, of the data points. With these two parameters, we are essentially able to calculate the *probability density function* (PDF) for the category. After calculating these parameters from the development data set, we can apply the following formula to generate the probability, *p*(x), of a sample, where x is the metric value we wish to classify.

$$p(x) = \frac{1}{\sqrt{2\pi\sigma}} \exp\left[-\frac{1}{2}\left(\frac{x-\mu}{\sigma} \right)^2 \right]$$

During the training step, the mean of a category is calculated. The following formula does this calculation, where n is the number of samples, and x_i is a particular metric of the ith sample:

$$\mu = \frac{\sum_{i=1}^{n} x_i}{n}$$

Also during the training step, the variance of a category is also calculated, with this formula:

$$\sigma^2 = \frac{\sum_{i=1}^{n} x_i^2 - \left(\sum_{i=1}^{n} x_i\right)^2 / n}{n}$$

For each type of entailment, there are two classifiers: one classifier for "YES" and one classifier for "NO", representing the two categories. During the *training* step, the mean and variance parameters are calculated directly from the metrics that

[1] For "good generalization performance, there are no context-independent or usage-independent reasons to favor one learning or classification method over another."

[2] Since we are creating the metrics, we are attempting to distribute the values in a Gaussian curve. This becomes a "context" which we can favor a classifier that will classify the data better, such as the univariate normal model. Our goal is to create a better metric and not necessarily to find a better classifier.

come from the development data. During the *testing* step, the specified metric is calculated for the T-H pair, and using the univariate normal formula, we can calculate the probability that the calculated metric is in the "YES" category or the "NO" category. Then which ever result is larger, that category is chosen as the answer.

To understand the limitations of this method, we have a quick example. Here is a parameter list of each category as well as the decisions that were made from them:

(IE,NO) = { μ = 0.6867668 , σ = 0.1824087}
(IE,YES) = { μ = 0.6874263 , σ = 0.1622136}
(IR,NO) = { μ = 0.3649016 , σ = 0.1984567}
(IR,YES) = { μ = 0.5888839 , σ = 0.2035728}
(QA,NO) = { μ = 0.4470804 , σ = 0.1821738}
(QA,YES) = { μ = 0.7330091 , σ = 0.1873602}
(SUM,NO) = { μ = 0.4470848 , σ = 0.2625011}
(SUM,YES) = { μ = 0.657442 , σ = 0.250246}

Overall correct entailments made: 492 out of 800.
Overall probability of success : 0.615

IE (200) [%47.5 with 95 correct]
  Predicted YES (0) [%NaN with 0 correct]
  Predicted NO (200) [%47.5 with 95 correct]
IR (200) [%66.5 with 133 correct]
  Predicted YES (76) [%63.16 with 48 correct]
  Predicted NO (124) [%68.55 with 85 correct]
QA (200) [%73.5 with 147 correct]
  Predicted YES (95) [%77.89 with 74 correct]
  Predicted NO (105) [%69.52 with 73 correct]
SUM (200) [%58.5 with 117 correct]
  Predicted YES (133) [%60.9 with 81 correct]
  Predicted NO (67) [%53.73 with 36 correct]

As we can see, the two categories (IE,NO) and (IE,YES) are very similar in mean, μ. This essentially translates to two Gaussian curves peaking at the same point, which would cause an overlap that would favor the curve with the larger variance during the calculation of p(x). If we look at the results using these parameters, we can see that in the "IE" type of entailment all decisions were made in favor of that category. This does not mean that there is an error, just that the distribution of this metric is too similar and so probably is not a good metric to use in deciding the classification for that category. Whereas in entailment type "QA", we find that this metric does indeed divide the categories into two curves that are quite separated, and so yields a good accuracy.

4.2 Maximizing the Discriminant Function

This is the easiest way the RTE tool calculates whether a T-H pair is in a specific category. If a metric is less-than a specific threshold, then the T-H pair is classified as "NO", and if it is above the threshold, then the pair is classified as "YES". Each type of entailment has its own discriminant function and therefore, there are only four classifiers or in this case, technically defined as four *dichotomizers*.

Each threshold is calculated using a brute force iterative technique. After the metric is calculated for each sample, the RTE tool simply increments the threshold a certain fixed amount (arbitrarily selected as 0.001 each each iteration) and records the accuracy over the entire development data set for that iteration. As the process concludes after one thousand iterations (that is, moving the threshold from 0 to 1 in .001 increments), the threshold with the maximum accuracy is selected as the threshold for that classifier. This, however, places a constraint on the way the metric needs to be defined, as described above in section 2.1.

5 Results

There are four result sets representing each of the metrics used paired with each of the classification strategies used. The first table below shows the actual results, broken down into each type of entailment, using the released annotated test set. The second table shows our results by randomly splitting the development dataset 80%/20% into a training set (80%) and a testing set (20%). From the results listed in the second table, it was decided which metric/classification pair would be used in our final submission.

Although we cannot truly compare results from this competition to last years RTE 2 competition, we found that our results seemed quite competitive. [Bar-Haim, Dagan, et al. 2006] We do recognize that some of our metrics have already been employed by other teams [Jijkoun and Rijke, 2005] and that our results may be different because of the thesaurus corpus we employed and the classification strategy we used.

5.1 Actual Results

The actual results are based on training the RTE tool we developed on the released annotated development dataset and then applying the trained classifiers on the test dataset. In this table, each column represents a training metric used with a classification method. For the two metrics used, "LS" represents Lexical Similarity, while "LR" represents Lexical Similarity with Synonym and Antonym Replacement (or Lexical Replacement for short). For the two types of classification used, "UN" represents the Univariate Normal model, while "DM" represents Linear Discriminant Maximization.

	LS+UN	LR+UN	LS+DM	LR+DM
Overall	0.615	**0.626**	**0.61**	0.629
IE	0.475	0.510	0.495	0.505
IR	0.665	0.630	0.635	0.640
QA	0.735	0.750	0.750	0.750
SUM	0.585	0.615	0.560	0.620

As the reader can see, our final submissions' scores were not the maximal ones from the table. Our first submission we submitted scored 61% and our second submission scored 62.62%. For our first submission, the Lexical Similarity metric was used in conjunction with the Linear Discriminant Maximization model for classification. For our second submission, our Lexical Replacement metric was used in combination with the Univariate Normal model of classification. These two combinations were chosen, however, from the training results below.

5.2 Training results

Using these results, it was decided to pick the maximal overall accuracy using both metrics. It was assumed that the same correlations found in the development dataset would be found in the testing dataset. Though this did not ring true in actuality, the final results using either method were quite close.

	LS+UN	LR+UN	LS+DM	LR+DM
Overall	0.669	**0.675**	**0.717**	0.644
IE	0.425	0.575	0.625	0.600
IR	0.688	0.667	0.688	0.646
QA	0.811	0.784	0.811	0.784
SUM	0.771	0.686	0.775	0.543

6 Conclusions and Future Enhancements

The lexical similarity metric and its variants obviously have some correlation to whether a Text-Hypothesis pair has entailment or not. Though we were surprised by the results (from our runs exceeding results from other teams' runs from previous years) and at how well they worked initially, further investigation found the accuracy of certain types of entailment, especially Information Extraction (IE), lacking and perhaps making some metrics almost irrelevant as a viable metric.

By focusing our efforts this year on developing a tool to test various methods of classification and metrics, we created an excellent way to develop our ideas and distribute our research efforts among researchers. The RTE Development Environment will help us coordinate our efforts and allow small gains in any individual metric to contribute to the overall classification in a proportionately significant way.

For future enhancements, we intend to apply the multivariate model to process a metric vector in determining classification instead of just considering one metric at a time (as we did in the univariate model). In addition, we intend to extend our metrics to consider semantic interpretations and comparisons between the Text-Hypothesis pair.

We feel that our overall success was illuminating to the larger task at hand and we are looking forward to applying our decision making framework to next year's submission. Judging by our results, the simplicity of our approach will quite possibly yield a competitive entailment strategy even in comparison to more syntactic or semantic decompositions of the sentence pairs at this time.

Our primary success, over the three week period in which we addressed this problem, was the development of a tool and a process by which members of our research group can interact. The pooling of expertise from our linguistics, computer science, and cognitive science disciplines and constructing our future plan of action culminated in the development of this tool, benchmarks for our group, and constraints in which we can operate efficiently and address this problem with more depth in the future.

7 Acknowledgements

We would like to thank Dr. Stuart Shapiro and Dr. William Rapaport of the SNePS Research Group, University at Buffalo, for their encouragement and guidance in this year and in the years to come.

Special thanks to Dr. Sargur Srihari of CEDAR, "Center of Excellence for Document Analysis and Recognition", University at Buffalo, for providing insight into various classification techniques. Finally, we congratulate our members of the SNePS Research Group for their contributions over the short amount of time we had to address this challenge this year.

References

Roy Bar-Haim, Ido Dagan, Bill Dolan, Lisa Ferro, Danilo Giampiccolo, Bernardo Magnini and Idan Szpektor. 2006. The Second PASCAL Recognising Textual Entailment Challenge. In *Proceedings of the Second PASCAL Challenges Workshop on Recognising Textual Entailment.*

Ronald J. Brachman and Hector J. Levesque. 2004. *Knowledge Representation and Reasoning.* Morgan Kaufmann Publishers, San Francisco, CA.

Richard O. Duda, Peter E. Hart, David G. Stork. *Pattern Classification.* Wily, New York, second edition, 2001.

Valentin Jijkoun and Maarten de Rijke. *Recognizing Textual Entailment Using Lexical Similarity.* Proceedings of the PASCAL Challenges Workshop on Recognising Textual Entailment, 2005.

The Role of Sentence Structure in Recognizing Textual Entailment

Catherine Blake
School of Information and Library Science
University of North Carolina at Chapel Hill
Chapel Hill, NC 27599-3360
cablake@email.unc.edu

Abstract

Recent research suggests that sentence structure can improve the accuracy of recognizing textual entailments and paraphrasing. Although background knowledge such as gazetteers, WordNet and custom built knowledge bases are also likely to improve performance, our goal in this paper is to characterize the syntactic features alone that aid in accurate entailment prediction. We describe candidate features, the role of machine learning, and two final decision rules. These rules resulted in an accuracy of 60.50 and 65.87% and average precision of 58.97 and 60.96% in $RTE3_{Test}$ and suggest that sentence structure alone can improve entailment accuracy by 9.25 to 14.62% over the baseline majority class.

1 Introduction

Understanding written language is a non-trivial task. It takes years for children to read, and ambiguities of written communication remain long after we learn the basics. Despite these apparent complexities, the bag-of-words (BOW) approach, which ignores structure both within a sentence and within a document, continues to dominate information retrieval, and to some extent document summarization and paraphrasing and entailment systems.

The rational behind the BOW approach is in part simplicity (it is much easier and less computationally expensive to compare terms in one sentence with terms in another, than to generate the sentence structure); and in part accuracy, the BOW approach continues to achieve similar if not improved performance than information retrieval systems employing deep language or logical based representations. This performance is surprising when you consider that a BOW approach could not distinguish between the very different meaning conveyed by: `(1)Slow down so that you don't hit the riders on the road` and `(2)Don't slow down so you hit the riders on the road.` A system that employed a syntactic representation of these sentences however, could detect that the `don't` modifier applies to `hit` in first sentence and to `slow` second.

In contrast to information retrieval, researchers in paraphrase and entailment detection have increased their use of sentence structure. Fewer than half of the submissions in the first Recognizing Textual Entailment challenge (RTE1) employed syntax (13/28, 46%) (Dagan, Glickman, & Magnini, 2005), but more than two-thirds (28/41, 68%) of the second RTE challenge (RTE2) submissions employed syntax (Bar-Haim et al., 2006). Furthermore, for the first time, the RTE2 results showed that systems employing deep language features, such as syntactic or logical representations of text, could outperform the purely semantic overlap approach typified by BOW. Earlier findings such as (Vanderwende, Coughlin, & Dolan, 2005) also suggest that sentence structure plays an important role in recognizing textual entailment and paraphrasing accurately.

Our goal in this paper is to explore the degree to which sentence structure alone influences the accuracy of entailment and paraphrase detection.

Proceedings of the Workshop on Textual Entailment and Paraphrasing, pages 101–106,
Prague, June 2007.

Other than a lexicon (which is used to identify the base form of a term), our approach uses no background knowledge, such as WordNet (Miller, 1995), extensive dictionaries (Litkowski, 2006) or custom-built knowledge-bases (Hickl et al., 2006) that have been successfully employed by other systems. While such semantic knowledge should improve entailment performance, we deliberately avoid these sources to isolate the impact of sentence structure alone.

2 System Architecture

2.1 Lexical Processing

Our approach requires an explicit representation of structure in both the hypothesis (HSent) and test (TSent) sentence(s). Systems in RTE challenges employ a variety of parsers. In RTE2 the most popular sentence structure was generated by Minipar (Lin, 1998), perhaps because it is also one of the fastest parsers. Our system uses the typed dependency tree generated by the Stanford Parser (Klein & Manning, 2002). A complete set of parser tags and the method used to map from a constituent to a typed dependency grammar can be found in (de Marneffe et al., 2006). Figure 1 shows an example typed dependency grammar for pair id 355 in the $\text{RTE3}_{\text{Test}}$ set.

2.2 Lexicon

Our proposed approach requires the base form of each term. We considered two lexicons for this purpose: WordNet (Miller, 1995) and the SPECIALIST lexicon (National Library of Medicine, 2000). The latter is part of the National Library of Medicine's (NLM) Unified Medical Language System (UMLS) and comprises terms drawn from medical abstracts, and dictionaries, both medical and contemporary.

With 412,149 entries, the SPECIALIST lexicon (version 2006AA) is substantially larger than the 5,947 entries in WordNet (Version 3.0). To understand the level of overlap between the lexicons we loaded both into an oracle database. Our subsequent analysis revealed that of the WordNet entries, 5008 (84.1%) had a morphological base form in the SPECIALIST lexicon. Of the 548 distinct entries that differed between the two lexicons, 389 differed because either the UMLS (214 terms) or WordNet (11 terms) did not have a base form. These results suggest that although the NLM did not develop their lexicon for news articles, the entries in the SPECIALIST lexicon subsumes most terms found in the more frequently used WordNet lexicon. Thus, our system uses the base form of terms from the SPECIALIST lexicon.

2.3 Collapsing Preposition Paths

Previous work (Lin & Pantel, 2001) suggests the utility of collapsing paths through prepositions. The type dependency does have a preposition tag, prep, however, we found that the parser typically assigns a more general tag, such as dep (see the dep tag in Figure 1 between wrapped and by). Instead of using the prep tag, the system collapses paths that contain a preposition from the SPECIALIST lexicon. For example, the system

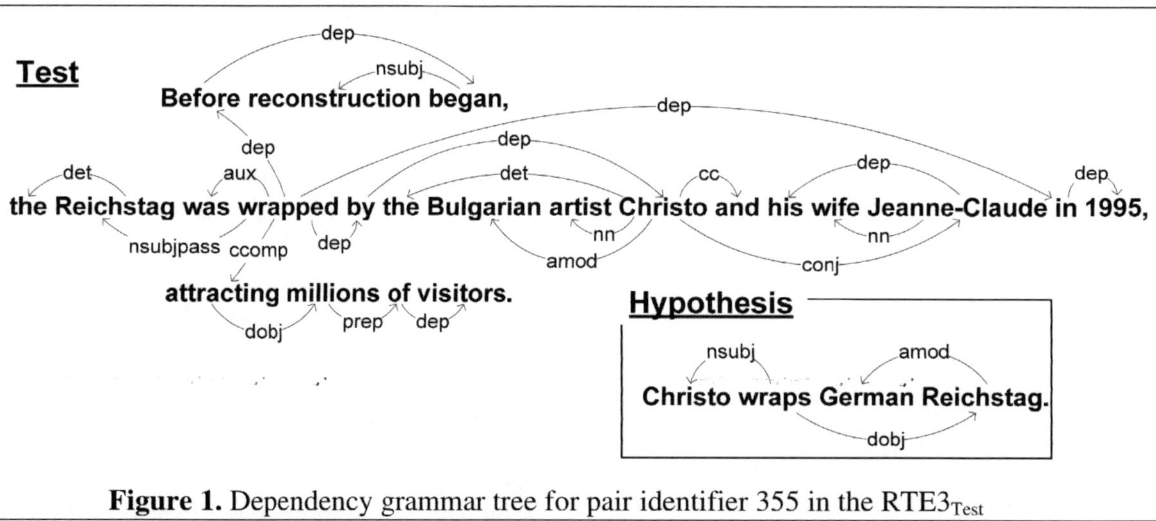

Figure 1. Dependency grammar tree for pair identifier 355 in the $\text{RTE3}_{\text{Test}}$

collapses four paths in $TSent_{EG}$ millions of visitors, wrapped in 1995, wrapped by Christo, and wrapped began before.

2.4 Base Level Sentence Features

The typed dependency grammar, such as that shown in Figure 1, can produce many different features that may indicate entailment. Our current implementation uses the following four base level features.

(1) Subject: The system identifies the subject(s) of a sentence using heuristics and the parser subject tags nsubjpass and nsubj.
(2) Object: The system uses the parser tag dobj to identify the object(s) in each sentence.
(3) Verb: The system tags all terms linked with either the subject or the object as a verb. For example, wrapped is tagged as the verb wrap from the link wrapped nsubjpass Reichstag shown in Figure 1.
(4) Preposition: As described in section 2.3 the system collapses paths that include a preposition.

The subject feature had the most coverage of the base level features and the system identified at least one subject for 789 of the 800 hypotheses sentences in $RTE3_{Devmt}$. We wrote heuristics that use the parser tags to identify the subject of the remaining 11 sentences. The system found subjects for seven of those eight remaining hypothesis sentences (3 were duplicate sentences). In contrast, the object feature had the least coverage, with the system identifying objects for only 480 of the 800 hypotheses in the RTE3 revised development set ($RTE3_{Devmt}$).

In addition to the head noun of a subject, modifying nouns can also be important to recognize entailment. Consider the underlined section of $TSent_{EG}$: which was later bought by <u>the Russian state-owned oil company Rosneft</u>. This sentence would lend support to hypotheses sentences that start with The Baikalfinasgroup was bought by … and end with any of the following phrases an oil company, a company, Rosneft, the Rosneft Company, the Rosneft oil company, a Russian company, a Russian Oil company, a state-owned company etc. Our system ensures the detection of these valid entailments by adding noun compounds and all modifiers associated with the subject and object term.

2.5 Derived Sentence Features

We reviewed previous RTE challenges and a subset of $RTE3_{Devmt}$ sentences before arriving at the following derived features that build on the base level features described in 2.4. The features that use 'opposite' approximate the difference between passive and active tense. For each hypothesis sentence, the system records both the number of matches (#match), and the percentage of matches (%match) that are supported by the test sentence(s).

(1) Triple: The system compares the subject-verb-objects in HSent with the corresponding triple in TSent.
(2) Triple Opposite: The system matches the verbs in both HSent and TSent, but matches the subject in HSent with the object in TSent.
(3) Triple Subject Object: This feature approximates the triple in (1) by comparing only the subject and the object in HSent with TSent, but ignoring the verb.
(4) Triple Subject Object Opposite: The system compares the objects in HSent with the subjects in TSent.
(5) Subject Subject: In addition to the triples used in the derived features 1-4, the system stores subject-verb and object-verb pairs. This feature compares the distinct number of subjects in HSent with those in TSent.
(6) Verb Verb: The system compares only the verb in the subject-verb, object-verb tuples in HSent with those in TSent.
(7) Subject Verb: The system compares the distinct subjects in HSent with the distinct verbs in TSent.
(8) Verb Subject: The system compares the verb in HSent with the subject in TSent.
(9) Verb Preposition: The system compares both the preposition and verb in HSent with those in TSent.
(10) Subject Preposition: The system compares both the subject and preposition in HSent with those in TSent.
(11) Subject Word: The system compares the distinct subjects in HSent with the distinct words in TSent. This is the most general of all 11 derived features used in the current system

2.6 Combining Features

A final decision rule requires a combination of the derived features in section 2.5. We used both previous RTE challenges and machine learning over the derived features to inform the final decision rules. For the latter, we chose a decision tree classifier because in addition to classification accuracy, we are also interested in gaining insight into the underlying syntactic features that produce the highest predictive accuracy.

The decision trees shown in Figure 2 were generated using the Oracle Data Miner 10.2.0.2. Tree (A) suggests that if there is less than a 63.33% similarity between the number of subjects in the hypothesis sentence and the words in any of the test sentences (feature 11), that the hypothesis sentence is not entailed by the test sentence(s). The NO prediction from this rule would be correct in 71% cases, and assigning NO would apply to 42% of sentences in the development set. A YES prediction would be correct in 69% of sentences, and a YES prediction would take place in 57% of sentences in the development set. Tree (B) also suggests that an increase in the number of matches between the subject in the hypothesis sentence and the words used in the test sentence(s) is indicative of an entailment.

```
Decision Tree (A)
  If Subject-Word match <= 63.3%

        NO                YES
  Accuracy=71%      Accuracy=69%
  Coverage=43%      Coverage= 57%

Decision Tree (B)
   If Subject-Word match <= 1.5

        NO                YES
   Accuracy=58%     Accuracy=64%
   Coverage=52%     Coverage=48%
```

Figure 2. Decision trees generated for the revised $RTE3_{Devmt}$ set during decision rule development.

Although tempting to implement the decision tree with the highest accuracy, we should first consider the greedy search employed by this algorithm. At each level of recursion, a decision tree algorithm selects the single feature that best improves performance (in this case, the purity of the resulting leaves, i.e. so that sentences in each leaf have all YES or all NO responses).

Now consider feature 1, where the subject, verb and object triple in the hypothesis sentence matches the corresponding triple in a test sentence. Even though the predictive accuracy of this feature is high (74.36%), it is unlikely that this feature will provide the best purity because only a small number of sentences (39 in $RTE3_{Devmt}$) match. Similarly, a subject-object match has the highest predictive accuracy of any feature in $RTE3_{Devmt}$ (78.79%), but again few sentences (66 in $RTE3_{Devm}$) match.

2.7 Final Decision Rules

We submitted two different decision rules to RTE3 based on thresholds set to optimize performance in $RTE3_{Devmt}$ set. The thresholds do not consider the source of a sentence, i.e. from information extraction, summarization, information retrieval or question answering activities.

The first decision rule adds the proportion of matches for each of the derived features described in section 2.5 and assigns YES when the total proportion is greater than or equal to a threshold 2.4. Thus, the first decision rule overly favors sentences where the subject, verb and object match both HSent and TSent because if a sentence pair matches on feature 1, then the system also counts a match for features 3, 4, 5, and 8. This lack of feature independence is intentional, and consistent with our intuition that feature 1 is a good indicator of entailment.

To arrive at the second decision rule, we considered the features proposed by decision trees with a non-greedy search strategy that favors high quality features even when only a small percentage of sentences match. The second rule predicts YES under the following conditions: when the subject, verb, and object of HSent match those in any TSent (feature 1), in either order (feature 2) or when the subject and object from the HSent triple match any TSent (feature 3), or when the TSent subject matches >= 80% of the HSent subject terms (feature 5) or when the TSent subject and preposition matches >=70% of those in HSent (feature 10) or when TSent word matches >= 70% of the subject terms in the HSent sentence (feature 11).

Feature		RTE3$_{Devmt}$			RTE3$_{Test}$			RTE2$_{All}$		
		Total	Pos	%Accy	Total	Pos	%Accy	Total	Pos	%Accy
1	Triple	35	26	74.29	37	24	64.86	47	35	74.47
2	Triple Opposite	4	3	75.00	9	4	44.44	2	1	50.00
3	Triple Subj Obj	66	52	78.79	76	47	61.84	102	69	67.65
4	Triple Subj Obj Opp.	9	4	44.44	16	7	43.75	10	5	50.00
5	Subject-Subject	750	397	52.93	760	404	53.16	777	391	50.32
6	Verb-Verb	330	196	59.39	345	181	52.46	395	208	52.66
7	Subject-Verb	297	178	59.93	291	168	57.73	292	154	52.74
8	Verb-Subject	348	196	56.32	369	207	56.10	398	212	53.27
9	Verb-Preposition	303	178	58.75	312	167	53.53	355	190	53.52
10	Subject-Preposition	522	306	58.62	540	310	57.41	585	303	51.79
11	Subject-Word	771	406	52.66	769	407	52.93	790	395	50.00

Table 1. Coverage and accuracy of each derived feature for RTE3 revised development collection (RTE3$_{Devmt}$), the RTE3 Test collection (RTE3$_{Test}$) and the entire RTE2 collection (RTE2$_{All}$).

3 Results

The experiments were completed using the revised RTE3 development set (RTE3$_{Devmt}$) before the RTE3$_{Test}$ results were released. The remaining RTE2 and RTE3$_{Test}$ analyses were then conducted.

3.1 Accuracy of Derived Features

Table 1 shows the accuracy of *any* match between the derived features described in section 2.5. Complete matching triples (feature 1), and matching subjects and objects in the triple (feature 2) provide the highest individual accuracy.

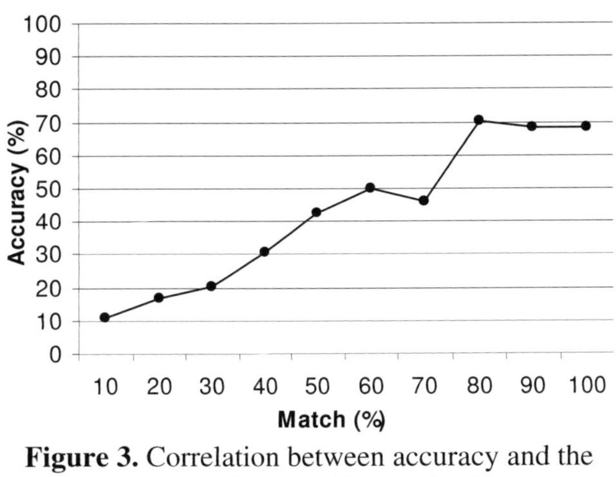

Figure 3. Correlation between accuracy and the percentage subjects in HSent that have a corresponding subject in TSent (feature 5).

The results in Table 1 do not consider the degree of feature match. For example, only one of the words from TSent in sentence 525's (RTE3$_{Devmt}$) matched the eight subject terms in corresponding HSent. If the derived features outlined in section 2.7 did capture the underlying structure of an entailment, you would expect an increased match would correlate with increased accuracy. We explored the correlations for each of the derived features. Figure 3 suggests entailment accuracy increases with an increase in the percentage of TSent subject terms that match HSent terms. (feature 5) and demonstrates why we set the 80% threshold for feature 5 in the second decision rule.

3.2 Accuracy of Decision Rules

Of the 800 sentences in RTE3$_{Devmt}$, the annotators labeled 412 as an entailment. Thus, without any information about HSent or TSent, the system would assign YES (the majority class) to each sentence, which would result in 51.50% accuracy.

The first decision rule considers the total percentage match of all features defined in section 2.5. We arrived at a threshold of 2.4 by ranking the development set in decreasing order the total percentage match and identifying where the threshold would lead to an accuracy of around 65%. Many sentences had a threshold of around 2.4, and the overall accuracy of the first decision on the RTE3$_{Devmt}$ set was 62.38%, compared to 60.50% in RTE3$_{Test}$. We consider the first decision rule a baseline and the second rule is our real submission.

The second rule uses only a sub-set of the derived features (1, 2, 3, 5, 10, and 11) and includes thresholds for features 5, 10 and 11. The accuracy of the second decision rule on RTE3$_{Devmt}$

set was 71.50%, compared with an accuracy of 65.87 % on $RTE3_{Test.}$

Our results are consistent with previous RTE2 findings (Bar-Haim et al., 2006) where task performance varies with respect to the sentence source. Both rules had similar (poor) performance for information extraction (50.00 vs. 50.50%). Both rules had moderate performance for summarization (56.50 vs. 60.50%) and good performance for information retrieval (70.00 vs. 75.50%). The second decision rule constantly out-performed the first, with the largest increase of 11.5% in the question answering activity (65.50 vs. 77.00%).

Both decision rules lend themselves well to ranking sentences in decreasing order from the most to the least certain entailment. Average precision is calculated using that ranking and produces a perfect score when all sentence pairs that are entailments (+ve) are listed before all the sentence pairs that are not (-ve) (Voorhees & Harman., 1999). The average precision of the first and second decision rules was 58.97% and 60.96% respectively. The variation in precision also varied with respect to the sentence source (IE, IR, QA and SUM) of 48.52, 65.93, 72.38, and 56.04% for the first decision rule and 48.32, 72.71, 78.75 and 56.69% for the second decision rule.

4 Conclusions

Although most systems include both syntax and semantics to detect entailment and paraphrasing, our goal in this paper was to measure the impact of sentence structure alone. We developed two decision rules that each use features from a typed dependency grammar representation the hypothesis and test sentences. The first decision rule considers all features and the second considers only a sub-set of features, and adds thresholds to ensure that the system does not consider dubious matches. Thresholds for both rules were established using sentences in $RTE3_{Devmt}$ only. The second rule out-performed the first on $RTE3_{Test}$, both with respect to accuracy (60.50% vs. 65.87%) and average precision (58.97% vs. 60.96%).

These results are particularly encouraging given that our approach requires no background knowledge (other than the lexicon) and that this was the first time we participated in RTE. The results suggest that sentence structure alone can improve entailment prediction by between 9.25-14.62% alone, over the majority class baseline (51.52% in $RTE3_{Test}$) and they provided additional support to the growing body of evidence that sentence structure will continue to play a role in the accurate detection of textual entailments and paraphrasing.

References

Bar-Haim, R., Dagan, I., Dolan, B., Ferro, L., Giampiccolo, D., Magnini, B., et al. (2006). *The Second PASCAL Recognising Textual Entailment Challenge.* Venice, Italy.

Dagan, I., Glickman, O., & Magnini, B. (2005). *The PASCAL Recognising Textual Entailment Challenge.* Southampton, U.K.

de Marneffe, M.-C., MacCartney, B., Grenager, T., Cer, D., Rafferty, A., & Manning, C. D. (2006). *Learning to distinguish valid textual entailments*, In *The Second PASCAL Challenges Workshop on Recognising Textual Entailment*, Venice, Italy.

Hickl, A., Williams, J., Bensley, J., Roberts, K., Rink, B., & Shi, Y. (2006). *Recognizing Textual Entailment with LCC's GROUNDHOG System* In *The Second PASCAL Recognising Textual Entailment Challenge,* Venice, Italy.

Klein, D., & Manning, C. D. (2002). *Fast Exact Inference with a Factored Model for Natural Language Parsing.* Paper presented at the Advances in Neural Information Processing Systems.

Lin, D. (1998). *Dependency-based Evaluation of MINIPAR.* In Workshop on the Evaluation of Parsing Systems, First International Conference on Language Resources and Evaluation, Granada,Spain.

Lin, D., & Pantel, P. (2001). Induction of semantic classes from natural language text. In *The 7th International conference on Knowledge discovery and Data Mining, San Francisco, CA.*

Litkowski, K. (2006). *Componential Analysis for Recognizing Textual Entailment.* In *The Second PASCAL Challenges Workshop on Recognising Textual Entailment*, Venice, Italy.

Miller, G. (1995). WordNet: A Lexical Database for English. *Communications of the ACM, 38*(11), 39-41.

National Library of Medicine. (2000). *The SPECIALIST Lexicon*, from www.nlm.nih.gov/pubs/factsheets/umlslex.html

Vanderwende, L., Coughlin, D., & Dolan, B. (2005). *What Syntax can Contribute in Entailment Task.* The PASCAL Challenges Workshop on Recognising Textual Entailment. Southhampton, UK.

Voorhees, E. M., & Harman., D. (1999). *Overview of the seventh text retrieval conference.* In *The Seventh Text REtrieval Conference* (TREC-7).

Semantic and Logical Inference Model for Textual Entailment

Dan Roth
University of Illinois
at Urbana-Champaign
Urbana, IL 61801
danr@cs.uiuc.edu

Mark Sammons
University of Illinois
at Urbana-Champaign
Urbana, IL 61801
mssammon@uiuc.edu

Abstract

We compare two approaches to the problem of Textual Entailment: SLIM, a compositional approach modeling the task based on identifying relations in the entailment pair, and BoLI, a lexical matching algorithm. SLIM's framework incorporates a range of resources that solve local entailment problems. A search-based inference procedure unifies these resources, permitting them to interact flexibly. BoLI uses WordNet and other lexical similarity resources to detect correspondence between related words in the Hypothesis and the Text. In this paper we describe both systems in some detail and evaluate their performance on the 3rd PASCAL RTE Challenge. While the lexical method outperforms the relation-based approach, we argue that the relation-based model offers better long-term prospects for entailment recognition.

1 Introduction

We compare two Textual Entailment recognition systems applied to the 3rd PASCAL RTE challenge. Both systems model the entailment task in terms of determining whether the Hypothesis can be "explained" by the Text.

The first system, BoLI (Bag of Lexical Items) uses WordNet and (optionally) other word similarity resources to compare individual words in the Hypothesis with the words in the Text.

The second system, the Semantic and Logical Inference Model (SLIM) system, uses a relational model, and follows the model-theory-based approach of (Braz et al., 2005).

SLIM uses a suite of resources to modify the original entailment pair by augmenting or simplifying either or both the Text and Hypothesis. Terms relating to quantification, modality and negation are detected and removed from the graphical representation of the entailment pair and resolved with an entailment module that handles basic logic.

In this study we describe the BoLI and SLIM systems and evaluate their performance on the 3rd PASCAL RTE Challenge corpora. We discuss some examples and possible improvements for each system.

2 System Description: Bag of Lexical Items (BoLI)

The BoLI system compares each word in the text with a word in the hypothesis. If a word is found in the Text that entails a word in the Hypothesis, that word is considered "explained". If the percentage of the Hypothesis that can be explained is above a certain threshold, the Text is considered to entail the Hypothesis. This threshold is determined using a training set (in this case, the Development corpus), by determining the percentage match for each entailment pair and selecting the threshold that results in the highest overall accuracy.

BoLI uses an extended set of stopwords including auxiliary verbs, articles, exclamations, and discourse markers in order to improve the distinction between Text and Hypothesis. Negation and modality are not explicitly handled.

The BoLI system can be changed by varying the comparison resources it uses. The available

Proceedings of the Workshop on Textual Entailment and Paraphrasing, pages 107–112,
Prague, June 2007.

resources are: WordNet-derived (Fellbaum, 1998) synonymy, meronymy, membership, and hypernymy; a filtered version of Dekang Lin's word similarity list (Lin, 1998) (only the ten highest-scored entries for each word); and a resource based on a lexical comparison of WordNet glosses.

We tried three main versions; one that used the four WordNet- derived resources ($BoLI$); a second that adds to the first system the Dekang Lin resource ($BoLI_D$); and a third that added to the second system the Gloss resource ($BoLI_G$). We ran them on the Development corpus, and determined the threshold that gave the highest overall score. We then used the highest-scoring version and the corresponding threshold to determine labels for the Test corpus. The results and thresholds for each variation are given in table 1.

3 System Description: Semantic and Logical Inference Model (SLIM)

The SLIM system approaches the problem of entailment via relations: the goal is to recognize the relations in the Text and Hypothesis, and use these to determine whether the Text entails the Hypothesis. A word in the Hypothesis is considered "covered" by a relation if it appears in that relation in some form (either directly or via abstraction). For the Text to entail the Hypothesis, sufficient relations in the Hypothesis must be entailed by relations in the Text to cover the underlying text.

The term "Relation" is used here to describe a predicate-argument structure where the predicate is represented by a verb (which may be inferred from a nominalized form), and the arguments by strings of text from the original sentence. These constituents may be (partially) abstracted by replacing tokens in some constituent with attributes attached to that or a related constituent (for example, modal terms may be dropped and represented with an attribute attached to the appropriate predicate).

Relations may take other relations as arguments. Examples include "before" and "after" (when both arguments are events) and complement structures.

3.1 Representation

The system compares the Text to the Hypothesis using a "blackboard" representation of the two text fragments (see figure 1). Different types of annotation are specified on different layers, all of which are "visible" to the comparison algorithm. All layers map to the original representation of the text, and each annotated constituent corresponds to some initial subset of this original representation. This allows multiple representations of the same surface form to be entertained.

Figure 1 shows some of the layers in this data structure for a simple entailment pair: the original text in the WORD layer; the relations induced from this text in the PREDICATE layer; and for the Text, a Coreference constituent aligned with the word "he" in the COREFERENCE layer. Note that the argument labels for "give" in the Text indicate that "he" is the theme/indirect object of the predicate "give".

Figure 1: "Blackboard" Representation of Entailment Pairs in SLIM

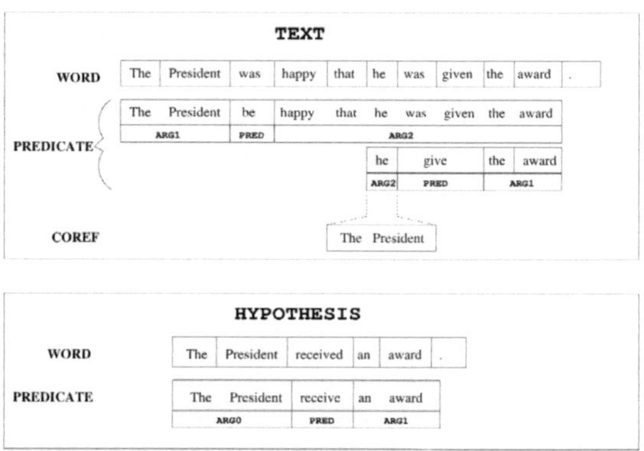

At compare-time, the coref constituent "The President" will be considered as a substitute for "he" when comparing the relation in the Hypothesis with the second relation in the Text. (The dashed lines indicate that the *coverage* of the coreference constituent is just that of the argument consisting of the word "he".) The relation comparator has access to a list of rules mapping between verbs and their argument types; this will allow it to recognize that the relation "give" can entail "receive", subject to the constraint that the agent of "give" must be the patient of "receive", and vice versa. This, together with the coreference constituent in the Text that aligns with the argument "he", will allow the system to recognize that the Text entails the Hypothesis.

3.2 Algorithm

The SLIM entailment system applies sequences of transformations to the original entailment pair in order to modify one or both members of the pair to make it easier to determine whether the Text entails the Hypothesis. The resources that make these transformations are referred to here as "operators". Each operator is required to use *Purposeful Inference*: before making a change to either entailment pair member, they must take the other member into account. For example, the conjunction expander will generate only those expansions in a text fragment that match structures in the paired text fragment more closely. This constrains the number of transformations considered and can reduce the amount of noise introduced by these operators.

Each such operator serves one of three purposes:

1. **ANNOTATE.** Make some implicit property of the meaning of the sentence explicit.
2. **SIMPLIFY/TRANSFORM.** Remove or alter some section of the Text in order to improve annotation accuracy or make it more similar to the Hypothesis.
3. **COMPARE.** Compare (some elements of) the two members of the entailment pair and assign a score that correlates to how successfully (those elements of) the Hypothesis can be subsumed by the Text.

The system's operators are applied to an entailment pair, potentially generating a number of new versions of that entailment pair. They may then be applied to these new versions. It is likely that only a subset of the operators will fire. It is also possible that multiple operators may affect overlapping sections of one or both members of the entailment pair, and so the resulting perturbations of the original pair may be sensitive to the order of application.

To explore these different subsets/orderings, the system is implemented as a search process over the different operators. The search terminates as soon as a satisfactory entailment score is returned by the comparison operator for a state reached by applying transformation operators, or after some limit to the depth of the search is reached. If entailment is determined to hold, the set of operations that generated the terminal state constitutes a proof of the solution.

3.2.1 Constraining the Search

To control the search to allow for the interdependence of certain operators, each operator may specify a set of pre- and post-conditions. Pre-conditions specify which operators must have fired to provide the necessary input for the current operator. Post-conditions typically indicate whether or not it is desirable to re-annotate the resulting entailment pair (e.g. after an operation that appends a new relation to an entailment pair member), or whether the Comparator should be called to check for entailment.

3.3 System Resources: Annotation

The SLIM system uses a number of standard annotation resources – Part-of-Speech, Shallow- and Full syntactic parsing, Named Entity tagging, and Semantic Role Labelling – but also has a number of more specialized resources intended to recognize implicit predicates from the surface representation in the text, and append these relations to the original text. These resources are listed below with a brief description of each.

Apposition Detector. Uses full parse information to detect appositive constructions, adding a relation that makes the underlying meaning explicit. It uses a set of rules specifying subtree structure and phrase labels.

Complex Noun Phrase Relation Detector. Analyzes long noun phrases and annotates them with their implicit relations. It applies a few general rules expressed at the shallow parse and named entity level.

Modality and Negation Annotator. Abstracts modifiers of relations representing modality or negation into attributes attached to the relation.

Discourse Structure Annotator. Scans the relation structure (presently only at the sentence level) to determine negation and modality of relations embedded in factive and other constructions. It marks the embedded relations accordingly, and where possible, discards the embedding relation.

Coreference Annotator. Uses Named Entity information to map pronouns to possible replacements.

Nominalization Rewriter. Detects certain common nominalized verb structures and makes the relation explicit. The present version applies a small set of very general rules instantiated with a list of embedding verbs and a mapping from nominalized to verbal forms.

3.4 System Resources: Simplification/Transformation

The simplification resources all demonstrate **purposeful inference**, as described in section 3.2.

Idiom Catcher. Identifies and replaces sequences of words corresponding to a list of known idioms, simplifying sentence structure. It can recognize a range of surface representations for each idiom.

Phrasal Verb Replacer. Checks for phrasal verb constructions, including those where the particle is distant from the main verb, replacing them with single verbs of equivalent meaning.

Conjunction Expander. Uses full parse information to detect and rewrite conjunctive argument and predicate structures by expanding them.

Multi-Word Expression Contractor. Scans both members of the entailment pair for compound noun phrases that can be replaced by just the head of the phrase.

3.5 System Resources: Main Comparator

All comparator resources are combined in a single operator for simplicity. This comparator uses the blackboard architecture described in 3.1.

The main comparator compares each relation in the Hypothesis to each relation in the Text, returning "True" if sufficient relations in the Hypothesis are entailed by relations in the Text to cover the underlying representation of the Hypothesis.

For a relation in the Text to entail a relation in the Hypothesis, the Text predicate must entail the Hypothesis predicate, and all arguments of the Hypothesis relation must be entailed by arguments of the Text relation. This entailment check also accounts for attributes such as negation and modality.

As part of this process, a set of rules that map between predicate- argument structures (some handwritten, most derived from VerbNet) are applied on-the-fly to the pair of relations being compared. These rules specify a mapping between predicates and a set of constraints that apply to the mappings between arguments of the predicates. For example, the agent of the relation "sell" should be the theme of the relation "buy", and vice versa.

When comparing the arguments of predicates, the system uses BoLI with the same configuration and threshold that give the best performance on the development set.

3.6 Comparison to Similar Approaches

Like (de Marneffe et al., 2005), SLIM's representation abstracts away terms relating to negation, modality and quantification. However, it uses them as part of the comparison process, not as features to be used in a classifier. In contrast to (Braz et al., 2005), SLIM considers versions of the entailment pair with and without simplifications offered by preprocessing modules, rather than reasoning only about the simplified version; and rather than formulating the subsumption (entailment) problem as a hierarchical linear program or classification problem, SLIM defers local entailment decisions to its modules and returns a positive label for a constituent only if these resources return a positive label for all subconstituents. Finally, SLIM returns an overall positive label if all words in the Hypothesis can be 'explained' by relations detected in the Hypothesis and matched in the Text, rather than requiring all detected relations in the Text to be entailed by relations in the Hypothesis.

4 Experimental Results

Table 3 presents the peformance of the BoLI and SLIM systems on the 3rd PASCAL RTE Challenge. The version of SLIM used for the Development corpus was incomplete, as several modules (Multi-word Expression, Conjunction, and Apposition) were still being completed at that time. Table 1 indicates the performance of 3 different versions of the BoLI system on the Development corpus as described in section 2.

To investigate the improvement of performance for the SLIM system relative to the available resources, we conducted a limited ablation study. Table 2 shows the performance for 3 different versions of the SLIM system on 100 entailment pairs each from the IE and QA subtasks of the Test corpus. The "full" (f) system includes all available resources. The "intermediate" (i) system excludes the resources we consider most likely to introduce errors, the Multiword Expression module and the most general Nominalization rewrite rules in the Nominalization Rewriter. The "strict" (s) system also omits the Apposition and Complex Noun Phrase

Table 1: Accuracy and corresponding threshold for versions of BoLI on the Development corpus.

TASK	Accuracy	Threshold
$BoLI$	0.675	0.667
$BoLI_D$	0.650	0.833
$BoLI_G$	0.655	0.833

Table 2: Results for different versions of SLIM on subsets of the Test and Develoment corpora.

System	SLIM s	SLIM i	SLIM f
Dev IE	-	-	0.650
Dev QA	-	-	0.660
Test IE	0.480	0.480	0.470
Test QA	0.680	0.710	0.710

modules. To give a sense of how well the complete SLIM system does on the Development corpus, the results for the full SLIM system on equal-sized subsets of the IE and QA subtasks of the Development corpus are also shown.

5 Discussion

From Table 3, it is clear that BoLI outperforms SLIM in every subtask.

The ablation study in Table 2 shows that adding new resources to SLIM has mixed benefits; from the samples we used for evaluation, the intermediate system would be the best balance between module coverage and module accuracy.

In the rest of this section, we analyze the results and each system's behavior on several examples from the corpus.

5.1 BoLI

There is a significant drop in performance of the BoLI from the Development corpus to the Test corpus, indicating that the threshold somewhat overfitted to the data used to train it. The performance drop when adding the gloss and Dekang Lin word similarity resources is not necessarily surprising, as these resources are clearly noisy, and so may increase similarity based on inappropriate word pairs.

In the following example, the word similarity is high, but the structure of the two text fragments gives the relevant words different overall meaning (here, that one subset of the matched words does not apply to the other):

id=26 Text: Born in Kingston-upon-Thames, Surrey, Brockwell played his county cricket for the very strong Surrey side of the last years of the 19th century.

Hypothesis: Brockwell was born in the last years of the 19th century.

From this example it is clear that in addition to the role of noise from these additional resources, the structure of text plays a major role in meaning, and this is exactly what BoLI cannot capture.

5.2 SLIM

The ablation study for the SLIM system shows a trade-off between precision and recall for some resources. In this instance, adding resources improves performance significantly, but including noisy resources also implies a ceiling on overall performance will ultimately be reached.

The following example shows the potentially noisy possessive rewrite operator permitting successful entailment:

id=19 Text: During Reinsdorf's 24 seasons as chairman of the White Sox, the team has captured Americal League division championships three times, including an AL Central title in 2000.

Transformed Text: During Reinsdorf have 24 seasons as chairman of the White Sox ...

Hypothesis: Reinsdorf was chairman of the White Sox for 24 seasons.

There are a number of examples where relaxed operators result in false positives, but where the negative label is debatable. In the next example, the apposition module adds a new relation and the Nominalization Rewriter detects the hypothesis using this new relation:

id=102 Hypothesis: He was initially successful, negotiating a 3/4 of 1 percent royalty on all cars sold by the Association of Licensed Automobile Manufacturers, the ALAM.

Transformed Text: ... Association of Licensed Automobile Manufacturers is the ALAM.

Hypothesis: The ALAM manufactured cars.

Finally, some modules did not fire as they should; for example 15, the conjunction module did not expand the conjunction over predicates. For example 24, the nominalization rewriter did not detect "plays in the NHL" from "is a NHL player". In example 35, the apposition module did not detect that "Harriet

Table 3: Results for SLIM and BoLI on the Pascal Development and Test Corpora. Results marked with an asterisk indicate not all system resources were available at the time the system was run.

Corpus	Development					Test				
Subtask	IE	IR	QA	SUM	OVERALL	IE	IR	QA	SUM	OVERALL
BoLI	0.560	0.700	0.790	0.690	0.675	0.510	0.710	0.830	0.575	0.656
SLIM	0.580*	0.595*	0.650*	0.545*	0.593*	0.485	0.6150	0.715	0.575	0.5975

Lane, niece of President James" could be rewritten.

Of course, there are also many examples where the SLIM system simply does not have appropriate resources (e.g. numerical reasoning, coreference requiring semantic categorization).

6 Conclusion

While BoLI outperforms SLIM on the PASCAL RTE 3 task, there is no clear way to improve BoLI. It is clear that for the PASCAL corpora, the distributions over word similarity between entailment pair members in positive and negative examples are different, allowing this simple approach to perform relatively well, but there is no guarantee that this is generally the case, and it is easy to create an adversarial corpus on which BoLI performs very badly (e.g., exchanging arguments or predicates of different crelations in the Text), no matter how good the word-level entailment resources are. This approach also offers no possibility of a meaningful explanation of the entailment decision.

SLIM, on the other hand, by offering a framework to which new resources can be added in a principled way, can be extended to cover new entailment phenomena in an incremental, local (i.e. compositional) way. The results of the limited ablation study support this conclusion, though the poor performance on the IE task indicates the problems with using lower-precision, higher-recall resources.

Overall, we find the results for the SLIM system very encouraging, as they support the underlying concept of incremental improvement, and this offers a clear path toward better performance.

6.1 Acknowledgements

We gratefully acknowledge the work on SLIM modules by Ming-Wei Chang, Michael Connor, Quang Do, Alex Klementiev, Lev Ratinov, and Vivek Srikumar. This work was funded by the Advanced Research and Development Activity (ARDA)'s Advanced Question Answering for Intelligence (AQUAINT) program, a grant from Boeing, and a gift from Google.

References

Johan Bos and Katja Markert. 2005. When logical inference helps determining textual entailment (and when it doesn't). In *Proceedings of the Second PASCAL Challenges Workshop on Recognizing Textual Entailment*.

R. Braz, R. Girju, V. Punyakanok, D. Roth, and M. Sammons. 2005. Knowledge representation for semantic entailment and question-answering. In *IJCAI-05 Workshop on Knowledge and Reasoning for Question Answering*.

Marie-Catherine de Marneffe, Bill MacCartney, Trond Grenager, Daniel Cer, Anna Rafferty, and Christopher Manning. 2005. Learning to distinguish valid textual entailments. In *Proceedings of the Second PASCAL Challenges Workshop on Recognizing Textual Entailment*.

C. Fellbaum. 1998. *WordNet: An Electronic Lexical Database*. MIT Press.

Sophia Katrenko and Peter Adriaans. 2005. Using maximal embedded syntactic subtrees for textual entailment recognition. In *Proceedings of the Second PASCAL Challenges Workshop on Recognizing Textual Entailment*.

D. Lin. 1998. An information-theoretic defi nition of similarity. In *Proc. of the International Conference on Machine Learning (ICML)*.

Marta Tatu, Brandon Iles, John Slavick, Adrian Novischi, and Dan Moldovan. 2005. Cogex at the second recognizing textual entailment challenge. In *Proceedings of the Second PASCAL Challenges Workshop on Recognizing Textual Entailment*.

SVO triple based Latent Semantic Analysis for recognising textual entailment

Gaston Burek **Christian Pietsch** **Anne De Roeck**

Centre for Research in Computing
The Open University
Walton Hall, Milton Keynes, MK7 6AA, UK
{g.g.burek,c.pietsch,a.deroeck}@open.ac.uk

Abstract

Latent Semantic Analysis has only recently been applied to textual entailment recognition. However, these efforts have suffered from inadequate bag of words vector representations. Our prototype implementation for the Third Recognising Textual Entailment Challenge (RTE-3) improves the approach by applying it to vector representations that contain semi-structured representations of words. It uses variable size n-grams of word stems to model independently verbs, subjects and objects displayed in textual statements. The system performance shows positive results and provides insights about how to improve them further.

1 Introduction

The Third Recognising Textual Entailment Challenge (RTE-3) task consists in developing a system for automatically determining whether or not a hypothesis (H) can be inferred from a text (T), which could be up to a paragraph long.

Our entry to the RTE-3 challenge is a system that takes advantage of Latent Semantic Analysis (LSA) (Landauer and Dumais, 1997). This numerical method for reducing noise generated by word choices within texts is extensively used for document indexing and word sense disambiguation. Recently, there have also been efforts to use techniques from LSA to recognise textual entailment (Clarke, 2006; de Marneffe et al., 2006). However, we argue that these efforts (like most LSA approaches in the past) suffer from an inadequate vector representation for textual contexts as bags of words. In contrast, we have applied LSA to vector representations of semi-structured text. Our representation takes into account the grammatical role (i.e. subject, verb or object) a word occurs in.

Within this system report, we describe and discuss our methodology in section 2, our current implementation in section 3, and system results in section 4. We conclude in section 5 with a discussion of the results obtained and with the presentation of possible steps to improve our system's performance.

2 Methodology for detecting Textual Entailment

2.1 Textual entailment formalisation

Our approach addresses the problem of the semantic gap that exists between low level linguistic entities (words) and concepts. Concepts can be described by means of predicate-argument structures or by a set of alternative natural language realisations. In this work we use terminology co-occurrence information to identify when different spans of text have common semantic content even if they do not share vocabulary. To achieve this, we use variable size n-grams to independently model subject, verb and object, and capture semantics derived from grammatical structure. In order to detect textual entailment we measure the semantic similarity between n-grams in each T–H pair.

2.2 Using n-grams to align SVOs

To align subjects, verbs and objects within H and T, we build the set of all n-grams for T, and do the same

Proceedings of the Workshop on Textual Entailment and Paraphrasing, pages 113–118,
Prague, June 2007.

for H. Section 3.5 describes this process in more detail.

2.3 Deriving word senses with Latent Semantic Analysis

Our approach is based on the assumption that a word sense can be derived from the textual contexts in which that words occurs. This assumption was formalised in the Distributional Hypothesis (Harris, 1954).

We implemented a vector space model (Salton et al., 1975) to capture word semantics from linguistic (i.e. grammatical role) and contextual (i.e. frequency) information about each word. To avoid high matrix sparsity our vector space model uses second order co-occurrence (Widdows, 2004, p. 174).

We assumed that the corpus we generated the vector space model from has a probabilistic word distribution that is characterised by a number of semantic dimensions. The LSA literature seems to agree that optimal number of dimensions is somewhere between two hundred and one thousand depending on corpus and domain. As specified by LSA we applied Singular Value Decomposition (SVD) (Berry, 1992) to identify the characteristic semantic dimensions.

The resulting model is a lower dimensional projection of the original model that captures indirect associations between the vectors in the original model. SVD reduces the noise in word categorisations by producing the best approximation to the original vector space model.

3 Implementation

3.1 Development data set

The development data set consists of eight hundred T–H pairs, half of them positive. By positive pair we mean a T–H pair in which T entails H. All other pairs we call negative. Each T–H pair belongs to a particular sub-task. Those sub-tasks are Information Extraction (IE), Information Retrieval (IR), Question Answering (QA) and Summarisation (SUM). In the current prototype, we ignored annotations about sub-tasks.

3.2 Corpus analysis

3.2.1 Corpora used

The only knowledge source we used in our implementation was a parsed newswire corpus (Reuters News Corpus) (Lewis et al., 2004). To derive contextual information about the meaning of words constituting the SVOs, we analysed the Reuters corpus as explained below.

3.2.2 SVO triple extraction

For parsing the corpus, we used Minipar[1] because of its speed and because its simple dependency triple output format (`-t` option) contains word stems and the grammatical relations between them. A simple AWK script was used to convert the parse results into Prolog facts, one file for each sentence. A straightforward Prolog program then identified SVOs in each of these fact files, appending them to one big structured text file.

Our algorithm currently recognises intransitive, transitive, ditransitive, and predicative clauses. Intransitive clauses are encoded as SVOs with an empty object slot. Transitive clauses result in a fully instantiated SVOs. Ditransitive clauses are encoded as two different SVOs: the first containing subject, verb and direct object; the second triple containing the subject again, an empty verb slot, and the indirect object. Predicatives (e.g. "somebody is something") are encoded just like transitive clauses.

In this first prototype, we only used one word (which could be a multi-word expression) for subject, verb and object slot respectively. We realise that this approach ignores much information, but given a large corpus, it might not be detrimental to be selective.

3.2.3 SVO Stemming and labeling

To reduce the dimensionality of our vector space model we stem the SVOs using Snowball[2]. Then, we calculate how many times stems co-occur as subject, verb or object with another stem within the same SVO instance.

[1] Minipar can be downloaded from http://www.cs.ualberta.ca/~lindek/minipar.htm. It is based on Principar, which is described in Lin (1994).

[2] Snowball is freely available from http://snowball.tartarus.org/. The English version is based on the original Porter Stemmer (Porter, 1980).

To keep track of the grammatical role (i.e. subject, verb, object) of the words we stem them and label the stems with the corresponding role.

3.3 Building vector spaces to represent stem semantics

From the corpus, we built a model $(\mathcal{S}, \mathcal{V}, \mathcal{O})$ of the English (news) language consisting of three matrices: $\mathcal{S}$ for subjects, $\mathcal{V}$ for verbs, and $\mathcal{O}$ for objects.

We built the three stem-to-stem matrices from labeled stem co-occurrences within the extracted triples. The entries to the matrices are the frequencies of the co-occurrence of each labeled stem with itself or with another labeled stem. In our current prototype, due to technical restrictions explained in Section 3.4, each matrix has 1000 rows and 5000 columns.

Columns of matrix $\mathcal{S}$ contain entries for stems labeled as subject, columns of matrix $\mathcal{V}$ contain entries for stems labeled as verb, and columns of matrix $\mathcal{O}$ contain entries for stems labeled as object. The frequency entries of each matrix correspond to the set of identically labeled stems with the highest frequency.

Rows of the three matrices contain entries corresponding to the same set of labeled stems. Those labeled stems are the ones with the highest frequency in the set of all labeled stems. Of these, 347 stems are labeled as subject, 356 are labeled as verb, and 297 are labeled as object. Each row entry is the frequency of co-occurrence of two labeled stems within the same triple.

Finally, each column entry is divided by the number of times the labeled stem associated with that column occurs within all triples.

3.4 Calculating the singular value decomposition

We calculated the Singular Value Decompositions (SVDs) for $\mathcal{S}$, $\mathcal{V}$ and $\mathcal{O}$. Each SVD of a matrix $\mathcal{A}$ is defined as a product of three matrices:

$$\mathcal{A} = U \times S \times V' \tag{1}$$

SVD is a standard matrix operation which is supported by many programming libraries and computer algebra applications. The problem is that only very few can handle the large matrices required for real-world LSA. It is easy to see that the memory required for representing a full matrix of 64 bit floating point values can easily exceed what current hardware offers. Fortunately, our matrices are sparse, so a library with sparse matrix support should be able to cope. Unfortunately, these are hard to find outside the Fortran world. We failed to find any Java library that can perform SVD on sparse matrices.[3] We finally decided to use SVDLIBC, a modernised version of SVDPACKC using only the LAS2 algorithm. In pre-tests with a matrix derived from a different text corpus (18371 rows $\times$ 3469 columns, density 0.73%), it completed the SVD task within ten minutes on typical current hardware. However, when we try to use it for this task on a matrix $\mathcal{S}$ of dimension 5000 $\times$ 5000 (density 1.4%), SVDLIBC did not terminate[4]. In theory, there is a Singular Value Decomposition for every given matrix, so we assume this is an implementation flaw in either SVDLIBC or GCC. With no time left to try Fortran alternatives, we resorted to reducing the size of our three matrices to 1000 $\times$ 5000, thus losing much information in our language model.

3.5 Looking for evidence of H in T using variable size n-grams

3.5.1 Building variable size n-grams

Our Minipar triple extraction algorithm is not able to handle SVOs that are embedded within other SVOs (as e.g. in "Our children play a new game that involves three teams competing for a ball."). Therefore, in order to determine if SVOs displayed in H are semantically similar to any of those displayed in T, we generate all n-grams of all lengths for each T and H: one set for subjects, one for verbs and another one for objects.

Example: "The boy played tennis."

Derived n-grams: the; the boy; the boy played; the boy played tennis; boy; boy played; boy played

[3]The popular JAMA library and the related Jampack library have no sparse matrix support at all. MTJ and Colt do support sparse matrices but cannot perform SVD on them without first converting them to full matrices.

[4]We tried various hardware / operating system / compiler combinations. On Linux systems, SVDLIBC would abort after about 15 minutes with an error message "imtqlb failed to converge". On Solaris and Mac OS X systems, the process would not terminate within several days.

tennis; played; played tennis; tennis.

We use n-grams to model subjects, verbs and objects of SVOs within T and H.

3.5.2 How to compare n-grams

We generate three vector representations for each n-gram. To do this, we add up columns from the Reuters Corpus derived matrices. To build the first vector representation, we use the $\mathcal{S}$ matrix, to build the second vector we use the $\mathcal{V}$ matrix, and to build the third vector we use the $\mathcal{O}$ matrix. Each of the three representations is the result of adding the columns corresponding to each stem within the n-gram.

To calculate the semantic similarity between n-grams, we fold the three vector representations of each n-gram into one of the dimensionally reduced matrices $\mathcal{S}_{200}$, $\mathcal{V}_{200}$ or $\mathcal{O}_{200}$. Vector representation originating from the $\mathcal{S}$ matrix are folded into $\mathcal{S}_{200}$. We proceed analogously for vector representations originating from $\mathcal{V}_{200}$ and $\mathcal{O}_{200}$. We apply equation 2 to fold vectors from G^r where $r \in \{\mathcal{S}, \mathcal{V}, \mathcal{O}\}$. G is a matrix which consists of all the vector representations of all the n-grams modeling T or H. S^r_{200} and U^r_{200} are SVD results reduced to 200 dimensions.

$$G^{r\prime} \times U^r_{200} \times (S^r_{200})^{-1} = G^r_{200} \qquad (2)$$

For each T–H pair we calculate the dot product between the G matrices for H and T as expressed in equation 3

$$^{text}G^r_{200} \times ^{hypothesis} G^{r\prime}_{200} = O^r \qquad (3)$$

The resulting matrix O^r contains the dot product similarity between all pairs of n-grams within the same set. Finally, for each T–H pair we obtain three similarity values s, v, o by selecting the entry of O^r with the highest value.

3.5.3 Scoring

Now we have calculated almost everything we need to venture a guess about textual entailment.

For each T–H pair, we have three scores s, v, o for for subject, verb and object slot respectively. The remaining task is to combine them in a meaningful way in order to make a decision. This requires some amount of training which in the current prototype is as simple as computing six average values: $\bar{s}_p$,

	$\bar{s}$	$\bar{v}$	$\bar{o}$
positive	0.244	$5.05 \cdot 10^{-7}$	0.323
negative	0.196	$4.76 \cdot 10^{-7}$	0.277

Table 1: Values computed for $\bar{s}_p, \bar{v}_p, \bar{o}_p, \bar{s}_n, \bar{v}_n, \bar{o}_n$

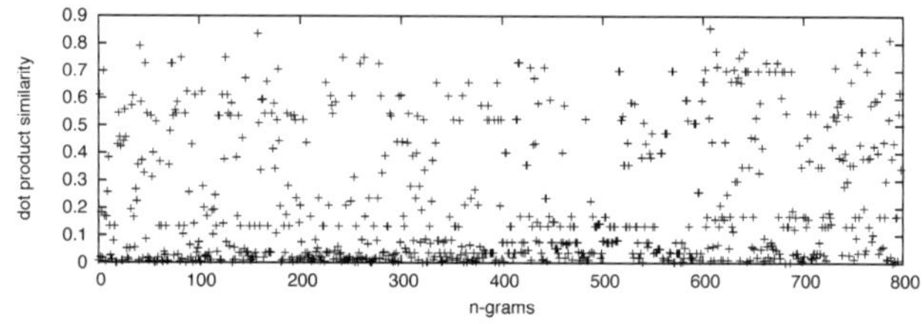

Figure 1: Subject similarities $s = \max O^{\mathcal{S}}$ for all H–T pairs

$\bar{v}_p$, $\bar{o}_p$ are the average scores of subject, verb and object slots over those T–H pairs for which textual entailment is known to hold. Conversely, $\bar{s}_n$, $\bar{v}_n$, $\bar{o}_n$ are the averages for those pairs that do not stand in a textual entailment relation. The (rounded) values were determined are shown in table 1.

Note that the average values for non-entailment are always lower than the average values for entailment, which indicates that our system indeed tends to discriminate correctly between these cases.

The very low values for the verb similarities (figure 3) compared to subject similarities (figure 1) and object similarities (figure 2) remind us that before we can combine slot scores, they should be scaled to a comparable level. This is achieved by dividing each slot score by its corresponding average. Ignoring the difference between positive and negative pairs for a moment, the basic idea of our scoring algorithm is to use the following threshold:

$$\frac{s}{\bar{s}} + \frac{v}{\bar{v}} + \frac{o}{\bar{o}} = 3 \qquad (4)$$

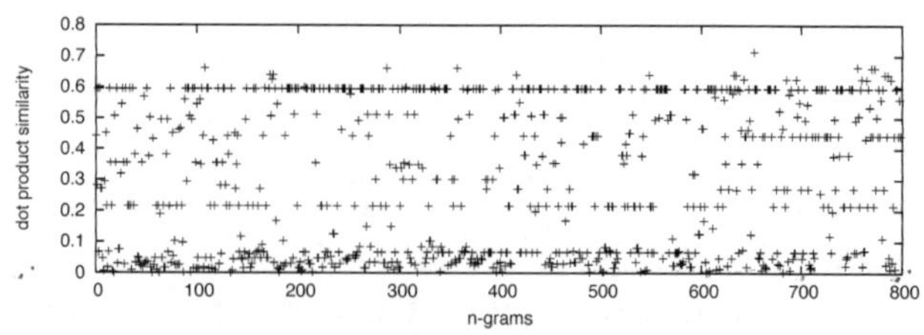

Figure 2: Object similarities $o = \max O^{\mathcal{O}}$ for all H–T pairs

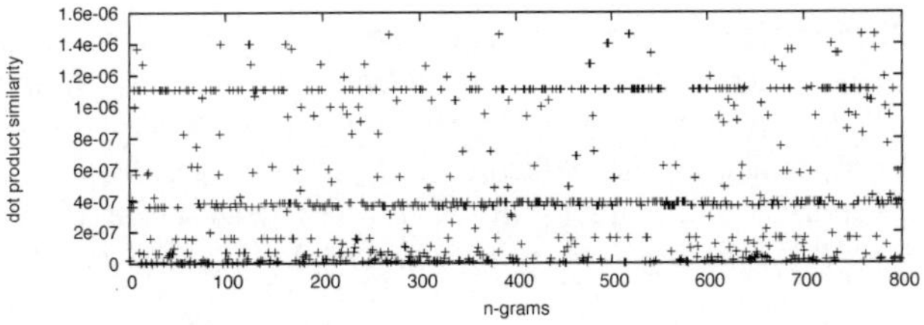

Figure 3: Verb similarities $v = \max O^{\mathcal{V}}$ for all H–T pairs

At this point we observed that scaling the verb similarities so much seemed to make results worse. It seems to be necessary to introduce weights:

$$\sigma\frac{s}{\bar{s}} + \phi\frac{v}{\bar{v}} + \omega\frac{o}{\bar{o}} = \sigma + \phi + \omega \quad (5)$$

Without loss of generality, we may assume $\phi = 1$:

$$\sigma\frac{s}{\bar{s}} + \frac{v}{\bar{v}} + \omega\frac{o}{\bar{o}} = \sigma + 1 + \omega \quad (6)$$

The complete scoring formula with both positive and negative scores is shown below. We assumed that the weights σ and ω are the same in the positive and in the negative case, so $\sigma = \sigma_p = \sigma_n$ and $\omega = \omega_p = \omega_n$.

$$\sigma\frac{s}{\bar{s}_p} + \frac{v}{\bar{v}_p} + \omega\frac{o}{\bar{o}_p} + \sigma\frac{s}{\bar{s}_n} + \frac{v}{\bar{v}_n} + \omega\frac{o}{\bar{o}_n} = 2(\sigma + 1 + \omega) \quad (7)$$

At this point, some machine learning over the development data set should be performed in order to determine optimal values for σ and ω. For lack of time, we simply performed a dozen or so of test runs and finally set $\sigma = \omega = 3$.

Our entailment threshold is thus simplified:

$$3\frac{s}{\bar{s}_p} + \frac{v}{\bar{v}_p} + 3\frac{o}{\bar{o}_p} + 3\frac{s}{\bar{s}_n} + \frac{v}{\bar{v}_n} + 3\frac{o}{\bar{o}_n} = q \quad (8)$$

If $q > 14$, our prototype predicts textual entailment. Otherwise, it predicts non-entailment.

4 Results

Using the scoring function described in section 3.5.3, our system achieved an overall accuracy of 0.5638 on the development dataset. Table 2 shows results for the system run on the test dataset. On this unseen dataset, the overall accuracy decreased only slightly to 0.5500. We take this as a strong indication that the thresholds we derived from the development dataset work well on other comparable input. Results show that our system has performed significantly above the 0.5 baseline that would result from a random decision.

	all	IE	IR	QA	SUM
accuracy	0.5500	0.4950	0.5750	0.5550	0.5750
av. prec.	0.5514	0.4929	0.5108	0.5842	0.6104

Table 2: Results on the test set

As shown in section 3.5.3, the values in the three similarity plots (see figures 1, 2 and 3) obtained with the development set seem to be scattered around the means. Therefore it seems that the threshold values used to the decide whether or not T entails H do not fully reflect the semantics underlying textual entailment.

The nature of the SVD calculations do not allow us directly to observe the performance of the variable size n-grams in independently aligning subject, verb and objects from T and from H. Nevertheless we can infer from figures 1, 2 and 3 that many of the values shown seem to be repeated. These value configurations can be observed in the three horizontal lines. These lines better visible in figures 2 and 3 are the effect of (a) many empty vectors resulting from the rather low number of stems represented by columns in our Reuters-derived matrices $\mathcal{S}$, $\mathcal{V}$ and $\mathcal{O}$, and (b) the effect of folding the n-gram vector representations into reduced matrices with two hundred dimensions.

5 Conclusion

Even though our system was developed from scratch in a very short period of time, it has already outperformed other LSA-based approaches to recognising textual entailment (Clarke, 2006), showing that it is both feasible and desirable to move away from a bag-of-words semantic representation to a semi-structured (here, SVO) semantic representation even when using LSA techniques.

Our system displays several shortcomings and limitations owing to its immature implementation state. These will be addressed in future work, and we are confident that without changing its theoretical basis, this will improve performance dramatically. Envisaged changes include:

- using larger matrices as input to SVD
- using the complete Reuters corpus, and adding Wikinews texts
- performing corpus look-up for unknown words
- extracting larger chunks from S and O slots
- using advanced data analysis and machine learning techniques to improve our scoring function

In addition, our approach currently does not take into consideration the directionality of the entailment relationship between the two text fragments. In cases where T1 entails T2 but T2 does not entail T1, our approach will treat (T1, T2) and (T2, T1) as the same pair. We expect to correct this misrepresentation by evaluating the degree of specificity of words composing the SVOs in asymmetric entailment relationships where the first text fragment is more general than the second one. For that purpose, one can use term frequencies as an indicator of specificity (Spärck Jones, 1972).

Obviously, system performance could be further improved by taking a hybrid approach as e.g. in de Marneffe et al. (2006), but we find it more instructive to take our pure LSA approach to its limits first.

6 Acknowledgements

We are grateful to Prof. Donia Scott, head of the Natural Language Generation group within the Centre for Research in Computing of the Open University, who made us aware of the RTE-3 Challenge and encouraged us to participate.

References

[Berry1992] M. W. Berry. 1992. Large-scale sparse singular value computations. *The International Journal of Supercomputer Applications*, 6(1):13–49, Spring.

[Clarke2006] Daoud Clarke. 2006. Meaning as context and subsequence analysis for entailment. In *Proceedings of the Second PASCAL Challenges Workshop on Recognising Textual Entailment*, Venice, Italy.

[de Marneffe et al.2006] Marie-Catherine de Marneffe, Bill MacCartney, Trond Grenager, Daniel Cer, Anna Rafferty, and Christopher D. Manning. 2006. Learning to distinguish valid textual entailments. In *Proceedings of the Second PASCAL Challenges Workshop on Recognising Textual Entailment*, Venice, Italy.

[Harris1954] Zelig S. Harris. 1954. Distributional structure. *WORD*, 10:146–162. Reprinted in J. Fodor and J. Katz, The structure of language: Readings in the philosophy of language, pp. 33–49, Prentice-Hall, 1964.

[Landauer and Dumais1997] T. K. Landauer and S. T. Dumais. 1997. A solution to Plato's Problem. The Latent Semantic Analysis theory of the acquisition, induction and representation of knowledge. *Psychological Review*, 104(2):211–240.

[Lewis et al.2004] D. D. Lewis, Y. Yang, T. Rose, and F. Li. 2004. RCV1: A new benchmark collection for text categorization research. *Journal of Machine Learning Research*, 5:361–397.

[Lin1994] Dekang Lin. 1994. PRINCIPAR – an efficient, broad-coverage, principle-based parser. In *Proc. COLING-94*, pages 42–488, Kyoto, Japan.

[Porter1980] M. F. Porter. 1980. An algorithm for suffix stripping. *Program*, 14(3):130–137.

[Salton et al.1975] G. Salton, A. Wong, and C. S. Yang. 1975. A vector space model for automatic indexing. *Commun. ACM*, 18(11):613–620.

[Spärck Jones1972] Karen Spärck Jones. 1972. A statistical interpretation of term specificity and its application in retrieval. *Journal of Documentation*, 28(1):11–21. Reprinted 2004 in 60(5):493–502 and in Spärck Jones (1988).

[Spärck Jones1988] Karen Spärck Jones. 1988. A statistical interpretation of term specificity and its application in retrieval. *Document retrieval systems*, pages 132–142.

[Widdows2004] Dominic Widdows. 2004. *Geometry and Meaning*. Number 172 in CSLI Lecture Notes. University of Chicago Press.

Textual Entailment Through Extended Lexical Overlap and Lexico-Semantic Matching

Rod Adams, Gabriel Nicolae, Cristina Nicolae and Sanda Harabagiu
Human Language Technology Research Institute
University of Texas at Dallas
Richardson, Texas
{rod, gabriel, cristina, sanda}@hlt.utdallas.edu

Abstract

This paper presents two systems for textual entailment, both employing decision trees as a supervised learning algorithm. The first one is based primarily on the concept of lexical overlap, considering a bag of words similarity overlap measure to form a mapping of terms in the hypothesis to the source text. The second system is a lexico-semantic matching between the text and the hypothesis that attempts an alignment between chunks in the hypothesis and chunks in the text, and a representation of the text and hypothesis as two dependency graphs. Their performances are compared and their positive and negative aspects are analyzed.

1 Introduction

Textual entailment is the task of taking a pair of passages, referred to as the *text* and the *hypothesis*, and labeling whether or not the hypothesis (H) can be fully inferred from the text (T), as is illustrated in Pair 1. In Pair 1, the knowledge that an attorney representing someone's interests entails that they work for that person.

Pair 1 (RTE2 IE 58)

T: "A force majeure is an act of God," said attorney Phil Wittmann, who represents the New Orleans Saints and owner Tom Benson's local interests.
H: Phil Wittmann works for Tom Benson.

The Third PASCAL Recognizing Textual Entailment Challenge[1] follows the experience of the second challenge (Bar-Haim et al., 2006), whose main task was to automatically detect if a hypothesis H is entailed by a text T. To increase the "reality" of the task, the text-hypothesis examples were taken from outputs of actual systems that solved applications like Question Answering (QA), Information Retrieval (IR), Information Extraction (IE) and Summarization (SUM).

In the challenge, there are two corpora, each consisting of 800 annotated pairs of texts and hypotheses. Pairs are annotated as to whether there exists a positive entailment between them and from which application domain each example came from. Instances are distributed evenly among the four tasks in both corpora, as are the positive and negative examples. One corpus was designated for development and training, while the other was reserved for testing.

In the Second PASCAL RTE Challenge (Bar-Haim et al., 2006), one of the best performing submissions was (Adams, 2006), which focused on strict lexical methods so that the system could remain relatively simple and be easily applied to various entailment applications. However, this simple approach did not take into account details like the syntactic structure, the coreference or the semantic relations between words, all necessary for a deeper understanding of natural language text. Thus, a new system, based on the same decision tree learning algorithm, was designed in an attempt to gain performance by adding alignment and dependency relations information. The two systems will be compared and their advantages and disadvantages discussed.

[1] http://www.pascal-network.org/Challenges/RTE3/

Proceedings of the Workshop on Textual Entailment and Paraphrasing, pages 119–124,
Prague, June 2007.

This paper is organized as follows: The first system is discussed in Section 2, followed by the second system in Section 3. The experimental results are presented in Section 4, and the paper concludes in Section 5.

2 Textual entailment through extended lexical overlap

The first system (Adams, 2006) follows a four step framework. The first step is a tokenization process that applies to the content words of the text and hypothesis. The second step is building a "token map" of how the individual tokens in the hypothesis are tied to those in the text, as explained in Section 2.1. Thirdly, several features, as described in Section 2.2, are extracted from the token map. Finally, the extracted features are fed into Weka's (Witten and Frank, 2005) J48 decision tree for training and evaluation.

2.1 The token map

Central to this system is the concept of the token map. This map is inspired by (Glickman et al., 2005)'s use of the most probable lexical entailment for each hypothesis pair, but has been modified in how each pair is evaluated, and that the mapping is stored for additional extraction of features. The complete mapping is a list of (H_i, T_j) mappings, where H_i represents the ith token in the hypothesis, and T_j is similarly the jth token in the text. Each mapping has an associated similarity score. There is one mapping per token in the hypothesis. Text tokens are allowed to appear in multiple mappings.

The mappings are created by considering each hypothesis token and comparing it to each token in the text and keeping the one with the highest similarity score.

Similarity scores A similarity score ranging from 0.0 to 1.0 is computed for any two tokens via a combination of two scores. This score can be thought of as the probability that the text token implies the hypothesis one, even though the methods used to produce it were not strictly probabilistic in nature.

The first score is derived from the cost of a WordNet (Fellbaum, 1998) path. The WordNet paths between two tokens are built with the method reported in (Hirst and St-Onge, 1998), and designated as $Sim_{WN}(H_i, T_j)$. Exact word matches are always given a score of 1.0, words that are morphologically related or that share a common sense are 0.9 and other paths give lower scores down to 0.0. This method of obtaining a path makes use of three groups of WordNet relations: *Up* (e.g. hypernym, member meronym), *Down* (e.g. hyponym, cause) and *Horizontal* (e.g. nominalization, derivation). The path can only follow certain combinations of these groupings, and assigns penalties for each link in the path, as well as for changing from one direction group to another.

The secondary scoring routine is the lexical entailment probability, $lep(u, v)$, from (Glickman et al., 2005). This probability is estimated by taking the page counts returned from the *AltaVista*[2] search engine for a combined u and v search term, and dividing by the count for just the v term. This can be precisely expressed as:

$$\text{Sim}_{AV}(H_i, T_j) = \frac{\text{AVCount}(H_i \,\&\, T_j)}{\text{AVCount}(T_j)}$$

The two scores are combined such that the secondary score can take up whatever slack the dominant score leaves available. The exact combination is:

$$\begin{aligned}\text{Sim}(H_i, T_j) &= \text{Sim}_{WN}(H_h, T_t) \\ &+ \alpha \cdot (1 - \text{Sim}_{WN}(H_h, T_t)) \cdot \text{Sim}_{AV}(H_h, T_t)\end{aligned}$$

where α is a tuned constant ($\alpha \in [0, 1]$). Empirical analysis found the best results with very low values of α[3]. This particular combination was chosen over a strict linear combination, so as to more strongly relate to Sim_{WN} when it's values are high, but allow Sim_{AV} to play a larger role when Sim_{WN} is low.

2.2 Feature extraction

The following three features were constructed from the token map for use in the training of the decision tree, and producing entailment predictions.

Baseline score This score is the product of the similarities of the mapped pairs, and is an extension of (Glickman et al., 2005)'s notion of $P(H|T)$. This

[2]http://www.av.com

[3]The results reported here used $\alpha = 0.1$

is the base feature of entailment.

$$Score_{BASE} = \prod_{(H_i,T_j)\in Map} \mathrm{Sim}(H_i, T_J)$$

One notable characteristic of this feature is that the overall score can be no higher than the lowest score of any single mapping. The failure to locate a strong similarity for even one token will produce a very low base score.

Unmapped negations A token is considered unmapped if it does not appear in any pair of the token map, or if the score associated with that mapping is zero. A token is considered a negation if it is in a set list of terms such as `no` or `not`. Both the text and the hypothesis are searched for unmapped negations, and total count of them is kept, with the objective of determining whether there is an odd or even number of them. A (possibly) modified, or flipped, score feature is generated:

n = # of negations found.

$$Score_{NEG} = \begin{cases} Score_{BASE} & \text{if } n \text{ is even,} \\ 1 - Score_{BASE} & \text{if } n \text{ is odd.} \end{cases}$$

Task The task domain used for evaluating entailment (i.e. IE, IR, QA or SUM) was also used as a feature to allow different thresholds among the domains.

3 Textual entailment through lexico-semantic matching

This second system obtains the probability of entailment between a text and a hypothesis from a supervised learning algorithm that incorporates lexical and semantic information extracted from WordNet and PropBank. To generate learning examples, the system computes features that are based upon the alignment between chunks from the text and the hypothesis. In the preliminary stage, each instance pair of text and hypothesis is processed by a chunker. The resulting chunks can be simple tokens or compound words that exist in WordNet, e.g., *pick up*. They constitute the lexical units in the next stages of the algorithm.

identity	1.0	coreference	0.8
synonymy	0.8	antonymy	-0.8
hypernymy	0.5	hyponymy	-0.5
meronymy	0.4	holonymy	-0.4
entailment	0.6	entailed by	-0.6
cause	0.6	caused by	-0.6

Table 2: Alignment relations and their scores.

3.1 Alignment

Once all the chunks have been identified, the system searches for alignment candidates between the chunks of the hypothesis and those of the text. The search pairs all the chunks of the hypothesis, in turn, with all the text chunks, and for each pair it extracts all the relations between the two nodes. Stop words and auxiliary verbs are discarded, and only two chunks with the same part of speech are compared (a noun must be transformed into a verb to compare it with another verb). The alignments obtained in this manner constitute a one-to-many mapping between the chunks of the hypothesis and the chunks of the text.

The following relations are identified: (a) identity (between the original spellings, lowercase forms or stems), (b) coreference and (c) WordNet relations (synonymy, antonymy, hypernymy, meronymy, entailment and causation). Each of these relations is attached to a score between -1 and 1, which is handcrafted by trial and error on the development set (Table 2).

The score is positive if the relation from the text word to the hypothesis word is compatible with an entailment, e.g., identity, coreference, synonymy, hypernymy, meronymy, entailment and causation, and negative in the opposite case, e.g., antonymy, hyponymy, holonymy, reverse entailment and reverse causation. This is a way of quantifying intuitions like: *"The cat ate the cake"* entails *"The animal ate the cake"*. To identify these relations, no word sense disambiguation is performed; instead, all senses from WordNet are considered. Negations present in text or hypothesis influence the sign of the score; for instance, if a negated noun is aligned with a positive noun through a negative link like antonymy, the two negations cancel each other and the score of the relation will be positive. The score of an alignment is the sum of the scores of all the

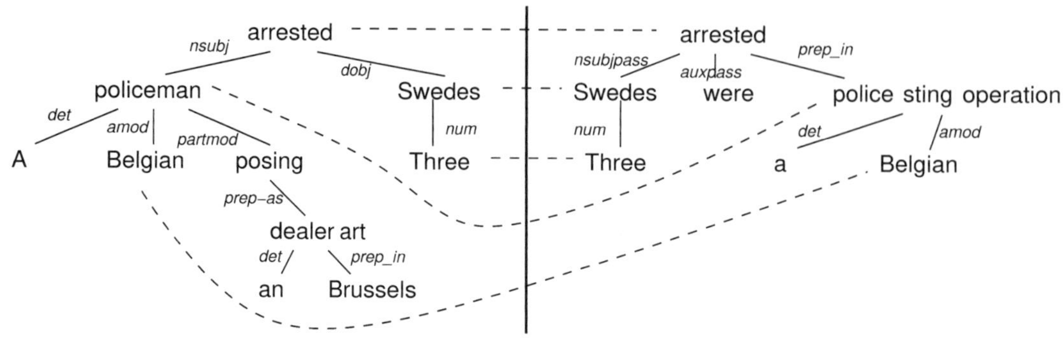

Figure 1: The dependency graphs and alignment candidates for Pair 2 (RTE3 SUM 633).

Category	*Feature name*	*Feature description*
alignment (score)	*totaligscore*	the total alignment score (sum of all scores)
	totminaligscore	the total alignment score when considering only the minimum scored relation for any two chunks aligned
	totmaxaligscore	the total alignment score when considering only the maximum scored relation for any two chunks aligned
alignment (count)	*allaligs*	the number of chunks aligned considering all alignments
	posaligs	the number of chunks aligned considering only positive alignments
	negaligs	the number of chunks aligned considering only negative alignments
	minposaligs	the number of alignments that have the minimum of their scores positive
	maxposaligs	the number of alignments that have the maximum of their scores positive
	minnegaligs	the number of alignments that have the minimum their scores negative
	maxnegaligs	the number of alignments that have the maximum of their scores negative
dependency	*edgelabels*	the pair of labels of non matching edges
	match	the number of relations that match when comparing the two edges
	nonmatch	the number of relations that don't match when comparing the two edges

Table 1: Features for lexico-semantic matching.

relations between the two words, and if the sum is positive, the alignment is considered positive.

3.2 Dependency graphs

The system then creates two dependency graphs, one for the text and one for the hypothesis. The dependency graphs are directed graphs with chunks as nodes, interconnected by edges according to the relations between them, which are represented as edge labels. The tool used is the dependency parser developed by (de Marneffe et al., 2006), which assigns some of 48 grammatical relations to each pair of words within a sentence. Further information is added from the predicate-argument structures in PropBank, e.g., a node can be the ARG0 of another node, which is a predicate.

Because the text can have more than one sentence, the dependency graphs for each of the sentences are combined into a larger one. This is done by collapsing together nodes (chunks) that are coreferent, identical or in an *nn* relation (as given by the parser). The relations between the original nodes and the rest of the nodes in the text (dependency links) and nodes in the hypothesis (alignment links) are all inherited by the new node. Again, each edge can have multiple relations as labels.

3.3 Features

With the alignment candidates and dependency graphs obtained in the previous steps, the system computes the values of the feature set. The features used are of two kinds (Table 1):

(a) The *alignment features* are based on the scores and counts of the candidate alignments. All the scores are represented as real numbers between -1 and 1, normalized by the number of concepts in the hypothesis.

(b) The *dependency features* consider each positively scored aligned pair with each of the other positively scored aligned pairs, and compare the set of

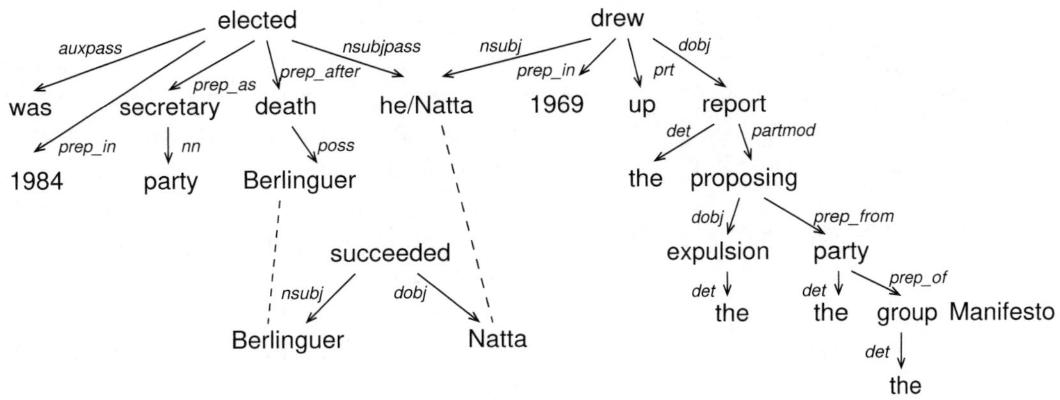

Figure 2: The dependency graphs and alignment candidates for Pair 3 (RTE3 IE 19).

relations between the two nodes in the text with the set of relations between the two nodes in the hypothesis. This comparison is performed on the dependency graphs, on the edges that immediately connect the two text chunks and the two hypothesis chunks, respectively. They have numerical values between 0 and 1, normalized by the square of the total number of aligned chunks.

3.4 Examples

Pair 2 (RTE3 SUM 633)

T: A Belgian policeman posing as an art dealer in Brussels arrested three Swedes.
H: Three Swedes were arrested in a Belgian police sting operation.

Figure 1 illustrates the dependency graphs and alignment candidates extracted for the instance in Pair 2. There is no merging of graphs necessary here, because the text is made up of a single sentence. The vertical line in the center divides the graph corresponding to the text from the one corresponding to the hypothesis. The dependency relations in the two graphs are represented as labels of full lines, while the alignment candidate pairs are joined by dotted lines. As can be observed, the alignment was done based on identity of spelling, e.g., *Swedes-Swedes*, and stem, e.g., *policeman-police*. For the sake of simplicity, the predicate-argument relations have not been included in the drawing. This is a case of a positive instance, and the dependency and alignment relations strongly support the entailment.

Pair 3 (RTE3 IE 19)

T: In 1969, he drew up the report proposing the expulsion from the party of the Manifesto group. In 1984, after Berlinguer's death, Natta was elected as party secretary.
H: Berlinguer succeeded Natta.

Figure 2 contains an example of a negative instance (Pair 3) that cannot be solved through the simple analysis of alignment and dependency relations. The graphs corresponding to the two sentences of the text have been merged into a single graph because of the coreference between the pronoun *he* in the first sentence and the proper name *Natta* in the second one. This merging has enriched the overall information about relations, but the algorithm does not take advantage of this. To correctly solve this problem of entailment, one needs additional information delivered by a temporal relations system. The chain of edges between *Berlinguer* and *Natta* in the text graph expresses the fact that the event of Natta's election happened after Berlinguer's death. Since the hypothesis states that Berlinguer succeeded Natta, the entailment is obviously false. The system presented in this section will almost certainly solve this kind of instance incorrectly.

4 Results

The experimental results are summarized in Tables 3 and 4. The first table presents the accuracy scores obtained by running the two systems through 10-fold crossvalidation on incremental RTE datasets. The first system, based on extended lexical overlap (ELO), almost consistently outperforms the second system, lexico-semantic matching (LSM),

Evaluation set	ELO	LSM	ELO+LSM	
	J48	J48	J48	JRip
RTE3Dev	66.38	63.63	65.50	67.50
+RTE2Dev	64.38	59.19	61.56	62.50
+RTE1Dev	62.11	56.67	60.36	59.62
+RTE2Test	61.04	57.77	61.51	61.20
+RTE1Test	60.07	56.57	59.04	60.42

Table 3: Accuracy for the two systems on various datasets.

Task	IE	IR	QA	SUM	All
Accuracy	53.50	73.50	80.00	61.00	67.00

Table 4: Accuracy by task for the Extended Lexical Overlap system tested on the RTE3Test corpus.

and the combination of the two. The only case when the combination gives the best score is on the RTE3 development set, using the rule-based classifier JRip. It can be observed from the table that the more data is added to the evaluation set, the poorer the results are. This can be explained by the fact that each RTE dataset covers a specific kind of instances. Because of this variety in the data, the results obtained on the whole collection of RTE datasets available are more representative than the results reported on each set, because they express the way the systems would perform in real-life natural language processing as opposed to an academic setup.

Since the ELO system was clearly the better of the two, it was the one submitted to the Third PASCAL Challenge evaluation. Table 4 contains the scores obtained by the system on the RTE3 testing set. The overall accuracy is 67%, which represents an increase from the score the system achieved at the Second PASCAL Challenge (62.8%). The task with the highest performance was Question Answering, while the task that ranked the lowest was Information Extraction. This is understandable, since IE involves a very deep understanding of the text, which the ELO system is not designed to do.

5 Conclusions

This paper has presented two different approaches of solving textual entailment: one based on extended lexical overlap and the other on lexico-semantic matching. The experiments have shown that the first approach, while simpler in concept, yields a greater performance when applied on the PASCAL RTE3 development set. At first glance, it seems puzzling that a simple approach has outperformed one that takes advantage of a deeper analysis of the text. However, ELO system treats the text naively, as a bag of words, and does not rely on any preprocessing application. The LSM system, while attempting an understanding of the text, uses three other systems that are not perfect: the coreference resolver, the dependency parser and the semantic parser. The performance of the LSM system is limited by the performance of the tools it uses. It will be of interest to evaluate this system again once they increase in accuracy.

References

Rod Adams. 2006. Textual entailment through extended lexical overlap. In *The Second PASCAL Recognising Textual Entailment Challenge (RTE-2)*.

Roy Bar-Haim, Ido Dagan, Bill Dolan, Lisa Ferro, Danilo Giampiccolo, Bernardo Magnini, and Idan Szpektor. 2006. The second pascal recognising textual entailment challenge. In *PASCAL RTE Challenge*.

Marie-Catherine de Marneffe, Bill MacCartney, and Christopher D. Manning. 2006. Generating typed dependency parses from phrase structure parses. In *5th International Conference on Language Resources and Evaluation (LREC 2006)*.

Christiane Fellbaum, editor. 1998. *WordNet: An Electronic Lexical Database*. The MIT Press.

Oren Glickman, Ido Dagan, and Moshe Koppel. 2005. Web based probabilistic textual entailment. In *PASCAL RTE Challenge*.

Graeme Hirst and David St-Onge. 1998. Lexical chains as representations of context for the detection and correction of malapropisms. In Christiane Fellbaum, editor, *WordNet: An electronic lexical database*, pages 305–332. The MIT Press.

Ian H. Witten and Eibe Frank. 2005. *Data Mining: Practical machine learning tools and techniques*. Morgan Kaufmann, 2nd edition.

Hypothesis Transformation and Semantic Variability Rules Used in Recognizing Textual Entailment

Adrian Iftene
„Al. I. Cuza" University, Faculty of Computer Science, Iasi, Romania
adiftene@info.uaic.ro

Alexandra Balahur-Dobrescu
„Al. I. Cuza" University, Faculty of Computer Science, Iasi, Romania
abalahur@info.uaic.ro

Abstract

Based on the core approach of the tree edit distance algorithm, the system central module is designed to target the scope of TE – semantic variability. The main idea is to transform the hypothesis making use of extensive semantic knowledge from sources like DIRT, WordNet, Wikipedia, acronyms database. Additionally, we built a system to acquire the extra background knowledge needed and applied complex grammar rules for rephrasing in English.

1 Introduction

Many NLP applications need to recognize when the meaning of one text can be expressed by, or inferred from, another text. Information Retrieval (IR), Question Answering (QA), Information Extraction (IE), Text Summarization (SUM) are examples of applications that need to assess such a semantic relationship between text segments. Textual Entailment Recognition (RTE) (Dagan et al., 2006) has recently been proposed as an application independent task to capture such inferences.

This year our textual entailment system participated for the first time in the RTE[1] competition. Next chapters present its main parts, the detailed results obtained and some possible future improvements.

2 System description

The process requires an initial pre-processing, followed by the execution of a core module which uses the output of the first phase and obtains in the end the answers for all pairs. Figure 1 shows how the pre-processing is realized with the MINIPAR (Lin, 1998) and LingPipe[2] modules which provide the input for the core module. This one uses four databases: DIRT, Acronyms, Background knowledge and WordNet.

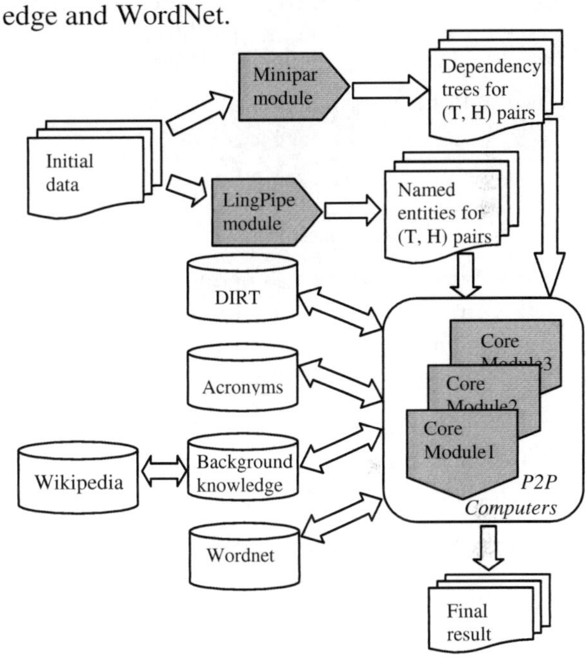

Figure 1: System architecture

The system architecture is based on a peer-to-peer networks design, in which neighboring computers collaborate in order to obtain the global fitness for every text-hypothesis pair. Eventually, based on the computed score, we decide for which pairs we have entailment. This type of architecture was used in order to increase the computation speed.

3 Initial pre-processing

The first step splits the initial file into pairs of files for text and hypothesis. All these files are then sent to the LingPipe module in order to find the Named entities.

[1] http://www.pascal-network.org/Challenges/RTE3/

[2] http://www.alias-i.com/lingpipe/

Proceedings of the Workshop on Textual Entailment and Paraphrasing, pages 125–130,
Prague, June 2007. ©2007 Association for Computational Linguistics

In parallel, we transform with MINIPAR both the text and the hypothesis into dependency trees. Figure 2 shows the output associated with the sentence: "*Le Beau Serge was directed by Chabrol.*".

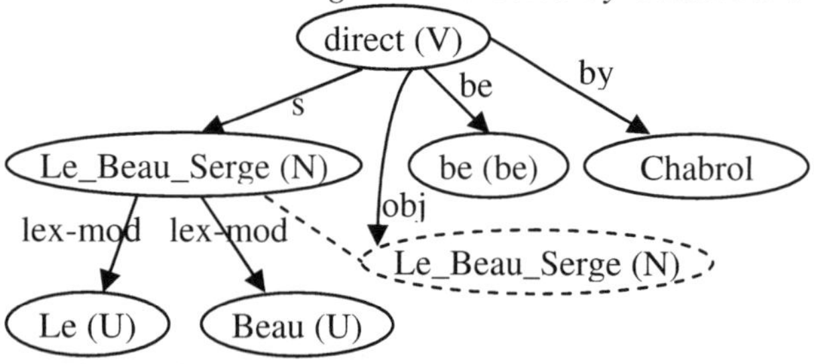

Figure 2: MINIPAR output – dependency tree

For every node from the MINIPAR output, we consider a stamp called **entity** with three main features: the node lemma, the father lemma and the edge label (which represents the relation between words) (like in Figure 3).

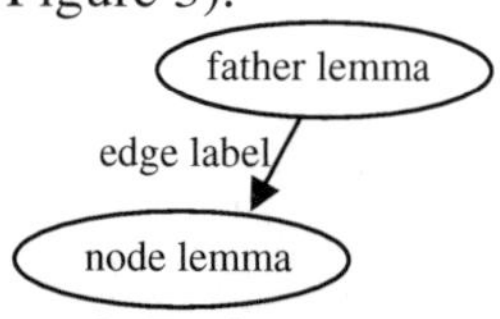

Figure 3: Entity components

Using this stamp, we can easily distinguish between nodes of the trees, even if these have the same lemma and the same father. In the example from Figure 1, for the "son" nodes we have two entities (*Le_Beau_Serge, direct, s*) and (*Le_Beau_Serge, direct, obj*).

4 The hypothesis tree transformation

Presently, the core of our approach is based on a tree edit distance algorithm applied on the dependency trees of both the text and the hypothesis (Kouylekov, Magnini 2005). If the distance (i.e. the cost of the editing operations) among the two trees is below a certain threshold, empirically estimated on the training data, then we assign an entailment relation between the two texts.

The main goal is to map every entity in the dependency tree associated with the hypothesis (called from now on *hypothesis tree*) to an entity in the dependency tree associated with the text (called from now on *text tree*).

For every mapping we calculate a **local fitness** value which indicates the appropriateness between entities. Subsequently, the global fitness is calculated from these partial values.

For every node (refers to the word contained in the node) which can be mapped directly to a node from the text tree, we consider the local fitness value to be 1. When we cannot map one word of the hypothesis to one node from the text, we have the following possibilities:

- If the word is a verb in the hypothesis tree, we use the DIRT resource (Lin and Pantel, 2001) in order to transform the hypothesis tree into an equivalent one, with the same nodes except the verb. Our aim in performing this transformation is to find a new value for the verb which can be better mapped in the text tree.

- If the word is marked as named entity by LingPipe, we try to use an acronyms' database[3] or if the word is a number we try to obtain information related to it from the background knowledge. In the event that even after these operations we cannot map the word from the hypothesis tree to one node from the text tree, no fitness values are computed for this case and we decide the final result: No entailment.

- Else, we use WordNet (Fellbaum, 1998) to look up synonyms for this word and try to map them to nodes from the text tree.

Following this procedure, for every transformation with DIRT or WordNet, we consider for local fitness the similarity value indicated by these resources. If after all checks, one node from the hypothesis tree cannot be mapped, some penalty is inserted in the value of the node local fitness.

4.1 The DIRT resource

For the verbs in the MINIPAR output, we extract templates with DIRT- like format. For the sample output in Figure 2, where we have a single verb "direct", we obtain the following list of "full" templates:N:s:V<direct>V:by:N and N:obj:V<direct>V:by:N. To this list we add a list of "partial" templates: N:s:V<direct>V:, :V<direct>V:by:N, :V<direct>V:by:N, and N:obj:V<direct>V:.

In the same way, we build a list with templates for the verbs in the text tree. With these two lists we perform a search in the DIRT database and extract the "best" trimming, considering the template type (full or partial) and the DIRT score.

According to the search results, we have the following situations:

[3] http://www.acronym-guide.com

a) *left – left* relations similarity

This case is described by the following two templates for the hypothesis and the text:
relation1 HypothesisVerb relation2
relation1 TextVerb relation3
This is the most frequent case, in which a verb is replaced by one of its synonyms or equivalent expressions

The transformation of the hypothesis tree is done in two steps:

1. Replace the relation2 with relation3,

2. Replace the verb from the hypothesis with the corresponding verb from the text. (see Figure 4).

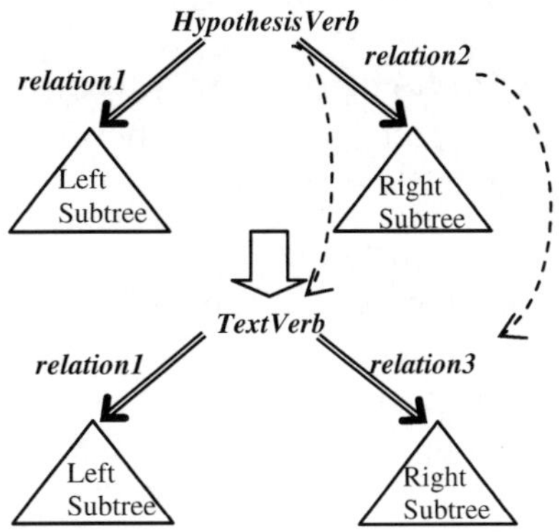

Figure 4: Left-left relation similarity

b) *right – right* relations similarity: the same idea from the previous case.

c) *left – right* relations similarity

This case can be described by the following two templates for the hypothesis and the text:
relation1 HypothesisVerb relation2
relation3 TextVerb relation1
The transformation of the hypothesis tree is:

1. Replace the relation2 with relation3,

2. Replace the verb from the hypothesis with the corresponding verb from the text.

3. Rotate the subtrees accordingly: left subtree will be right subtree and vice-versa right subtree will become left-subtree (as it can be observed in Figure 5).

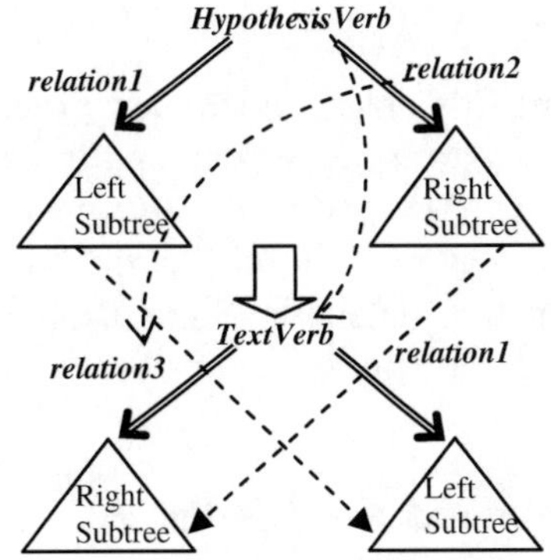

Figure 5: Left-right relation similarity

This case appears for pair 161 with the verb "attack":
T: "The demonstrators, convoked by the solidarity with Latin America committee, verbally attacked Salvadoran President Alfredo Cristiani."
H: "President Alfredo Cristiani was attacked by demonstrators."
In this case, for the text we have the template N:subj:V<attack>V:obj:N, and for the hypothesis the template N:obj:V<attack>V:by:N. Using DIRT, hypothesis H is transformed into:
H': Demonstrators attacked President Alfredo Cristiani.
Under this new form, H is easier comparable to T.

d) *right – left* relations similarity: the same idea from the previous case

For every node transformed with DIRT, we consider its local fitness as being the similarity value indicated by DIRT.

4.2 Extended WordNet

For non-verbs nodes from the hypothesis tree, if in the text tree we do not have nodes with the same lemma, we search for their synonyms in the extended WordNet[4]. For every synonym, we check to see if it appears in the text tree, and select the mapping with the best value according to the values from Extended WordNet. Subsequently, we change the word from the hypothesis tree with the word from WordNet and also its fitness with its indicated similarity value. For example, the relation between "relative" and "niece" is accomplished with a score of 0.078652.

[4] http://xwn.hlt.utdallas.edu/downloads.html

4.3 Acronyms

The acronyms' database helps our program find relations between the acronym and its meaning: "*US - United States*", and "*EU - European Union*". We change the word with the corresponding expression from this database. Since the meaning is the same, the local fitness is considered maximum, i.e. 1.

4.4 Background Knowledge

Some information cannot be deduced from the already used databases and thus we require additional means of gathering extra information of the form:

Argentine [is] Argentina
Netherlands [is] Holland
2 [is] two
Los Angeles [in] California
Chinese [in] China

Table 1: Background knowledge

Background knowledge was built semi-automatically, for the named entities (NEs) and for numbers from the hypothesis without correspondence in the text. For these NEs, we used a module to extract from Wikipedia[5] snippets with information related to them. Subsequently, we use this file with snippets and some previously set patterns of relations between NEs, with the goal to identify a known relation between the NE for which we have a problem and another NE.

If such a relation is found, we save it to an output file. Usually, not all relations are correct, but those that are will help us at the next run.

Our patterns identify two kinds of relations between words:

- "is", when the module extracts information of the form: *'Argentine Republic' (Spanish: 'Republica Argentina', IPA)'* or when explanations about the word are given in brackets, or when the extracted information contains one verb used to define something, like "is", "define", "represent": *'2' ('two') is a number.*

- "in" when information is of the form: *'Chinese' refers to anything pertaining to China* or in the form *Los Angeles County, California*, etc.

[5] http://en.wikipedia.org/wiki/Main_Page

In this case, the local fitness for the node is set to the maximum value for the [is]-type relations, and it receives some penalties for the [in]-type relation.

5 Determination of entailment

After transforming the hypothesis tree, we calculate a global fitness score using the ***extended local fitness*** value for every node from the hypothesis - which is calculated as sum of the following values:

1. local fitness obtained after the tree transformation and node mapping,

2. parent fitness after parent mapping,

3. mapping of the node edge label from the hypothesis tree onto the text tree,

4. node position (left, right) towards its father in the hypothesis and position of the mapping nodes from the text.

After calculating this extended local fitness score, the system computes a total fitness for all the nodes in the hypothesis tree and a negation value associated to the hypothesis tree. Tests have shown that out of these parameters, some are more important (the parameter at 1.) and some less (the parameter at 3.). Below you can observe an example of how the calculations for 3 and 4 are performed and what the negation rules are.

5.1 Edge label mapping

After the process of mapping between nodes, we check how edge labels from the hypothesis tree are mapped onto the text tree. Thus, having two adjacent nodes in the hypothesis, which are linked by an edge with a certain label, we search on the path between the nodes' mappings in the text tree this label. (see Figure 6)

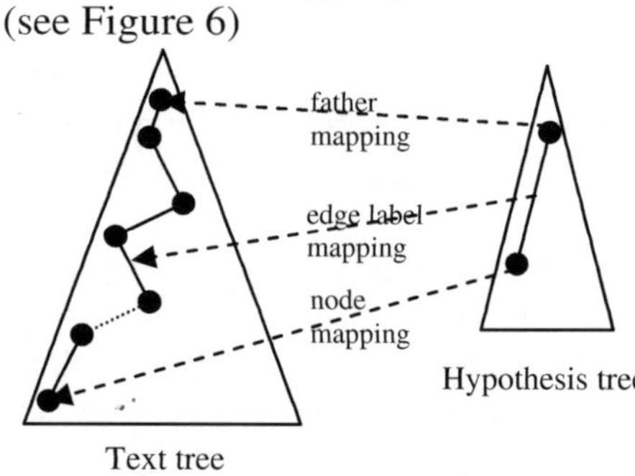

Figure 6: Entity mapping

It is possible that more nodes until the label of the edge linking the nodes in the hypothesis exist, or it is possible that this label is not even found on this path. According to the distance or to the case in which the label is missing, we insert some penalties in the extended local fitness.

5.2 Node position

After mapping the nodes, one of the two following possible situations may be encountered:

- The position of the node towards its father and the position of the mapping node towards its father's mapping are the same (left-left or right-right). In this case, the extended local fitness is incremented.

- The positions are different (left-right or right-left) and in this case a penalty is applied accordingly.

5.3 Negation rules

For every verb from the hypothesis we consider a Boolean value which indicates whether the verb has a negation or not, or, equivalently, if it is related to a verb or adverb "diminishing" its sense or not. Consequently, we check in its tree on its descending branches to see whether one or more of the following words are to be found (pure form of negation or modal verb in indicative or conditional form): "not, may, might, cannot, should, could, etc.". For each of these words we successively negate the initial truth value of the verb, which by default is "false". The final value depends on the number of such words.

Since the mapping is done for all verbs in the text and hypothesis, regardless of their original form in the snippet, we also focused on studying the impact of the original form of the verb on its overall meaning within the text. Infinitives can be identified when preceded by the particle "to". Observing this behavior, one complex rule for negation was built for the particle "to" when it precedes a verb. In this case, the sense of the infinitive is strongly influenced by the active verb, adverb or noun before the particle "to", as follows: if it is being preceded by a verb like "allow, impose, galvanize" or their synonyms, or adjective like "necessary, compulsory, free" or their synonyms or noun like "attempt", "trial" and their synonyms, the meaning of the verb in infinitive form is stressed upon and becomes "certain". For all other cases, the particle "to" diminish the certainty of the action expressed in the infinitive-form verb. Based on the synonyms database with the English thesaurus[6], we built two separate lists – one of "certainty stressing (preserving)" – "positive" and one of "certainty diminishing" – "negative" words. Some examples of these words are "probably", "likely" – from the list of "negative" words and "certainly", "absolutely" – from the list of "positive" words.

5.4 Global fitness calculation

We calculate for every node from the hypothesis tree the value of the extended local fitness, and afterwards consider the normalized value relative to the number of nodes from the hypothesis tree. We denote this result by *TF* (*total fitness*):

$$TF = \frac{\sum_{node \in H} ExtendedLocalFitness_{node}}{HypothesisNodesNumber}$$

After calculating this value, we compute a value *NV* (the *negation value*) indicating the number of verbs with the same value of negation, using the following formula:

$$NV = \frac{Positive\_VerbsNumber}{TotalNumberOfVerbs}$$

where the *Positive_VerbsNumber* is the number of non-negated verbs from the hypothesis using the negation rules, and *TotalNumberOfVerbs* is the total number of verbs from the hypothesis.

Because the maximum value for the extended fitness is 4, the complementary value of the *TF* is *4-TF* and the formula for the **global fitness** used is:

$$GlobalFitness = NV * TF + (1 - NV) * (4 - TF)$$

For pair 518 we have the following:

Initial entity	Node Fitness	Extended local fitness
(the, company, det)	1	3.125
(French, company, nn)	1	3.125
(railway, company, nn)	1	3.125
(company, call, s)	1	2.5
(be, call, be)	1	4
(call, -, -)	0.096	3.048
(company, call, obj)	1	1.125
(SNCF, call, desc)	1	2.625

Table 2: Entities extended fitness

[6] http://thesaurus.reference.com/

TF = (3.125 + 3.125 + 3.125 + 2.5 + 4 + 3.048 + 1.125 + 2.625)/8 = 22.673/8 = 2.834
NV = 1/1 = 1
GlobalFitness = 1*2.834+(1−1)*(4-2.834) = 2.834

Using the development data, we establish a threshold value of 2.06. Thus, pair 518 will have the answer "yes".

6 Results

Our system has a different behavior on different existing tasks, with higher results on Question Answering (0.87) and lower results on Information Extraction (0.57). We submitted two runs for our system, with different parameters used in calculating the extended local fitness. However, the results are almost the same (see Table 3).

	IE	IR	QA	SUM	Global
Run01	0.57	0.69	0.87	0.635	**0.6913**
Run02	0.57	0.685	0.865	0.645	**0.6913**

Table 3: Test results

To be able to see each component's relevance, the system was run in turn with each component removed. The results in the table below show that the system part verifying the NEs is the most important.

System Description	Precision	Relevance
Without DIRT	0.6876	**0.54 %**
Without WordNet	0.6800	**1.63 %**
Without Acronyms	0.6838	**1.08 %**
Without BK	0.6775	**2.00 %**
Without Negations	0.6763	**2.17 %**
Without NEs	0.5758	**16.71 %**

Table 4: Components relevance

7 Conclusions

The system's core algorithm is based on the tree edit distance approach, however, focused on transforming the hypothesis. It presently uses widespread syntactic analysis tools like Minipar, lexical resources like WordNet and LingPipe for Named Entities recognition and semantic resources like DIRT. The system's originality resides firstly in creating a part-of and equivalence ontology using an extraction module for Wikipedia data on NEs (the background knowledge), secondly in using a distinct database of acronyms from different domains, thirdly acquiring a set of important context influencing terms and creating a semantic equivalence set of rules based on English rephrasing concepts and last, but not least, on the technical side, using a distributed architecture for time performance enhancement.

The approach unveiled some issues related to the dependency to parsing tools, for example separating the verb and the preposition in the case of phrasal verbs, resulting in the change of meaning.

Another issue was identifying expressions that change context nuances, which we denoted by "positive" or "negative" words. Although we applied rules for them, we still require analysis to determine their accurate quantification.

For the future, our first concern is to search for a method to establish more precise values for penalties, in order to obtain lower values for pairs with No entailment. Furthermore, we will develop a new method to determine the multiplication coefficients for the parameters in the extended local fitness and the global threshold.

8 Acknowledgements

The authors thank the members of the NLP group in Iasi for their help and support at different stages of the system development. Special thanks go to Daniel Matei which was responsible for preparing all the input data.

The work on this project is partially financed by Siemens VDO Iaşi and by the CEEX Rotel project number 29.

References

Dagan, I., Glickman, O., and Magnini, B. 2006. *The PASCAL Recognising Textual Entailment Challenge*. In Quiñonero-Candela et al., editors, *MLCW 2005, LNAI Volume 3944*, pages 177-190. Springer-Verlag.

Fellbaum, C. 1998. *WordNet: An Electronic Lexical Database*. MIT Press, Cambridge, Mass.

Kouylekov, M. and Magnini, B. 2005. *Recognizing Textual Entailment with Tree Edit Distance Algorithms*. In Proceedings of the First Challenge Workshop Recognising Textual Entailment, Pages 17-20, 25–28 April, 2005, Southampton, U.K.

Lin, D. 1998. *Dependency-based Evaluation of MINIPAR*. In Workshop on the Evaluation of Parsing Systems, Granada, Spain, May, 1998.

Lin, D., and Pantel, P. 2001. *DIRT - Discovery of Inference Rules from Text*. In Proceedings of ACM Conference on Knowledge Discovery and Data Mining (KDD-01). pp. 323-328. San Francisco, CA.

Semantic Inference at the Lexical-Syntactic Level for Textual Entailment Recognition

Roy Bar-Haim[†]**,Ido Dagan**[†]**, Iddo Greental**[‡]**, Idan Szpektor**[†] and **Moshe Friedman**[†]
[†]Computer Science Department, Bar-Ilan University, Ramat-Gan 52900, Israel
[‡]Linguistics Department, Tel Aviv University, Ramat Aviv 69978, Israel
{barhair,dagan}@cs.biu.ac.il,greenta@post.tau.ac.il,
{szpekti,friedmm}@cs.biu.ac.il

Abstract

We present a new framework for textual entailment, which provides a modular integration between knowledge-based exact inference and cost-based approximate matching. Diverse types of knowledge are uniformly represented as entailment rules, which were acquired both manually and automatically. Our proof system operates directly on parse trees, and infers new trees by applying entailment rules, aiming to strictly *generate* the target *hypothesis* from the source *text*. In order to cope with inevitable knowledge gaps, a cost function is used to measure the remaining "distance" from the hypothesis.

1 Introduction

According to the traditional formal semantics approach, inference is conducted at the logical level. However, practical text understanding systems usually employ shallower lexical and lexical-syntactic representations, augmented with partial semantic annotations. Such practices are typically partial and quite ad-hoc, and lack a clear formalism that specifies how inference knowledge should be represented and applied. The current paper proposes a step towards filling this gap, by defining a principled semantic inference mechanism over parse-based representations.

Within the textual entailment setting a system is required to recognize whether a hypothesized statement h can be inferred from an asserted text t. Some inferences can be based on available knowledge, such as information about synonyms and paraphrases. However, some gaps usually arise and it is often not possible to derive a complete "proof" based on available inference knowledge. Such situations are typically handled through approximate matching methods.

This paper focuses on knowledge-based inference, while employing rather basic methods for approximate matching. We define a proof system that operates over syntactic parse trees. New trees are derived using entailment rules, which provide a principled and uniform mechanism for incorporating a wide variety of manually and automatically-acquired inference knowledge. Interpretation into stipulated semantic representations, which is often difficult to obtain, is circumvented altogether. Our research goal is to explore how far we can get with such an inference approach, and identify the scope in which semantic interpretation may not be needed. For a detailed discussion of our approach and related work, see (Bar-Haim et al., 2007).

2 Inference Framework

The main contribution of the current work is a principled semantic inference mechanism, that aims to generate a target text from a source text using entailment rules, analogously to logic-based proof systems. Given two parsed text fragments, termed *text* (t) and *hypothesis* (h), the inference system (or *prover*) determines whether t entails h. The prover applies entailment rules that aim to transform t into h through a sequence of intermediate parse trees. For each generated tree p, a heuristic cost function is employed to measure the likelihood of p entailing h.

Proceedings of the Workshop on Textual Entailment and Paraphrasing, pages 131–136,
Prague, June 2007.

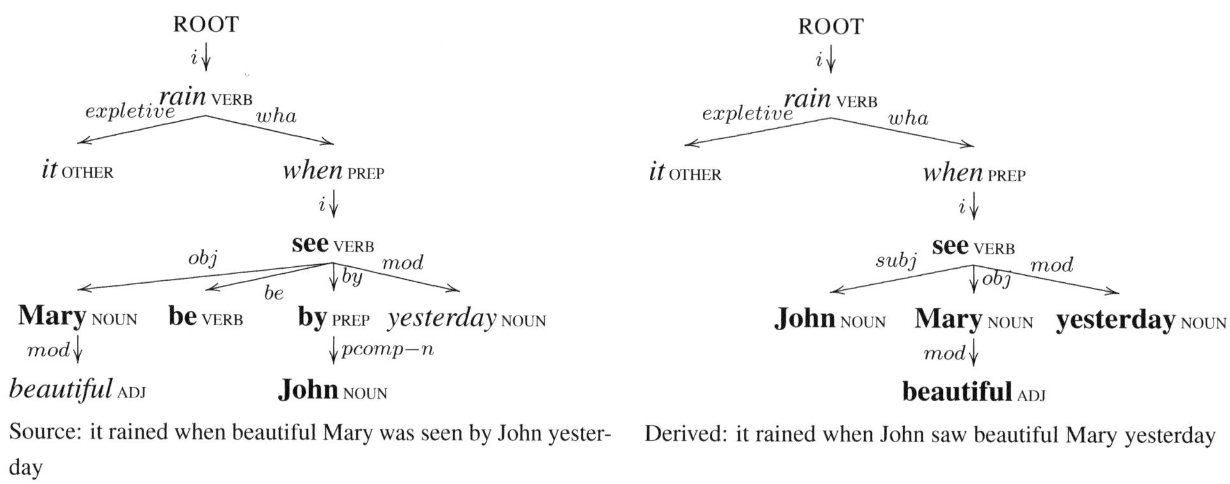

(a) Application of passive to active transformation

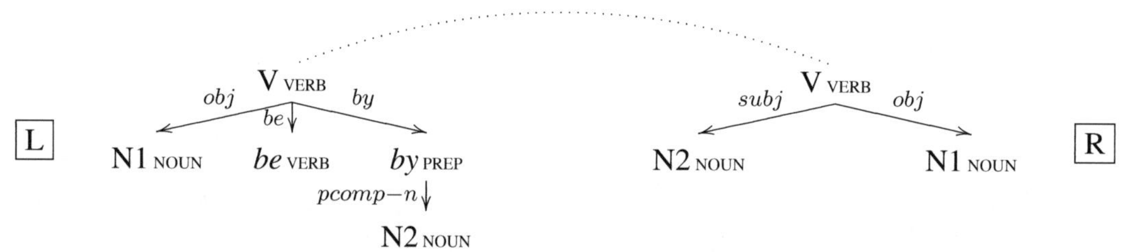

(b) Passive to active transformation (substitution rule). The dotted arc represents alignment.

Figure 1: Application of inference rules. POS and relation labels are based on Minipar (Lin, 1998b)

If a complete proof is found (h was generated), the prover concludes that entailment holds. Otherwise, entailment is determined by comparing the minimal cost found during the proof search to some threshold θ.

3 Proof System

Like logic-based systems, our proof system consists of *propositions* (t, h, and intermediate premises), and *inference (entailment) rules*, which derive new propositions from previously established ones.

3.1 Propositions

Propositions are represented as dependency trees, where nodes represent words, and hold a set of features and their values. In our representation these features include the word lemma and part-of-speech, and additional features that may be added during the proof process. Edges are annotated with dependency relations.

3.2 Inference Rules

At each step of the proof an inference rule generates a *derived* tree d from a *source* tree s. A rule is primarily composed of two templates, termed *left-hand-side* (L), and *right-hand-side* (R). *Templates* are dependency subtrees which may contain *variables*. Figure 1(b) shows an inference rule, where V, $N1$ and $N2$ are common variables. L specifies the subtree of s to be modified, and R specifies the new generated subtree. Rule application consists of the following steps:

L matching The prover first tries to match L in s. L is *matched* in s if there exists a one-to-one node mapping function f from L to s, such that: (i) For each node u, $f(u)$ has the same features and feature values as u. Variables match any lemma value in $f(u)$. (ii) For each edge $u \to v$ in L, there is an edge $f(u) \to f(v)$ in s, with the same dependency relation. If matching fails, the rule is not applicable to s. Otherwise, successful matching induces *vari-*

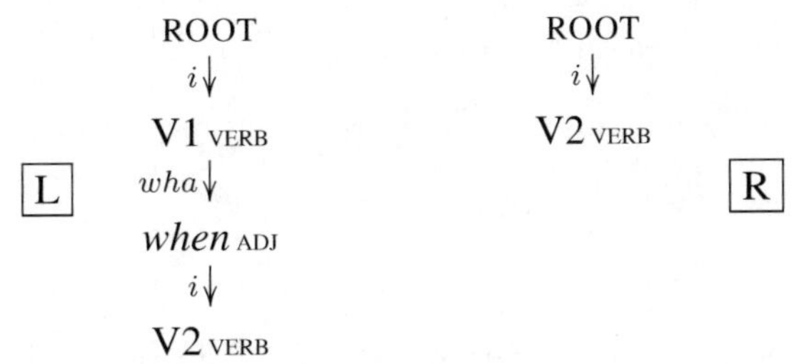

Figure 2: Temporal clausal modifier extraction (introduction rule)

able binding $b(X)$, for each variable X in L, defined as the full subtree rooted in $f(X)$ if X is a leaf, or $f(X)$ alone otherwise. We denote by l the subtree in s to which L was mapped (as illustrated in bold in Figure 1(a), left tree).

R instantiation An instantiation of R, which we denote r, is generated in two steps: (i) creating a copy of R; (ii) replacing each variable X with a copy of its binding $b(X)$ (as set during L matching). In our example this results in the subtree *John saw beautiful Mary*.

Alignment copying the *alignment* relation between pairs of nodes in L and R specifies which modifiers in l that are not part of the rule structure need to be copied to the generated tree r. Formally, for any two nodes u in l and v in r whose matching nodes in L and R are aligned, we copy the daughter subtrees of u in s, which are not already part of l, to become daughter subtrees of v in r. The bold nodes in the right part of Figure 1(b) correspond to r after alignment. *yesterday* was copied to r due to the alignment of its parent verb node.

Derived tree generation by rule type Our formalism has two methods for generating the derived tree: *substitution* and *introduction*, as specified by the rule type. With *substitution* rules, the derived tree d is obtained by making a local modification to the source tree s. Except for this modification s and d are identical (a typical example is a lexical rule, such as *buy* → *purchase*). For this type, d is formed by copying s while replacing l (and the descendants of l's nodes) with r. This is the case for the passive rule. The right part of Figure 1(a) shows the derived tree for the passive rule application. By contrast, *introduction* rules are used to make inferences from a subtree of s, while the other parts of s are ignored and do not affect d. A typical example is inference of a proposition embedded as a relative clause in s. In this case the derived tree d is simply taken to be r. Figure 2 presents such a rule that derives propositions embedded within temporal modifiers. Note that the derived tree does not depend on the main clause. Applying this rule to the right part of Figure 1(b) yields the proposition *John saw beautiful Mary yesterday*.

3.3 Annotation Rules

Annotation rules add features to parse tree nodes, and are used in our system to annotate negation and modality. Annotation rules do not have an R. Instead, nodes of L may contain annotation features. If L is matched in a tree then the annotations are copied to the matched nodes. Annotation rules are applied to t and to each inferred premise prior to any entailment rule application and these features may block inappropriate subsequent rule applications, such as for negated predicates.

4 Rules for Generic Linguistic Structures

Based on the above framework we have manually created a rule base for generic linguistic phenomena.

4.1 Syntactic-Based Rules

These rules capture entailment inferences associated with common syntactic structures. They have three major functions: (i) simplification and canonization of the source tree (categories 6 and 7 in Table 1); (ii) extracting embedded propositions (categories 1, 2, 3); (iii) inferring propositions from non-propositional subtrees (category 4).

4.2 Polarity-Based Rules

Consider the following two examples:

John *knows* that Mary is here ⇒ Mary is here.
John *believes* that Mary is here ⇏ Mary is here.

Valid inference of propositions embedded as verb complements depends on the verb properties, and the polarity of the context in which the verb appears (positive, negative, or unknown) (Nairn et al., 2006). We extracted from the polarity lexicon of Nairn et al. a list of verbs for which inference is allowed in positive polarity context, and generated entailment

#	Category	Example: source	Example: derived
1	Conjunctions	Helena's very experienced and has played a long time on the tour.	⇒ Helena has played a long time on the tour.
2	Clausal modifiers	But celebrations were muted as many Iranians observed a Shi'ite mourning month.	⇒ Many Iranians observed a Shi'ite mourning month.
3	Relative clauses	The assailants fired six bullets at the car, which carried Vladimir Skobtsov.	⇒ The car carried Vladimir Skobtsov.
4	Appositives	Frank Robinson, a one-time manager of the Indians, has the distinction for the NL.	⇒ Frank Robinson is a one-time manager of the Indians.
5	Determiners	The plaintiffs filed **their** lawsuit last year in U.S. District Court in Miami.	⇒ The plaintiffs filed **a** lawsuit last year in U.S. District Court in Miami.
6	Passive	We have been approached by the investment banker.	⇒ The investment banker approached us.
7	Genitive modifier	Malaysia's crude palm oil output is estimated to have risen by up to six percent.	⇒ The crude palm oil output of Malasia is estimated to have risen by up to six percent.
8	Polarity	Yadav was forced to resign.	⇒ Yadav resigned.
9	Negation, modality	What we've **never** seen is actual costs come down.	What we've never $\overline{\text{seen}}$ is actual costs come down. (⇏ What we've seen is actual costs come down.)

Table 1: Summary of rule base for generic linguistic structures.

rules for these verbs (category 8). The list was complemented with a few reporting verbs, such as *say* and *announce*, assuming that in the news domain the speaker is usually considered reliable.

4.3 Negation and Modality Annotation Rules

We use annotation rules to mark negation and modality of predicates (mainly verbs), based on their descendent modifiers. Category 9 in Table 1 illustrates a negation rule, annotating the verb *seen* for negation due to the presence of *never*.

4.4 Generic Default Rules

Generic default rules are used to define default behavior in situations where no case-by-case rules are available. We used one default rule that allows removal of any modifiers from nodes.

5 Lexical-based Rules

These rules have open class lexical components, and consequently are numerous compared to the generic rules described in section 4. Such rules are acquired either lexicographically or automatically.

The rules described in the section 4 are applied whenever their L template is matched in the source premise. For high fan-out rules such as lexical-based rules (e.g. words with many possible synonyms), this may drastically increase the size of the search space. Therefore, the rules described below are applied only if L is matched in the source premise p and R is matched in h.

5.1 Lexical Rules

Lexical entailment rules, such as 'steal → take' and 'Britain → UK' were created based on WordNet (Fellbaum, 1998). Given p and h, a lexical rule $lemma_p \rightarrow lemma_h$ may be applied if $lemma_p$ and $lemma_h$ are lemmas of open-class words appearing in p and h respectively, and there is a path from $lemma_h$ to $lemma_p$ in the WordNet ontology, through synonym and hyponym relations.

5.2 Lexical-Syntactic Rules

In order to find lexical-syntactic paraphrases and entailment rules, such as 'X strike $Y \rightarrow X$ hit Y' and 'X buy $Y \rightarrow X$ own Y' that would bridge between p and h, we applied the DIRT algorithm (Lin and Pantel, 2001) to the first CD of the Reuters RCV1 corpus[1]. DIRT does not identify the entailment direction, hence we assumed bi-directional entailment.

We calculate off-line only the feature vector of every template found in the corpus, where each path between head nouns is considered a template instance. Then, given a premise p, we first mark all lexical noun alignments between p and h. Next, for every pair of alignments we extract the path between the two nouns in p, labeled $path_p$, and the corresponding path between the aligned nouns in h, labeled $path_h$. We then on-the-fly test whether there is a rule '$path_p \rightarrow path_h$' by extracting the stored feature vectors of $path_p$ and $path_h$ and measuring

[1]http://about.reuters.com/researchandstandards/corpus/

their similarity. If the score exceeds a given threshold[2], we apply the rule to p.

Another enhancement that we added to DIRT is template canonization. At learning time, we transform every template identified in the corpus into its canonized form[3] using a set of morpho-syntactic rules, similar to the ones described in Section 4. In addition, we apply nominalization rules such as 'acquisition of Y by $X \rightarrow X$ acquire Y', which transform a nominal template into its related verbal form. We automatically generate these rules (Ron, 2006), based on Nomlex (Macleod et al., 1998).

At inference time, before retrieving feature vectors, we canonize $path_p$ into $path_p^c$ and $path_h$ into $path_h^c$. We then assess the rule '$path_p^c \rightarrow path_h^c$', and if valid, we apply the rule '$path_p \rightarrow path_h$' to p. In order to ensure the validity of the implicature '$path_p \rightarrow path_p^c \rightarrow path_h^c \rightarrow path_h$', we canonize $path_p$ using the same rule set used at learning time, but we apply only bi-directional rules to $path_h$ (e.g. conjunct heads are not removed from $path_h$).

6 Approximate Matching

As mentioned in section 2, approximate matching is incorporated into our system via a cost function, which estimates the likelihood of h being entailed from a given premise p. Our cost function $C(p, h)$ is a linear combination of two measures: lexical cost, $C_{lex}(p, h)$ and lexical-syntactic cost $C_{lexSyn}(p, h)$:

$$C(p, h) = \lambda C_{lexSyn}(p, h) + (1 - \lambda) C_{lex}(p, h) \quad (1)$$

Let $\hat{m}()$ be a (possibly partial) 1-1 mapping of the nodes of h to the nodes of p, where each node is mapped to a node with the same lemma, such that the number of matched edges is maximized. An edge $u \rightarrow v$ in h is matched in p if $\hat{m}(u)$ and $\hat{m}(v)$ are both defined, and there is an edge $\hat{m}(u) \rightarrow \hat{m}(v)$ in p, with the same dependency relation. $C_{lexSyn}(p, h)$ is then defined as the percentage of unmatched edges in h.

Similarly, $C_{lex}(p, h)$ is the percentage of unmatched lemmas in h, considering only open-class words, defined as:

$$C_{lex}(p, h) = 1 - \frac{\sum_{l \in h} Score(l)}{\#OpenClassWords(h)} \quad (2)$$

where $Score(l)$ is 1 if it appears in p, or if it is a derivation of a word in p (according to WordNet). Otherwise, $Score(l)$ is the maximal Lin dependency-based similarity score between l and the lemmas of p (Lin, 1998a) (synonyms and hypernyms/hyponyms are handled by the lexical rules).

7 System Implementation

Deriving the initial propositions t and h from the input text fragments consists of the following steps: (i) Anaphora resolution, using the MARS system (Mitkov et al., 2002). Each anaphor was replaced by its antecedent. (ii) Sentence splitting, using mxterminator (Reynar and Ratnaparkhi, 1997). (iii) Dependency parsing, using Minipar (Lin, 1998b).

The proof search is implemented as a depth-first search, with maximal depth (i.e. proof length) of 4. If the text contains more than one sentence, the prover aims to prove h from each of the parsed sentences, and entailment is determined based on the minimal cost. Thus, the only cross-sentence information that is considered is via anaphora resolution.

8 Evaluation

		Full (run1)		Lexical (run2)	
Dataset	Task	Acc.	Avg.P	Acc.	Avg.P
Test	IE	0.4950	0.5021	0.5000	0.5379
Official	IR	0.6600	0.6174	0.6450	0.6539
Results	QA	0.7050	0.8085	0.6600	0.8075
	SUM	0.5850	0.6200	0.5300	0.5927
	All	**0.6112**	**0.6118**	**0.5837**	**0.6093**
Dev.	All	0.6443	0.6699	0.6143	0.6559

Table 2: Empirical evaluation - results.

The results for our submitted runs are listed in Table 2, including per-task scores. **run1** is our full system, denoted $\mathcal{F}$. It was tuned on a random sample of 100 sentences from the development set, resulting in $\lambda = 0.6$ and $\theta = 0.6242$ (entailment threshold). **run2** is a lexical configuration, denoted $\mathcal{L}$, in which $\lambda = 0$ (lexical cost only), $\theta = 0.2375$ and the only inference rules used were WordNet Lexical rules. We found that the higher accuracy achieved by $\mathcal{F}$ as compared to $\mathcal{L}$ might have been merely due to a lucky choice of threshold. Setting the threshold to its optimal value with respect to the test set resulted in an accuracy of 62.4% for $\mathcal{F}$, and 62.9% for

[2]We set the threshold to 0.01

[3]The active verbal form with direct modifiers

$\mathcal{L}$. This is also hinted by the very close average precision scores for both systems, which do not depend on the threshold. The last row in the table shows the results obtained for 7/8 of the development set that was not used for tuning, denoted *Dev*, using the same parameter settings. Again, $\mathcal{F}$ performs better than $\mathcal{L}$. $\mathcal{F}$ is still better when using an optimal threshold (which increases accuracy up to 65.3% for $\mathcal{F}$ and 63.9% for $\mathcal{L}$. Overall, $\mathcal{F}$ does not show yet a consistent significant improvement over $\mathcal{L}$.

Initial analysis of the results (based on *Dev*) suggests that the coverage of the current rules is still rather low. Without approximate matching (h must be fully proved using the entailment rules) the recall is only 4.3%, although the precision (92%) is encouraging. Lexical-syntactic rules were applied in about 3% of the attempted proofs, and in most cases involved only morpho-syntactic canonization, with no lexical variation. As a result, entailment was determined mainly by the cost function. Entailment rules managed to reduce the cost in about 30% of the attempted proofs.

We have qualitatively analyzed a subset of false negative cases, to determine whether failure to complete the proof is due to deficient components of the system or due to higher linguistic and knowledge levels. For each pair, we assessed the reasoning steps a successful derivation of h from t would take. We classified each pair according to the most demanding type of reasoning step it would require. We allowed rules that are presently unavailable in our system, as long as they are similar in power to those that are currently available. We found that while the single dominant cause for proof failure is lack of world knowledge, e.g. *the king's son is a member of the royal family*, the combination of missing lexical-syntactic rules and parser failures equally contributed to proof failure.

9 Conclusion

We defined a novel framework for semantic inference at the lexical-syntactic level, which allows a unified representation of a wide variety of inference knowledge. In order to reach reasonable recall on RTE data, we found that we must scale our rule acquisition, mainly by improving methods for automatic rule learning.

Acknowledgments

We are grateful to Cleo Condoravdi for making the polarity lexicon developed at PARC available for this research. We also wish to thank Ruslan Mitkov, Richard Evans, and Viktor Pekar from University of Wolverhampton for running the MARS system for us. This work was partially supported by ISF grant 1095/05, the IST Programme of the European Community under the PASCAL Network of Excellence IST-2002-506778, the Israel Internet Association (ISOC-IL) grant 9022 and the ITC-irst/University of Haifa collaboration.

References

Roy Bar-Haim, Ido Dagan, Iddo Greental, and Eyal Shnarch. 2007. Semantic inference at the lexical-syntactic level. In *AAAI (to appear)*.

Christiane Fellbaum, editor. 1998. *WordNet: An Electronic Lexical Database*. Language, Speech and Communication. MIT Press.

Dekang Lin and Patrik Pantel. 2001. Discovery of inference rules for question answering. *Natural Language Engineering*, 4(7):343–360.

Dekang Lin. 1998a. Automatic retrieval and clustering of similar words. In *Proceedings of COLING/ACL*.

Dekang Lin. 1998b. Dependency-based evaluation of minipar. In *Proceedings of the Workshop on Evaluation of Parsing Systems at LREC*.

C. Macleod, R. Grishman, A. Meyers, L. Barrett, and R. Reeves. 1998. Nomlex: A lexicon of nominalizations. In *EURALEX*.

Ruslan Mitkov, Richard Evans, and Constantin Orasan. 2002. A new, fully automatic version of Mitkov's knowledge-poor pronoun resolution method. In *Proceedings of CICLing*.

Rowan Nairn, Cleo Condoravdi, and Lauri Karttunen. 2006. Computing relative polarity for textual inference. In *Proceedings of ICoS-5*.

Jeffrey C. Reynar and Adwait Ratnaparkhi. 1997. A maximum entropy approach to identifying sentence boundaries. In *Proceedings of ANLP*.

Tal Ron. 2006. Generating entailment rules based on online lexical resources. Master's thesis, Computer Science Department, Bar-Ilan University, Ramat-Gan, Israel.

An Extensible Probabilistic Transformation-based Approach to the Third Recognizing Textual Entailment Challenge

Stefan Harmeling
Institute of Adaptive and Neural Computation
School of Informatics, Edinburgh University, Scotland
stefan.harmeling@ed.ac.uk

Abstract

We introduce a system for textual entailment that is based on a probabilistic model of entailment. The model is defined using some calculus of transformations on dependency trees, which is characterized by the fact that derivations in that calculus preserve the truth only with a certain probability. We also describe a possible set of transformations (and with it implicitly a calculus) that was successfully applied to the RTE3 challenge data. However, our system can be improved in many ways and we see it as the starting point for a promising new approach to textual entailment.

1 Introduction

Textual entailment recognition asks the question whether a piece of text like

> The Cassini Spacecraft has taken images from July 22, 2006 that show rivers and lakes present on Saturn's moon Titan.

implies a hypothesis like

> The Cassini Spacecraft reached Titan.

There exists already many interesting approaches to this problem, see (Dagan et al., 2005; Bar-Haim et al., 2006) for various recent efforts and our paper wont try to fully reinvent the wheel. Instead it will present some work in progress that tries to model the probability of entailment in terms of ideas motivated by approaches like the edit-distance (Kouylekov and Magnini, 2005; Kouylekov and Magnini, 2006; Tatu et al., 2006; Adams, 2006). However, instead of defining some distance based on edits, we will generate derivations in some calculus that is able to transform dependency parse trees. The special property of our calculus is that the truth is only preserved with a certain probability along its derivations. This might sound like a disadvantage. However, in commonsense reasoning there is usual a lot of uncertainty due the fact that it is impossible to formalize *all* world knowledge. We think that probabilities might help us in such situations where it is impossible to include everything into the model, but in which nonetheless we want to do reasoning.

2 Main idea

First of all, let us assume that the text and the hypothesis of an textual entailment example are represented as dependency trees T and H. We would like to formalize the probability that T entails H with some model $p_\theta(T \models H)$ parametrized by a vector θ. In order to define $p_\theta(T \models H)$ we first introduce the probability of preserving truth along syntactic derivations in some calculus $T \vdash_\tau H$ which we informally introduce next.

Suppose we are given n transformations $\mathsf{TF}_1, \ldots, \mathsf{TF}_n$ that are designed to modify dependency trees. For each such transformation TF_j, the probability of preserving truth is modelled as a constant value θ_j independent of the dependency tree T it is applied to, i.e.

$$p_\theta(T \vdash_{\mathsf{TF}_j} \mathsf{TF}_j(T)) = \theta_j \quad \text{for all } T, \qquad (1)$$

with parameter θ being the vector of all θ_j. The idea

Proceedings of the Workshop on Textual Entailment and Paraphrasing, pages 137–142,
Prague, June 2007.

is that applying a transformation to T could also create a dependency tree that is sometimes not entailed by T anymore. Consider e.g. the transformation that extracts an appositive and adds a new sentence for it. Usually this is correct, but there are situations in which the appositive appears inside a quote, where it might lead to a wrong conclusion. Thus it makes sense to consider probabilities to deal with imperfect calculi.

We call an n-tuple of such transformations a derivation, which we denote by τ with $\ell(\tau) = n$. Let τ_j count the number of times TF_j appears in τ. Furthermore, let $\tau(T)$ be the result of applying the transformations in τ to some dependency tree T, e.g. for $\tau = (\mathsf{TF}_3, \mathsf{TF}_3, \mathsf{TF}_{17})$ with $\ell(\tau) = 3$ we have $\tau(T) = \mathsf{TF}_{17}(\mathsf{TF}_3(\mathsf{TF}_3(T)))$.

Suppose that a derivation $\tau = (t_1, \ldots, t_{\ell(\tau)})$ derives H from T, i.e. $\tau(T) = H$. Then we define the probability of preserving the truth along the derivation τ as the product of the preservation probabilities of the transformations involved[1]:

$$p_\theta(T \vdash_\tau H) = \prod_{i=1}^{\ell(\tau)-1} p_\theta(T_i \vdash_{t_i} T_{i+1}) = \prod_{j=1}^{n} \theta_j^{\tau_j} \quad (2)$$

with $T_1 = T$, $T_{i+1} = t_i(T_i)$ and $T_{\ell(\tau)} = H$. Note that even though for a certain dependency tree T applying different derivations τ and σ can result in the same tree, i.e. $\tau(T) = \sigma(T)$, their probabilities of preserving truth can be different, since the probabilities depend only the transformations applied.

In the previous paragraphs we have defined probabilities of preserving truth for all finite length derivations in the calculus. This allows us now to define the probability of $T \models H$ to be the maximal probability over all possible derivations,

$$p_\theta(T \models H) = \max_{\tau:\tau(T)=H} p_\theta(T \vdash_\tau H) = \max_{\tau:\tau(T)=H} \prod_{j=1}^{n} \theta_j^{\tau_j}. \quad (3)$$

In the following we introduce a set of transformations that is able to transform any text into any hypothesis and we will propose a heuristic that generates such derivations.

[1]Note, that this definition is similar to the idea of "transitive chaining" introduced in (Dagan and Glickman, 2004).

3 Details

3.1 Preprocessing and parsing

For preprocessing we apply the following steps to the text string and the hypothesis string:

(1) Remove white space, dots and quotations marks at beginning and end.
(2) Remove trailing points of abbreviations.
(3) Remove space between names, e.g. 'Pat Smith' becomes 'PatSmith'.
(4) Unify numbers, e.g. resolve 'million'.
(5) Unify dates, e.g. '5 June' becomes 'June 5'.

We then split the text string into sentences simply by splitting at all locations containing a dot followed by a space. The resulting strings are fed to the Stanford Parser (de Marneffe et al., 2006; Klein and Manning, 2003) with its included pretrained model and options '-retainTmpSubcategories' and '-splitTMP 1'. This allows us to generate dependency trees the nodes of which contain a single stemmed word, its part-of-speech tag and its dependency tag (as produced using the parser's output options 'wordsAndTags' and 'typedDependencies', see (de Marneffe et al., 2006)). For the stemming we apply the function 'morphy' of the NLTK-LITE toolbox (Bird, 2005). If the text string contains more than one sentence, they will be combined to a single dependency tree with a common root node. Let us from now on refer to the dependency trees of text and hypothesis by T and H.

3.2 Generating derivations

The heuristic described in the following generates a derivation that transforms T into H. For brevity we will use in the text the abbreviations of the transformations as listed in Tab. 1.

(1) Resolve appositives and relative clauses. All derivations for some T and H start by converting any existing appositives and relative clauses in T to new sentences that are added to T. For each sentence that was added in this step, the applied transformation, ATS or RTS, is appended to τ.

(2) Calculate how H can clamp to T. Often there are several possibilities to assign all or some of the words in H to words in T. For simplicity our system currently ignores certain grammatical parts which

SS	substitute synonym
SN	substitute number
SNE	substitute named entity
SI	substitute identity
SHE	substitute hypernym
SHO	substitute hyponym
SC	substitute currency
SP	substitute pronoun
GTC	grammar tag change
CP	change prep
SA	substitute antonym
DOS	del other sents
RUP	remove unclamped parts
RUN	remove unclamped negs
RUNO	remove unclamped negs oddity
MCU	move clamped up
RRN	restructure remove noun
RAN	restructure add noun
RRV	restructure remove verb
RAV	restructure add verb
RPD	restructure pos depth
RND	restructure neg depth
RHNC	restructure h neg count
RHNO	restructure h neg oddity
ATP	active to passive
PTA	passive to active
ATS	appos to sent
RTS	rcmod to sent

Table 1: Current transformations with their abbr.

are auxiliaries ('aux'), determiners ('det'), prepositions ('prep') and possessives ('poss'). Furthermore, we currently ignore words of those parts of speech (POS) that are not verbs ('VB'), nouns ('NN'), adjectives ('JJ'), adverbs ('RB'), pronouns ('PR'), cardinals ('CD') or dollar signs ('$'). For all other words w_H in H and words w_T in T we calculate whether w_T can be substituted by w_H. For this we employ amongst simple heuristics also WordNet 2.1 (Fellbaum, 1998) as described next:

(1) Are the tokens and POS tags of w_T and w_H identical? If yes, return (1, *'identity'*).

(2) If the POS tags of w_T and w_H indicate that both words appear in WordNet continue with (3) otherwise with (8).

(3) Are they antonyms in WordNet? If yes, return (2, *'antonym'*).

(4) Are they synonyms in WordNet? If yes, return (2, *'synonym'*).

(5) Does w_H appear in the hypernym hierarchy of w_T in WordNet? If yes, return (z, *'hyponym'*) with z being the distance, i.e. w_T is a hyponym of w_H.

(6) Does w_T appear in the hypernym hierarchy of w_H in WordNet? If yes, return (z, *'hypernym'*) with z being the distance, i.e. w_T is a hypernym of w_H

(7) Are they named entities that share certain parts of their strings? If yes, return (z, *'named entity'*) with z being larger dependent on how different they are.

(8) Is w_T a pronoun and w_H a noun? If yes, return (2, *'pronoun'*).

(9) Are w_T and w_H exactly matching cardinals? If yes, return (1, *'number'*).

(10) Are w_T and w_H identical currencies? If yes, return (1, *'currency'*).

(11) Are w_T and w_H both currencies? If yes, return (2, *'currency'*).

Note that along the hierarchy in WordNet we also look one step along the "derived form" pointer to allow a noun like 'winner' be substitutable by the verb 'win'. If a word w_T is substitutable by a word w_H, we say that w_T and w_H are *clamped*. We call the whole assignment that assigns some or all words of H to words in T a *clamp*. Since usually a single word w_H is clamped to several words in T, we will often have several different clamps. E.g. if H has three words each of which is clamped to four words in T there are sixty-four possible clamps in total, i.e. sixty-four possible ways to clamp the words in H to words in T.

Each of these different clamps gives rise to a different derivation. However, let us for simplicity continue to focus on a single clamp and see how to complete a single derivation τ.

(3) Substitute the clamped words. If w_H and w_T are clamped, we know what their relationship is: e.g. (3, *hypernym*) means that we have to go three steps up w_H's hypernym-hierarchy in WordNet to reach w_T. Thus we have to apply three times the transformation SHE to substitute w_T by w_H, which we reflect in τ by appending three times SHE to it. Similarly, we add other transformations for other relations. The substitution of w_T with w_H might also trigger other transformations, such as PTA, ATP, CP and GTC which try to adjust the surrounding grammatical structure. All applied transformations will be appended to the derivation τ.

(4) Pick the sentence with the most clamps. After substituting all clamped words, we simply pick the sentence in T with the most clamped words and delete the others using DOS. E.g. if T consists of three sentences, after this step T will only contain the single sentence with the most clamps and DOS will be appended twice to τ.

(5) Remove subtrees that do not contain clamped nodes. After this step we add for each removed node the transformation RUP to τ. Then we add RUN for each removed negation modifier ('neg') and additionally RUNO if the number of removed negation is odd. RUNO is a somewhat artificial transformation and acts more like a flag. This might be changed in future sets of transformation to better comply with the transformation metaphor.

(6) Move the clamped nodes closer to the root and remove unclamped subtree. Again we do some counting before and after this step, which determines the transformations to add to τ. In particular we count how many verbs are passed by moving clamped nodes up. For each passed verb we add MCU to τ.

(7) Restructure and add the missing pieces. The definition in Eq. (3) requires that any T can be transformed into any H, otherwise the maximum is undefined. In the last step we will thus remove all words in T which are not needed for H and add all missing words to T and restructure until T becomes H. For the bookkeeping we count the number of nouns, verbs and negation modifier that have to be added and removed. Furthermore, we count how many levels up or down we need to move words in T such that they match the structure in H. For all these countings we add accordingly as many transformations RRN, RRV, RAN, RAV, RPD, RND, RHNC, RHNO (see Tab. 1 for short explanations).

Finally, the completed derivation τ with $\tau(T) = H$ is converted to a 28-dimensional feature vector $[\tau_1, \ldots, \tau_{28}]^\top$ using the notion of τ_j which has been defined in Sec. 2.

3.3 Estimating the parameters

Let $D_{tr} = \{(T_1, H_1, y_1), \ldots, (T_{800}, H_{800}, y_{800})\}$ be the training examples with $y_i \in \{0, 1\}$ indicating entailment. For brevity we define

$$f_i(\theta) = p_\theta(T_i \models H_i) \tag{4}$$

to abbreviate the probability of entailment modelled as outline in Sec. 2. Then the data likelihood can be written as:

$$p_\theta(D_{tr}) = \prod_{i=1}^{800} f_i(\theta)^{y_i}(1 - f_i(\theta))^{(1-y_i)} \tag{5}$$

We would like to maximize $p_\theta(D_{tr})$ in term of the vector θ. However, the maxima in Eq. (3) make this optimization difficult. For the submission to the RTE3 challenge we choose the following way to approximate it:

(1) Generate for each example pair several derivations (as described in the previous section) and choose the eight shortest ones. If there are less than eight derivations available, copy the shortest ones to end up with eight (some of which could be identical).

(2) There are now $8 \cdot 800$ derivations in total. We denote the corresponding feature vectors by $x_1, \ldots, x_{6400}$. Note that x_i is a vector containing the countings of the different transformations. E.g. if the corresponding derivation was τ, then $x_{ij} = \tau_j$.

(3) Similarly copy the training labels y_i to match those 6400 feature vectors, i.e. now our data becomes $D_{tr} = \{(x_1, y_1), \ldots, (x_{6400}, y_{6400})\}$.

(4) Replacing $f_i(\theta)$ by

$$g_i(\theta) = \prod_j \theta_j^{x_{ij}} \tag{6}$$

the data likelihood becomes:

$$p_\theta(D_{tr}) = \prod_{i=1}^{6400} g_i(\theta)^{y_i}(1 - g_i(\theta))^{(1-y_i)} \tag{7}$$

(5) Replace furthermore each θ_j by

$$\sigma(z_j) = \frac{1}{1 + \exp(-z_j)} \tag{8}$$

with σ being the sigmoidal function, which ensures that the values for θ_j stay between zero and one.

(6) Maximize $p_z(D_{tr})$ in terms of $z = [z_1, \ldots, z_n]^\top$ using gradient ascent.

(7) Calculate $\theta_j = \sigma(z_j)$ for all j.

3.4 Classifying the test data

Having estimated the parameter vector θ we can apply the trained model to the test data D_{te} to infer its unknown labels. Since we only generate some derivations and can not try all possible—as would be required by Eq. (3)—we again transform the test data into 6400 feature vectors $x_1, \ldots, x_{6400}$. Note that $x_1, \ldots, x_8$ are the feature vectors belonging to the first test example (T_1, H_1), and so forth. To approximate the probability of entailment we take the maximum over the eight feature vectors assigned to each test example, e.g. for (T_1, H_1),

$$p_\theta(T_1 \models H_1) \approx \max_{i \in \{1,\ldots,8\}} \prod_{j=1}^{28} \theta_j^{x_{ij}} \tag{9}$$

and analogously for the other test examples. The class label and herewith the answer to the question whether T_i entails H_i is obtained be checking whether $p_\theta(T_i \models H_i)$ is above a certain threshold, which we can determine using the training set. This completes the description of the system behind our first run of our RTE3 submission.

3.5 Logistic Regression

The second run of our RTE3 submission is motivated by the following observation: introducing a weight vector with entries $w_j = \log \theta_j$ and using logarithms, we can rewrite Eq. (3) as

$$\log p_\theta(T \models H) = \max_{\tau:\tau(T)=H} \sum_{j=1}^{n} \tau_j w_j. \tag{10}$$

The probability of entailment becomes the maximum of several linear expressions with the additional constraint $w_j < 0$ for all j which ensures that θ_j is a probability. In order to compare with another linear classifier we applied as the second run logistic regression to the data. Again we used eight derivations/feature vectors per training example to estimate the parameters of the logistic regression. Also with the test data we applied the weight vector to eight derivations/feature vectors per test example and choose the largest result which was then threshold to obtain a label.

4 Results

The first fact we see from the official RTE3 results in Tab. 3 is that our system is better than random.

RTE 2	overall	IE	IR	QA	SUM
AccTr	0.5950	0.5700	0.5850	0.5500	0.6750
AccTe	0.5675	0.5000	0.5850	0.5600	0.6250
AccTr	0.6050	0.5700	0.5550	0.5800	0.7150
AccTe	0.5725	0.5000	0.5800	0.5800	0.6300

Table 2: Results for the RTE2 data. Shown are the accuracies on the training and test sets. First two lines for the first run (transformation-based model) and the next two lines for the second run (logistic regression).

RTE 3	overall	IE	IR	QA	SUM
AccTr	0.6475	0.5750	0.6350	0.7600	0.6200
AccTe	0.5600	0.4700	0.6250	0.6450	0.5000
PreTe	0.5813	0.5162	0.6214	0.6881	0.5607
AccTr	0.6550	0.5600	0.6300	0.7850	0.6450
AccTe	0.5775	0.5000	0.6300	0.6700	0.5100
PreTe	0.5952	0.5562	0.6172	0.7003	0.5693

Table 3: Official results on the RTE3 test data and inofficial results on the corresponding training data. Shown are the accuracies and average precision on the test data. First three lines for the first run (transformation-based model) and the next three lines for the second run (logistic regression).

However, with 56% and 57.75% it is not much better. From the task specific data we see that it completely failed on the information extraction (IE) and the summarization (SUM) data. On the other hand it has reached good results well above 60% for the information retrieval (IR) and question answering (QA) data. From the accuracies of the training data in Tab. 3 we see that there was some overfitting.

We also applied our system to the RTE2 challenge data. The results are shown in Tab. 2 and show that our system is not yet competitive with last year's best systems. It is curious that in the RTE2 data the SUM task appears simpler than the other tasks while in this year's data IR and QA seem to be the easiest.

5 Future work and conclusion

As already mentioned, this paper presents work in progress and we hope to improve our system in the near future. For the RTE3 challenge our main goal was to get a system running before the deadline. However, we had to make a lot of compromises/simplifications to achieve that goal.

Even though our current results suggest that right now our system might not be able to compete with the better systems from last year's challenge we see the potential that our architecture provides a useful platform on which one can test and evolve different sets of transformations on dependency trees. Again, we note that such a set of transformations can be seen as a calculus that preserves truth only with a certain probability, which is an interesting concept to follow up on. Furthermore, this idea of a probabilistic calculus is not limited to dependency trees but could equally well applied to other representations of text.

Besides working on more powerful and faithful transformations, our system might be improved also simply by replacing our ad hoc solutions for the preprocessing and sentence-splitting. We should also try different parsers and see how they compare for our purposes. Since our approach is based on a probabilistic model, we could also try to incorporate several optional parse trees (as a probabilistic parser might be able to create) with their respective probabilities and create a system that uses probabilities in a consistent way all the way from tagging/parsing to inferring entailment.

Acknowledgement

The author is grateful for valuable discussions with Chris Williams and Amos Storkey. This research was supported by the EU-PASCAL network of excellence (IST- 2002-506778) and through a European Community Marie Curie Fellowship (MEIF-CT-2005-025578). Furthermore, the author is thankful to the organizers of the RTE challenges and to the creators of WordNet, NLTK-LITE and the Stanford Parser for sharing their software with the scientific community.

References

R. Adams. 2006. Textual entailment through extended lexical overlap. In *Proceedings of the Second PASCAL Challenges Workshop on Recognising Textual Entailment.*

R. Bar-Haim, I. Dagan, B. Dolan, L. Ferro, D. Giampiccolo, B. Magnini, and I. Szpektor, editors. 2006. *Proceedings of the Second PASCAL Challenges Workshop on Recognising Textual Entailment.*

S. Bird. 2005. NLTK-Lite: Efficient scripting for natural language processing. In *4th International Conference on Natural Language Processing*, pages 1–8.

I. Dagan and O. Glickman. 2004. Probabilistic textual entailment: Generic applied modeling of language variability. In *PASCAL Workshop on Learning Methods for Text Understanding and Mining, Grenoble.*

I. Dagan, O. Glickman, and B. Magnini, editors. 2005. *Proceedings of the PASCAL Challenges Workshop on Recognising Textual Entailment.*

M.-C. de Marneffe, B. MacCartney, and C.D. Manning. 2006. Generating typed dependency parses from phrase structure parses. In *International Conference on Language Resources and Evaluation (LREC).*

C. Fellbaum. 1998. *WordNet: an electronic lexical database.* MIT Press.

D. Klein and C.D. Manning. 2003. Accurate unlexicalized parsing. In *Proceedings of the 41st Meeting of the Association for Computational Linguistics.*

M. Kouylekov and B. Magnini. 2005. Recognizing textual entailment with tree edit distance algorithms. In *Proceedings of the PASCAL Challenges Workshop on Recognising Textual Entailment.*

M. Kouylekov and B. Magnini. 2006. Tree edit distance for recognizing textual entailment: Estimating the cost of insertion. In *Proceedings of the Second PASCAL Challenges Workshop on Recognising Textual Entailment.*

M. Tatu, B. Iles, J. Slavick, A. Novischi, and D. Moldovan. 2006. COGEX at the second recognizing textual entailment challenge. In *Proceedings of the Second PASCAL Challenges Workshop on Recognising Textual Entailment.*

Mutaphrase: Paraphrasing with FrameNet

Michael Ellsworth and **Adam Janin**
{infinity,janin}@icsi.berkeley.edu
International Computer Science Institute
1947 Center Street, Suite 600
Berkeley, CA 94704-1105 USA

Abstract

We describe a preliminary version of Mutaphrase, a system that generates paraphrases of semantically labeled input sentences using the semantics and syntax encoded in FrameNet, a freely available lexico-semantic database. The algorithm generates a large number of paraphrases with a wide range of syntactic and semantic distances from the input. For example, given the input "I like eating cheese", the system outputs the syntactically distant "Eating cheese is liked by me", the semantically distant "I fear sipping juice", and thousands of other sentences. The wide range of generated paraphrases makes the algorithm ideal for a range of statistical machine learning problems such as machine translation and language modeling as well as other semantics-dependent tasks such as query and language generation.

1 Introduction

A central tenet of statistical natural language processing (NLP) is "there's no data like more data". One method for generating more data is to restate each phrase in a corpus, keeping similar semantics while changing both the words and the word sequence. The efficacy of this approach has been well-established in many areas, including automated evaluation of machine translation systems (Kauchak and Barzilay, 2006), text summarization (Kittredge, 2002), question answering (Rinaldi et al., 2003), document retrieval (Zukerman and Raskutti, 2002), and many others.

Most of the reported work on paraphrase generation from arbitrary input sentences uses machine learning techniques trained on sentences that are known or can be inferred to be paraphrases of each other (Bannard and Callison-Burch, 2005; Barzilay and Lee, 2003; Barzilay and McKeown, 2001; Callison-Burch et al., 2006; Dolan et al., 2004; Ibrahim et al., 2003; Lin and Pantel, 2001; Pang et al., 2003; Quirk et al., 2004; Shinyama et al., 2002). Mutaphrase instead generates paraphrases algorithmically using an input sentence and FrameNet, a freely available lexico-semantic resource (information regarding FrameNet, including relevant terminology, is presented in Section 2).

Figure 1: Syntactic and semantic similarity to *I like eating cheese*.

Conceptually, the Mutaphrase algorithm takes a semantic specification of a sentence, provided by an automatic semantic parser such as Shalmaneser (Erk

Proceedings of the Workshop on Textual Entailment and Paraphrasing, pages 143–150,
Prague, June 2007.

and Padó, 2006), and recursively replaces each semantically parsed phrase with a semantically similar phrase. To generate each new phrase, each of the semantic parts of the original phrase is mapped, using FrameNet data, onto a new word or phrase whose position and syntactic marking may be quite different.

The Mutaphrase algorithm outputs a large set of paraphrases with a variety of distances from the input in terms of both syntax and semantics; see Figure 1. Depending on the needs of the application, filtering can be applied to limit the distance to a desired range. For example, language modeling may benefit from a wider variety of semantic outputs, since if *I like eating cheese* is in-domain, then *I like sipping juice* is also likely in-domain. Other applications, e.g. Question Answering, require more stringent limits on semantic distance. See Section 4.

1.1 Current Limitations

The current implementation of Mutaphrase suffers from several limitations. Perhaps the most significant is that the input sentences must be semantically labeled using FrameNet annotations. Since no automated systems for FrameNet-specific annotation are currently incorporated into our algorithm, input is limited to hand-annotated sentences. Also, certain types of semantic ill-formedness are permitted (e.g. *I like sipping meat*), and some types of syntax are not well supported (e.g. conjunctions, relative-clauses). We believe all these factors can be addressed; they are covered briefly in Future Work (Section 4). We confine ourselves in other sections to describing the core Mutaphrase algorithm as currently implemented.

2 FrameNet

The primary resource used in Mutaphrase is FrameNet (Fontenelle, 2003; FrameNet, 2007b), a lexico-semantic database that describes concepts and their interrelations, wordform and word-sequence information, syntactic categories, and mappings between conceptual and lexical/syntactic information. All of these are grounded in hand-annotated examples of real-world sentences. At a slightly more abstract level, FrameNet can be described as providing a two-way mapping between meaning (semantics) and form (syntax, wordforms, sequences).

2.1 Semantics

The conceptual information is represented using **frames**, where a frame is a type of schema or scenario (e.g. Motion, Commercial_transaction), and **frame elements** (FEs), which are the participants and parameters of the frames (e.g. Motion.Path, Commercial_transaction.Buyer). Frames and their frame elements are related and mapped with a limited type of conceptual ontology involving Inheritance (i.e. subtype), Subframe (i.e. temporal subpart), Using (i.e. presupposition) and a few other relation types.

2.2 Syntax

On the form side, the representation is more minimal. **Wordforms** and word-sequences are represented so that words with multiple wordforms (e.g. *take/took*) and word sequences with wordforms (e.g. *take/took off*) can be referred to as unitary objects. We have a category **Support** (and the more specific label 'Copula') for pieces of multi-word expressions that are optional for expressing the semantics of the whole (e.g. *take* in *take a bath*). FrameNet also represents a small but sufficiently rich set of syntactic categories of English (i.e. **phrase types** or PTs, such as 'Sfin', i.e. finite sentence) and syntactic relations (i.e. **grammatical functions** or GFs, e.g. 'Object').

2.3 Syntax-Semantics Bindings

The most vital part of the FrameNet data for our Mutaphrase algorithm is the mappings between semantics and syntax. There are several categories pertaining to this in the data. **Lexical units** (LUs) are a pairing of words/word sequences with the frame each evokes. The **valences** for each LU are sequences in which semantic and form information pertinent to phrases are paired. They are not stored in the database, so we have created a process that produces them entirely automatically (see 3.2). For example, for the LU *hand* in the Giving frame and *possible* in the Likelihood frame, we have the following annotated sentences:

1. [She]$_{Donor/NP/Ext}$ [**handed**]$_{Target}$
   [a bag]$_{Theme/NP/Obj}$
   [to Nob]$_{Recipient/PP(to)/Dep}$

2. [It]$_{Null}$ [was]$_{Copula}$ **[possible]**$_{Target}$ [that he had been hoping to frighten Steve]$_{Hypothetical\_event/Sfin(that)/Dep}$

Example 1 above shows a typical valence, in which most of the positions are semantically labeled with a frame element which is paired with syntactic GF and PT information. The second annotation (2) is more complex, exemplifying each of the major categories that make up the positions of a valence. The categories are:

1. a Null element, with syntax but no semantics (usually *there* or *it*)

2. a Support or Copula with its wordforms

3. a Target (i.e. an LU or word that is part of an LU) with its wordforms, conceptually representing a frame

4. a frame-element/phrase-type/grammatical-function phrase description, which puts together semantic (FE) information with syntax (GF and PT); the PT also indicates fixed words (e.g. the word *that* in the example above)

We can abstract away from the individual sentences, preserving only the sequences of positions with their features, as in the following representation of sentence 2 above:
Null(it), Copula, Target(possible), Hypothetical_event/Dep/Sfin(that)

These abstract valences are the basis for the algorithm we present here. There are typically between two and ten basic patterns associated with each annotated lexical unit, encompassing alternations in the realization of FEs such as Active/Passive (*I recommended her* vs. *She was recommended by me*), the Dative Alternation (*He handed the paper to Stephen* vs. *He handed Stephen the paper*), optional elements (*I ate dinner* vs. *I ate*) and many more.

Basing our algorithm on rearranging the fillers of these FEs allows us to abstract away from syntax, since the FEs of a frame express the same relations regardless of the LU or syntax they occur with. Some meaning differences between LUs within the same frame (e.g. *drink* vs. *eat*) are not overtly modeled in FrameNet. Other resources, such as WordNet, could provide added information in cases requiring finer granularity (see Section 4).

3 Mutaphrase Algorithm

At a very high level, the paraphrase algorithm that we use is as follows: we begin with a sentence with frame-semantic annotation, replace each lexical unit and its associated frame Elements with an alternative valence, then filter the output for its syntactic and semantic fit with the original sentence. The valences may be drawn from either the same LU, an LU of the same frame, or an LU of a related frame.

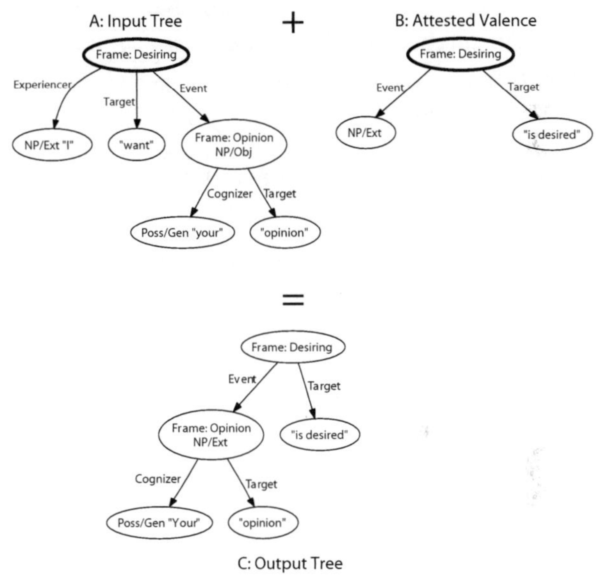

Figure 2: Algorithm Sketch: A syntactic/semantic tree of the original sentence (A) is rearranged to match a different valence (B), producing a new tree (C); thus *I want your opinion* yields the paraphrase *Your opinion is desired.*

Figure 2 shows an example of one step of the algorithm. An input tree for the sentence *I want your opinion* is shown in Figure 2A. The particular valence for the Desiring frame in Figure 2B describes the relations between the word *desire* and its dependents in sentences like *A meeting was desired.* Because the phrase types and grammatical functions of the FEs between the input and the attested valence are compatible, it is possible to replace the input frame with the new valence. The output is shown in Figure 2C.

The remainder of this section describes in more detail how this algorithm is implemented.

3.1 Building a Syntax/Semantics Tree from FrameNet Data

Because the FEs of the original sentence are often filled by phrases with their own annotation, the initial syntactic/semantic annotation is (conceptually, at least) in the form of a graph. Typically, the graph is nearly a tree, with few or no non-tree edges[1]. Hereafter, we will use the term 'tree' even for the cases where there are non-tree edges.

Since the data are not organized in this format in the FrameNet output, we have implemented a routine which can turn FrameNet data into a syntactico-semantic tree; tree examples can be seen in Figure 2A and Figure 2C.

3.2 Building Ordered Valences from FrameNet Data

As mentioned in Section 2.3, we have constructed a routine to parse FrameNet data to produce the valences for each LU of a frame. The basic output is an ordered list of syntactico-semantic elements, optional apositional features (e.g. passive +/-), and the frequency of the pattern.[2]

One innovation of our algorithm is its ability to handle multiword LUs. It simply identifies each word of the LU as a separate element in the list, marking each with the label 'Target'. Thus the ordered valences of *take off.v* in the Undressing frame include, among others:

- Wearer/NP/Ext, take/Target, off/Target, Clothing/NP/Obj; Frequency: 57/68
  (e.g. *I TOOK OFF my watch*)

- Wearer/NP/Ext, take/Target, Clothing/NP/Obj, off/Target; Frequency: 7/68
  (e.g. *You TAKE your shoes OFF*)

One way of thinking about the valence set is that it represents possible orderings of subparts of a phrase that is semantically a frame instance and syntactically a phrase headed by the Target (see, for example, Figure 2B). This semantic/syntactic information is detailed enough to build the syntax of a phrase, given FrameNet-style semantics.

3.3 Core algorithm

Once the input has been turned into a tree and there is a set of alternative ways of expressing each frame that is in the input, the algorithm then recurses downward and then, as it returns up, replaces each phrase/frame node with a set of alternative phrases. In the simplest case, these phrases are built from all the valences that are attested for the frame that the original phrase expressed [3]. In other words, our algorithm is a recursive tree-rewrite in which the current valence of the current LU is replaced by many alternate valences of many different LUs.

In the recursion, word and phrase nodes not headed by an LU are kept the same (except for pronouns, which are expanded to all their wordforms, e.g. *me* to *I/me/my/mine*). The child phrases of such an unparaphrased node, if they are headed by an LU or pronoun, can be paraphrased as long as the paraphrases match the phrase type and grammatical function of the original child phrase.

In Figure 2, the original sentence (represented in Figure 2A) has the phrase representing the Desiring frame replaced with an alternative phrase evoking the same frame (Figure 2B) to produce a new, roughly semantically equivalent sentence (Figure 2C) by expressing the same set of frames in the same FE relations to each other.

In practice, we have to throw away at the outset many of the valences because they include FEs that are not in the input sentence[4] or because they have syntactic requirements of their child phrases which

[1]These non-tree edges are introduced when a phrase is an FE of more than one frame. In keeping with normal syntactic analysis, we treat the node as non-local to all but one parent.

[2]Although frequency of a particular pattern in the FrameNet data is not strictly representative of the frequency of that pattern in the corpus, a close examination reveals that the rank order of patterns is largely identical, i.e. the most common pattern in FrameNet represents the most common pattern in the corpus. How useful this inexact statistical data will be is the subject of future research.

[3]Our algorithm will work just as well with related frames as long as the relevant FEs are mapped in the FrameNet data. Controlling the distance, direction, and relation-types of related frames that are included for paraphrase (if any) is one way to control the degree of semantic diversity of the paraphrase output. See further Section 3.4.

[4]Thus attempting to use the valence Experiencer/NP/Ext, Degree/AVP/Dep, want/Target, Event/NP/Obj (e.g. *I really*

cannot be filled by a paraphrase of the child phrases. For example, for the input sentence *I gave presents to friends*, the code can output 560 (unfiltered) paraphrases. A random selection from the output includes *Presents bequeathed to friends*, *I handed in presents*, and *Presents donated by I*. Of these, the first and last are filtered out as not filling the original sentential context and the last, in addition, is filtered out because of the mismatch between the pronoun wordform *I* and the non-subject grammatical function.

To further refine the paraphrases, we must eliminate examples that are not compatible with the input sentence. In our current implementation, our algorithm filters out incorrect syntax during the recursion over the tree. Ultimately, we will also filter out malformed semantics. The rest of this section is devoted to an explication of the details of this filtering.

3.4 Syntactic/Semantic Compatibility

For both syntax and semantics, the degree of viability of a paraphrase can be divided up into two components: well-formedness and similarity. Syntactic and semantic well-formedness is always desirable and the algorithm seeks to maximize it in ways that are outlined below. Similarity between the original sentence and its paraphrases (or among the paraphrases), however, may be more or less desirable depending on the task. Figure 1 shows an example of the various degrees of syntactic and semantic similarity of the paraphrase output. To maintain flexibility, we will need several control parameters to allow us to filter our output for syntactic/semantic similarity.

3.4.1 Syntactic Compatibility

Syntactic incompatibilities most commonly result from gross mismatches between the Phrase Type called for in a new valence and the Phrase Type possibilities available for the child phrase.

For example, if the initial sentence for paraphrase is *I want your opinion* as in 1 below (repeated from Figure 2), Valence 2 below represents a PT mismatch, since *I*, an NP filler of the Experiencer role in the original sentence, is not modifiable into an adjective phrase (AJP).

1. Experiencer/NP/Ext, want/Target, Event/NP/Obj

2. There/Null, be/Copula, Experiencer/AJP/Dep, desire/Target, Event/PP(for)/Dep (e.g. *There is a public desire for transparency*)

3. There/Null, be/Copula, desire/Target, Experiencer/PP(in)/Dep, Event/PP(for)/Dep (e.g. *There was a desire in America for home rule*)

This filtering is vital, as otherwise valence 2 would yield the awful *There is me desire for your opinion*.

However, phrase types that are not exact matches may nevertheless be compatible with each other. Valence 3, for example, is compatible with the original valence, since the original Experiencer and Event FEs were filled by NPs, to which prepositions can be added to match the PP realizations required by Valence 3. This yields another paraphrase of the sentence in Figure 2: *There is a desire in me for your opinion*. Similarly, full sentential clauses can be modified to match VPs by truncation of the External (subject) argument, etc. A phrase from the original sentence may also be omitted to match an empty phrase in the paraphrase, as seen in the omission of the Experiencer in the paraphrase in Figure 2.

These alternations provide more variety in the potential phrase types of the paraphrases. Which syntactic modifications are allowed should be an externally controllable parameter, but this has not yet been implemented. In general, allowing fewer types of modification should move the average output leftward in the syntax/semantic similarity graph in Figure 1 (toward more syntactic similarity).

Although every annotated valence represents a grammatical structure, some of these structures will more likely be judged as well-formed than others; in particular, infrequent patterns are more likely ill-formed than frequent ones. An additional controllable parameter, allowing a trade-off between recall and precision, is a frequency cut-off for accepting a valence pattern based on the number of times

want another chance) when paraphrasing the initial sentence in Figure 2 will not work, since there is nothing in the original to fill the Degree FE mentioned here.

the pattern is found in the FrameNet data. Our algorithm currently produces a ranked list of paraphrases based on exactly this frequency parameter, and downstream processing can choose a cut-off frequency or n-best to reduce the total output.

3.4.2 Semantic Filtering

Lexical units of the same frame are not necessarily synonyms; they may be antonyms or coordinate terms (i.e. co-hyponyms). For example, *cheese* and *juice* are both in the Food frame, but *I like eating cheese* and *I like eating juice* are certainly not a semantic match! In fact, the second is a semantically ill-formed modification of the first. Similarly, *like* and *hate* are both in the Experiencer_subject frame. While *I hate eating cheese* is similar to *I like eating cheese* in describing an attitude toward eating cheese, they are not an exact semantic match either; in this case, however, the lack of semantic similarity does not lead to semantic ill-formedness.

For some tasks such as expanding a language model, exact semantic match is not necessary, but for tasks that require strict semantic match, there are several simple ways to increase robustness.

Tighter filtering, of whatever kind, will move the average output of the algorithm downward in the syntax/semantic similarity graph in Figure 1 (toward more semantic similarity).

3.5 Preliminary Results

We have implemented the above algorithm to the point that it is capable of producing paraphrases of arbitrary input sentences that have received proper FrameNet annotation. A large number of paraphrases with a variety of phrase types are produced, but the lack of semantic filtering occasionally leads to semantically ill-formed results. The output is ranked purely according to the frequency in the FrameNet data of the valences used to build the paraphrase.

For the sentence *I like eating cheese*, the paraphraser produced 8403 paraphrases, of which the following was top-ranked: *I resented drinking cheese*, which suffers from the semantic mismatch problems discussed in Section 3.4.2. Some other output at random:

- I am interested in cheese devouring.
- I was nervous that cheese's ingested.
- I'm worried about gobbling down cheese.
- My regrets were that cheese was eaten by me.

Since most of the annotation in the Ingestion frame (the frame for *eat*, etc.) concerns eating rather than drinking, the majority of the output is semantically well-formed. The paraphrases generated from the Experiencer_subject frame (the frame for *like, interested, regret*, etc.) are more uniformly felicitous, even if semantically quite divergent from the meaning of the original. Both the infelicity of *drinking cheese* and the semantic divergence appear to be addressable by refining semantic tightness using WordNet. Averaging over senses, words like *gobble* and *ingest* have lower WordNet-based semantic distance from *eat* than *drink*.

For the sentence *Nausea seems a commonplace symptom*, the paraphraser outputs 502 paraphrases, of which the following was top-ranked: *It seems a commonplace sign*. Other output at random:

- Tiredness looks indicative.
- Queasiness smelt of a commonplace sign.
- Sleepiness appears a commonplace sign.
- Queasiness smelt indicative queasiness.
- Somnolence appears to be indicative.

Longer sentences (e.g. *Locally elected school boards, especially in our larger cities, become the prey of ambitious, generally corrupt, and invariably demagogic local politicians or would-be politicians*) currently take excessive amounts of time and memory to run, but typically produce 10,000+ paraphrases. Pruning earlier during paraphrase generation should help address this issue.

4 Future Work

Currently, Mutaphrase requires the input sentences to have been marked with FrameNet annotations prior to processing. Although automatic semantic parsing is a large and growing field (Moldovan et al., 2004; Litkowski, 2004; Baldewein et al., 2004), two problems present themselves. First, output from an automated parser is not typically compatible with FrameNet markup. Although this is mostly "a simple matter of programming", some linguistic tools must be developed to convert between formats (e.g. to infer FrameNet phrase types from part-of-speech tags).[5] Second, it is not yet clear how the inevitable errors introduced by the parser will affect the Mutaphrase algorithm[6]. We plan to use application-dependent measures to judge the effects of parsing errors.

Certain types of semantic ill-formedness cannot be detected by the current version of Mutaphrase. A typical example is *I like sipping beef* as a paraphrase of *I like eating cheese*. We can guarantee semantic well-formedness by limiting paraphrases to morphologically related words (e.g. *consume, consumption*) and/or by choosing only the FrameNet LUs which are in the same WordNet (Fellbaum, 1998; WordNet, 2006) synset or higher in the WN hierarchy than the original LU (e.g. *eat* to *consume*). Clearly this will exclude many well-formed paraphrases, so for tasks in which breadth is more important than accuracy of paraphrase, we anticipate experimenting with WordNet hierarchy distances between the original and paraphrase LUs as a quantitative measure of semantic similarity as a proxy for semantic well-formedness.

Currently, paraphrase scores are computed simply from the frequency of a particular valence in FrameNet data. We plan to significantly extend scoring to simultaneously rate each paraphrase on its WordNet similarity, syntactic edit distance[7], and language model scores. We also plan to measure the correlation between these estimated scores and both human-judged paraphrase accuracy and application dependent metrics, e.g. extension of in-domain language models by paraphrase.

WordNet can also be used to provide additional paraphrases beyond the particular valences attested in FrameNet. For example, we plan to use WordNet to generate synonyms of target words so that, for example, *adore* could be used anywhere *like* is used even if *adore* never appears in the FrameNet data.

Finally, the structure of the Mutaphrase algorithm makes multi-lingual paraphrase possible. This requires FrameNet-like data in other languages, and several projects are underway to provide just such a resource (FrameNet, 2007d; FrameNet, 2007c; SALSA, 2007). We plan to exploit these as they become available.

5 Conclusions

We have presented the Mutaphrase algorithm, a system for generating a large set of paraphrases of semantically marked input sentences using FrameNet. The generated sentences range widely in their similarity to the input sentence both in terms of syntax and semantics. Various methods of filtering the output for well-formedness and semantic and syntactic similarity were presented.

Although the current implementation suffers from a number of limitations, we believe these can be addressed, eventually providing a fully automated paraphrase system suitable for use in a variety of statistical natural language processing systems.

Acknowledgments

This work was partly supported by the European Union 6th FWP IST Integrated Project AMI (Augmented Multi-party Interaction, FP6-506811), and by the Swiss National Science Foundation through NCCR's IM2 project.

References

U. Baldewein, K. Erk, S. Padó, and D. Prescher. 2004. Semantic role labelling with similarity-based generalization using EM-based clustering. In R. Mihalcea and P. Edmonds, editors, *Senseval-3: Third International Workshop on the Evaluation of Systems for the Semantic Analysis of Text*, pages 64–68, Barcelona, Spain, July. Association for Computational Linguistics.

C. Bannard and C. Callison-Burch. 2005. Paraphrasing with bilingual parallel corpora. In *Proceedings of the 43rd annual meeting of the Association for Computational Linguistics (ACL)*, pages 597–604, Ann Arbor, June.

R. Barzilay and L. Lee. 2003. Learning to paraphrase: An unsupervised approach using multiple-sequence

[5]It is worth noting that the current SemEval competition (FrameNet, 2007a) should lead to more complete automatic FrameNet-style annotation.

[6]An anecdotal example from a semantic parse of *I was prepared for a hound, but not for such a creature as this.* (Doyle, 1902) assigns *prepared* to the Cooking_creation frame, leading to the interesting paraphrase *I was tenderized for a hound....*

[7]We plan to base the syntactic distance on the edit distance between the original and paraphrase syntactic valences.

alignment. In *Proceedings of the Human Language Technology Conference (HLT)*, pages 16–23, Edmonton, Canada, May.

R. Barzilay and K. McKeown. 2001. Extracting paraphrases from a parallel corpus. In *Proceedings of the Annual Meeting of the Association for Computational Linguistics (ACL)*, pages 50–57, Toulouse, July.

C. Callison-Burch, P. Koehn, and M. Osborne. 2006. Improved statistical machine translation using paraphrases. In *Proceedings of the Human Language Technology Conference (HLT)*, pages 17–24, New York City, June.

W. Dolan, C. Quirk, and C. Brockett. 2004. Unsupervised construction of large paraphrase corpora: Exploiting massively parallel news sources. In *Proceedings of the 20th International Conference on Computational Linguistics (COLING)*, Geneva, Switzerland, August.

A.C. Doyle. 1902. Hound of the Baskervilles. Project Gutenburg web site. http://www.gutenberg.org/dirs/etext02/bskrv11a.txt.

K. Erk and S. Padó. 2006. Shalmaneser — a flexible toolbox for semantic role assignment. In *Proceedings of the Fifth International Conference on Language Resources and Evaluation (LREC)*, pages 527–532, Genoa, Italy, May.

C. Fellbaum. 1998. *WordNet: An Electronic Lexical Database*. The MIT Press, May.

T. Fontenelle, editor. 2003. *International Journal of Lexicography Special Issue on FrameNet and Frame Semantics*. Oxford University Press, September. volume 16(3).

FrameNet. 2007a. The FrameNet task on SemEval web site. http://nlp.cs.swarthmore.edu/semeval/tasks/task19/summary.shtml.

FrameNet. 2007b. FrameNet web site. http://framenet.icsi.berkeley.edu.

Japanese FrameNet. 2007c. Japanese FrameNet web site. http://jfn.st.hc.keio.ac.jp/.

Spanish FrameNet. 2007d. Spanish FrameNet web site. http://gemini.uab.es:9080/SFNsite.

A. Ibrahim, B. Katz, and J. Lin. 2003. Extracting structural paraphrases from aligned monolingual corpora. In *Proceedings of the Second International Workshop on Paraphrasing*, pages 57–64, Sapporo, Japan, July.

D. Kauchak and R. Barzilay. 2006. Paraphrasing for automatic evaluation. In *Proceedings of the Human Language Technology Conference (HLT)*, pages 455–462, New York City, June.

R. Kittredge. 2002. Paraphrasing for condensation in journal abstracting. *Journal of Biomedical Informatics*, 35(4):265–277.

D. Lin and P. Pantel. 2001. Discovery of inference rules for question-answering. *Natural Language Engineering*, 7(4):343–360.

K. Litkowski. 2004. Senseval-3 task: Automatic labeling of semantic roles. In R. Mihalcea and P. Edmonds, editors, *Senseval-3: Third International Workshop on the Evaluation of Systems for the Semantic Analysis of Text*, pages 9–12, Barcelona, Spain, July. Association for Computational Linguistics.

D. Moldovan, R. Gîrju, M. Olteanu, and O. Fortu. 2004. SVM classification of FrameNet semantic roles. In Rada Mihalcea and Phil Edmonds, editors, *Senseval-3: Third International Workshop on the Evaluation of Systems for the Semantic Analysis of Text*, pages 167–170, Barcelona, Spain, July. Association for Computational Linguistics.

B. Pang, K. Knight, and D. Marcu. 2003. Syntax-based alignment of multiple translations: Extracting paraphrases and generating new sentences. In *Proceedings of the Human Language Technology Conference (HLT)*, pages 102–109, Edmonton, Canada, May.

C. Quirk, C. Brockett, and W. Dolan. 2004. Monolingual machine translation for paraphrase generation. In *Proceedings of the 2004 Conference on Empirical Methods in Natural Language Processing*, pages 142–149, Barcelona Spain, July.

F. Rinaldi, J. Dowdall, K. Kaljurand, M. Hess, and D. Mollá. 2003. Exploiting paraphrases in a question answering system. In *Proceedings of the Second International Workshop on Paraphrasing*, pages 25–32, July.

SALSA. 2007. SALSA Project web site. http://www.coli.uni-saarland.de/projects/salsa/.

Y. Shinyama, S. Sekine, K. Sudo, and R. Grishman. 2002. Automatic paraphrase acquisition from news articles. In *Proceedings of Human Language Technology Conference (HLT)*, pages 40–46, San Diego, March.

WordNet. 2006. WordNet web site. http://wordnet.princeton.edu.

I. Zukerman and B. Raskutti. 2002. Lexical query paraphrasing for document retrieval. In *Proceedings of the 19th International Conference on Computational Linguistics (COLING)*, pages 1–7, Taipei, Taiwan, August.

A Compositional Approach toward Dynamic Phrasal Thesaurus

Atsushi Fujita Shuhei Kato Naoki Kato Satoshi Sato
Graduate School of Engineering, Nagoya University
{fujita,ssato}@nuee.nagoya-u.ac.jp
{shuhei,naoki}@sslab.nuee.nagoya-u.ac.jp

Abstract

To enhance the technology for computing semantic equivalence, we introduce the notion of phrasal thesaurus which is a natural extension of conventional word-based thesaurus. Among a variety of phrases that conveys the same meaning, i.e., paraphrases, we focus on syntactic variants that are compositionally explainable using a small number of atomic knowledge, and develop a system which dynamically generates such variants. This paper describes the proposed system and three sorts of knowledge developed for dynamic phrasal thesaurus in Japanese: (i) transformation pattern, (ii) generation function, and (iii) lexical function.

1 Introduction

Linguistic expressions that convey the same meaning are called paraphrases. Handling paraphrases is one of the key issues in a broad range of natural language processing tasks, including machine translation, information retrieval, information extraction, question answering, summarization, text mining, and natural language generation.

Conventional approaches to computing semantic equivalence between two expressions are five-fold. The first approximates it based on the similarities between their constituent words. If two words belong to closer nodes in a thesaurus or semantic network, they are considered more likely to be similar. The second uses the family of tree kernels (Collins and Duffy, 2001; Takahashi, 2005). The degree of equivalence of two trees (sentences) is defined as the number of common subtrees included in both trees. The third estimates the equivalence based on word alignment composed using templates or translation probabilities derived from a set of parallel text (Barzilay and Lee, 2003; Brockett and Dolan, 2005). The fourth espouses the distributional hypothesis (Harris, 1968): given two words are likely to be equivalent if distributions of their surrounding words are similar (Lin and Pantel, 2001; Weeds et al., 2005). The final regards two expressions equivalent if they can be associated by using a set of lexico-syntactic paraphrase patterns (Mel'čuk, 1996; Dras, 1999; Yoshikane et al., 1999; Takahashi, 2005).

Despite the results previous work has achieved, no system that robustly recognizes and generates paraphrases is established. We are not convinced of a hypothesis underlying the word-based approaches because the structure of words also conveys some meaning. Even tree kernels, which take structures into account, do not have a mechanism for identifying typical equivalents: e.g., dative alternation and passivization, and abilities to generate paraphrases. Contrary to the theoretical basis, the two lines of corpus-based approaches have problems in practice, i.e., data sparseness and computation cost. The pattern-based approaches seem steadiest. Yet no complete resource or methodology for handling a wide variety of paraphrases has been developed.

On the basis of this recognition, we introduce the notion of **phrasal thesaurus** to directly compute semantic equivalence of phrases such as follows.

(1) a. be in our favor / be favorable for us
  b. its reproducibility / if it is reproducible
  c. decrease sharply / show a sharp decrease
  d. investigate the cause of a fire /
   investigate why there was a fire /
   investigate what started a fire /
   make an investigation into the cause of a fire

Proceedings of the Workshop on Textual Entailment and Paraphrasing, pages 151–158,
Prague, June 2007.

Phrasal thesaurus is a natural extension of conventional word-based thesaurus. It is thus promised that it will bring us the following benefits:

Enhancement of NLP applications: As conventional thesauri, phrasal thesaurus must be useful to handle paraphrases having different structures in a wide range of NLP applications.

Reading and writing aids: Showing more appropriate alternative phrases must be a powerful aid at certain situations such as writing text. Controlling readability of text by altering phrases must also be beneficial to readers.

Our aim is to develop resources and mechanisms for computing semantic equivalence on the working hypothesis that phrase is the appropriate unit for that purpose. This paper describes the first version of our paraphrase generation system and reports on our ongoing work on constructing resources for realizing phrasal thesaurus.

The following sections describe the range of phenomena we treat (Section 2), the overall architecture of our paraphrase generation system which functions as phrasal thesaurus (Section 3), the implementation of knowledge bases (Section 4) followed by discussion (Section 5), and conclusion (Section 6).

2 Dynamic phrasal thesaurus

2.1 Issue

Toward realizing phrasal thesaurus, the following two issues should be discussed.

- What sorts of phrases should be treated
- How to cope with a variety of expressions

Although technologies of shallow parsing have been dramatically improved in the last decade, it is still difficult to represent arbitrary expression in logical form. We therefore think it is reasonable to define the range relying on lexico-syntactic structure instead of using particular semantic representation. According to the work of (Chklovski and Pantel, 2004; Torisawa, 2006), predicate phrase (simple sentence) is a reasonable unit because it approximately corresponds to the meaning of single event.

Combination of words and a variety of construction coerce us into handling an enormous number of expressions than word-based approaches. One may think taking phrase is like treading a thorny path because one of the arguments in Section 1 is about coverage. On this issue, we speculate that one of the feasible approach to realize a robust system is to divide phenomena into compositional and non-compositional (idiosyncratic) ones[1], and separately develop resources to handle them as described in (Fujita and Inui, 2005).

To compute semantic equivalence of idiosyncratic paraphrases, pairs or groups of paraphrases have to be **statically** compiled into a dictionary as word-based thesaurus. The corpus-based approach is valuable for that purpose, although they are not guaranteed to collect all idiosyncratic paraphrases. On the other hand, compositional paraphrases can be captured by a relatively small number of rules. Thus it seems tolerable approach to generate them **dynamically** by applying such rules. Our work is targeted at compositional paraphrases and the system can be called **dynamic phrasal thesaurus**. Hereafter, we refer to paraphrases that are likely to be explained compositionally as **syntactic variants**.

2.2 Target language: Japanese

While the discussion above does not depend on particular language, our implementation of dynamic phrasal thesaurus is targeted at Japanese. Several methods for paraphrasing Japanese predicate phrases have been proposed (Kondo et al., 1999; Kondo et al., 2001; Kaji et al., 2002; Fujita et al., 2005). The range they treat is, however, relatively narrow because they tend to focus on particular paraphrase phenomena or to rely on existing resources. On the other hand, we define the range of phenomena from a top-down viewpoint. As a concrete definition of predicate phrase in Japanese,

noun phrase + case marker + predicate

is employed which is hereafter referred to "phrase."

Noun phrase and predicate in Japanese themselves subcategorize various syntactic variants as shown in Figure 1 and paraphrase phenomena for above phrase also involve those focused on their interaction. Thus the range of phenomena is not so narrow, and intriguing ones, such as shown in examples[2] (2) and (3), are included.

[1] We regard lexical paraphrases (e.g., "scope" ⇔ "range") and idiomatic paraphrases (e.g., "get the sack" ⇔ "be dismissed from employment") as idiosyncratic.

[2] In each example, "s" and "t" denote an original sentence and its paraphrase, respectively. SMALLCAPS strings indicate the syntactic role of their corresponding Japanese expressions. [N] indicates a nominalizer.

(2) Head switching

s. *kakunin-o isogu.*
checking-ACC to hurry-PRES
We hurry checking it.

t. *isoide kakunin-suru.*
in a hurry to check-PRES
We check it in a hurry.

(3) Noun phrase ⇔ sub-clause

s. *kekka-no saigensei-o kenshou-suru.*
result-GEN reproducibility-ACC to validate-PRES
We validate its reproducibility.

t. [*kekka-o saigen-dekiru*]
result-ACC to reproduce-to be able
ka-douka-o kenshou-suru.
[N]-whether-ACC to validate-PRES
We validate whether it is reproducible.

We focus on syntactic variants at least one side of which is subcategorized into the definition of phrase above. For the sake of simplicity, we hereafter represent those expressions using part-of-speech (POS) patterns. For instance, (2s) is called $N : C : V$ type, and (3s) is $N_1 : no : N_2 : C : V$ type.

3 Paraphrase generation system

Given a phrase, the proposed system generates its syntactic variants in the following four steps:

1. Morphological analysis
2. Syntactic transformation
3. Surface generation with lexical choice
4. SLM-based filtering

where no particular domain, occasion, and media is assumed[3]. Candidates of syntactic variants are first over-generated in step 2 and then anomalies among them are filtered out in steps 3 and 4 using rule-based lexical choice and statistical language model.

The rest of this section elaborates on each component in turn.

3.1 Morphological analysis

Technologies of morphological analysis in Japanese have matured by introducing machine learning techniques and large-scale annotated corpus, and there are freely available tools. Since the structure of input phrase is assumed to be quite simple, employment of dependency analyzer was put off. We simply use a morphological analyzer MeCab[4].

[3]This corresponds to the linguistic transformation layer of KURA (Takahashi et al., 2001).

[4]http://mecab.sourceforge.net/

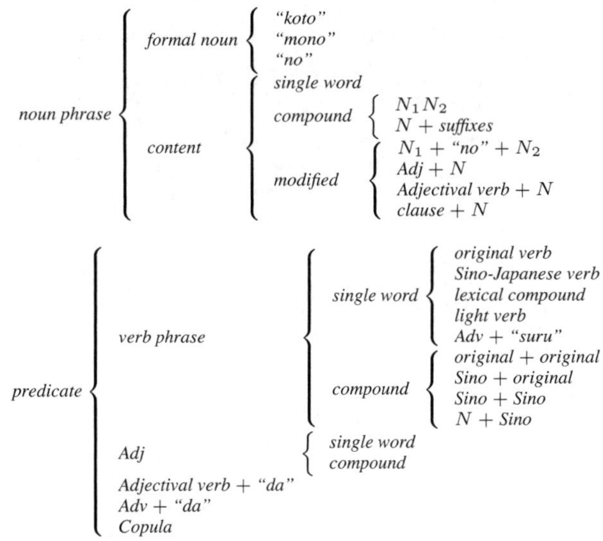

Figure 1: Classification of syntactic variants of noun phrase and predicate in Japanese.

Our system has a post-analysis processing. If either of Sino-Japanese verbal nouns (e.g., "*kenshou* (validation)" and "*kandou* (impression)") or transliteration of verbs in foreign language (e.g., "*doraibu* (to drive)" and "*shifuto* (to shift)") is immediately followed by "*suru* (to do)" or "*dekiru* (to be able)," these adjacent two morphemes are joined into a single morpheme to avoid incorrect transformation.

3.2 Syntactic transformation

The second step over-generates syntactic variants using the following three sorts of knowledge:

(i) Transformation pattern: It gives skeletons of syntactic variants. Each variant is represented by POS symbols designating the input constituents and triggers of the generation function and lexical function below.

(ii) Generation function: It enumerates different expressions that are constituted with the same set of words and subcategorized into the required syntactic category. Some of generation functions handle base phrases, while the rest generates functional words. Base phrases the former generates are smaller than that transformation patterns treat. Since some functional words are disjunctive, the latter generates all candidates with a separator "/" and leaves the selection to the following step.

Table 1: Grammar in Backus-Naur form, example, and instantiation for each knowledge.

<table>
<tr><th>Knowledge type</th><th>Grammar / Example / Instantiation</th></tr>
<tr><td rowspan="3">(i) Transformation pattern</td><td><transformation_pattern> ::= <left_pattern> ⇒ <right_pattern>
<left_pattern> ::= (<POS_symbol>|<word_form>)+
<POS_symbol> ::= ($N \mid C \mid V \mid Adj \mid Adv$)
<word_form> ::= (<hiragana>|<katakana>|<kanji>)+
<right_pattern> ::=
(<POS_symbol>|<word_form>|<function_definition>|<lexical_function>)+</td></tr>
<tr><td>(a) $N : C : V \Rightarrow adv(V) : vp(N)$
(b) N_1 : no : $N_2 : C : V \Rightarrow N_1$: $genCase()$: $vp(N_2)$: ka-douka : $C : V$</td></tr>
<tr><td>(a) kakunin : o : isogu ⇒ adv(isogu) : vp(kakunin)
checking ACC to hurry adv(to hurry) vp(checking)
(b) kekka : no : saigensei : o : kenshou-suru
result GEN reproducibility ACC to validate-PRES
⇒ kekka : $genCase()$: vp(saigensei) : ka-douka : o : kenshou-suru
result case marker vp(reproducibility) [N]-whether ACC to validate-PRES</td></tr>
<tr><td rowspan="3">(ii) Generation function</td><td><generation_function> ::= <function_definition> ⇒ '{'<right_pattern>+'}'
<function_definition> ::= <syntactic_category>'('<POS_symbol>*')'
<syntactic_category> ::= ($np \mid vp \mid lvc$)</td></tr>
<tr><td>(a) $vp(N) \Rightarrow \{v(N) : genVoice() : genTense()\}$
(b) $np(N_1, N_2) \Rightarrow \{N_1, N_2, N_1 : N_2, N_1$: no : $N_2, vp(N_1) : N_2, wh(N_2) : vp(N_1)$: ka, ...}</td></tr>
<tr><td>(a) vp(kakunin) ⇒ { v(kakunin) : $genVoice()$: $genTense()$ }
vp(verification) v(verification) verbal suffix for voice verbal suffix for tense
(b) np(shukka, gen-in)
np(starting fire, reason)
⇒ { shukka , gen-in , shukka : gen-in , shukka : no : gen-in ,
starting fire reason starting fire reason starting fire GEN reason
vp(shukka) : gen-in , wh(gen-in) : vp(shukka) : ka , ... }
vp(starting fire) reason wh(reason) vp(starting fire) [N]</td></tr>
<tr><td rowspan="3">(iii) Lexical function</td><td><lexical_function> ::= <relation>'('<POS_symbol>')'
<relation> ::= ($n \mid v \mid adj \mid adjv \mid adv \mid wh$)</td></tr>
<tr><td>(a) $adv(V)$
(b) $wh(N)$</td></tr>
<tr><td>(a) adv(isogu) (⇒ isoide (given by a verb–adverb dictionary))
adv(to hurry) in a hurry
(b) wh(gen-in) (⇒ { naze , doushite } (given by a noun–interrogative dictionary))
wh(reason) why why</td></tr>
</table>

(iii) Lexical function: It generates different lexical items in certain semantic relations, such as derivative form, from a given lexical item. The back-end of this knowledge is a set of pre-compiled dictionaries as described in Section 4.2.

Table 1 gives a summary of grammar in Backus-Naur form, examples, and instantiations of each knowledge. Figure 2 illustrates an example of knowledge application flow for transforming (4s) into (4t), where ":" denotes delimiter of constituents.

(4) s. "*kakunin*:*o*:*isogu*"
t. "*isoide*:{*kakunin-suru*:
{ϕ, *reru*/*rareru*, *seru*/*saseru*}:{ϕ, *ta*/*da*}}"

First, transformation patterns that match to the given input are applied. Then, the skeletons of syntactic variants given by the pattern are lexicalized by consecutively invoking generation functions and lexical functions. Plural number of expressions that generation function and lexical function generate are enumerated within curly brackets. Transformation is ended when the skeletons are fully lexicalized.

In fact, knowledge design for realizing the transformation is not really new, because we have been inspired by the previous pattern-based approaches. Transformation pattern is thus alike that in the Meaning-Text Theory (MTT) (Mel'čuk, 1996), Synchronous Tree Adjoining Grammar (STAG) (Dras, 1999), meta-rule for Fastr (Yoshikane et al., 1999),

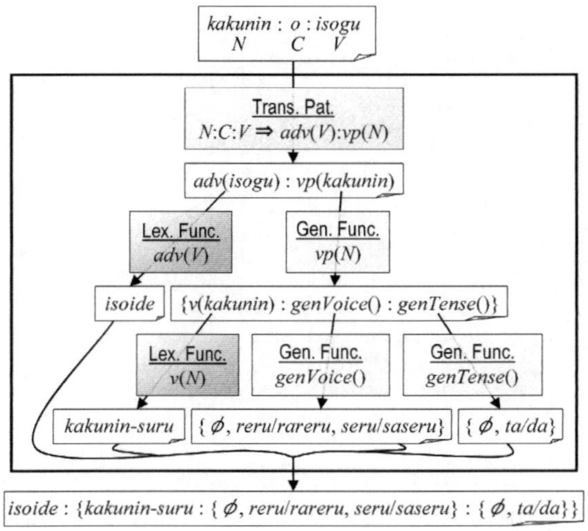

Figure 2: Syntactic transformation (for (2)).

and transfer pattern for KURA (Takahashi et al., 2001). Lexical function is also alike that in MTT. However, our aim in this research is beyond the design. In other words, as described in Section 1, we are aiming at the following two: to develop resources for handling syntactic variants in Japanese, and to confirm if phrasal thesaurus really contribute to computing semantic equivalence.

3.3 Surface generation with lexical choice

The input of the third component is a bunch of candidate phrases such as shown in (4t). This component does the following three processes in turn:

Step 1. Unfolding: All word sequences are generated by removing curly brackets one by one.

Step 2. Lexical choice: Disjunctive words are concatenated with "/" (e.g., "*reru/rareru*" in (4t)). One of them is selected based on POS and conjugation types of the preceding word.

Step 3. Conjugation: In the transformation step, conjugative words are moved to different positions and some of them are newly generated. Inappropriate conjugation forms are corrected.

3.4 SLM-based filtering

In the final step, we assess the correctness of each candidate of syntactic variants using a statistical language model. Our model simply rejects candidate phrases that never appear in a large size of raw text corpus consisting of 15 years of newspaper articles (Mainichi 1991–2005, approximately 1.8GB). Although it is said that Japanese language has a degree of freedom in word ordering, current implementation does not yet employ structured language models because phrases we handle are simple.

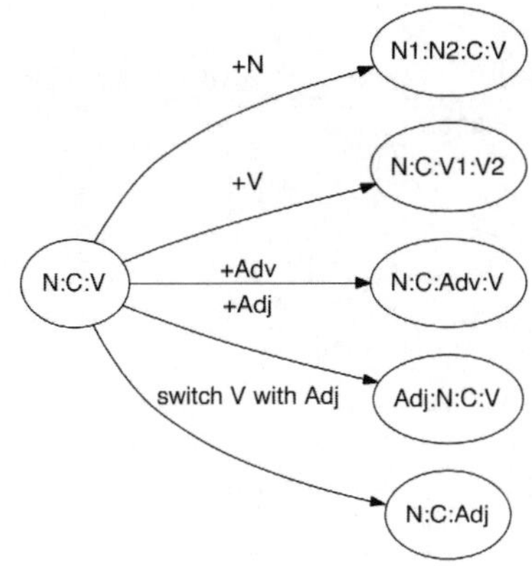

Figure 3: Derivations of phrase types.

4 Knowledge implementation

4.1 Transformation patterns and generation functions

An issue of developing resources is how to ensure their coverage. Our approach to this issue is to describe transformation patterns by extending those for simpler phrases. We first described following three patterns for $N : C : V$ type phrases which we consider the simplest according to Figure 1.

(5) a. $N : C : V \Rightarrow vp(N)$
b. $N : C : V \Rightarrow N : genCase() : lvc(V)$
c. $N : C : V \Rightarrow adv(V) : vp(N)$

While the pattern (5c) is induced from example (2), the patterns (5a-b) are derived from examples (6) and (7), respectively.

(6) s. *shigeki-o* *ukeru*
inspiration-ACC to receive
to receive an inspiration
t. *shigeki-sareru*
to inspire-PASS
to be inspired

(7) s. *hada-o* *shigeki-suru*
skin-ACC to stimulate
to stimulate skin
t. *hada-ni* *shigeki-o* *ataeru*
skin-DAT stimulus-ACC to give
to give skin a stimulus

Regarding the patterns in (8) as the entire set of compositional paraphrases for $N : C : V$ type phrases, we then extended them to a bit more complex phrases as in Figure 3. For instance, 10 patterns

Table 2: Transformation patterns.

Target phrase	# of patterns
$N : C : V$	3
$N_1 : N_2 : C : V$	10
$N : C : V_1 : V_2$	10
$N : C : Adv : V$	7
$Adj : N : C : V$	4
$N : C : Adj$	3
Total	37

Table 3: Generation functions.

Definition	Syntactic category	# of returned value
$np(N_1, N_2)$	noun phrase	9
$vp(N)$	verb phrase	1
$vp(N_1, N_2)$	verb phrase	2
$vp(V_1, V_2)$	verb phrase	3
$lvc(V)$	light verb construction	1
$genCase()$	case marker	4
$genVoice()$	verbal suffix for voice	3
$genTense()$	verbal suffix for tense	2
$genAspect()$	verbal suffix for aspect	2

for $N_1 : N_2 : C : V$ type phrases shown in (8) have been described based on patterns in (5), mainly focusing on interactions between newly introduced N_1 and other constituents.

(8) a. $N_1 : N_2 : C : V \Rightarrow vp(N_1, N_2)$ (5a)
b. $N_1 : N_2 : C : V \Rightarrow$ $N_1 : genCase() : vp(N_2)$ (5a)
c. $N_1 : N_2 : C : V \Rightarrow$ $N_2 : genCase() : vp(N_1)$ (5a)
d. $N_1 : N_2 : C : V \Rightarrow$ $np(N_1, N_2) : genCase() : lvc(V)$ (5b)
e. $N_1 : N_2 : C : V \Rightarrow N_1 : genCase() :$ $N_2 : genCase() : lvc(V)$ (5b)
f. $N_1 : N_2 : C : V \Rightarrow N_2 : genCase() :$ $N_1 : genCase() : lvc(V)$ (5b)
g. $N_1 : N_2 : C : V \Rightarrow$ $adv(V) : vp(N_1, N_2)$ (5c)
h. $N_1 : N_2 : C : V \Rightarrow$ $adv(V) : N_1 : genCase() : vp(N_2)$ (5c)
i. $N_1 : N_2 : C : V \Rightarrow$ $adv(V) : N_2 : genCase() : vp(N_1)$ (5c)
j. $N_1 : N_2 : C : V \Rightarrow$ $np(N_1, N_2) : C : V$ (new)

The number of transformation patterns we have so far developed is shown in Table 2.

Generation functions shown in Table 3 are developed along with creating transformation patterns. Although this is the heart of the proposed model, two problems are remained: (i) the granularity of each generation function is determined according to our linguistic intuition, and (ii) they do not ensure of generating all possible phrases. Therefore, we have to establish the methodology to create this knowledge more precisely.

Table 4: Dictionaries for lexical functions.

ID POS-pair	$\|D\|$	$\|C\|$	$\|D \cup C\|$	$\|J\|$
(a) noun–verb	3,431	-	3,431	3,431
(b) noun–adjective	308	667	906	475 †
(c) noun–adjectival verb	1,579	-	1,579	1,579
(d) noun–adverb	271	-	271	271
(e) verb–adjective	252	-	252	192 †
(f) verb–adjectival verb	74	-	74	68 †
(g) verb–adverb	74	-	74	64 †
(h) adjective–adjectival verb	66	95	159	146 †
(i) adjective–adverb	33	-	33	26 †
(j) adjectival verb–adverb	70	-	70	70
Total	6,158	762	6,849	6,322

4.2 Lexical functions

Except $wh(N)$, which generates interrogatives as shown in the bottom line of Table 1, the relations we have so far implemented are lexical derivations. These roughly correspond to **S**, **V**, **A**, and **Adv** in MTT. The back-end of these lexical functions is a set of dictionaries built by the following two steps:

Step 1. Automatic candidate collection: Most derivatives in Japanese share the beginning of words and are characterized by the correspondences of their suffixes. For example, "*amai* (be sweet)" and "*amami* (sweetness)" has a typical suffix correspondence "∗-i:∗-mi" of adjective–noun derivation. Using this clue, candidates are collected by two methods.

- *From dictionary*: Retrieve all word pairs from the given set of words those satisfying the following four conditions: (i) beginning with *kanji* character, (ii) having different POSs, (iii) sharing at least the first character and the first sound, and (iv) having a suffix pattern which corresponds to at least two pairs.
- *Using dictionary and corpus*: Generate candidates from a set of words by applying a set of typical suffix patterns, and then check if each candidate is an actual word using corpus. This is based on (Langkilde and Knight, 1998).

Step 2. Manual selection: The set of word pairs collected in the previous step includes those do not have particular semantic relationship. This step involves human to discard noises.

Table 4 shows the size of 10 dictionaries, where each column denotes the number of word pairs retrieved from IPADIC[5] ($|D|$), those using IPADIC, seven patterns and the same corpus as in Section 3.4 ($|C|$), their union ($|D \cup C|$), and those manually judged correct ($|J|$), respectively. The sets of word pairs J are used as bi-directional lexical functions, although manual screening for four dictionaries without dagger (†) are still in process.

5 Discussion

5.1 Unit of processing

The working hypothesis underlying our work is that phrase is the appropriate unit for computing semantic equivalence. In addition to the arguments in Section 1, the hypothesis is supported by what is done in practice. Let us see two related fields.

The first is the task of word sense disambiguation (WSD). State-of-the-art WSD techniques refer to context as a clue. However, the range of context is usually not so wide: words and their POSs within small window centered the target word and content words within the same sentence of the target word. The task therefore can be viewed as determining the meaning of phrase based on its constituent words and surrounding content words.

Statistical language model (SLM) is another field. SLMs usually deal with various things within word sequence (or structure) at the same time. However, relations within a phrase should be differentiated from that between phrases, because checking the former is for grammaticality, while the latter for cohesion. We think SLMs should take the phrase to determine boundaries for assessing the correctness of generated expressions more accurately.

5.2 Compositionality

We examined how large part of manually created paraphrases could be generated in our compositional approach. First, a set of paraphrase examples were created in the following procedure:

Step 1. Most frequent 400 phrases typed $N_1 : N_2 : C : V$ were sampled from one year of newspaper articles (Mainichi 1991).

Step 2. An annotator produced paraphrases for each phrase. We allowed to record more than one paraphrase for a given phrase and to give up producing paraphrases. As a result, we obtained 211 paraphrases for 170 input phrases.

Manual classification revealed that 42% (88 / 211) of paraphrases could be compositionally explainable, and the (theoretical) coverage increases to 86% (182 / 211) if we have a synonym dictionary. This ratio is enough high to give these phenomena preference as the research target, although we cannot reject a possibility that data has been biased.

5.3 Sufficient condition of equivalence

In our system, transformation patterns and generation functions offer necessary conditions for generating syntactic variants for given input. However, we have no sufficient condition to control the application of such a knowledge.

It has not been thoroughly clarified what clue can be sufficient condition to ensure semantic equivalence, even in a number of previous work. Though, at least, roles of participants in the event have to be preserved by some means, such as the way presented in (Pantel et al., 2007). Kaji et al. (2002) introduced a method of case frame alignment in paraphrase generation. In the model, arguments of main verb in the source are taken over by that of the target according to the similarities between arguments of the source and target. Fujita et al. (2005) employed a semantic representation of verb to realize the alignment of the role of participants governed by the source and target verbs. According to an empirical experiment in (Fujita et al., 2005), statistical language models do not contribute to calculating semantic equivalence, but to filtering out anomalies. We therefore plan to incorporate above alignment-based models into our system, for example, within or after the syntactic transformation step (Figure 2).

5.4 Ideas for improvement

The knowledge and system presented in Section 3 are quite simple. Thus the following features should be incorporated to improve the system in addition to the one described in Section 5.3.

- *Dependency structure*: To enable flexible matching, such as $Adv : N : C : V$ type input and transformation pattern for $N : C : Adv : V$ type phrases.
- *Sophisticated SLM*: The generation phase should also take the structure into account to

[5] http://mecab.sourceforge.jp/

evaluate generated expressions flexibly.

- *Knowledge development*: Although we have not done intrinsic evaluation of knowledge, we are aware of its incompleteness. We are continuing manual screening for the dictionaries and planning to enhance the methodology of knowledge development.

6 Conclusion

To enhance the technology for computing semantic equivalence, we have introduced the notion of phrasal thesaurus, which is a natural extension of conventional word-based thesaurus. Plausibility of taking phrase as the unit of processing has been discussed from several viewpoints. On the basis of that, we have been developing a system to dynamically generate syntactic variants in Japanese predicate phrases which utilizes three sorts of knowledge that are inspired by MTT, STAG, Fastr, and KURA.

Future work includes implementing more precise features and larger resources to compute semantic equivalence. We also plan to conduct an empirical evaluation of the resources and the overall system.

Acknowledgments

This work was supported in part by MEXT Grants-in-Aid for Young Scientists (B) 18700143, and for Scientific Research (A) 16200009, Japan.

References

Regina Barzilay and Lillian Lee. 2003. Learning to paraphrase: an unsupervised approach using multiple-sequence alignment. In *Proceedings of the 2003 Human Language Technology Conference and the North American Chapter of the Association for Computational Linguistics (HLT-NAACL)*, pages 16–23.

Chris Brockett and William B. Dolan. 2005. Support Vector Machines for paraphrase identification and corpus construction. In *Proceedings of the 3rd International Workshop on Paraphrasing (IWP)*, pages 1–8.

Timothy Chklovski and Patrick Pantel. 2004. VerbOcean: mining the Web for fine-grained semantic verb relations. In *Proceedings of the 2004 Conference on Empirical Methods in Natural Language Processing (EMNLP)*, pages 33–40.

Michael Collins and Nigel Duffy. 2001. Convolution kernels for natural language. In *Advances in Neural Information Processing Systems 14: Proceedings of the 2001 Conference*, pages 625–632.

Mark Dras. 1999. *Tree adjoining grammar and the reluctant paraphrasing of text*. Ph.D. thesis, Division of Information and Communication Science, Macquarie University.

Atsushi Fujita, Kentaro Inui, and Yuji Matsumoto. 2005. Exploiting Lexical Conceptual Structure for paraphrase generation. In *Proceedings of the 2nd International Joint Conference on Natural Language Processing (IJCNLP)*, pages 908–919.

Atsushi Fujita and Kentaro Inui. 2005. A class-oriented approach to building a paraphrase corpus. In *Proceedings of the 3rd International Workshop on Paraphrasing (IWP)*, pages 25–32.

Zellig Harris. 1968. *Mathematical structures of language*. New York: Interscience Publishers.

Nobuhiro Kaji, Daisuke Kawahara, Sadao Kurohashi, and Satoshi Sato. 2002. Verb paraphrase based on case frame alignment. In *Proceedings of the 40th Annual Meeting of the Association for Computational Linguistics (ACL)*, pages 215–222.

Keiko Kondo, Satoshi Sato, and Manabu Okumura. 1999. Paraphrasing of "sahen-noun + suru". *IPSJ Journal*, 40(11):4064–4074. (in Japanese).

Keiko Kondo, Satoshi Sato, and Manabu Okumura. 2001. Paraphrasing by case alternation. *IPSJ Journal*, 42(3):465–477. (in Japanese).

Irene Langkilde and Kevin Knight. 1998. Generation that exploits corpus-based statistical knowledge. In *Proceedings of the 36th Annual Meeting of the Association for Computational Linguistics and the 17th International Conference on Computational Linguistics (COLING-ACL)*, pages 704–710.

Dekang Lin and Patrick Pantel. 2001. Discovery of inference rules for question answering. *Natural Language Engineering*, 7(4):343–360.

Igor Mel'čuk. 1996. Lexical functions: a tool for the description of lexical relations in a lexicon. In Leo Wanner, editor, *Lexical Functions in Lexicography and Natural Language Processing*, pages 37–102. John Benjamin Publishing Company.

Patrick Pantel, Rahul Bhagat, Bonaventura Coppola, Timothy Chklovski, and Eduard Hovy. 2007. Isp: Learning inferential selectional preferences. In *Proceedings of Human Language Technologies 2007: The Conference of the North American Chapter of the Association for Computational Linguistics (NAACL-HLT)*, pages 564–571.

Tetsuro Takahashi, Tomoya Iwakura, Ryu Iida, Atsushi Fujita, and Kentaro Inui. 2001. KURA: a transfer-based lexico-structural paraphrasing engine. In *Proceedings of the 6th Natural Language Processing Pacific Rim Symposium (NLPRS) Workshop on Automatic Paraphrasing: Theories and Applications*, pages 37–46.

Tetsuro Takahashi. 2005. *Computation of semantic equivalence for question answering*. Ph.D. thesis, Graduate School of Information Science, Nara Institute of Science and Technology.

Kentaro Torisawa. 2006. Acquiring inference rules with temporal constraints by using Japanese coordinated sentences and noun-verb co-occurrences. In *Proceedings of the Human Language Technology Conference of the North American Chapter of the Association for Computational Linguistics (HLT-NAACL)*, pages 57–64.

Julie Weeds, David Weir, and Bill Keller. 2005. The distributional similarity of sub-parses. In *Proceedings of the ACL Workshop on Empirical Modeling of Semantic Equivalence and Entailment*, pages 7–12.

Fuyuki Yoshikane, Keita Tsuji, Kyo Kageura, and Christian Jacquemin. 1999. Detecting Japanese term variation in textual corpus. In *Proceedings of the 4th International Workshop on Information Retrieval with Asian Languages*, pages 97–108.

Machine Learning Based Semantic Inference: Experiments and Observations at RTE-3

Baoli Li[1], Joseph Irwin[1], Ernest V. Garcia[2], and Ashwin Ram[1]

[1] College of Computing
Georgia Institute of Technology
Atlanta, GA 30332, USA
baoli@gatech.edu
gtg519g@mail.gatech.edu
ashwin@cc.gatech.edu

[2] Department of Radiology
School of Medicine, Emory University
Atlanta, GA 30322, USA
Ernest.Garcia@emoryhealthcare.org

Abstract

Textual Entailment Recognition is a semantic inference task that is required in many natural language processing (NLP) applications. In this paper, we present our system for the third PASCAL recognizing textual entailment (RTE-3) challenge. The system is built on a machine learning framework with the following features derived by state-of-the-art NLP techniques: lexical semantic similarity (LSS), named entities (NE), dependent content word pairs (DEP), average distance (DIST), negation (NG), task (TK), and text length (LEN). On the RTE-3 test dataset, our system achieves the accuracy of 0.64 and 0.6488 for the two official submissions, respectively. Experimental results show that LSS and NE are the most effective features. Further analyses indicate that a baseline dummy system can achieve accuracy 0.545 on the RTE-3 test dataset, which makes RTE-3 relatively easier than RTE-2 and RTE-1. In addition, we demonstrate with examples that the current Average Precision measure and its evaluation process need to be changed.

1 Introduction

Textual entailment is a relation between two text snippets in which the meaning of one snippet, called the *hypothesis* (*H*), can be inferred from the other snippet, called the *text* (*T*). Textual entailment recognition is the task of deciding whether a given *T* entails a given *H*. An example pair (pair id 5) from the RTE-3 development dataset is as follows:

T: A bus collision with a truck in Uganda has resulted in at least 30 fatalities and has left a further 21 injured.
H: 30 die in a bus collision in Uganda.

Given such a pair, a recognizing textual entailment (RTE) system should output its judgement about whether or not an entailment relation holds between them. For the above example pair, *H* is entailed by *T*.

The PASCAL Recognizing Textual Entailment Challenge is an annual challenge on this task which has been held since 2005 (Dagan et al., 2006; Bar-Haim et al. 2006). As textual entailment recognition is thought to be a common underlying semantic inference task for many natural language processing applications, such as Information Extraction (IE), Information Retrieval (IR), Question Answering (QA), and Document Summarization (SUM), the PASCAL RTE Challenge has been gaining more and more attention in the NLP community. In the past challenges, various approaches to recognizing textual entailment have been proposed, from syntactic analysis to logical inference (Bar-Haim et al. 2006).

As a new participant, we have two goals by attending the RTE-3 Challenge: first, we would like to explore how state-of-the-art language techniques help to deal with this semantic inference problem; second, we try to obtain a more thorough knowledge of this research and its state-of-the-art.

Inspired by the success of machine learning techniques in RTE-2, we employ the same strategy in our RTE-3 system. Several lexical, syntactical, and semantical language analysis techniques are

Proceedings of the Workshop on Textual Entailment and Paraphrasing, pages 159–164,
Prague, June 2007.

explored to derive effective features for determining textual entailment relation. Then, a general machine learning algorithm is applied on the transformed data for training and prediction. Our two official submissions achieve accuracy 0.64 and 0.6488, respectively.

In the rest of this paper we describe the detail of our system and analyze the results. Section 2 gives the overview of our system, while Section 3 discusses the various features in-depth. We present our experiments and discussions in Section 4, and conclude in Section 5.

2 System Description

Figure 1 gives the architecture of our RTE-3 system, which finishes the process of both training and prediction in two stages. At the first stage, a *T-H* pair goes through language processing and feature extraction modules, and is finally converted to a set of feature-values. At the second stage, a machine learning algorithm is applied to obtain an inference/prediction model when training or output its decision when predicting.

In the language processing module, we try to analyze *T-H* pairs with the state-of-the-art NLP techniques, including lexical, syntactical, and semantical analyses. We first split text into sentences, and tag the Part of Speech (POS) of each word. The text with POS information is then fed into three separate modules: a named entities recognizer, a word sense disambiguation (WSD) module, and a dependency parser. These language analyzers output their own intermediate representations for the feature extraction module.

We produce seven features for each *T-H* pair: lexical semantic similarity (LSS), named entities (NE), dependent content word pairs (DEP), average distance (DIST), negation (NG), task (TK), and text length (LEN). The last two features are extracted from each pair itself, while others are based on the results of language analyzers.

The resources that we used in our RTE-3 system include:

OAK: a general English analysis tool (Sekine 2002). It is used for sentence splitting, POS tagging, and named entities recognition.

WordNet::SenseRelate::Allwords package: a word sense disambiguation (WSD) module for assigning each content word a sense from WordNet (Pedersen et al., 2005). It is used in WSD module.

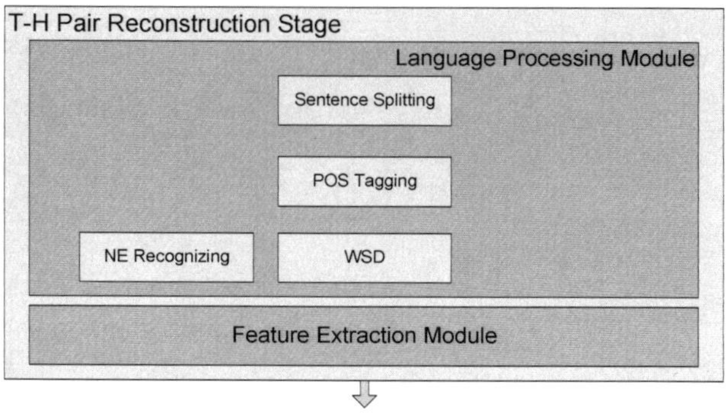

package to calculate the semantic similarity of two content words in WordNet (Fellbaum 1998). This package provides many different semantic relatedness measures. In our system, we use the *Lesk* relatedness measure for function *SSim*, as it can be used to make comparisons between concepts of different parts of speech (POS) (Banerjee&Pedersen, 2002). Because the value of *SSim* may be larger than 1, we normalize the original value from the WordNet::Similarity package to guarantee it fall between 0 and 1.

For the words out of WordNet, e.g. new proper nouns, we use the following strategy: if two words match exactly, the similarity between them is 1; otherwise, the similarity is 0.

It needs to be pointed out that Equation (1) is a variant of the text semantic similarity proposed in (Mihalcea et al. 2006). However, in Equation (1), we take into account out of vocabulary words and normalization for some word-to-word similarity metrics that may be larger than 1.

In addition, we use an IDF dictionary from MEAD (Radev et al. 2001; http://www.summarization.com/mead/) for retrieving the IDF value for each word. For the words out of the IDF dictionary, we assign a default value 3.0.

3.2 Named Entities (NE)

Named Entities are important semantic information carriers, which convey more specific information than individual component words. Intuitively, we can assume that all named entities in a hypothesis would appear in a textual snippet which entails the hypothesis. Otherwise, it is very likely that the entailment relation in a *T-H* pair doesn't hold. Based on this assumption, we derive a NE feature for each *T-H* pair as follows:

$$NE(H,T)=\begin{cases} 1 & ,if\ |NE\_S(H)|=0, \\ \dfrac{|NE\_S(H)\cap NE\_S(T)|}{|NE\_S(H)|} & ,if\ |NE\_S(H)|>0. \end{cases}$$

Function NE_S derives the set of named entities from a textual snippet. When we search in *T* the counterpart of a named entity in *H*, we use a looser matching strategy: if a named entity *neA* in *H* is consumed by a named entity *neB* in *T*, *neA* and *neB* are thought to be matched. We use the English analysis tool OAK (Sekine 2002) to recognize named entities in textual snippets.

3.3 Dependent Content Word Pairs (DEP)

With the NE feature, we can capture some local dependency relations between words, but we may miss many dependency relations expressed in a long distance. These missed long distance dependency relations may be helpful for determining whether entailment holds between *H* and *T*. So, we design a DEP feature as follows:

$$DEP(H,T)=\begin{cases} 1 & ,if\ |DEP\_S(H)|=0, \\ \dfrac{|DEP\_S(H)\cap DEP\_S(T)|}{|DEP\_S(H)|} & ,if\ |DEP\_S(H)|>0. \end{cases}$$

Function DEP_S derives the set of dependent content word pairs from a textual snippet. We require that the two content words of each pair should be dependent directly or linked with at most one function word. We use C&C parser (Clark and Curran 2004) to parse the dependency structure of a textual snippet and then derive the dependent content word pairs. We don't consider the type of dependency relation between two linked words.

3.4 Average Distance (DIST)

The DIST feature measures the distance between unmapped tokens in the text. Adams (2006) uses a simple count of the number of unmapped tokens in the text that occur between two mapped tokens, scaled to the length of the hypothesis. Our system uses a different approach, i.e. measuring the average length of the gaps between mapped tokens. The number of tokens in the text between each consecutive pair of mapped tokens is summed up, and this sum is divided by the number of gaps (equivalent to the number of tokens – 1). In this formula, consecutive mapped tokens in the text count as gaps of 0, so a prevalence of consecutive mapped tokens lowers the value for this feature. The purpose of this approach is to reduce the effect of long appositives, which may not be mapped to the hypothesis but should not rule out entailment.

3.5 Negation (NG)

The Negation feature is very simple. We simply count the occurrences of negative words from a list in both the hypothesis (n_h) and the text (n_t). The list includes some common negating affixes. Then the value is:

$$NEG(H,T)=\begin{cases} 1, if\ n_h\ and\ n_t\ have\ the\ same\ parity \\ 0, otherwise \end{cases}$$

3.6 Task (TK)

The Task feature is simply the task domain from which the text-hypothesis pair was drawn. The values are Question Answering (QA), Information Retrieval (IR), Information Extraction (IE), and Multi-Document Summarization (SUM).

3.7 Text Length (LEN)

The Text Length feature is drawn directly from the length attribute of each *T-H* pair. Based on the length of *T*, its value is either "short" or "long".

4 Experiments and Discussions

We run several experiments using various datasets to train and test models, as well as different combinations of features. We also experiment with several different machine learning algorithms, including support vector machine, decision tree, k-nearest neighbor, naïve bayes, and so on. Decision tree algorithm achieves the best results in all experiments during development. Therefore, we choose to use decision tree algorithm (J48 in WEKA) at the machine learning stage.

4.1 RTE-3 Datasets

RTE-3 organizers provide two datasets, i.e. a development set and a test set, each consisting of 800 *T-H* pairs. In both sets pairs are annotated according to the task the example was drawn from and its length. The length annotation is introduced in this year's competition, and has a value of either "long" or "short." In addition, the development set is annotated as to whether each pair is in an entailment relation or not.

In order to aid our analysis, we compile some statistics on the datasets of RTE-3. Statistics on the development dataset are given in Table 1, while those on the test dataset appear in Table 2.

From these two tables, we found the distribution of different kinds of pairs is not balanced in both the RTE-3 development dataset and the RTE-3 test dataset. 412 entailed pairs appear in the development dataset, where 410 pairs in the test dataset are marked as "YES". Thus, the first baseline system that outputs all "YES" achieves accuracy 0.5125. If we consider task information (IE, IR, QA, and SUM) and assume the two datasets have the same "YES" and "NO" distribution for each task, we will derive the second baseline system, which can get accuracy 0.5450. Similarly, if we further consider length information (short and long) and assume the two datasets have the same "YES" and "NO" distribution for each task with length information, we will derive the third baseline system, which can also get accuracy 0.5450.

Long (135)	IE	NO	11	1.38%
		YES	17	2.13%
	IR	NO	22	2.75%
		YES	21	2.63%
	QA	NO	20	2.50%
		YES	27	3.38%
	SUM	NO	4	0.50%
		YES	13	1.63%
Short (665)	IE	NO	80	10.00%
		YES	92	11.50%
	IR	NO	89	11.13%
		YES	68	8.50%
	QA	NO	73	9.13%
		YES	80	10.00%
	SUM	NO	89	11.13%
		YES	94	11.75%

Table 1. Statistical Information of the RTE-3 Development Dataset.

Long (117)	IE	NO	11	1.38%
		YES	8	1.00%
	IR	NO	31	3.88%
		YES	23	2.88%
	QA	NO	13	1.63%
		YES	22	2.75%
	SUM	NO	4	0.50%
		YES	5	0.63%
Short (683)	IE	NO	84	10.50%
		YES	97	12.13%
	IR	NO	82	10.25%
		YES	64	8.00%
	QA	NO	81	10.13%
		YES	84	10.50%
	SUM	NO	84	10.50%
		YES	107	13.38%

Table 2. Statistical Information of the RTE-3 Test Dataset.

As different kinds of pairs are evenly distributed in RTE-1 and RTE-2 datasets, the baseline system for RTE-1 and RTE-2 that assumes all "YES" or all "NO" can only achieve accuracy 0.5. The relatively higher baseline performance for RTE-3 datasets (0.545 vs. 0.5) makes us expect that the average accuracy may be higher than those in previous RTE Challenges.

Another observation is that the numbers of long pairs in both datasets are very limited. Only

16.88% and 14.63% pairs are long in the development dataset and the test dataset respectively.

4.2 Evaluation Measures

Systems are evaluated by simple accuracy as in Equation (2); that is, the number of pairs (*C*) classified correctly over the total number of pairs (*N*). This score can be further broken down according to task.

$$Accuracy = \frac{C}{N}. \quad (2)$$

There is another scoring available for ranked results, Average Precision, which aims to evaluate the ability of systems to rank all the *T-H* pairs in the test set according to their entailment confidence (in decreasing order from the most certain entailment to the least certain). It is calculated as in Equation (3).

$$AvgP = \frac{1}{R}\sum_{i=1}^{N}\frac{E(i) * Nep(i)}{i}. \quad (3)$$

Where R is the total number of positive pairs in the test set, $E(i)$ is 1 if the i-th pair is positive and 0 otherwise, and $Nep(i)$ returns the number of positive pairs in the top i pairs.

RUN	Overall Accuracy	Accuracy by Task			
		IE	IR	QA	SUM
1	0.6400	0.5100	0.6600	0.7950	0.5950
2	0.6488	0.5300	0.6350	0.8050	0.6250

Table 3. Our Official RTE-3 Run Results.

4.3 Official RTE-3 Results

The official results for our system are shown in Table 3. For our first run, the model was trained on all the datasets from the two previous challenges as well as the RTE-3 development set, using only the LSS, NE, and TK features. This feature combination achieves the best performance on the RTE-3 development dataset in our experiments. For the second run, the model was trained only on the RTE-3 development dataset, but adding other two features LEN and DIST. We hope these two features may be helpful for differentiating pairs with different length.

RUN2 with five features achieves better results than RUN1. It performs better on IE, QA and SUM tasks than RUN1, but poorer on IR task. Both runs obtain the best performance on QA task, and perform very poor on IE task. For the IE task itself, a baseline system can get accuracy 0.525. RUN1 cannot beat this baseline system on IE task, while RUN2 only has a trivial advantage over it. In further analysis on the detailed results, we found that our system tends to label all IE pairs as entailed ones, because most of the IE pairs exhibit higher lexical overlapping between *T* and *H*. In our opinion, word order and long syntactic structures may be helpful for dealing with IE pairs. We will explore this idea and other methods to improve RTE systems on IE pairs in our future research.

Feature Set	Accuracy by Task				Acc.
	IE	IR	QA	SUM	
LSS	0.530	*0.660*	0.720	0.595	0.6263
NE	0.520	0.620	0.780	0.580	0.6250
DEP	0.495	0.625	0.575	0.570	0.5663
TK	0.525	0.565	0.530	0.560	0.5450
DIST	0.525	*0.435*	*0.530*	0.560	*0.5125*
NG	*0.555*	0.505	0.590	*0.535*	0.5463
LEN	0.525	*0.435*	*0.530*	0.560	*0.5125*
LSS+NE	0.525	0.645	0.805	0.585	0.6400
LSS+NE+DEP	0.520	0.650	*0.810*	0.580	0.6400
LSS+NE+TK	0.530	0.625	0.805	0.595	0.6388
LSS+NE+TK+LEN	0.530	0.630	0.805	0.625	0.6475
LSS+NE+TK+DEP	0.530	0.625	0.805	0.620	0.6450
LSS+NE+TK+DEP+NG	*0.460*	0.625	0.785	*0.655*	0.6313
LSS+NE+TK+LEN+DEP	0.525	0.615	0.790	0.600	0.6325
LSS+NE+TK+LEN+DIST (run2)	0.530	0.635	0.805	0.625	*0.6488*
All Features	0.500	0.590	0.790	0.630	0.6275

Table 4. Accuracy by task and selected feature set on the RTE-3 Test dataset (Trained on the RTE-3 development dataset).

4.4 Discussions

4.4.1 Feature Analysis

Table 4 lays out the results of using various feature combinations to train the classifier. All of the models were trained on the RTE 3 development dataset only.

It is obvious that the LSS and NE features have the most utility. The DIST and LEN features seem useless for this dataset, as these features themselves can not beat the baseline system with accuracy 0.545. Systems with individual features perform similarly on SUM pairs except NG, and on IE pairs except NG and DEP features. However, on IR and QA pairs, they behave quite differently. For example, system with NE feature achieves accuracy 0.78 on QA pairs, while system with DEP feature obtains 0.575. NE and LSS features have similar effects, but NE is more useful for QA pairs.

It is interesting to note that some features improve the score in some combinations, but in others they decrease it. For instance, although DEP scores above the baseline at 0.5663, when added to the combination of LSS, NE, TK, and LEN it lowers the overall accuracy by 1.5%.

4.4.2 About Average Precision Measure

As we mentioned in section 4.2, Average Precision (AvgP) is expected to evaluate the ranking ability of a system according to confidence values. However, we found that the current evaluation process and the measure itself have some problems and need to be modified for RTE evaluation.

On one hand, the current evaluation process doesn't consider tied cases where many pairs may have the same confidence value. It is reasonable to assume that the order of tied pairs will be random. Accordingly, the derived Average Precision will vary.

Let's look at a simple example: suppose we have two pairs *c* and *d*, and *c* is the only one positive entailment pair. Here, R=1, N=2 for Equation (3). Two systems X and Y output ranked results as $\{c, d\}$ and $\{d, c\}$ respectively. According to Equation (3), the AvgP value of system X is 1, where that of system Y is 0.5. If these two systems assign same confidence value for both pairs, we can not conclude that system X is better than system Y.

To avoid this problem, we suggest requiring that each system for ranked submission output its confidence for each pair. Then, when calculating Average Precision measure, we first re-rank the list with these confidence values and true answers for each pair. For tied pairs, we rank pairs with true answer "NO" before those with positive entailment relation. By this way, we can produce a stable and more reasonable Average Precision value. For example, in the above example, the modified average precisions for both systems will be 0.5.

On the other hand, from the Equation (3), we know that the upper bound of Average Precision is 1. At the same time, we can also derive a lower bound for this measure as in Equation (4). It corresponds to the worst system which places all the negative pairs before all the positive pairs. The lower bound of Average Precision for RTE-3 test dataset is 0.3172.

$$LB\_AvgP = \frac{1}{R}\sum_{j=0}^{R-1}\frac{R-j}{N-j}. \quad (4)$$

As the values of *N* and *R* change, the lower bound of Average Precision will vary. Therefore, the original Average Precision measure as in Equation (3) is not an ideal one for comparison across datasets.

To solve this problem, we propose a normalized Average Precision measure as in Equation (5).

$$Norm\_AvgP = \frac{AvgP - LB\_AvgP}{1 - LB\_AvgP}. \quad (5)$$

5 Conclusion and Future Work

In this paper, we report our RTE-3 system. The system was built on a machine learning framework with features produced by state-of-the-art NLP techniques. Lexical semantic similarity and Named entities are the two most effective features. Data analysis shows a higher baseline performance for RTE-3 than RTE-1 and RTE-2, and the current Average Precision measure needs to be changed.

As *T-H* pairs from IE task are the most difficult ones, we will focus on these pairs in our future research.

References

Rod Adams. 2006. Textual Entailment Through Extended Lexical Overlap. In *Proceedings of RTE-2 Workshop*.

Satanjeev Banerjee and Ted Pedersen. 2002. An Adapted Lesk Algorithm for Word Sense Disambiguation Using WordNet. In *Proceedings of CICLING-02*.

Roy Bar-Haim et al. 2006. The Second PASCAL Recognising Textual Entailment Challenge. In *Proceedings of RTE-2 Workshop*.

Stephen Clark and James R. Curran. 2004. Parsing the WSJ using CCG and Log-Linear Models. In *Proceedings of ACL-04*.

Ido Dagan, Oren Glickman, and Bernardo Magnini. 2006. The PASCAL Recognising Textual Entailment Challenge. In Quiñonero-Candela et al. (editors.), *MLCW 2005, LNAI Volume 3944*.

Christiane Fellbaum. 1998. *WordNet: an Electronic Lexical Database*. MIT Press.

Rada Mihalcea, Courtney Corley, and Carlo Strapparava. 2006. Corpus-based and Knowledge-based Measures of Text Semantic Similarity. *In Proceedings of AAAI-06*.

Ted Pedersen et al. 2005. *Maximizing Semantic Relatedness to Perform Word Sense Disambiguation*. Research Report UMSI 2005/25, Supercomputing Institute, University of Minnesota.

Dragomir Radev, Sasha Blair-Goldensohn, and ZhuZhang. 2001. Experiments in single and multidocument summarization using MEAD. In *Proceedings of DUC 2001*.

Satoshi Sekine. 2002. Manual of Oak System (version 0.1). Computer Science Department, New York University, *http://nlp.cs.nyu.edu/oak*.

Ian H. Witten and Eibe Frank. 2005. *Data Mining: Practical machine learning tools and techniques*. Morgan Kaufmann, San Francisco.

Learning Alignments and Leveraging Natural Logic

Nathanael Chambers, Daniel Cer, Trond Grenager, David Hall, Chloe Kiddon
Bill MacCartney, Marie-Catherine de Marneffe, Daniel Ramage
Eric Yeh, Christopher D. Manning
Computer Science Department
Stanford University
Stanford, CA 94305
{natec,dcer,grenager,dlwh,loeki,wcmac,mcdm,dramage,yeh1,manning}@stanford.edu

Abstract

We describe an approach to textual inference that improves alignments at both the typed dependency level and at a deeper semantic level. We present a machine learning approach to alignment scoring, a stochastic search procedure, and a new tool that finds deeper semantic alignments, allowing rapid development of semantic features over the aligned graphs. Further, we describe a complementary semantic component based on natural logic, which shows an added gain of 3.13% accuracy on the RTE3 test set.

1 Introduction

Among the many approaches to textual inference, alignment of dependency graphs has shown utility in determining entailment without the use of deep understanding. However, discovering alignments requires a scoring function that accurately scores alignment and a search procedure capable of approximating the optimal mapping within a large search space. We address the former requirement through a machine learning approach for acquiring lexical feature weights, and we address the latter with an approximate stochastic approach to search.

Unfortunately, the most accurate aligner cannot capture deeper semantic relations between two pieces of text. For this, we have developed a tool, Semgrex, that allows the rapid development of dependency rules to find specific entailments, such as familial or locative relations, a common occurence in textual entailment data. Instead of writing code by hand to capture patterns in the dependency graphs, we develop a separate rule-base that operates over aligned dependency graphs. Further, we describe a separate natural logic component that complements our textual inference system, making local entailment decisions based on monotonic assumptions.

The next section gives a brief overview of the system architecture, followed by our proposal for improving alignment scoring and search. New coreference features and the Semgrex tool are then described, followed by a description of natural logic.

2 System Overview

Our system is a three stage architecture that conducts linguistic analysis, builds an alignment between dependency graphs of the text and hypothesis, and performs inference to determine entailment.

Linguistic analysis identifies semantic entities, relationships, and structure within the given text and hypothesis. Typed dependency graphs are passed to the aligner, as well as lexical features such as named entities, synonymity, part of speech, etc. The alignment stage then performs dependency graph alignment between the hypothesis and text graphs, searching the space of possible alignments for the highest scoring alignment. Improvements to the scorer, search algorithm, and automatically learned weights are described in the next section.

The final inference stage determines if the hypothesis is entailed by the text. We construct a set of features from the previous stages ranging from antonyms and polarity to graph structure and semantic relations. Each feature is weighted according to a set of hand-crafted or machine-learned weights over

Proceedings of the Workshop on Textual Entailment and Paraphrasing, pages 165–170,
Prague, June 2007.

the development dataset. We do not describe the features here; the reader is referred to de Marneffe et al. (2006a) for more details. A novel component that leverages natural logic is also used to make the final entailment decisions, described in section 6.

3 Alignment Model

We examine three tasks undertaken to improve the alignment phase: (1) the construction of manually aligned data which enables automatic learning of alignment models, and effectively decouples the alignment and inference development efforts, (2) the development of new search procedures for finding high-quality alignments, and (3) the use of machine learning techniques to automatically learn the parameters of alignment scoring models.

3.1 Manual Alignment Annotation

While work such as Raina et al. (2005) has tried to learn feature alignment weights by credit assignment backward from whether an item is answered correctly, this can be very difficult, and here we follow Hickl et al. (2006) in using supervised gold-standard alignments, which help us to evaluate and improve alignment and inference independently.

We built a web-based tool that allows annotators to mark semantic relationships between text and hypothesis words. A table with the hypothesis words on one axis and the text on the other allows relationships to be marked in the corresponding table cell with one of four options. These relationships include text to hypothesis entailment, hypothesis to text entailment, synonymy, and antonymy. Examples of entailment (from the RTE 2005 dataset) include pairs such as *drinking/consumption*, *coronavirus/virus*, and *Royal Navy/British*. By distinguishing between these different types of alignments, we can capture some limited semantics in the alignment process, but full exploitation of this information is left to future work.

We annotated the complete RTE2_dev and RTE3_dev datasets, for a total of 1600 aligned text/hypothesis pairs (the data is available at http://nlp.stanford.edu/projects/rte/).

3.2 Improving Alignment Search

In order to find "good" alignments, we define both a formal model for scoring the quality of a proposed alignment and a search procedure over the alignment space. Our goal is to build a model that maximizes the total alignment score of the full dataset $\mathcal{D}$, which we take to be the sum of the alignment scores for all individual text/hypothesis pairs (t, h).

Each of the text and hypothesis is a semantic dependency graph; $n(h)$ is the set of nodes (words) and $e(h)$ is the set of edges (grammatical relations) in a hypothesis h. An alignment $a\colon n(h) \mapsto n(t) \cup \{null\}$ maps each hypothesis word to a text word or to a *null* symbol, much like an IBM-style machine translation model. We assume that the alignment score $s(t, h, a)$ is the sum of two terms, the first scoring aligned word pairs and the second the match between an edge between two words in the hypothesis graph and the corresponding path between the words in the text graph. Each of these is a sum, over the scoring function for individual word pairs s_w and the scoring function for edge path pairs s_e:

$$s(t,h,a) = \sum_{h_i \in n(h)} s_w(h_i, a(h_i)) + \sum_{(h_i,h_j) \in e(h)} s_e((h_i,h_j),(a(h_i),a(h_j)))$$

The space of alignments for a hypothesis with m words and a text with n words contains $(n+1)^m$ possible alignments, making exhaustive search intractable. However, since the bulk of the alignment score depends on local factors, we have explored several search strategies and found that *stochastic local search* produces better quality solutions.

Stochastic search is inspired by Gibbs sampling and operates on a complete state formulation of the search problem. We initialize the algorithm with the complete alignment that maximizes the greedy word pair scores. Then, in each step of the search, we seek to randomly replace an alignment for a single hypothesis word h_i. For each possible text word t_j (including *null*), we compute the alignment score if we were to align h_i with t_j. Treating these scores as log probabilities, we create a normalized distribution from which we sample one alignment. This Gibbs sampler is guaranteed to give us samples from the posterior distribution over alignments defined implicitly by the scoring function. As we wish to find a maximum of the function, we use simulated annealing by including a temperature parameter to smooth the sampling distribution as a function of time. This allows us to initially explore the space widely, but later to converge to a local maximum which is hopefully the global maximum.

3.3 Learning Alignment Models

Last year, we manually defined the alignment scoring function (de Marneffe et al., 2006a). However, the existence of the gold standard alignments described in section 3.1 enables the automatic learning of a scoring function. For both the word and edge scorers, we choose a linear model where the score is the dot product of a feature and a weight vector:

$$s_w(h_i, t_j) = \theta_w \cdot \mathbf{f}(h_i, t_j), \text{and}$$
$$s_e((h_i, h_j), (t_k, t_\ell)) = \theta_e \cdot \mathbf{f}((h_i, h_j), (t_k, t_\ell)).$$

Recent results in machine learning show the effectiveness of online learning algorithms for structure prediction tasks. Online algorithms update their model at each iteration step over the training set. For each datum, they use the current weight vector to make a prediction which is compared to the correct label. The weight vector is updated as a function of the difference. We compared two different update rules: the *perceptron update* and the *MIRA update*. In the perceptron update, for an incorrect prediction, the weight vector is modified by adding a multiple of the difference between the feature vector of the correct label and the feature vector of the predicted label. We use the adaptation of this algorithm to structure prediction, first proposed by (Collins, 2002). The *MIRA update* is a proposed improvement that attempts to make the *minimal* modification to the weight vector such that the score of the incorrect prediction for the example is lower than the score of the correct label (Crammer and Singer, 2001).

We compare the performance of the perceptron and MIRA algorithms on 10-fold cross-validation on the RTE2_dev dataset. Both algorithms improve with each pass over the dataset. Most improvement is within the first five passes. Table 1 shows runs for both algorithms over 10 passes through the dataset. MIRA consistently outperforms perceptron learning. Moreover, scoring alignments based on the learned weights marginally outperforms our hand-constructed scoring function by 1.7% absolute.

A puzzling problem is that our overall performance decreased 0.87% with the addition of RTE3_dev alignment data. We believe this is due to a larger proportion of "irrelevant" and "relation" pairs. Irrelevant pairs are those where the text and hypothesis are completely unrelated. Relation pairs are those where the correct entailment judgment relies on the extraction of relations such as *X* works for *Y*, *X* is located in *Y*, or *X* is the wife of *Y*. Both of these categories do not rely on alignments for entailment decisions, and hence introduce noise.

	Perfectly aligned	
	Individual words	Text/hypothesis pairs
Perceptron	4675	271
MIRA	4775	283

Table 1: Perceptron and MIRA results on 10-fold cross-validation on RTE2_dev for 10 passes.

4 Coreference

In RTE3, 135 pairs in RTE3_dev and 117 in RTE3_test have lengths classified as "long," with 642 personal pronouns identified in RTE3_dev and 504 in RTE3_test. These numbers suggest that resolving pronomial anaphora plays an important role in making good entailment decisions. For example, identifying the first "he" as referring to "Yunus" in this pair from RTE3_dev can help alignment and other system features.

P: Yunus, who shared the 1.4 million prize Friday with the Grameen Bank that he founded 30 years ago, pioneered the concept of "microcredit."
H: Yunus founded the Grameen Bank 30 years ago.

Indeed, 52 of the first 200 pairs from RTE3_dev were deemed by a human evaluator to rely on reference information. We used the OpenNLP[1] package's maximum-entropy coreference utility to perform resolution on parse trees and named-entity data from our system. Found relations are stored and used by the alignment stage for word similarity.

We evaluated our system with and without coreference over RTE3_dev and RTE3_test. Results are shown in Table 3. The presence of reference information helped, approaching significance on the development set ($p < 0.1$, McNemar's test, 2-tailed), but not on the test set. Examination of alignments and features between the two runs shows that the alignments do not differ significantly, but associated

[1]http://opennlp.sourceforge.net/

weights do, thus affecting entailment threshold tuning. We believe coreference needs to be integrated into all the featurizers and lexical resources, rather than only with word matching, in order to make further gains.

5 Semgrex Language

A core part of an entailment system is the ability to find semantically equivalent patterns in text. Previously, we wrote tedious graph traversal code by hand for each desired pattern. As a remedy, we wrote Semgrex, a pattern language for dependency graphs. We use Semgrex atop the typed dependencies from the Stanford Parser (de Marneffe et al., 2006b), as aligned in the alignment phase, to identify both semantic patterns in a single text and over two aligned pieces of text. The syntax of the language was modeled after tgrep/Tregex, query languages used to find syntactic patterns in trees (Levy and Andrew, 2006). This speeds up the process of graph search and reduces errors that occur in complicated traversal code.

5.1 Semgrex Features

Rather than providing regular expression matching of atomic tree labels, as in most tree pattern languages, Semgrex represents nodes as a (non-recursive) attribute-value matrix. It then uses regular expressions for subsets of attribute values. For example, `{word:run;tag:/^NN/}` refers to any node that has a value *run* for the attribute *word* and a *tag* that starts with *NN*, while {} refers to any node in the graph.

However, the most important part of Semgrex is that it allows you to specify relations between nodes. For example, `{} <nsubj {}` finds all the dependents of `nsubj` relations. Logical connectives can be used to form more complex patterns and node naming can help retrieve matched nodes from the patterns. Four base relations, shown in figure 1, allow you to specify the type of relation between two nodes, in addition to an alignment relation (@) between two graphs.

5.2 Entailment Patterns

A particularly useful application of Semgrex is to create relation entailment patterns. In particular, the IE subtask of RTE has many characteristics that are not well suited to the core alignment features of our system. We began integrating Semgrex into our system by creating semantic alignment rules for these IE tasks.

Semgrex Relations

Symbol	#Description
{A} >reln {B}	A is the governor of a reln relation with B
{A} <reln {B}	A is the dependent of a reln relation with B
{A} >>reln {B}	A dominates a node that is the governor of a reln relation with B
{A} <<reln {B}	A is the dependent of a node that is dominated by B
{A} @ {B}	A aligns to B

Figure 1: Semgrex relations between nodes.

T: Bill Clinton's wife Hillary was in Wichita today, continuing her campaign.
H: Bill Clinton is married to Hillary. (*TRUE*)
Pattern:

```
({}=1
  <nsubjpass ({word:married} >pp_to {}=2))
@ ({} >poss ({lemma:/wife/} >appos {}=3))
```

This is a simplified version of a pattern that looks for marriage relations. If it matches, additional programmatic checks ensure that the nodes labeled 2 and 3 are either aligned or coreferent. If they are, then we add a MATCH feature, otherwise we add a MISMATCH. Patterns included other familial relations and employer-employee relations. These patterns serve both as a necessary component of an IE entailment system and as a test drive of Semgrex.

5.3 Range of Application

Our rules for marriage relations correctly matched six examples in the RTE3 development set and one in the test set. Due to our system's weaker performance on the IE subtask of the data, we analyzed 200 examples in the development set for Semgrex applicability. We identified several relational classes, including the following:

- **Work**: works for, holds the position of
- **Location**: lives in, is located in
- **Relative**: wife/husband of, are relatives
- **Membership**: is an employee of, is part of
- **Business**: is a partner of, owns
- **Base**: is based in, headquarters in

These relations make up at least 7% of the data, suggesting utility from capturing other relations.

6 Natural Logic

We developed a computational model of *natural logic*, the NatLog system, as another inference engine for our RTE system. NatLog complements our core broad-coverage system by trading lower recall for higher precision, similar to (Bos and Markert, 2006). Natural logic avoids difficulties with translating natural language into first-order logic (FOL) by forgoing logical notation and model theory in favor of natural language. Proofs are expressed as incremental edits to natural language expressions. Edits represent conceptual *contractions* and *expansions*, with truth preservation specified natural logic. For further details, we refer the reader to (Sánchez Valencia, 1995).

We define an entailment relation $\sqsubseteq$ between nouns (*hammer* $\sqsubseteq$ *tool*), adjectives (*deafening* $\sqsubseteq$ *loud*), verbs (*sprint* $\sqsubseteq$ *run*), modifiers, connectives and quantifiers. In ordinary (*upward-monotone*) contexts, the entailment relation between compound expressions mirrors the entailment relations between their parts. Thus *tango in Paris* $\sqsubseteq$ *dance in France*, since *tango* $\sqsubseteq$ *dance* and *in Paris* $\sqsubseteq$ *in France*. However, many linguistic constructions create *downward-monotone* contexts, including negation (*didn't sing* $\sqsubseteq$ *didn't yodel*), restrictive quantifiers (*few beetles* $\sqsubseteq$ *few insects*) and many others.

NatLog uses a three-stage architecture, comprising linguistic pre-processing, alignment, and entailment classification. In pre-processing, we define a list of expressions that affect monotonicity, and define Tregex patterns that recognize each occurrence and its scope. This *monotonicity marking* can correctly account for multiple monotonicity inversions, as in *no soldier without a uniform*, and marks each token span with its final effective monotonicity.

In the second stage, word alignments from our RTE system are represented as a sequence of *atomic edits* over token spans, as entailment relations are described across incremental edits in NatLog. Aligned pairs generate *substitution* edits, unaligned premise words yield *deletion* edits, and unaligned hypothesis words yield *insertion* edits. Where possible, contiguous sequences of word-level edits are collected into span edits.

In the final stage, we use a decision-tree classifier to predict the *elementary entailment relation* (table 2) for each atomic edit. Edit features include the type, effective monotonicity at affected tokens, and their lexical features, including syntactic category, lemma similarity, and WordNet-derived measures of synonymy, hyponymy, and antonymy. The classifier was trained on a set of 69 problems designed to exercise the feature space, learning heuristics such as *deletion in an upward-monotone context yields* $\sqsubset$, *substitution of a hypernym in a downward-monotone context yields* $\sqsupset$, and *substitution of an antonym yields* $|$.

relation	symbol	in terms of $\sqsubseteq$	RTE
equivalent	$p = h$	$p \sqsubseteq h, h \sqsubseteq p$	yes
forward	$p \sqsubset h$	$p \sqsubseteq h, h \not\sqsubseteq p$	yes
reverse	$p \sqsupset h$	$h \sqsubseteq p, p \not\sqsubseteq h$	no
independent	$p \# h$	$p \not\sqsubseteq h, h \not\sqsubseteq p$	no
exclusive	$p \mid h$	$p \sqsubseteq \neg h, h \sqsubseteq \neg p$	no

Table 2: NatLog's five elementary entailment relations. The last column indicates correspondences to RTE answers.

To produce a top-level entailment judgment, the atomic entailment predictions associated with each edit are composed in a fairly obvious way. If r is any entailment relation, then $(= \circ r) \equiv r$, but $(\# \circ r) \equiv \#$. $\sqsubset$ and $\sqsupset$ are transitive, but $(\sqsubset \circ \sqsupset) \equiv \#$, and so on.

We do not expect NatLog to be a general-purpose solution for RTE problems. Many problems depend on types of inference that it does not address, such as paraphrase or relation extraction. Most pairs have large edit distances, and more atomic edits means a greater chance of errors propagating to the final output: given the entailment composition rules, the system can answer *yes* only if all atomic-level predictions are either $\sqsubset$ or $=$. Instead, we hope to make reliable predictions on a subset of the RTE problems.

Table 3 shows NatLog performance on RTE3. It makes positive predictions on few problems (18% on development set, 24% on test), but achieves good precision relative to our RTE system (76% and 68%, respectively). For comparison, the FOL-based system reported in (Bos and Markert, 2006) attained a precision of 76% on RTE2, but made a positive prediction in only 4% of cases. This high precision suggests that superior performance can be achieved by hybridizing NatLog with our core RTE system.

The reader is referred to (MacCartney and Man-

ID	Premise(s)	Hypothesis	Answer
518	The French railway company SNCF is cooperating in the project.	The French railway company is called SNCF.	*yes*
601	NUCOR has pioneered a giant mini-mill in which steel is poured into continuous casting machines.	Nucor has pioneered the first mini-mill.	*no*

Table 4: Illustrative examples from the RTE3 test suite

RTE3 Development Set (800 problems)				
System	% yes	precision	recall	accuracy
Core +coref	50.25	68.66	66.99	67.25
Core -coref	49.88	66.42	64.32	64.88
NatLog	18.00	**76.39**	26.70	58.00
Hybrid, bal.	50.00	69.75	67.72	68.25
Hybrid, opt.	55.13	69.16	**74.03**	**69.63**

RTE3 Test Set (800 problems)				
System	% yes	precision	recall	accuracy
Core +coref	50.00	61.75	60.24	60.50
Core -coref	50.00	60.25	58.78	59.00
NatLog	23.88	**68.06**	31.71	57.38
Hybrid, bal.	50.00	64.50	62.93	63.25
Hybrid, opt.	54.13	63.74	**67.32**	**63.62**

Table 3: Performance on the RTE3 development and test sets. *% yes* indicates the proportion of *yes* predictions made by the system. Precision and recall are shown for the *yes* label.

ning, 2007) for more details on NatLog.

7 System Results

Our core system makes *yes*/*no* predictions by thresholding a real-valued *inference score*. To construct a hybrid system, we adjust the inference score by $+x$ if NatLog predicts *yes*, $-x$ otherwise. x is chosen by optimizing development set accuracy when adjusting the threshold to generate balanced predictions (equal numbers of *yes* and *no*). As another experiment, we fix x at this value and adjust the threshold to optimize development set accuracy, resulting in an excess of *yes* predictions. Results for these two cases are shown in Table 3. Parameter values tuned on development data yielded the best performance. The optimized hybrid system attained an absolute accuracy gain of 3.12% over our RTE system, corresponding to an extra 25 problems answered correctly. This result is statistically significant ($p < 0.01$, McNemar's test, 2-tailed).

The gain cannot be fully attributed to NatLog's success in handling the kind of inferences about monotonicity which are the staple of natural logic. Indeed, such inferences are quite rare in the RTE data. Rather, NatLog seems to have gained primarily by being more precise. In some cases, this precision works against it: NatLog answers *no* to problem 518 (table 4) because it cannot account for the insertion of *called*. On the other hand, it correctly rejects the hypothesis in problem 601 because it cannot account for the insertion of *first*, whereas the less-precise core system was happy to allow it.

Acknowledgements

This material is based upon work supported in part by the Disruptive Technology Office (DTO)'s AQUAINT Phase III Program.

References

Johan Bos and Katja Markert. 2006. When logical inference helps determining textual entailment (and when it doesn't). In *Proceedings of the Second PASCAL RTE Challenge*.

Michael Collins. 2002. Discriminative training methods for hidden markov models: Theory and experiments with perceptron algorithms. In *Proceedings of EMNLP-2002*.

Koby Crammer and Yoram Singer. 2001. Ultraconservative online algorithms for multiclass problems. In *Proceedings of COLT-2001*.

Marie-Catherine de Marneffe, Bill MacCartney, Trond Grenager, Daniel Cer, Anna Rafferty, and Christopher D. Manning. 2006a. Learning to distinguish valid textual entailments. In *Second Pascal RTE Challenge Workshop*.

Marie-Catherine de Marneffe, Bill MacCartney, and Christopher D. Manning. 2006b. Generating typed dependency parses from phrase structure parses. In *5th Int. Conference on Language Resources and Evaluation (LREC 2006)*.

Andrew Hickl, John Williams, Jeremy Bensley, Kirk Roberts, Bryan Rink, and Ying Shi. 2006. Recognizing textual entailment with LCC's GROUNDHOG system. In *Proceedings of the Second PASCAL RTE Challenge*.

Roger Levy and Galen Andrew. 2006. Tregex and Tsurgeon: tools for querying and manipulating tree data structures. In *Proceedings of the Fifth International Conference on Language Resources and Evaluation*.

Bill MacCartney and Christopher D. Manning. 2007. Natural logic for textual inference. In *ACL Workshop on Textual Entailment and Paraphrasing*.

Rajat Raina, Andrew Y. Ng, and Christopher D. Manning. 2005. Robust textual inference via learning and abductive reasoning. In *AAAI 2005*, pages 1099–1105.

Victor Sánchez Valencia. 1995. Parsing-driven inference: Natural logic. *Linguistic Analysis*, 25:258–285.

A Discourse Commitment-Based Framework for Recognizing Textual Entailment

Andrew Hickl and Jeremy Bensley
Language Computer Corporation
1701 North Collins Boulevard
Richardson, Texas 75080 USA
{andy, jeremy}@languagecomputer.com

Abstract

In this paper, we introduce a new framework for recognizing textual entailment which depends on extraction of the set of publicly-held beliefs – known as *discourse commitments* – that can be ascribed to the author of a text or a hypothesis. Once a set of commitments have been extracted from a *t-h* pair, the task of recognizing textual entailment is reduced to the identification of the commitments from a *t* which support the inference of the *h*. Promising results were achieved: our system correctly identified more than 80% of examples from the RTE-3 Test Set correctly, without the need for additional sources of training data or other web-based resources.

1 Introduction

Systems participating in the previous two PASCAL Recognizing Textual Entailment (RTE) Challenges (Bar-Haim et al., 2006) have successfully employed a variety of "shallow" techniques in order to recognize instances of textual entailment, including methods based on: (1) sets of heuristics (Vanderwende et al., 2006), (2) measures of term overlap (Jijkoun and de Rijke, 2005), (3) the alignment of graphs created from syntactic or semantic dependencies (Haghighi et al., 2005), or (4) statistical classifiers which leverage a wide range of features, including the output of paraphrase generation (Hickl et al., 2006) or model building systems (Bos and Markert, 2006).

While relatively "shallow" approaches have shown much promise in RTE for entailment pairs where the text and hypothesis remain short, we expect that performance of these types of systems will ultimately degrade as longer and more syntactically complex entailment pairs are considered. In order to remain effective as texts get longer, we believe that RTE systems will need to employ techniques that will enable them to enumerate the set of propositions which are inferable – whether asserted, presupposed, or conventionally or conversationally implicated – from a text-hypothesis pair.

In this paper, we introduce a new framework for recognizing textual entailment which depends on extraction of the set of publicly-held beliefs – or *discourse commitments* – that can be ascribed to the author of a text or a hypothesis. We show that once a set of discourse commitments have been extracted from a text-hypothesis pair, the task of recognizing textual entailment can be reduced to the identification of the one (or more) commitments from the text which are most likely to support the inference of each commitment extracted from the hypothesis. More formally, we assume that given a commitment set $\{c_t\}$ consisting of the set of discourse commitments inferable from a text t and a hypothesis h, we define the task of RTE as a search for the commitment $c \in \{c_t\}$ which maximizes the likelihood that c textually entails h.

The rest of this paper is organized in the following way. Section 2 provides a sketch of the system we used in the PASCAL RTE-3 Challenge. Sections 3, 4, and 5 describe details of our systems for Commitment Extraction, Commitment Se-

Proceedings of the Workshop on Textual Entailment and Paraphrasing, pages 171–176,
Prague, June 2007.

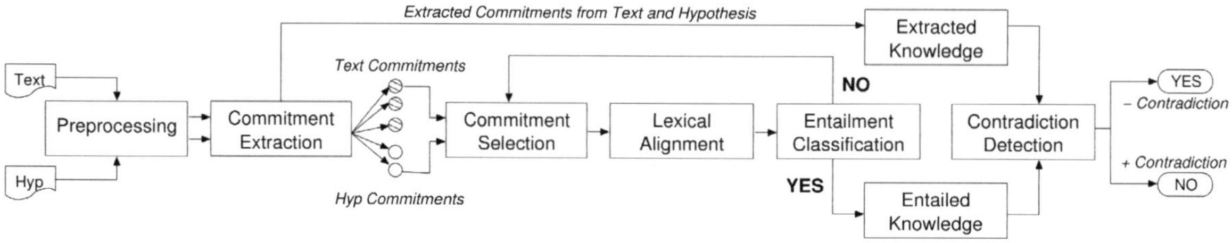

Figure 1: System Architecture.

lection, and Entailment Classification, respectively. Finally, Section 6 discusses results from this year's evaluation, and Section 7 provides our conclusions.

2 System Overview

The architecture of our system for recognizing textual entailment (RTE) is presented in Figure 1.

In our system, *text-hypothesis* (*t-h*) pairs are initially submitted to a *Preprocessing* module which (1) syntactic parses each passage (using an implementation of the (Collins, 1999) parser), (2) identifies semantic dependencies (using a semantic dependency parser trained on PropBank (Palmer et al., 2005) and NomBank (Meyers et al., 2004)), (3) annotates named entities (using LCC's *CiceroLite* named entity recognition system), (4) resolves instances of pronominal and nominal coreference (using a system based on (Luo et al., 2004)), and (5) normalizes temporal and spatial expressions to fully-resolved instances (using a technique first introduced in (Aarseth et al., 2006)).

Annotated passages are then sent to a *Commitment Extraction* module, which uses a series of extraction heuristics in order to enumerate a subset of the discourse commitments that are inferable from either the *text* or *hypothesis*. Following (Gunlogson, 2001; Stalnaker, 1979), we assume that a discourse commitment (c) represents the any of the set of propositions that can necessarily be inferred to be true, given a conventional reading of a text passage. The complete list of commitments that our system is able to extract from from the t used in examples 34 and 36 from the RTE-3 Test Set is presented in Figure 2. (Details of our commitment extraction approach are presented in Section 3.)

Commitments are then sent to a *Commitment Selection* module, which uses a weighted bipartite matching algorithm first described in (Taskar et al., 2005b) in order to identify the commitment from the t which features the best alignment for each commitment extracted from the h. The commitment pairs identified for the hypotheses from 34 and 36 are highlighted in Figure 2. (Details of our method for selecting and aligning commitments are provided in Section 4.)

Each pair of commitments are then considered in turn by an *Entailment Classification* module, which follows (Bos and Markert, 2006; Hickl et al., 2006) in using a decision tree classifier in order to compute the likelihood that a commitment extracted from a t textually entails a commitment extracted from an h.

If a commitment pair is judged to be a positive instance of TE, it is sent to an *Entailment Validation* module, which uses a system for recognizing instances of textual contradiction (RTC) based on (Harabagiu et al., 2006) in order to determine whether the (presumably) entailed hypothesis is contradicted by any of other commitments extracted from the t during commitment extraction. If no text commitment can be identified which contradicts the hypothesis, it is presumed to be textually entailed, and a judgment of YES is returned. Alternatively, if the entailed h is textually contradicted by one (or more) of the commitments extracted from the t, the h is considered to be contradicted by the t, the entailment pair is classified as a negative instance of TE, and a judgment of NO is returned.

In contrast, when commitment pairs are judged to be negative instances of TE by the Entailment Classifier, the current pair is removed from further consideration by the system, and the next most likely commitment pair is considered. Commitment pairs are considered in decreasing order of the probability output by the Commitment Selection module until a positive instance of TE is identified – or until there are no more commitment pairs with a selection probability greater than a pre-defined threshold.

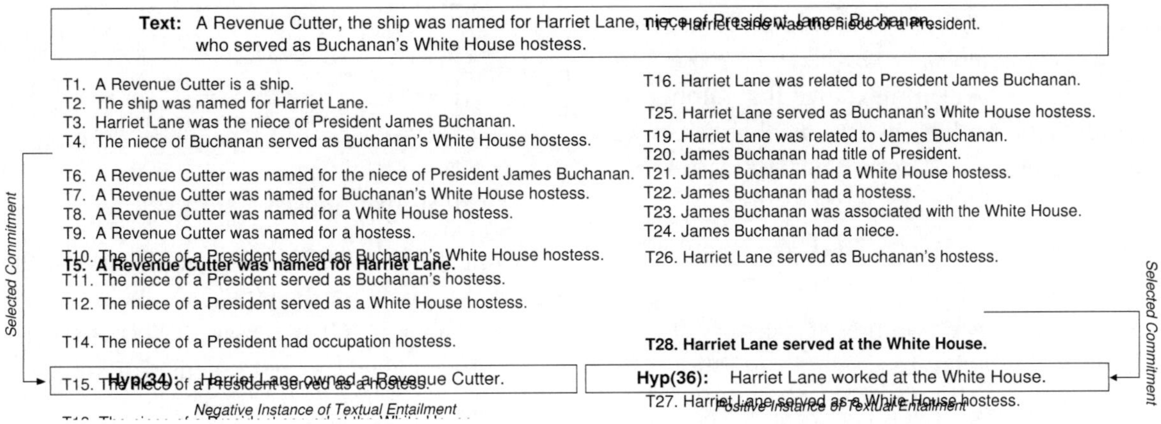

Figure 2: Text Commitments Extracted from Examples 34 and 36.

3 Extracting Discourse Commitments

Following Preprocessing, our system for RTE leverages a series of heuristics in order to extract a subset of the discourse commitments available from a text-hypothesis pair. In this section, we outline the five classes of heuristics we used to extract commitments for the RTE-3 Challenge.

Sentence Segmentation: We use a sentence segmenter to break text passages into sets of individual sentences; commitments are then extracted from each sentence independently.

Syntactic Decomposition: We use heuristics to syntactically decompose sentences featuring coordination and lists into well-formed sentences that only include a single conjunct or list element.

Supplemental Expressions: Recent work by (Potts, 2005; Huddleston and Pullum, 2002) has demonstrated that the class of supplemental expressions – including appositives, *as*-clauses, parentheticals, parenthetical adverbs, non-restrictive relative clauses, and epithets – trigger conventional implicatures (CI) whose truth is necessarily presupposed, even if the truth conditions of a sentence are not satisfied. In our current system, heuristics were used to extract supplemental expressions from each sentence under consideration and to create new sentences which specify the CI conveyed by the expression.

Relation Extraction: We used an in-house relation extraction system to recognize six types of semantic relations between named entities, including: (1) *artifact* (e.g. OWNER-OF), (2) *general affiliation* (e.g. LOCATION-OF), (3) *organization affiliation* (e.g. EMPLOYEE-OF), (4) *part-whole*, (5) *social affiliation* (e.g. RELATED-TO), and (6) *physical location* (e.g. LOCATED-NEAR) relations. Again, as with supplemental expressions, heuristics were used to generate new commitments which expressed the semantics conveyed by these nominal relations.

Coreference Resolution: We used systems for resolving pronominal and nominal coreference in order to expand the number of commitments available to the system. After a set of co-referential entity mentions were detected (e.g. *Harriet Lane*, *the niece*, *Buchanan's White House hostess*), new commitments were generated from the existing set of commitments which incorporated each co-referential mention.

4 Commitment Selection

Following Commitment Extraction, we used an word alignment technique first introduced in (Taskar et al., 2005b) in order to select the commitment extracted from *t* (henceforth, c_t) which represents the best alignment for each of the commitments extracted from *h* (henceforth, c_h).

We assume that the alignment of two discourse commitments can be cast as a maximum weighted matching problem in which each pair of words (t_i,h_j) in an commitment pair (c_t,c_h) is assigned a score $s_{ij}(t, h)$ corresponding to the likelihood that t_i is aligned to h_j.[1] As with (Taskar et al., 2005b), we use the large-margin structured prediction model

[1] In order to ensure that content from the *h* is reflected in the *t*, we assume that each word from the *h* is aligned to exactly one or zero words from the *t*.

introduced in (Taskar et al., 2005a) in order to compute a set of parameters w (computed with respect to a set of features f) which maximize the number of correct alignment predictions ($\bar{y}_i$) made given a set of training examples (x_i), as in Equation (1).

$$y_i = \arg\max_{\bar{y}_i \in Y} w^\top f(x_i, \bar{y}_i), \forall i \quad (1)$$

We used three sets of features in our model: (1) string features (including Levenshtein edit distance, string equality, and stemmed string equality), (2) lexico-semantic features (including WordNet Similarity (Pedersen et al., 2004) and named entity similarity equality), and (3) word association features (computed using the Dice coefficient (Dice, 1945)[2]). In order to provide a training set which most closely resembled the RTE-3 Test Set, we hand-annotated token alignments for each of the 800 entailment pairs included in the Development Set.

Following alignment, we used the sum of the edge scores ($\sum_{i,j=1}^{n} s_{ij}(t_i, h_j)$) computed for each of the possible (c_t, c_h) pairs in order to search for the c_t which represented the *reciprocal best hit* (Mushegian and Koonin, 2005) of each c_h extracted from the hypothesis. This was performed by selecting a commitment pair (c_t, c_h) where c_t was the top-scoring alignment candidate for c_h and c_h was the top-scoring alignment candidate for c_t. If no reciprocal best-hit could be found for any of the commitments extracted from the *h*, the system automatically returned a TE judgment of NO.

We compared the performance of our word alignment and commitment selection algorithms against an implementation of the lexical alignment classifier described in (Hickl et al., 2006) on commitments extracted from the entailment pairs from the RTE-2 Test Set. Table 1 presents results from evaluations of these two models on the token alignment and commitment selection tasks. (Gold standard annotations for each task were created by hand by a team of 3 annotators following the RTE-3 evaluations.)

[2]The Dice coefficient was computed as $Dice(i) = \frac{2C_{th}(i)}{C_t(i)C_h(i)}$, where C_{th} is equal to the number of times a word i was found in both the *t* and an *h* of a single entailment pair, while C_t and C_h were equal to the number of times a word was found in any *t* or *h*, respectively. A hand-crafted corpus of 100,000 entailment pairs was used to compute values for C_t, C_h, and C_{th}.

Task	Measurement	Current Work	Hickl et al.
Token Alignment	Precision	94.55%	92.22%
Token Alignment	MRR	0.9219	0.8797
Commitment Selection	Precision	89.50%	72.50%
Commitment Selection	MRR	0.8853	0.7410

Table 1: Alignment and Selection Performance

5 Entailment Classification

Following work done by (Bos and Markert, 2006; Hickl et al., 2006) for the RTE-2 Challenge, we used a decision tree (C5.0 (Quinlan, 1998)) to estimate the likelihood that a commitment pair represented a valid instance of textual entailment.[3] Confidence values associated with each leaf node (i.e. YES or NO) were normalized and used to rank examples for the official submission.

In a departure from previous work (such as (Hickl et al., 2006)) which leveraged large corpora of entailment pairs to train an entailment classifier, our model was only trained on the 800 text-hypothesis pairs found in the RTE-3 Development Set (DevSet). Features were selected manually by performing ten-fold cross validation on the DevSet. Maximum performance of the entailment classifier on the DevSet is provided in Table 2.

	IE	IR	QA	SUM	Total
Accuracy	0.8450	0.8750	0.8850	0.8600	0.8663
Average Precision	0.8522	0.8953	0.9005	0.8959	0.8860

Table 2: Entailment Classifier Performance.

A partial list of the features used in the Entailment Classifier used in our official submission is provided in Figure 3.

6 Experiments and Results

We submitted one ranked run in our official submission for this year's evaluation. Official results from the RTE-3 Test Set are presented in Table 3.

	IE	IR	QA	SUM	Total
Accuracy	0.6750	0.8000	0.9000	0.8400	0.8038
Average Precision	0.7760	0.8133	0.9308	0.8974	0.8815

Table 3: Official RTE-3 Results.

Accuracy and average precision varied significantly ($p < 0.05$) across each of the four tasks. Performance (in terms of accuracy and average precision) was highest on the QA set (90.0% precision) and lowest on the IE set (67.5%).

The length of the *text* (either *short* or *long*) did not significantly impact performance, however; in fact,

[3]We used a pruning confidence of 20% in our model.

ALIGNMENT FEATURES: Derived from the results of the alignment of each pair of commitments performed during Commitment Selection.
◇1◇ LONGEST COMMON STRING: This feature represents the longest contiguous string common to both texts.
◇2◇ UNALIGNED CHUNK: This feature represents the number of chunks in one text that are not aligned with a chunk from the other
◇3◇ LEXICAL ENTAILMENT PROBABILITY: Defined as in (Glickman and Dagan, 2005).

DEPENDENCY FEATURES: Computed from the semantic dependencies identified by the PropBank- and NomBank-based semantic parsers.
◇1◇ ENTITY-ARG MATCH: This is a boolean feature which fires when aligned entities were assigned the same argument role label.
◇2◇ ENTITY-NEAR-ARG MATCH: This feature is collapsing the arguments Arg_1 and Arg_2 (as well as the Arg_M subtypes) into single categories for the purpose of counting matches.
◇3◇ PREDICATE-ARG MATCH: This boolean feature is flagged when at least two aligned arguments have the same role.
◇4◇ PREDICATE-NEAR-ARG MATCH: This feature is collapsing the arguments Arg_1 and Arg_2 (as well as the Arg_M subtypes) into single categories for the purpose of counting matches.

SEMANTIC/PRAGMATIC FEATURES: Extracted during preprocessing.
◇1◇ NAMED ENTITY CLASS: This feature has a different value for each of the 150 named entity classes.
◇2◇ TEMPORAL NORMALIZATION: This boolean feature is flagged when the temporal expressions are normalized to the same ISO 9000 equivalents.
◇3◇ MODALITY MARKER: This boolean feature is flagged when the two texts use the same modal verbs.
◇4◇ SPEECH-ACT: This boolean feature is flagged when the lexicons indicate the same speech act in both texts.
◇5◇ FACTIVITY MARKER: This boolean feature is flagged when the factivity markers indicate either TRUE or FALSE in both texts simultaneously.
◇6◇ BELIEF MARKER: This boolean feature is set when the belief markers indicate either TRUE or FALSE in both texts simultaneously.

Figure 3: Features used in the Entailment Classifier

as can be seen in Table 4, total accuracy was nearly the same for examples featuring *short* or *long texts*.

	Short		Long	
	n	Accuracy	*n*	Accuracy
IE	181	0.6685	19	0.7368
IR	146	0.8082	54	0.7778
QA	165	0.8909	35	0.9429
SUM	191	0.8482	9	0.6667
Total	683	0.8023	117	0.8120

Table 4: Short vs. Long Pairs.

In experiments conducted following the RTE-3 submission deadline, we found that using a system for recognizing textual contradiction to validate judgments output by the entailment classifier had only a slight positive impact on the overall performance of our system. Table 5 compares performance of our RTE system when four different configurations of our system for recognizing textual contradiction was used.

When used with its default threshold (λ = 0.85), we discovered that using textual contradiction enabled us to identify 17 additional examples (2.13% overall) that were not available when using our system for RTE alone.[4] When we hand-tuned λ to maximize performance on the RTE-3 Test Set, we found that accuracy could be increased by 3.0% over the baseline (to 81.25% overall). Despite its limited effectiveness on this year's Test Set, we believe that net positive effect of using textual contradiction to validate textual entailment judgments suggests that this technique has merit and should be explored in future evaluations.

Validation?	λ	IE	IR	QA	SUM	Total
Yes *(RTE-3)*	0.85	0.6750	0.8000	0.9000	0.8400	0.8038
Yes	0.75	0.6900	0.8100	0.8850	0.8650	0.8125
Yes	0.65	0.6550	0.8000	0.8850	0.8250	0.7913
No	–	0.6550	0.8000	0.8650	0.8250	0.7865

Table 5: Impact of Validation.

In a second post hoc experiment, we sought to quantify the impact that additional sources of training data could have on the performance of our RTE system. Although our official submission was only trained on the 800 *t-h* pairs found in the RTE-3 Development Set, we followed (Hickl et al., 2006) in using a large, hand-crafted training set of 100,000 text-hypothesis pairs in order to train our entailment classifier. Even though previous work has shown that RTE accuracy increased with the size of the training set, our experiments showed no correlation between the size of the training corpus and the overall accuracy of the system. Table 6 summarizes the performance of our RTE system when trained on increasing amounts of training data. While increasing the training data to approximately 10,000 training examples did positively impact performance, we discovered that using a training corpus of a size equal to (Hickl et al., 2006)'s had nearly no measurable impact on the observed performance of our system.

Training Corpus	Accuracy	Average Precision
800 pairs (RTE-3 Dev)	0.8038	0.8815
10,000 pairs	0.8150	0.8939
25,000 pairs	0.8225	0.8834
50,000 pairs	0.8125	0.8355
100,000 pairs	0.8050	0.8003

Table 6: Impact of Training Corpus Size.

While large training corpora (like (Hickl et al., 2006)'s or the one compiled for this work) may provide an important source of lexico-semantic information that can be leveraged in performing an entailment classification, these results suggest that our approach based on commitment extraction may nullify

[4]We learned the default threshold by training on the textual contradiction corpus compiled by (Harabagiu et al., 2006).

the gains in performance seen by these approaches.

7 Conclusions

This paper introduced a new framework for recognizing textual entailment which depends on the extraction of the discourse commitments that can be inferred from a conventional interpretation of a text passage. By explicitly enumerating the set of inferences that can be drawn from a *t* or *h*, our approach is able to reduce the task of RTE to the identification of the set of commitments that support the inference of each corresponding commitment extracted from a hypothesis. In our current work, we show that this approach can be used to correctly classify more than 80% of examples from the RTE-3 Test Set, without the need for additional sources of training data or web-based resources.

References

Paul Aarseth, John Lehmann, Murat Deligonul, and Luke Nezda. 2006. TASER: A Temporal and Spatial Expression Recognition and Normalization System. In *Proceedings of the Automatic Content Extraction (ACE) Conference*.

Roy Bar-Haim, Ido Dagan, Bill Dolan, Lisa Ferro, Danilo Giampiccolo, Bernardo Magnini, and Idan Szpektor. 2006. The Second PASCAL Recognising Textual Entailment Challenge. In *Proceedings of the Second PASCAL Challenges Workshop*.

Johan Bos and Katya Markert. 2006. When logical inference helps in determining textual entailment (and when it doesn't). In *Proceedings of the Second PASCAL Recognizing Textual Entailment Conference*, Venice, Italy.

Michael Collins. 1999. *Head-Driven Statistical Models for Natural Language Parsing*. Ph.D. thesis, Univ. of Pennsylvania.

L.R. Dice. 1945. Measures of the Amount of Ecologic Association Between Speices. In *Journal of Ecology*, volume 26, pages 297–302.

Oren Glickman and Ido Dagan. 2005. A Probabilistic Setting and Lexical Co-occurrence Model for Textual Entailment. In *Proceedings of the ACL Workshop on Empirical Modeling of Semantic Equivalence and Entailment*, Ann Arbor, USA.

Christine Gunlogson. 2001. *True to Form: Rising and Falling Declaratives as Questions in English*. Ph.D. thesis, University of California, Santa Cruz.

Aria Haghighi, Andrew Ng, and Christopher Manning. 2005. Robust textual inference via graph matching. In *Proceedings of Human Language Technology Conference and Conference on Empirical Methods in Natural Language Processing*, pages 387–394.

Sanda Harabagiu, Andrew Hickl, and Finley Lacatusu. 2006. Negation, Contrast, and Contradiction in Text Processing. In *Proceedings of AAAI*, Boston, MA.

Andrew Hickl, John Williams, Jeremy Bensley, Kirk Roberts, Bryan Rink, and Ying Shi. 2006. Recognizing Textual Entailment with LCC's Groundhog System. In *Proceedings of the Second PASCAL Challenges Workshop*.

Rodney Huddleston and Geoffrey Pullum, editors, 2002. *The Cambridge Grammar of the English Language*. Cambridge-University Press.

V. Jijkoun and M. de Rijke. 2005. Recognizing Textual Entailment Using Lexical Similarity. In *Proceedings of the First PASCAL Challenges Workshop*.

X. Luo, A. Ittycheriah, H. Jing, N. Kambhatla, and S. Roukos. 2004. A mention-synchronous coreference resolution algorithm based on the Bell Tree. In *Proceedings of the ACL-2004*, Barcelona, Spain.

A. Meyers, R. Reeves, C. Macleod, R. Szekely, V. Zielinska, B. Young, and R. Grishman. 2004. The nombank project: An interim report. In A. Meyers, editor, *HLT-NAACL 2004 Workshop: Frontiers in Corpus Annotation*, pages 24–31, Boston, Massachusetts, USA, May 2 - May 7. Association for Computational Linguistics.

Arcady Mushegian and Eugene Koonin. 2005. A minimal gene set for cellular life derived by compraison of complete bacterial genomes. In *Proceedings of the National Academies of Science*, volume 93, pages 10268–10273.

Martha Palmer, Daniel Gildea, and Paul Kingsbury. 2005. The Proposition Bank: An Annotated Corpus of Semantic Roles. *Computational Linguistics*, 31(1):71–106.

T. Pedersen, S. Patwardhan, and J. Michelizzi. 2004. WordNet::Similarity - Measuring the Relatedness of Concepts. In *Proceedings of the Nineteenth National Conference on Artificial Intelligence (AAAI-04)*, San Jose, CA.

Christopher Potts, editor, 2005. *The Logic of Conventional Implicatures*. Oxford University Press.

R. Quinlan. 1998. C5.0: An Informal Tutorial. RuleQuest.

Robert Stalnaker, 1979. *Assertion*, volume 9, pages 315–332.

Ben Taskar, Simone Lacoste-Julien, and Michael Jordan. 2005a. Structured prediction via the extragradient method. In *Proceedings of Neural Information Processing Systems*, Vancouver, Canada.

Ben Taskar, Simone Lacoste-Julien, and Dan Klein. 2005b. A discriminative matching approach to word alignment. In *Proceedings of Human Language Technology Conference and Empirical Methods in Natural Language Processing (HLT/EMNLP 2005)*, Vancouver, Canada.

Lucy Vanderwende, Arul Menezes, and Rion Snow. 2006. Microsoft Research at RTE-2: Syntactic Contributions in the Entailment Task: an implementation. In *Proceedings of the Second PASCAL Challenges Workshop*.

Biology Based Alignments of Paraphrases for Sentence Compression

João Cordeiro
CLT and Bioinformatics
University of Beira Interior
Covilhã, Portugal
jpaulo@di.ubi.pt

Gäel Dias
CLT and Bioinformatics
University of Beira Interior
Covilhã, Portugal
ddg@di.ubi.pt

Guillaume Cleuziou
LIFO - University of Orléans
Orléans, France
guillaume.cleuziou@univ-orleans.fr

Abstract

[1] In this paper, we present a study for extracting and aligning paraphrases in the context of Sentence Compression. First, we justify the application of a new measure for the automatic extraction of paraphrase corpora. Second, we discuss the work done by (Barzilay & Lee, 2003) who use clustering of paraphrases to induce rewriting rules. We will see, through classical visualization methodologies (Kruskal & Wish, 1977) and exhaustive experiments, that clustering may not be the best approach for automatic pattern identification. Finally, we will provide some results of different biology based methodologies for pairwise paraphrase alignment.

1 Introduction

Sentence Compression can be seen as the removal of redundant words or phrases from an input sentence by creating a new sentence in which the gist of the original meaning of the sentence remains unchanged. Sentence Compression takes an important place for Natural Language Processing (NLP) tasks where specific constraints must be satisfied, such as length in summarization (Barzilay & Lee, 2002; Knight & Marcu, 2002; Shinyama et al., 2002; Barzilay & Lee, 2003; Le Nguyen & Ho, 2004; Unno et al., 2006), style in text simplification (Marsi & Krahmer, 2005) or sentence simplification for subtitling (Daelemans et al., 2004).

[1]Project partially funded by Portuguese FCT (Reference: POSC/PLP/57438/2004)

Generally, Sentence Compression involves performing the following three steps: (1) Extraction of paraphrases from comparable corpora, (2) Alignment of paraphrases and (3) Induction of rewriting rules. Obviously, each of these steps can be performed in many different ways going from totally unsupervised to totally supervised.

In this paper, we will focus on the first two steps. In particular, we will first justify the application of a new measure for the automatic extraction of paraphrase corpora. Second, we will discuss the work done by (Barzilay & Lee, 2003) who use clustering of paraphrases to induce rewriting rules. We will see, through classical visualization methodologies (Kruskal & Wish, 1977) and exhaustive experiments, that clustering may not be the best approach for automatic pattern identification. Finally, we will provide some results of different biology based methodologies for pairwise paraphrase alignment.

2 Related Work

Two different approaches have been proposed for Sentence Compression: purely statistical methodologies (Barzilay & Lee, 2003; Le Nguyen & Ho, 2004) and hybrid linguistic/statistic methodologies (Knight & Marcu, 2002; Shinyama et al., 2002; Daelemans et al., 2004; Marsi & Krahmer, 2005; Unno et al., 2006).

As our work is based on the first paradigm, we will focus on the works proposed by (Barzilay & Lee, 2003) and (Le Nguyen & Ho, 2004).

(Barzilay & Lee, 2003) present a knowledge-lean algorithm that uses multiple-sequence alignment to

Proceedings of the Workshop on Textual Entailment and Paraphrasing, pages 177–184,
Prague, June 2007.

learn generate sentence-level paraphrases essentially from unannotated corpus data alone. In contrast to (Barzilay & Lee, 2002), they need neither parallel data nor explicit information about sentence semantics. Rather, they use two comparable corpora. Their approach has three main steps. First, working on each of the comparable corpora separately, they compute lattices compact graph-based representations to find commonalities within groups of structurally similar sentences. Next, they identify pairs of lattices from the two different corpora that are paraphrases of each other. Finally, given an input sentence to be paraphrased, they match it to a lattice and use a paraphrase from the matched lattices mate to generate an output sentence.

(Le Nguyen & Ho, 2004) propose a new sentence-reduction algorithm that do not use syntactic parsing for the input sentence. The algorithm is an extension of the template-translation algorithm (one of example-based machine-translation methods) via innovative employment of the Hidden Markov model, which uses the set of template rules learned from examples.

In particular, (Le Nguyen & Ho, 2004) do not propose any methodology to automatically extract paraphrases. Instead, they collect a corpus by performing the decomposition program using news and their summaries. After correcting them manually, they obtain more than 1,500 pairs of long and reduced sentences. Comparatively, (Barzilay & Lee, 2003) propose to use the N-gram Overlap metric to capture similarities between sentences and automatically create paraphrase corpora. However, this choice is arbitrary and mainly leads to the extraction of quasi-exact or exact matching pairs. For that purpose, we introduce a new metric, the *Sumo-Metric*.

Unlike (Le Nguyen & Ho, 2004), one interesting idea proposed by (Barzilay & Lee, 2003) is to cluster similar pairs of paraphrases to apply multiple-sequence alignment. However, once again, this choice is not justified and we will see by classical visualization methodologies (Kruskal & Wish, 1977) and exhaustive experiments by applying different clustering algorithms, that clustering may not be the best approach for automatic pattern identification. As a consequence, we will study global and local biology based sequence alignments compared to multi-sequence alignment that may lead to better results for the induction of rewriting rules.

3 Paraphrase Corpus Construction

Paraphrase corpora are golden resources for learning monolingual text-to-text rewritten patterns. However, such corpora are expensive to construct manually and will always be an imperfect and biased representation of the language paraphrase phenomena. Therefore, reliable automatic methodologies able to extract paraphrases from text and subsequently corpus construction are crucial, enabling better pattern identification. In fact, text-to-text generation is a particularly promising research direction given that there are naturally occurring examples of comparable texts that convey the same information but are written in different styles. Web news stories are an obvious example. Thus, presented with such texts, one can pair sentences that convey the same information, thereby building a training set of rewriting examples i.e. a paraphrase corpus.

3.1 Paraphrase Identification

A few unsupervised metrics have been applied to automatic paraphrase identification and extraction (Barzilay & Lee, 2003; Dolan & Brockett, 2004). However, these unsupervised methodologies show a major drawback by extracting quasi-exact[2] or even exact match pairs of sentences as they rely on classical string similarity measures such as the *Edit Distance* in the case of (Dolan & Brockett, 2004) and *word N-gram overlap* for (Barzilay & Lee, 2003). Such pairs are clearly useless.

More recently, (Anonymous, 2007) proposed a new metric, the *Sumo-Metric* specially designed for asymmetrical entailed pairs identification, and proved better performance over previous established metrics, even in the specific case when tested with the *Microsoft Paraphrase Research Corpus* (Dolan & Brockett, 2004). For a given sentence pair, having each sentence x and y words, and with λ exclusive links between the sentences, the *Sumo-Metric* is defined in Equation 1 and 2.

[2]Almost equal strings, for example: *Bush said America is addicted to oil.* and *Mr. Bush said America is addicted to oil.*

$$S(S_a, S_b) = \begin{cases} S(x,y,\lambda) & if \;\; S(x,y,\lambda) < 1.0 \\ 0 & if \;\; \lambda = 0 \\ e^{-k*S(x,y,\lambda)} & otherwise \end{cases} \quad (1)$$

where

$$S(x, y, \lambda) = \alpha \log_2(\frac{x}{\lambda}) + \beta \log_2(\frac{y}{\lambda}) \quad (2)$$

with $\alpha, \beta \in [0, 1]$ and $\alpha + \beta = 1$.

(Anonymous, 2007) show that the *Sumo-Metric* outperforms all state-of-the-art metrics over all tested corpora. In particular, it shows systematically better F-Measure and Accuracy measures over all other metrics showing an improvement of (1) at least 2.86% in terms of F-Measure and 3.96% in terms of Accuracy and (2) at most 6.61% in terms of F-Measure and 6.74% in terms of Accuracy compared to the second best metric which is also systematically the word N-gram overlap similarity measure used by (Barzilay & Lee, 2003).

3.2 Clustering

Literature shows that there are two main reasons to apply clustering for paraphrase extraction. On one hand, as (Barzilay & Lee, 2003) evidence, clusters of paraphrases can lead to better learning of text-to-text rewriting rules compared to just pairs of paraphrases. On the other hand, clustering algorithms may lead to better performance than stand-alone similarity measures as they may take advantage of the different structures of sentences in the cluster to detect a new similar sentence.

However, as (Barzilay & Lee, 2003) do not propose any evaluation of which clustering algorithm should be used, we experiment a set of clustering algorithms and present the comparative results. Contrarily to what expected, we will see that clustering is not a worthy effort.

Instead of extracting only sentence pairs from corpora[3], one may consider the extraction of paraphrase sentence clusters. There are many well-known clustering algorithms, which may be applied to a corpus sentence set $S = \{s_1, ..., s_n\}$. Clustering implies the definition of a similarity or (distance) matrix $A_{n \times n}$, where each each element a_{ij} is the similarity (distance) between sentences s_i and s_j.

[3] A pair may be seen as a cluster with only two elements.

3.2.1 Experimental Results

We experimented four clustering algorithms on a corpus of *web news stories* and then three human judges manually cross-classified a random sample of the generated clusters. They were asked to classify a cluster as a "wrong cluster" if it contained at least two sentences without any entailment relation between them. Results are shown in the next table 1.

Table 1: Precision of clustering algorithms

BASE	S-HAC	C-HAC	QT	EM
0.618	0.577	0.569	0.640	0.489

The "BASE" column is the baseline, where the *Sumo-Metric* was applied rather than clustering. Columns "S-HAC" and "C-HAC" express the results for *Single-link* and *Complete-link Hierarchical Agglomerative Clustering* (Jain et al., 1999). The "QT" column shows the *Quality Threshold* algorithm (Heyer et al., 1999) and the last column "EM" is the *Expectation Maximization* clustering algorithm (Hogg et al., 2005).

One main conclusion, from table 1 is that clustering tends to achieve worst results than simple paraphrase pair extraction. Only the QT achieves better results, but if we take the average of the four clustering algorithms it is equal to 0.568, smaller than the 0.618 baseline. Moreover, these results with the QT algorithm were applied with a very restrictive value for cluster attribution as it is shown in table 2 with an average of almost two sentences per cluster.

Table 2: Figures about clustering algorithms

Algorithm	# Sentences/# Clusters
S-HAC	6,23
C-HAC	2,17
QT	2,32
EM	4,16

In fact, table 2 shows that most of the clusters have less than 6 sentences which leads to question the results presented by (Barzilay & Lee, 2003) who only keep the clusters that contain more than 10 sentences. In fact, the first conclusion is that the number of experimented clusters is very low, and more important, all clusters with more than 10 sentences showed to be of very bad quality.

The next subsection will reinforce the sight that

clustering is a worthless effort for automatic paraphrase corpora construction.

3.2.2 Visualization

In this subsection, we propose a visual analysis of the different similarity measures tested previously: the Edit Distance (Levenshtein, 1966), the BLEU metric (Papineni et al., 2001), the word N-gram overlap and the *Sumo-Metric*. The goal of this study is mainly to give the reader a visual interpretation about the organization each measure induces on the data.

To perform this study, we use a Multidimensional Scaling (MDS) process which is a traditional data analysis technique. MDS (Kruskal & Wish, 1977) allows to display the structure of distance-like data into an Euclidean space.

Since the only available information is a similarity in our case, we transform similarity values into distance values as in Equation 3.

$$d_{ij} = (s_{ii} - 2s_{ij} + s_{jj})^{1/2} \qquad (3)$$

This transformation enables to obtain a (pseudo) distance measure satisfying properties like minimality, identity and symmetry. On a theoretical point of view, the measure we obtain is a pseudo-distance only, since triangular inequality is not necessary satisfied. In practice, the projection space we build with the MDS from such a pseudo-distance is sufficient to have an idea about whether data are organized into classes.

We perform the MDS process on 500 sentences[4] randomly selected from the Microsoft Research Paraphrase Corpus. In particular, the projection over the three first eigenvectors (or proper vectors) provides the best visualization where data are clearly organized into several classes (at least two classes). The obtained visualizations (Figure 1) show distinctly that no particular data organization can be drawn from the used similarity measures. Indeed, we observe only one central class with some "satellite" data randomly placed around the class.

The last observation allows us to anticipate on the results we could obtain with a clustering step. First, clustering seems not to be a natural way to manage such data. Then, according to the clustering method used, several types of clusters can be expected: very small clusters which contain "satellite" data (pretty relevant) or large clusters with part of the main central class (pretty irrelevant). These results confirm the observed figures in the previous subsection and reinforce the sight that clustering is a worthless effort for automatic paraphrase corpora construction, contrarily to what (Barzilay & Lee, 2003) suggest.

4 Biology Based Alignments

Sequence alignments have been extensively explored in bioinformatics since the beginning of the *Human Genome Project*. In general, one wants to align two sequences of symbols (genes in Biology) to find structural similarities, differences or transformations between them.

In NLP, alignment is relevant in sub-domains like Text Generation (Barzilay & Lee, 2002). In our work, we employ alignment methods for aligning words between two sentences, which are paraphrases. The words are the *base blocks* of our sequences (sentences).

There are two main classes of pairwise alignments: the global and local classes. In the first one, the algorithms try to fully align both sequences, admitting gap insertions at a certain cost, while in the local methods the goal is to find pairwise sub-alignments. How suitable each algorithm may be applied to a certain problem is discussed in the next two subsections.

4.1 Global Alignment

The well established and widely used Needleman-Wunsch algorithm for pairwise global sequence alignment, uses dynamic programming to find the best possible alignment between two sequences. It is an optimal algorithm. However, it reveals space and time inefficiency as sequence length increases, since an $m * n$ matrix must be maintained and processed during computations. This is the case with DNA sequence alignments, composed by many thousands of nucleotides. Therefore, a huge optimization effort were engaged and new algorithms appeared like *k-tuple*, not guaranteeing to find optimal alignments but able to tackle the complexity problem.

In our alignment tasks, we do not have these com-

[4] The limitation to 500 data is due to computation costs since MDS requires the diagonalization of the square similarity or distance matrix.

plexity obstacles, because in our corpora the mean length of a sentence is equal to 20.9 words, which is considerably smaller than in a DNA sequence. Therefore an implementation of the Needleman-Wunsch algorithm has been used to generate optimal global alignments.

The figure 2 exemplifies a global word alignment on a paraphrase pair.

4.2 Local Alignment

The Smith-Waterman (SW) algorithm is similar to the Needleman Wunsch (NW) one, since dynamic programming is also followed hence denoting the similar complexity issues, to which our alignment task is immune. The main difference is that SW seeks optimal sub-alignments instead of a global alignment and, as described in the literature, it is well tailored for pairs with considerable differences[5], in length and type. In table 3 we exemplify this by showing two character sequences[6] where one may clearly see that *SW* is preferable:

N	Char. Sequences	Alignments
1	ABBAXYTRVRVTTRVTR FWHWWHGWGFXYTVWGF	XYTRV XYT-V
2	ABCDXYDRQR DQZZSTABZCD	AB-CD ABZCD

Table 3: Preferable local alignment cases.

Remark that in the second pair, only the maximal local sub-alignment is shown. However, there exists another sub-alignment: (DRQ, D-Q). This means that local alignment may be tuned to generate not only the maximum sub-alignment but a set of sub-alignments that satisfy some criterium, like having alignment value greater than some minimum threshold. In fact, this is useful in our word alignment problem and were experimented by adapting the Smith Waterman algorithm.

4.3 Dynamic Alignment

According to the previous two subsections, where two alignment strategies were presented, a natural question rises: which alignment algorithm to use for our problem of inter-sentence word alignment? Initially, we thought to use only the global alignment *Needleman Wunsch* algorithm, since a complete inter-sentence word alignment is obtained. However, we noticed that this strategy is unappropriate for certain pairs, specially when there are syntactical alternations, like in the next example:

> ***During his magnificent speech,*** *the president remarkably praised IBM research.*
>
> *The president praised IBM research,* ***during his speech.***

If a global alignment is applied for such a pair, then weird alignments will be generated, like the one that is shown in the next representation (we use character sequences for space convenience and try to preserve the word first letter, from the previous example):

```
D H M S T P R Q I S _ _ _
_ _ _ _ T P _ Q I S D H S
```

Here it would be more adequate to apply local alignment and extract all relevant sub-alignments. In this case, two sub-alignments would be generated:

```
|D H M S|     |T P R P I R|
|D H _ S|     |T P _ P I R|
```

Therefore, for inter-paraphrase word alignments, we propose a dynamic algorithm which chooses the best alignment to perform: global or local. To compute this pre-scan, we regard the notion of link-crossing between sequences as illustrated in the figure 3, where the 4 crossings are signalized with the small squares.

It is easily verifiable that the maximum number of crossings, among two sequences with n exclusive links in between is equal to $\theta = \frac{1}{2} * n * (n-1)$. We suggest that if a fraction of these crossings holds, for example $0.4 * \theta$ or $0.5 * \theta$, then a local alignment should be used. Remark that the more this fraction tends to 1.0 the more unlikely it is to use global alignment.

Crossings may be calculated by taking index pairs $\langle x_i, y_i \rangle$ to represent links between sequences, where x_i and y_i are respectively the first and second sequence indexes, for instance in figure 3 the "U" link has pair $\langle 5, 1 \rangle$. It is easily verifiable that two links $\langle x_i, y_i \rangle$ and $\langle x_j, y_j \rangle$ have a crossing point if: $(x_i - x_j) * (y_i - y_j) < 0$.

4.4 Alignment with Similarity Matrix

In bioinformatics, DNA sequence alignment algorithms are usually guided by a scoring function, related to the field of expertise, that defines what is

[5] With sufficient similar sequences there is no difference between NW and SW.

[6] As in DNA subsequences and is same for word sequences.

the mutation probability between nucleotides. These scoring functions are defined by PAM[7] or BLOSUM[8] matrices and encode evolutionary approximations regarding the rates and probabilities of amino acid mutations. Different matrices might produce different alignments.

Subsequently, this motivated the idea of modeling word mutation. It seems intuitive to allow such a word mutation, considering the possible relationships that exit between words: lexical, syntactical or semantic. For example, it seems evident that between *spirit* and *spiritual* there exists a stronger relation (higher mutation probability) than between *spiritual* and *hamburger*.

A natural possibility to choose a word mutation representation function is the *Edit-distance* (Levenshtein, 1966) (edist(.,.)) as a negative reward for word alignment. For a given word pair $\langle w_i, w_j \rangle$, the greater the *Edit-distance* value, the more unlikely the word w_i will be aligned with word w_j. However, after some early experiments with this function, it revealed to lead to some problems by enabling alignments between very different words, like $\langle total, israel \rangle$, $\langle fire, made \rangle$ or $\langle troops, members \rangle$, despite many good alignments also achieved. This happens because the *Edit-distance* returns relatively small values, unable to sufficiently penalize different words, like the ones listed before, to inhibit the alignment. In bioinformatics language, it means that even for such pairs the mutation probability is still high. Another problem of the *Edit-distance* is that it does not distinguish between long and small words, for instance the pairs $\langle in, by \rangle$ and $\langle governor, governed \rangle$ have both the *Edit-distance* equals to 2.

As a consequence, we propose a new function (Equation 4) for word mutation penalization, able to give better answers for the mentioned problems. The idea is to divide the *Edit-distance* value by the length of the normalized[9] maximum common subsequence $maxseq(.,.)$ between both words. For example, the longest common subsequence for the pair $\langle w_1, w_2 \rangle = \langle reinterpretation, interpreted \rangle$ is "$interpret$", with length equal to 9 and $maxseq(w_1, w_2) = \frac{9}{max\{16,11\}} = 0.5625$

$$costAlign(w_i, w_j) = -\frac{edist(w_i, w_j)}{\varepsilon + maxseq(w_i, w_j)} \quad (4)$$

where ε is a small value[10] that acts like a "safety hook" against divisions by zero, when $maxseq(w_i, w_j) = 0$.

word 1	word 2	-edist	costAlign
rule	ruler	-1	-1.235
governor	governed	-2	-2.632
pay	paying	-3	-5.882
reinterpretation	interpreted	-7	-12.227
hamburger	spiritual	-9	-74.312
in	by	-2	-200.000

Table 4: Word mutation functions comparision.

Remark that with the $costAlign(.,.)$ scoring function the problems with pairs like $\langle in, by \rangle$ simply vanish. The smaller the words, the more constrained the mutation will be.

5 Experiments and Results

5.1 Corpus of Paraphrases

To test our alignment method, we used two types of corpora. The first is the "DUC 2002" corpus (DUC2002) and the second is automatically extracted from related *web news stories* (WNS) automatically extracted. For both original corpora, paraphrase extraction has been performed by using the *Sumo-Metric* and two corpora of paraphrases were obtained. Afterwards the alignment algorithm was applied over both corpora.

5.2 Quality of Dynamic Alignment

We tested the proposed alignment methods by giving a sample of 201 aligned paraphrase sentence pairs to a human judge and ask to classify each pair as *correct*, *acorrect*[11], *error* [12], and *merror*[13]. We also asked to classify the local alignment choice[14] as *adequate* or *inadequate*. The results are shown in the next table:

[7] Point Access Mutation.

[8] Blocks Substitution Matrices.

[9] The length of the longest common subsequence divided by the word with maximum length value.

[10] We take $\varepsilon = 0.01$.

[11] Almost correct - minor errors exist

[12] With some errors.

[13] With many errors

[14] Global or local alignment.

	Global				Local
not para	*correct*	*acorrect*	*error*	*merror*	*adequate*
31	108	28	12	8	12/14
15.5%	63.5%	16.5%	7.1%	4.7%	85.7%

Table 5: Precision of alignments.

For global alignments[15] we have 11.8% pairs with relevant errors and 85.7% (12 from 14) of all local alignment decisions were classified as *adequate*. The *not para* column shows the number of false paraphrases identified, revealing a precision value of 84.5% for the *Sumo-Metric*.

6 Conclusion and Future Work

A set of important steps toward automatic construction of aligned paraphrase corpora are presented and inherent relevant issues discussed, like clustering and alignment. Experiments, by using 4 algorithms and through visualization techniques, revealed that clustering is a worthless effort for paraphrase corpora construction, contrary to the literature claims (Barzilay & Lee, 2003). Therefore simple paraphrase pair extraction is suggested and by using a recent and more reliable metric (*Sumo-Metric*) (Anonymous, 2007) designed for asymmetrical entailed pairs. We also propose a dynamic choosing of the alignment algorithm and a word scoring function for the alignment algorithms.

In the future we intend to clean the automatic constructed corpus by introducing syntactical constraints to filter the wrong alignments. Our next step will be to employ *Machine Learning* techniques for rewriting rule induction, by using this automatically constructed aligned paraphrase corpus.

References

Barzilay R. and Lee L. 2002. *Bootstrapping Lexical Choice via Multiple-Sequence Alignment.* Proceedings of the Conference on Empirical Methods in Natural Language Processing, (EMNLP), 164-171.

Barzilay, R., and Lee, L. 2003. *Learning to paraphrase: An unsupervised approach using multiple-sequence alignment.* Proceedings of HLT-NAACL.

[15] Percentage are calculated by dividing by 170 (201 − 31) the number of true paraphrases that exists.

Dolan W.B. and Brockett C. 2004. *Unsupervised construction of large paraphrase corpora: Exploiting massively parallel news sources.* Proceedings of 20th International Conference on Computational Linguistics (COLING 2004).

Anonymous 2007. *Learning Paraphrases from WNS Corpora.* Proceedings of 20th International FLAIRS Conference. AAAI Press. Key West, Florida.

Daelemans W., Hothker A., and Tjong E. 2004. *Automatic Sentence Simplification for Subtitling in Dutch and English.* In Proceedings of LREC 2004, Lisbon, Portugal.

Heyer L.J., Kruglyak S. and Yooseph S. 1999. Exploring Expression Data: Identification and Analysis of Coexpressed Genes. *Genome Research*, 9:1106-1115.

Hogg R., McKean J., and Craig A. 2005 *Introduction to Mathematical Statistics.* Upper Saddle River, NJ: Pearson Prentice Hall, 359-364.

Jain A., Murty M. and Flynn P. Data clustering: a review. *ACM Computing Surveys*, 31:264-323

Knight K. and Marcu D. 2002. Summarization beyond sentence extraction: A probabilistic approach to sentence compression. *Artificial Intelligence*, 139(1):91-107.

Kruskal J. B. and Wish M. 1977. *Multidimensional Scaling.* Sage Publications. Beverly Hills. CA.

Le Nguyen M., Horiguchi S., A. S., and Ho B. T. 2004. Example-based sentence reduction using the hidden markov model. *ACM Transactions on Asian Language Information Processing (TALIP)*, 3(2):146-158.

Levenshtein V. 1966. Binary Codes Capable of Correcting Deletions, Insertions, and Reversals. Soviet Physice-Doklady, 10:707-710.

Marsi E. and Krahmer E. 2005. Explorations in sentence fusion. In Proceedings of the 10th European Workshop on Natural Language Generation.

Papineni K., Roukos S., Ward T., Zhu W.-J. 2001. BLEU: a Method for Automatic Evaluation of Machine Translation. IBM Research Report RC22176.

Shinyama Y., Sekine S., and Sudo K. 2002. *Automatic Paraphrase Acquisition from News Articles.* Sao Diego, USA.

Unno Y., Ninomiya T., Miyao Y. and Tsujii J. 2006. *Trimming CFG Parse Trees for Sentence Compression Using Machine Learning Approaches.* In the Proceedings of the COLING/ACL 2006 Main Conference Poster Sessions.

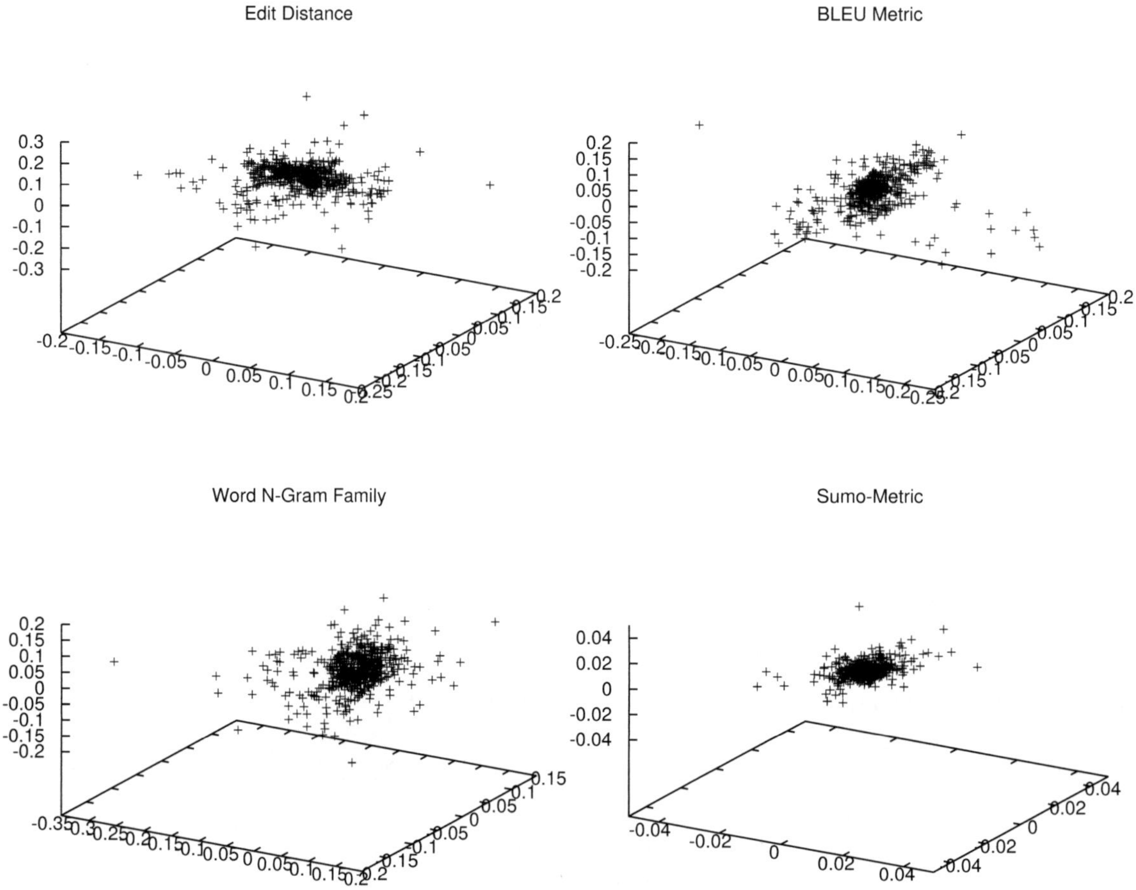

Figure 1: MDS on 500 sentences with the Edit Distance (top left), the BLEU Metric (top right), the Word N-Gram Family (bottom left) and the Sumo-Metric (bottom right).

```
To the horror of their television fans , Miss Ball and Arnaz were divorced in 1960.
__ ___ ______ __ _____ __________ ____ _ ____ Ball and Arnaz ____ divorced in 1960.
```

Figure 2: Global aligned words in a paraphrase pair.

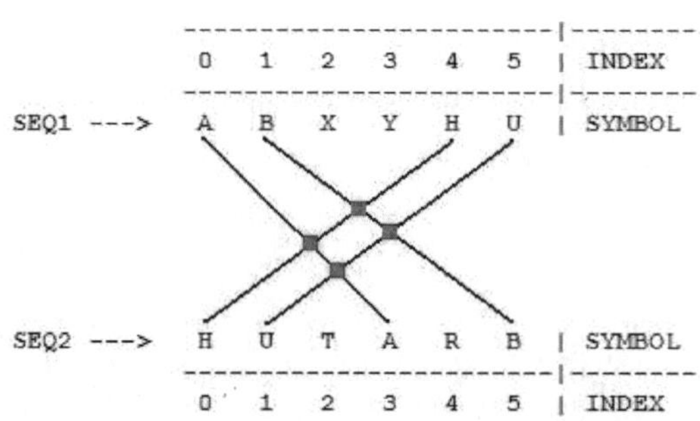

Figure 3: Crossings between a sequence pair.

A first order semantic approach to adjectival inference

Marilisa Amoia
INRIA/Université de Nancy 1 &
University of the Saarland
Saarbrücken, Germany
amoia@coli.uni-saarland.de

Claire gardent
CNRS/Loria
Campus Scientifique BP 239
54506 Vandoeuvre-les-Nancy, France
claire.gardent@loria.fr

Abstract

As shown in the formal semantics literature, adjectives can display very different inferential patterns depending on whether they are intersective, privative, subsective or plain non-subsective. Moreover, many of these classes are often described using second order constructs. In this paper, we adopt Hobbs's ontologically promiscuous approach and present a first order treatment of adjective semantics which opens the way for a sophisticated treatment of adjectival inference. The approach was implemented and tested using first order automated reasoners.

1 Introduction

As has often been observed, not all of natural language meaning can be represented by first order logic. There are expressions such as, *most, former, I didn't* whose meaning intuitively involve higher-order constructs.

Nevertheless, as (Hobbs, 1985) and others have argued, semantic representations for natural language need not be higher-order in that ontological promiscuity can solve the problem. That is, by reifying all objects that can be predicated of, it is possible to retain a semantic representation scheme for NL that is first-order.

This observation is crucial for computational applications for two reasons. First, logics that goes beyond first order are highly undecidable. Second and more importantly, there is no off the shelf higher order automated reasoners that could be put to use to reason about the meaning of higher-order formulae.

In this paper, we present a semantics for adjectives that adopts an ontologically promiscuous approach and thereby supports first order inference for all types of adjectives including extensional ones.

Indeed, traditional semantic classifications of adjectives such as (Chierchia and Connell-Ginet, 1990; Kamp, 1975; Kamp and Partee, 1995) subdivide adjectives into two classes namely extensional vs. intensional adjectives, the latter grouping together adjectives which intuitively denote functions from properties to properties, i.e. second order objects.

We present a compositional semantics for adjectives which both (i) defines a first order representation and (ii) integrates interactions with other sources of linguistic information such as lexical semantics and morpho-derivational relations. We then show that the proposed semantics correctly predicts the inferential patterns observed to hold of the various adjective subclasses identified in the literature (Chierchia and Connell-Ginet, 1990; Kamp, 1975; Kamp and Partee, 1995; Amoia and Gardent, 2006).

This paper is structured as follows. We start by presenting a classification of adjectives which is motivated by the different inferential patterns observed. We then propose a compositional semantics for each class and show that it correctly predicts their inferential behaviour. We conclude with a brief discussion of related work and pointers for further research.

2 Inferential patterns and adjective classes

In the literature (Chierchia and Connell-Ginet, 1990; Kamp, 1975; Kamp and Partee, 1995; Amoia and

Proceedings of the Workshop on Textual Entailment and Paraphrasing, pages 185–192,
Prague, June 2007. ©2007 Association for Computational Linguistics

Gardent, 2006), adjectives are usually divided into four main classes namely, intersective, subsective, privative and plain non subsective depending on whether or not the [Adj N]$_{AP}$ phrase entails the properties expressed by the noun and/or the adjective. More specifically, each of the four classes is characterised as follows.

Intersective adjectives. This class includes common categorical (e.g., *red, rectangular, French*) and tautological (e.g., *real, present*) adjectives. It is characterised by the inferential patterns:

$$[A\ N] \models N$$
$$[A\ N] \models A$$

For instance, saying that there is *a red table* implies both that there is something red and that there is a table.

Subsective adjectives form an ontologically heterogeneous class including for instance denominal (e.g., *gastronomical*) and measure (e.g. *big*) adjectives. They are characterised by the fact that the [Adj N]$_{AP}$ phrase does not entail the Adj property:

$$[A\ N] \models N$$
$$[A\ N] \not\models A$$

For instance, *a big mouse* is a mouse but is not big. Instead it is "big for a mouse". In other words, 'bigness' cannot be directly inferred as, e.g. a big mouse and a big elephant are big in very different ways.

Privative adjectives denote adjectives such that the [Adj N]$_{AP}$ phrase entails the negation of the N property:

$$[A\ N] \models \neg N$$

For instance, *the former king* is not the king and *a fake weapon* is not a weapon.

Plain non-subsective adjectives are adjectives which preclude any inference wrt to the N property:

$$[A\ N] \models (N \vee \neg N)$$
$$[A\ N] \not\models A$$

Thus, if *Peter is an alleged murderer*, it is impossible to know whether or not he is a murderer.

Now, the class of *intensional* adjectives groups together adjectives with a syntactic and semantic idiosyncratic behaviour. Syntactically, *intensional* adjectives are not gradable (e.g. cannot be modified by *very*) and most of them can only be used attributively (*He is a former president* but not *The president is former*). Semantically, they are usually taken to denote second order properties, i.e. functions of the type $\langle\langle e,t\rangle, \langle e,t\rangle\rangle$.

Intensional adjectives include denominal (or relational) adjectives (e.g *polar bear, atomic scientist*), manner (or adverbial) adjectives (e.g. *a poor liar, a fast car*), emotive (e.g. *a poor man*) and modals, i.e. all adjectives which are related to adverbs, quantifiers or determiners (e.g. *a feeble excuse, the specific reason, a fake nose*, etc.).

3 Assigning FOL Representation to Intensional adjectives

We now show how adjectives can be assigned an appropriate first order logic representation which appropriately reflects their inferential behaviour.

Following Hobbs, we adopt a promiscuous ontology and assume that for every predication that can be made in natural language, there corresponds an "eventuality". As Hobbs has argued, this allows for higher order predications to remain first order in that they become predications over (first order) eventualities.

Thus, in the domain there are entities which are either *eventualities* or *individuals* and *relations* between individuals. Moreover like Hobbs, we assume a model to describe a platonic universe containing everything that can be spoken about whether or not these things exist in the real world. To express existence in the real world, a special predicate (*Exists*) is introduced.

We use the following notation:

- e_i, for eventuality variables,
- x_i, for individuals,
- P_i, for properties of individuals.

And the following types:

- e will denote the type of individuals,
- ev the type of eventualities and

- $\mathtt{t}$ a truth value.

3.1 The intuition

As shown in section 2, the semantics of [Adj N]$_{AP}$ phrases has very different inferential properties depending on the type of the adjective Adj. The differences stem from three main points.

The number of individuals introduced by the [Adj N]$_{AP}$ phrase. Thus, *the red table* evokes a single individual x which is both *red* and a *table* whilst *the gastronomical book* refers to a book x which is about the gastronomy concept y. More generally, the variables predicated of by the noun and by the adjective can refer either to the same or to two distinct individual(s).

The properties licensed by the adjective and the noun to contribute to the meaning of the [Adj N]$_{AP}$ phrase. Depending on the adjective type, the properties denoted by Adj and N will contribute either directly or indirectly to the meaning of the [Adj N]$_{AP}$ phrase. Thus in an intersective [Adj N]$_{AP}$ phrase, the meaning contributed by Adj and N are simply the properties they denote. By contrast, the privative *fake* forces the negation of the N property to be part of the Adj N meaning whilst the subsective *gastronomical* induces a relation to the morphoderivationally related noun concept (*about gastronomy*) to be included in the the Adj N meaning. More generally, the properties that compose the meaning of the Adj N phrase can be the denotation of Adj and/or N, the negation of N, its denotation in the past or some property derived from it.

The existence in the real world of the entity denoted by the NP. In all cases the [Adj N]$_{AP}$ phrase denotes a set of individuals but whilst in most cases the [Adj N]$_{AP}$ phrase is neutral with respect to the existence in the real world of these individuals, plain non-subsective [Adj N]$_{AP}$ phrases (e.g. *alleged murderer*) explicitly question it (an *alleged murderer* may or not exist in the real world).

3.2 The semantics of nouns

In designing a semantics for adjectives, we assume a semantics for nouns which reflect their possible interactions with the different types of adjectives

(1) a. **noun:** $\lambda Pol \lambda e \lambda x.[Pol(\textsf{table}(e)) \wedge e = x]$

As we shall shortly see, the additional lambda variable e is imposed by the treatment of adjective semantics we propose and more specifically by the necessity to sometimes distinguish between the individual described by the noun and the individual described by the adjective. The variable Pol accounts for the polarity of the noun, i.e. whether it occurs with the negation or not.

We give here also the semantics assigned to the pronouns *someone/something* which will be used in the derivations throughout this paper:

(2) a. **someone/something:** $\lambda P \exists x.P(x)$

3.3 The semantics of the copula

Following the proposal of Mantague, we assign a unique representation for both the uses of the copula in identity statements (e.g. *John is Mary* $\rightarrow$ john=mary) and in predicative assertions (e.g. *John is a man* $\rightarrow$ man(john)):

(3) a. **be:** $\lambda K \lambda x.K(\lambda y(x = y))$

In the case of predicative assertions in which the predicate is an adjective (e.g. *John is brave*), we adjust the type of the argument of the copula in the following way:

(4) a. **be Adj:** $\textsf{be}(Adj(\lambda Pol \lambda e \lambda x.true))$

3.4 The semantics of adjectives

Given such a representation for nouns, we represent adjectives using the schema given in Figure 1.

Briefly, schema 1 captures the observations made in section (3.1) as follows. First it introduces an existential quantification (in the platonic universe) over not one but two variables (e_a and e_n) – depending on how the formula is instantiated (and in particular on the value of R_1 and R_2) these two variables may or not denote the same object. This accounts for the first observation according to which an [Adj N]$_{AP}$ phrase may refer to either one or two individuals.

Second, the meaning of the [Adj N]$_{AP}$ phrase is a function not of the Adj and N meaning but rather of properties derived from these meanings (A' for Adj and N, as modified by its three arguments, for N). This accounts for the second observation.

Third, the use of the $\textsf{exists}$ predicate will permit distinguishing between existence in the universe of discourse and existence in the real world.

$$\lambda N \lambda x \exists e_a \exists e_n.[A'(e_a) \wedge R_1(x, e_a) \wedge R_2(e_n, e_a) \wedge N(Pol)(e_n)(x)]$$

with A' the property licensed by the adjective, R_1, R_2 two arbitrary relations licensed by the adjective, N the property denoted by the noun and Pol a polarity argument of value either $\lambda S.S$ or $\lambda S.\neg S$

Figure 1: Semantics schema for all adjectives

We now show how this general schema receives different instantiations depending on the adjectival class being considered; and how each instantiation predicts the correct inferential pattern for the four adjectival classes.

3.4.1 Intersective adjectives

The semantic representation of an [Adj N]$_{AP}$ adjectival phrase involving an intersective adjective is given in Figure 2 together with the derivation of the [Adj N]$_{AP}$ phrase *red table*. As can be seen, in this case, the relation R_1 holding between the lambda bound variable x and the entity introduced by the adjective is one of identity. Similarly, the entity e_n introduced is equated with x and the relation R_2 is $\lambda x, y.\textsf{true}$ (i.e. there is no modifying relation between e_a and e_n). Hence the [Adj N]$_{AP}$ phrase licenses in effect a single entity x and the resulting semantics is the traditional $\lambda x.[A(x) \wedge N(x)]$ with A the semantics of the adjective and N that of the noun. Assuming further that determiners have the semantics:

a/the $\lambda P \lambda Q \exists x.[P(\lambda S.S)(x) \wedge Q(x)]$

then the semantics of *Something is a red table* is

(5) $\exists x \exists e_a \exists e_n.[\textsf{red}(e_a) \wedge x = e_a \wedge \textsf{table}(e_n) \wedge e_n = x]$

which correctly entails that there is an entity x which is both red and a table i.e.,

(5) $\models \exists x.[\textsf{red}(x)]$ *something is red*
(5) $\models \exists x.[\textsf{table}(x)]$ *something is a table*

3.4.2 Subsective adjectives

As recalled above, subsective adjectives are characterised by the fact that the [Adj N]$_{AP}$ phrase entails N but not A. Relatedly, the adjective phrase introduces not one but two individuals, one linked to the adjective and the other to the noun. For instance, the phrase *the gastronomical book* refers to a book x which is about the gastronomy concept e_n.

Thus in such cases, we take the R_2 relation holding between x, the NP quantified variable, and e_a, the entity introduced by the adjective, to be distinct from identity, while the R_1 relation is empty.

(6) $\exists x \exists e_a \exists e_n.[\textsf{gastronomy}(e_a) \wedge \textsf{about}(e_n, e_a) \wedge \textsf{book}(e_n) \wedge e_n = x]$

This ensures that the NP refers to two entities, one bound by the determiner and licenced by N, the other existentially quantified and licensed by A. For instance, the sentence *John read every gastronomical books* is interpreted as meaning that John read all books that are about gastronomy.

More generally, this ensures that *[A N]* $\not\models$ *A* (and in fact, adjectives like *gastronomical* cannot be used predicatively), e.g.

(6) $\models$ *something is a book*
$\models \exists x.[\textsf{book}(x)]$
(6) $\models$ *something is about gastronomy*
$\models \exists x \exists e_a.[\textsf{about}(x, e_a) \wedge \textsf{gastronomy}(e_a)]$
(6) $\not\models$ *something is a book and a gastronomy*
$\not\models \exists x[\textsf{book}(x) \wedge \textsf{gastronomy}(x)]$
(6) $\not\models$ *something is gastronomical*
$\not\models \exists x[\textsf{gastronomical}(x)]$

As shown in (Amoia and Gardent, 2006), subsective adjectives can be further divided into at least four classes. Because of space restrictions, we only show here how to represent two of these subclasses namely denominal (e.g. *gastronomical*) and measure subsective adjectives (e.g. *big*). In both cases, the idea is to decompose the meaning of the adjectives into a finer grained lexical meaning. Depending on the lexical meaning involved, this decomposition induces different instantiation patterns for the

Intersective Adjectives
$\lambda N \lambda x \exists e_a \exists e_n.[A(e_a) \wedge x = e_a \wedge N(\lambda S.S)(e_n)(x)]$

Red table
$\lambda N \lambda x \exists e_a \exists e_n.[\textsf{red}(e_a) \wedge x = e_a \wedge N(\lambda S.S)(e_n)(x)](\lambda Pol \lambda e \lambda x.[Pol(\textsf{table}(e)) \wedge e = x])$
$\equiv \lambda x \exists e_a \exists e_n.[\textsf{red}(e_a) \wedge x = e_a \wedge \textsf{table}(e_n) \wedge e_n = x])$
$\equiv \lambda x.[\textsf{red}(x) \wedge \textsf{table}(x)])$

Figure 2: Semantics of Intersective Adjectives

Subsective Adjectives
$\lambda N \lambda x \exists e_a \exists e_n.[A'(e_a) \wedge R_2(e_n, e_a) \wedge N(\lambda S.S)(e_n)(x)]$
with A' an arbitrary complex relation derived from the lexical meaning of the adjective and
R_2 a relation other than identity

Gastronomical book
$\lambda N \lambda x \exists e_a \exists e_n.[\textsf{gastronomy}(e_a) \wedge about(e_n, e_a) \wedge N(\lambda S.S)(e_n)(x)](\lambda Pol \lambda e \lambda x.[Pol(\textsf{book}(e)) \wedge e = x])$
$\equiv \lambda x \exists e_a \exists e_n.[\textsf{gastronomy}(e_a) \wedge about(e_n, e_a) \wedge \textsf{book}(e_n) \wedge e_n = x])$

Figure 3: Semantics of Subsective Adjectives

R relation mentioned in the general schema for adjective semantic representation.

Thus, the meaning of the adjectival phrase containing an adjective of measure, e.g. *big mouse* will be represented as:

$$\lambda N \lambda x \exists e_a \exists e_n.[\textsf{size}(e_a) \wedge highFor(e_a, C) \wedge has(e_n, e_a) \wedge N(\lambda S.S)(e_n)(x)] (\lambda Pol \lambda e \lambda x.[\textsf{mouse}(e) \wedge e = x])$$

$$\equiv \lambda x \exists e_a \exists e_n.[\textsf{size}(e_a) \wedge highFor(e_a, C) \wedge has(e_n, e_a) \wedge \textsf{mouse}(e_n) \wedge e_n = x])$$

where C is a contextually given parameter which determine the scale size is measured against. In this case, C would be, e.g. "mouse" so that the formula above can be glossed as *x is a mouse with a size e_a which is high for a mouse.* In particular, *Daisy is a big mouse* entails that *Daisy is a mouse* and that *Daisy is big for a mouse*, but not that *Daisy is big*.

3.4.3 Privative adjectives

As seen above, privative adjectives entail that the entity described by the NP is not N, e.g. a fake gun is not a gun. For such adjectives, it is the entity introduced by the adjective that is being quantified over, hence e_a is identified with x (cf. Figure 4). Further, the N property is either denied or subject to a modality (*former, potential*). As shown in Figure 4, this is accounted for by providing the appropriate relation R (e.g. R_2 being the relation $\textsf{time}$ introduced by *former* or R_1 being the identity relation x = e_a introduced by *fake*).

This representation presupposes that each sentence in which such modality adjectives do not occur has a default value for time and/or modality. Thus, for instance that

(7) John is a former president. $\not\models$ John is the president.

(8) John is a possible president. $\not\models$ John is the president.

can only be accounted for if the base forms are assigned the following default representations:

(7) $\exists e_a \exists x \quad [\textsf{president}(x) \wedge \textsf{time}(x, e_a) \wedge \textsf{present}(e_a)]$
(8) $\exists e_a \exists x \quad [\textsf{president}(x) \wedge \textsf{mod}(x, e_a) \wedge \textsf{possible}(e_a)]$

3.4.4 Plain non-subsective adjectives

Finally, plain non-subsective adjectives fail to make any prediction about the existence of an in-

Privative Adjectives (e.g., *fake,potential,former,future*)
(e.g. *fake, fictitious*)
$\lambda N \lambda x \exists e_a \exists e_n.[A(e_a) \wedge x = e_a \wedge N(\lambda S.\neg S)(e_n)(x)]$ OR
$\lambda N \lambda x \exists e_a \exists e_n.[A'(e_a) \wedge \textsf{mod/time}(e_a, e_n) \wedge N(\lambda S.S)(e_n)(x)]$
with R_2 being the relation *mod/time* specifying the modality or the time indicated by the adjective

Fake gun
$\lambda N \lambda x \exists e_a \exists e_n.[\textsf{fake}(e_a) \wedge x = e_a \wedge N(\lambda S.\neg S)(e_n)(x)](\lambda Pol \lambda e \lambda x.[Pol(\textsf{gun}(e)) \wedge e = x])$
$\equiv \lambda x \exists e_a \exists e_n.[\textsf{fake}(e_a) \wedge x = e_a \wedge \neg \textsf{gun}(e_n) \wedge e_n = x])$

Former president
$\lambda N \lambda x \exists e_a \exists e_n.[\textsf{former}(e_a) \wedge \textsf{time}(e_n, e_a) \wedge N(\lambda S.S)(e_n)(x)]$
$(\lambda Pol \lambda e \lambda x.[Pol(\textsf{president}(e)) \wedge e = x])$
$\equiv \lambda x \exists e_a \exists e_n[\textsf{former}(e_a) \wedge \textsf{time}(x, e_a) \wedge \textsf{president}(e_n) \wedge x = e_n]$

Figure 4: Semantics of Privative Adjectives

dividual having the N property. Thus for instance, if John is an alleged murderer, there might or might not exist a murderer.

To account for this fact, we follow Hobbs' approach in distinguishing between existence in the universe of discourse and existence in the real world. Thus, the logical existential connective $\exists$ is used to denote existence in the discourse world while the special predicate *Exists* is used to denote existence in the real world. We assume further a theory that permits determining when an individual exists in the universe of discourse and when it exists in the real world.

Given these caveats, the semantics of plain non-subsective adjectives is as indicated in Figure 5 and simply specifies that the alleged murderer is an individual x which exists in the universe of discourse (but not necessarily in the real world) and which is alleged to be a murderer. Moreover, as stated in (Hobbs, 1985), we assume that the *alleged* predicate is existentially opaque in its second argument. That is, an *alleged* predication does not imply the existence in the real world of its second argument.

4 Implementation

The semantics of adjectives presented in this paper was tested using (Blackburn and Bos, 2005) computational semantics framework.

First, based on the classification of 300 English adjectives presented in (Amoia and Gardent, 2006), which identifies 17 different adjectival subclasses for the four main classes proposed by (Kamp, 1975; Kamp and Partee, 1995), we have built a test suite of about 150 examples in the following way. We have chosen for each class a representant adjective and written for it the set of sentence pairs (H/T) illustrating the inference patterns displayed by the class the adjective belongs to. In particular, we have built examples which test:

1. whether the adjective partecipates in both predicative and attributive constructions, so that the resulting sentences (H and T) are paraphrastic,
2. whether the two sentences contain adjectives which are synonyms,
3. what kind of antonymic relation links the given adjective with its antonym,
4. which of the three inference patterns described in (Kamp and Partee, 1995) holds for the given adjective,
5. hyperonymy,
6. derivational morphology.

For instance, the test suite contains for an adjective such as *fake*, belonging to a subclass of the privative adjectives, the H/T pairs in (9).

(9) a. H:*This is a fake gun* / T:*This gun is fake*

Plain non subsective Adjectives (e.g., *alleged*)
$\lambda N \lambda x \exists e_a \exists e_n.[A'(e_a, e_n) \wedge x = e_a \wedge N(\lambda S.S)(e_n)(e_n)]$
with R_1 being the identity relation between x and e_a and R_2 being the relation introduced by the adjective $A'(e_a, e_n)$

Alleged murderer
$\lambda N \lambda x \exists e_a \exists e_n.[\textsf{alleged}(e_a, e_n) \wedge x = e_a \wedge N(\lambda S.S)(e_n)(e_n)](\lambda Pol \lambda e \lambda x.[Pol(\textsf{murderer}(e)) \wedge e = x])$
$\equiv \lambda x \exists e_a \exists e_n.[\textsf{alleged}(e_a, e_n) \wedge x = e_a \wedge \textsf{murderer}(e_n) \wedge e_n = e_n])$

Figure 5: Semantics of plain non-subsective Adjectives

b. H:*This is a fake gun* / T:*This is a false gun*

c. H:*This is a fake gun* / T:*This gun is not genuine*

d. H:*This is not a fake gun* $\models$ *This gun is real*

e. H:*This is a fake gun* / T:*This is a gun*

f. H:*This is a fake gun* / T:*This is not a gun*

g. H:*This is a fake gun* / T:*This is fake*

h. H:*This is a fake gun* / T:*This is a fake weapon*

i. H:*This is a fake gun* / T:*This gun is a counterfeit*

Second, a grammar fragment was implemented which integrates the semantics of nouns and adjectives presented here. This grammar fragment was then used together with the appropriate lexicon to automatically associate with each sentence of the test suite a representation of its meaning.

Third, lexical Knowledge pertaining to each class of adjectives is captured through a set of axioms describing the specific lexical relationships adjectives are involved in.

Synonymy is captured introducing equality axioms which describe the equivalence of the two properties expressed by the two adjectives $\texttt{Adj}_1$ and $\texttt{Adj}_2$ asserting:

$$\forall e[\text{Adj}_1(e) \leftrightarrow \text{Adj}_2(e)]$$

Hyponymy (for example big/giant vs. small/minuscule) is captured by introducing the axioms such as:

$$\forall e[\text{Adj}_1(e) \rightarrow \text{Adj}_2(e)]$$

Antonymy is captured by introducing different axioms depending on the type of opposition relation in which the adjectives are involved, i.e. binary, contrary or multiple opposition. The axiom below for example introduces a binary antonymic relation:

$$\forall e[\text{Adj}_1(e) \leftrightarrow \neg \text{Adj}_2(e)]$$

Fourth, entailment (H$\models$T) was checked for each sentence pair using the first order theorem provers available in the system and the results compared with the expected result. A first evaluation shows that the methodology proposed yields the expected results: we could correctly predict all the inferential patterns presented above from 1 to 5 (136 pairs, 89%). The results for other patterns, describing morphoderivational relations of adjectives, depend on the amount of information implemented in the grammar which for the moment is very limited.

5 Perspectives and Comparison with related works

The approach presented here lays the basis for a computational treatment of adjectival inference in that it provides a fine grained characterisation of the various types of inferential patterns licenced by adjectives.

In future work, we believe three main points are worth investigating.

First, previous work (Amoia and Gardent, 2006) has shown that the classification presented here can be further detailed and even finer-grained classes identified thereby permitting the creation of syntactically and semantically homogeneous adjectival classes. The advantages of identifying such homogeneous classes has been well demonstrated for verbs. It permits structuring the lexicon and facilitates development and maintenance. Based on the idea that syntax (and in particular, so-called syntactic alternations) helps define such classes, we are currently investigating in how far adjectival syntax helps further refine adjectival classes.

Second, the proposed classification need to be applied and combined with ontological and lexical semantic information. That is, each adjective should be classified wrt the 4 types of model theoretic semantics described here and related to such a lexical semantics ontology as e.g., WordNet, the MikroKosmos ontology of the SIMPLE lexicon.

Thus (Raskin and Nirenburg, 1995) describe the methodology used to encode adjectival entries in the lexicon of the MikroKosmos semantic analyser. The MikroKosmos lexicon contains 6,000 entries for English and 1,500 entries for Spanish adjectives. Adjectives are organised in an ontology which distinguishes between the following three main adjectival classes: (i) `Scalar Adjectives`, which are represented as *property-value* pairs, (ii) `Denominal Adjectives`, (e.g. *atomic, civil, gastronomical*) represented as nouns and (iii) `Deverbal Adjectives`, (e.g. *eager, abusive, readable*) is related to the meaning of the verb they are derived to.

The classification of adjectives proposed in SIMPLE (SIMPLE, 2000) is also ontology-based. A lexical entry for an adjective is characterised by a set of semantic and syntactic information. Semantic information describes: (i) the hierarchy of ontological properties expressed by the particular adjective, for example the adjective expresses the property of COLOUR and this is a physical property; (ii) whether the adjective is intersective or subsective; (iii) whether the adjective has a persistent duration (i.e. is stable) or not. Moreover, syntactic information describes adjectival features such as (i) predicative/attributive usage, and (ii) gradability.
SIMPLE has actually added semantic information to approximately 3,500 lexical entries (about 10,000 senses) for each of the 12 European languages considered in the project.

It would be interesting to see whether any of these resources can be used to create an adjective lexicon rich enough to support both syntactic processing and semantic inference.

Finally, a third point of interest concerns the integration of the compositional semantics proposed here for adjectives into a robust semantic processing system. We plan to integrate this semantics into the CCG2Sem semantic parsing system (Bos, 2005) and to investigate in how far, this would help deal with entailment recognition.

References

Marilisa Amoia and Claire Gardent. 2006. Adjective based inference. In *Proceedings of KRAQ'06 (Knowledge and Reasoning for Answering Questions)*, Trento, Italy.

Patrick Blackburn and Johan Bos. 2005. *Representation and Inference for Natiral Language. A first Course in Computational Semantics.* CSLI Studies in Computational Linguistics.

Johan Bos. 2005. Towards wide-coverage semantic interpretation. In *In Proceedings of the Sixth International Workshop on Computational Semantics IWCS-6*, pages 42–53.

G. Chierchia and S. Mc Connell-Ginet. 1990. *Meaning and Grammar: An Introduction to Semantics.* The MIT Press, Cambridge, MA.

Jerry R. Hobbs. 1985. Ontological promiscuity. In *Proceedings of the 23rd Annual Meeting of the Association for Computational Linguistics*, pages 61–69, Chicago, Illinois, July.

Hans Kamp and Barbara Partee. 1995. Prototype theory and compositionality. *Cognition*, (57):129–191.

Hans Kamp. 1975. Two theories about adjectives. In Edward L. Keenan (ed.), *Formal Semantics of Natural Language*, pages 123–155. Cambridge University Press.

V. Raskin and S. Nirenburg. 1995. *Lexical Semantics of Adjectives, a micro-theory of adjectival meaning.* MCCS Report.

Specification Group SIMPLE. 2000. Specification simple work package 2. Linguistic specifications deliverable d2.1.

Natural Logic for Textual Inference

Bill MacCartney
Stanford University
wcmac@cs.stanford.edu

Christopher D. Manning
Stanford University
manning@cs.stanford.edu

Abstract

This paper presents the first use of a computational model of *natural logic*—a system of logical inference which operates over natural language—for textual inference. Most current approaches to the PASCAL RTE textual inference task achieve robustness by sacrificing semantic precision; while broadly effective, they are easily confounded by ubiquitous inferences involving monotonicity. At the other extreme, systems which rely on first-order logic and theorem proving are precise, but excessively brittle. This work aims at a middle way. Our system finds a low-cost edit sequence which transforms the premise into the hypothesis; learns to classify entailment relations across atomic edits; and composes atomic entailments into a top-level entailment judgment. We provide the first reported results for any system on the FraCaS test suite. We also evaluate on RTE3 data, and show that hybridizing an existing RTE system with our natural logic system yields significant performance gains.

1 Introduction

The last five years have seen a surge of interest in the problem of *textual inference*, that is, automatically determining whether a natural-language *hypothesis* can be inferred from a given *premise*. A broad spectrum of approaches have been explored, ranging from shallow-but-robust to deep-but-brittle. Up to now, the most successful approaches have used fairly impoverished semantic representations, relying on measures of lexical or semantic overlap (Jijkoun and de Rijke, 2005), pattern-based relation extraction (Romano et al., 2006), or approximate matching of predicate-argument structure (Hickl et al., 2006). Such methods, while robust and broadly effective, are imprecise, and are easily confounded by ubiquitous inferences involving monotonicity, particularly in negative polarity contexts, as in:

P: *No case of indigenously acquired rabies infection has been confirmed in the past 2 years.*

H: *No rabies cases have been confirmed.*

Because it drops important qualifiers in a negative context, the hypothesis does not follow; yet both the lexical content and the predicate-argument structure of the hypothesis closely match the premise.

At the other extreme, textual inference can be approached as deduction, building on work in formal computational semantics to translate sentences into first-order logic (FOL), and then applying a theorem prover or a model builder (Akhmatova, 2005; Fowler et al., 2005). However, such approaches tend to founder on the difficulty of accurately translating natural language in FOL—tricky issues include idioms, intensionality and propositional attitudes, modalities, temporal and causal relations, certain quantifiers, and so on. FOL-based systems that have attained high precision (Bos and Markert, 2006) have done so at the cost of very poor recall.

In this work, we explore a different point on the spectrum, by developing a computational model of *natural logic*, that is, a logic whose vehicle of inference is natural language.[1] Natural logic eschews logical notation and model theory. Its proofs proceed by incremental edits to expressions of natural language, and its inference rules specify conditions under which semantic expansions or contractions preserve truth. It thus permits us to do precise reasoning about monotonicity, while sidestepping the difficulties of translating sentences into FOL.

It should be emphasized that there are many

[1]Natural logic should not be confused with *natural deduction*, a proof system for first-order logic.

Proceedings of the Workshop on Textual Entailment and Paraphrasing, pages 193–200,
Prague, June 2007.

important kinds of inference which are not addressed by a natural logic system, including temporal reasoning, causal reasoning (*Khan sold nuclear plans* $\Rightarrow$ *Khan possessed nuclear plans*), paraphrase (*McEwan flew to Rome* $\Rightarrow$ *McEwan took a flight to Rome*), relation extraction (*Bill Gates and his wife, Melinda...* $\Rightarrow$ *Melinda Gates is married to Bill Gates*), etc. Moreover, a natural logic system will struggle with inferences requiring model-building or deep proof search, which are more suitable for formal deduction systems. However, the applicability of natural logic is broader than it might at first appear, and a natural logic system can be designed to integrate with other kinds of reasoners.

2 Foundations of natural logic

Natural logic aims to explain inferences involving monotonicity, in which the concepts or constraints expressed are expanded or contracted. Consider, for example, the sentence *Every meal without wine is a terrible crime*. Some semantic elements can be expanded (but not contracted) *salva veritate*, and are therefore said to have positive polarity: *wine* may be broadened to *drink*, *terrible crime* may be relaxed to *crime*, or *every* may be weakened to *some*. Other elements can only be contracted (not expanded) *salva veritate*, and thus have negative polarity: *meal* can be narrowed to *dinner*. The monotonicity calculus developed in (Sánchez Valencia, 1991) explains these polarity effects by (1) defining an entailment relation over multifarious expressions of natural language, (2) defining monotonicity properties of semantic functions, and finally (3) specifying how monotonicities combine during Fregean composition of semantic functions.

The entailment relation. Most work in textual inference reflects a simple concept of entailment: one sentence entails another, or does not. In natural logic, however, entailment is a semantic containment relation (analogous to the set containment relation $\subseteq$) over expressions of all types, including words and phrases as well as sentences. We define the entailment relation $\sqsubseteq$ recursively over the semantic types familiar from Montague semantics. If c and d are of type t (truth values), then $c \sqsubseteq d$ iff $c \rightarrow d$. If c and d are of type e (entities), then $c \sqsubseteq d$ iff $c = d$. Finally, if c and d are of functional type $\langle\alpha, \beta\rangle$, then $c \sqsubseteq d$ iff for all $a \in \alpha$, $c(a) \sqsubseteq d(a)$. Otherwise, if $c \not\sqsubseteq d$ and $d \not\sqsubseteq c$, we write $c \# d$.

Using these formal definitions, we can establish entailment relations between common nouns (*penguin* $\sqsubseteq$ *bird*), common and proper adjectives (*tiny* $\sqsubseteq$ *small*, *French* $\sqsubseteq$ *European*), transitive and intransitive verbs (*kick* $\sqsubseteq$ *strike*, *hover* $\sqsubseteq$ *fly*), temporal and locative modifiers (*this morning* $\sqsubseteq$ *today*, *in Beijing* $\sqsubseteq$ *in China*), connectives (*and* $\sqsubseteq$ *or*), and quantifiers (*everyone* $\sqsubseteq$ *someone*, *all* $\sqsubseteq$ *most* $\sqsubseteq$ *some*).[2] Among noun phrases, we have *everyone* $\sqsubseteq$ *Einstein* $\sqsubseteq$ *some physicist*. Finally, observe that dropping a modifier generally yields entailment (*eat quickly* $\sqsubseteq$ *eat*) though this heuristic can be violated, e.g., by operator adjectives (*fake vaccine* $\not\sqsubseteq$ *vaccine*).

Monotonicity. Under the Fregean hypothesis, the meaning of a compound expression is the result of function application. In semantics as in mathematics, we can describe a function as *upward monotone* if "larger" inputs yield larger outputs. Formally, given a function f of functional type $\langle\alpha, \beta\rangle$:

- f is upward-monotone ($\uparrow$) iff for all $x, y \in \alpha$, $x \sqsubseteq y$ entails $f(x) \sqsubseteq f(y)$.
- f is downward-monotone ($\downarrow$) iff for all $x, y \in \alpha$, $x \sqsubseteq y$ entails $f(y) \sqsubseteq f(x)$.
- f is non-monotone ($\not\updownarrow$) iff it is neither upward- nor downward-monotone.

Most linguistic expressions may be regarded as upward-monotone semantic functions. Thus *tango in Paris* $\sqsubseteq$ *dance in France*, since *tango* $\sqsubseteq$ *dance* and *in Paris* $\sqsubseteq$ *in France*. However, a number of important linguistic constructions are downward-monotone, including negation (*not*), restrictive quantifiers (*no*, *few*, *at most* n), restrictive verbs (*lack*, *fail*, *prohibit*), certain adverbs (*without*, *except*), the antecedent of a conditional, and so on. We thus have *didn't dance* $\sqsubseteq$ *didn't tango*, *few athletes* $\sqsubseteq$ *few sprinters*, *lack weapons* $\sqsubseteq$ *lack guns*,

[2]The entailment relations among quantifiers may be counterintuitive to those prone to what Peter Geach called "quantificatious thinking", who might consider *someone* "smaller" than *everyone*. But in the theory of generalized quantifiers, the denotation of a quantified noun phrase is the set of predicates which it satisfies, and the predicates satisfied by *everyone* are a subset of those satisfied by *someone*. Note also that logicians will deny that the universal entails the existential: $\forall x\ P(x) \not\rightarrow \exists x\ P(x)$. However, most people are happy to infer *someone is hungry* from *everyone is hungry*.

without clothes $\sqsubseteq$ *without pants*, and *If stocks rise, we win* $\sqsubseteq$ *If stocks soar, we win*. Finally, a few expressions must be considered non-monotone, including superlative adjectives and quantifiers such as *most*. Thus *prettiest butterfly # prettiest insect* and *most boats # most vehicles*. Note that certain generalized quantifiers must be treated as binary functions having different monotonicities in different arguments. Thus *every* is downward-monotone in its first argument (*every fish swims* $\sqsubseteq$ *every shark swims*) but upward-monotone in its second argument (*every shark swims* $\sqsubseteq$ *every shark moves*).

Composition of monotonicity. Finally, we must specify how monotonicities combine during Fregean composition of semantic functions. In Sánchez Valencia's *marking algorithm*, we represent each input expression as a parse in the Lambek categorial grammar. We then (1) mark leaf nodes with appropriate lexical monotonicity values, (2) project monotonicities to internal nodes representing function applications, and finally (3) compose monotonicities along the path from the root to each leaf in order to determine effective polarities. The composition of monotonicities is straightforward. Suppose $h = f \circ g$. If either f or g is non-monotone, then so is h. Otherwise, if the monotonicities of f and g are the same, then h is upward-monotone; if they are different, then h is downward-monotone. (Thus, *wine* has positive polarity in *no meal without wine* because it falls under two downward-monotone operators.)

3 The NatLog System

Our natural logic system, dubbed the *NatLog* system, has a three-stage architecture similar to those in (Marsi and Krahmer, 2005; MacCartney et al., 2006), comprising (1) linguistic pre-preprocessing, (2) alignment, and (3) entailment classification.

3.1 Linguistic pre-processing

Relative to other textual inference systems, the NatLog system does comparatively little linguistic preprocessing. We rely on the Stanford parser (Klein and Manning, 2003), a Treebank-trained statistical parser, for tokenization, part-of-speech tagging, and phrase-structure parsing. By far the most important analysis performed at this stage is *monotonicity marking*, in which we compute the effective monotonicity for each token span in each input sentence. For this, we use an adaptation of the marking algorithm of Sánchez Valencia (section 2); however, our choice of a Treebank-trained parser (driven by the goal of broad coverage) requires us to modify the algorithm substantially. Unlike the categorial grammar parses assumed by Sánchez Valencia, the nesting of constituents in phrase-structure parses does not always correspond to the composition of semantic functions, which introduces a number of complications. We define a list of downward-monotone and non-monotone expressions, and for each item we specify its arity and a Tregex pattern (Levy and Andrew, 2006) which permits us to identify its occurrences. We also specify, for each argument, both the monotonicity and another Tregex pattern which helps us to determine the sentence span over which the monotonicity is projected. (Figure 1 shows some example definitions.) The marking process computes these projections, performs monotonicity composition where needed, and marks each token span with its final effective monotonicity.

```
unary operator: without
  pattern: IN < /^[Ww]ithout\$/
  argument 1: monotonicity ↓ on dominating PP
    pattern: __ > PP=proj

binary operator: most
  pattern: JJS < /^[Mm]ost\$/ !> QP
  argument 1: monotonicity ↑̸↓̸ on dominating NP
    pattern: __ >+(NP) (NP=proj !> NP)
  argument 2: monotonicity ↑ on dominating S
    pattern: __ >+(/.*/) (S=proj !> S)
```

Figure 1: Two examples of monotonicity operator definitions. The patterns employ Tregex syntax.

3.2 Alignment

The second stage of processing establishes an *alignment* between the premise and the hypothesis. While there are many notions of alignment, in this work we have chosen to represent alignments as sequences of *atomic edits* over spans of word tokens. We define four types of atomic edits: *deletion* of a span from the premise, *insertion* of a span into the hypothesis, *substitution* of a hypothesis span for a premise span, and *advance* over a span without modification. Each atomic edit is parameterized by the token indices at which it operates. As an example, the first problem in table 3 may be aligned using following edits:

An Irishman	$\Longrightarrow$	An Irishman	ADV
won	$\Longrightarrow$	won	ADV
a	$\Longrightarrow$	the	SUB
Nobel prize	$\Longrightarrow$	Nobel prize	ADV
	$\Longrightarrow$	for literature	INS
.	$\Longrightarrow$	.	ADV

Clearly, this representation imposes certain limitations: there is no atomic edit type representing the movement of a token span from one sentence location to another (instead a combination of deletion and insertion must be used), and there can be no alignments to non-contiguous sets of tokens. However, the span edit representation also offers important benefits. First, there is always a well-defined sequence of intermediate forms through which the sentence progresses during editing, which is important for the computation of monotonicity features. Second, given a cost function over edits, it is possible to construct an efficient dynamic program to find the lowest-cost edit sequence between any pair of sentences, using a straightforward extension of the Levenshtein string-edit algorithm.

For this purpose, we have designed a cost function which prefers edits which operate on longer spans; penalizes edits operating on spans which are not parse-tree constituents; imposes nomimal cost on substitutions of words having the same lemma; and imposes little cost on certain "light" edits, involving prepositions, articles, auxiliaries, etc. When applied to problems like those in the FraCaS test suite (section 4), this cost model gives intuitively pleasing results. However, because our focus in this work is on entailment, we have not devoted much energy to optimizing our alignment model, and will not discuss it further. (For the RTE experiments described in section 5, we use alignments derived from an independent RTE system. Translating those alignments into the span edit representation requires relaxing some of its constraints, as we'll explain.)

3.3 Entailment classification

The edit sequence obtained during the alignment stage effectively decomposes the global entailment problem into a sequence of atomic entailment problems, one for each atomic edit. In the final stage, we train a model for atomic entailment classification, and predict an entailment relation for each atomic edit. We then compose our atomic entailment predictions to produce a global entailment prediction.

relation	symbol	in terms of $\sqsubseteq$	FraCaS	RTE
equivalent	$p = h$	$p \sqsubseteq h, h \sqsubseteq p$	yes	yes
forward	$p \sqsubset h$	$p \sqsubseteq h, h \not\sqsubseteq p$	yes	yes
reverse	$p \sqsupset h$	$h \sqsubseteq p, p \not\sqsubseteq h$	unk	no
independent	$p \# h$	$p \not\sqsubseteq h, h \not\sqsubseteq p$	unk	no
exclusive	$p \mid h$	$p \sqsubseteq \neg h$	no	no

Table 1: The five elementary entailment relations. The last two columns indicate correspondences to FraCaS and RTE answers; see sections 4 and 5.

The atomic entailment model uses a classifier to predict one of five *elementary entailment relations* (table 1) for each atomic edit. This model uses a feature representation designed to capture characteristics of the edit pertinent to a natural logic analysis: the type of the edit (DEL, INS, or SUB), the effective monotonicity at the affected token span ($\uparrow$, $\downarrow$, or $\not\updownarrow$), and various lexical features of the affected tokens. In the case of a SUB edit, the lexical features help to indicate whether the substitution constitutes a semantic expansion, contraction, equivalence, or exclusion, using WordNet-derived measures of synonymy, hyponymy, and antonymy, and a measure of lemma similarity based on Levenshtein string-edit distance. In addition, for edits of all types, we have found it useful to generate a "light edit" feature indicating whether the affected tokens belong to categories which are usually negligible for inferential purposes, including prepositions, articles, auxiliaries, and punctuation.

The entailment model uses a decision tree classifier, trained on a small data set of 69 problems custom-designed to exercise diverse regions of the feature space.[3] From these examples, the decision tree effectively learns such heuristics as *deletion in an upward-monotone context yields* $\sqsubset$, *substitution of a hypernym in a downward-monotone context yields* $\sqsupset$, and *substitution of an antonym yields* $\mid$.

To produce a top-level entailment judgment, the atomic entailment predictions associated with each

[3]Thus, in using learning, we are not trying to estimate statistical properties of some natural distribution of data. Rather, the learning framework provides (1) a modular way to add features which may impact the entailment decision, (2) a principled way to combine evidence from diverse features, such as real-valued lexical features, and (3) a convenient way to verify the proper functioning of the system.

atomic edit: SUB(*a*, *the*)
features:
type: SUB, *monotonicity*: $\uparrow$, *isLightEdit*: true,
wnSyno: 0.0, *wnHypo*: 0.0, *wnAnto*: 0.0, *lemmaSim*: 0.0
predicted entailment relation: $=$

atomic edit: INS(*for literature*)
features:
type: INS, *monotonicity*: $\uparrow$, *isLightEdit*: false
predicted entailment relation: $\sqsupset$

top-level inference:
composition of entailment relations: $= \circ \sqsupset \Rightarrow \sqsupset$
mapping to FraCaS answer: $\sqsupset \Rightarrow$ *unk*

Figure 2: The operation of the entailment model on FraCaS problem 33 (see table 3).

§	Category	Count	% Acc.
1	Quantifiers	44	84.09
2	Plurals	24	41.67
3	Anaphora	6	50.00
4	Ellipsis	25	28.00
5	Adjectives	15	60.00
6	Comparatives	16	68.75
7	Temporal	36	61.11
8	Verbs	8	62.50
9	Attitudes	9	55.56
Applicable sections: 1, 5, 6		75	76.00
All sections		183	59.56

Table 2: NatLog's accuracy on the FraCaS test suite, by section. We exclude degenerate problems and multiple-premise problems; see text.

edit are composed in a fairly obvious way. If r is any entailment relation, then $= \circ r \equiv r$, but $\# \circ r \equiv \#$. $\sqsubset$ and $\sqsupset$ are transitive, but $\sqsubset \circ \sqsupset \equiv \#$, and so on. Compositions are commutative and associative.

Figure 2 shows an example of the operation of the entailment model.

4 Experiments with the FraCaS test suite

The FraCaS test suite (Cooper et al., 1996) was developed as part of a collaborative research effort in computational semantics. It contains 346 inference problems reminiscent of a textbook on formal semantics. In the authors' view, "inferencing tasks [are] the best way of testing an NLP system's semantic capacity." Yet, to our knowledge, this work is the first to present a quantitative system evaluation using FraCaS.[4]

The problems are divided into nine sections, each focused on a category of semantic phenomena, such as quantifiers or anaphora (see table 2). Each problem consists of one or more premise sentences, followed by a one-sentence question. For this project, the questions were converted into declarative hypotheses. Each problem also has an answer, which (usually) takes one of three values: *yes* (the hypothesis can be inferred from the premise(s)), *no* (the negation of the hypothesis can be inferred), or *unk* (neither the hypothesis nor its negation can be inferred). Some examples are shown in table 3.

Not all of the 346 problems were used in this work. First, 12 of the problems were excluded because they are degenerate, lacking either a hypothesis or a well-defined answer. Second, an additional 151 problems (about 45% of the total) were excluded because they involve multiple premises. While many of the multiple-premise problems should be feasible for NatLog in the future, such inferences require search, and for now we have chosen to sidestep this complexity.

Finally, it should be noted that several sections of the test suite involve semantic phenomena, such as ellipsis, which the NatLog system makes no attempt to model. While we report results for these sections, we do not expect performance to be good, and in development we have concentrated on the sections where we expect NatLog to have relevant expertise. In table 2, results for these sections are aggregated under the label "applicable sections".

Results are shown in table 2. On the "applicable" sections, performance is good. (Not suprisingly, we make little headway with, e.g., ellipsis.) Of course, this does not constitute a proper evaluation on unseen test data—but on the other hand, the system was never trained on the FraCaS problems, and has had no opportunity to learn biases implicit in the data.[5] Our main goal in testing on FraCaS is to evaluate the representational and inferential adequacy of our model of natural logic, and from that perspective, the strong performance in quantifiers,

[4]Indeed, our first step was to put the FraCaS data into machine-readable form, which we make publicly available at *http://nlp.stanford.edu/~wcmac/downloads/fracas.xml*.

[5]This also explains why NatLog's performance on some FraCaS sections falls below that of a baseline most-common-label classifier.

§	ID	Premise(s)	Hypothesis	Ans
1	33	An Irishman won a Nobel prize.	An Irishman won the Nobel prize for literature.	*unk*
1	38	No delegate finished the report.	Some delegate finished the report on time.	*no*
2	99	Clients at the demonstration were all impressed by the system's performance. Smith was a client at the demonstration.	Smith was impressed by the system's performance.	*yes*
9	335	Smith believed that ITEL had won the contract in 1992.	ITEL won the contract in 1992.	*unk*

Table 3: Illustrative examples from the FraCaS test suite

	guess			
answer	*yes*	*unk*	*no*	total
yes	62	40	–	102
unk	15	45	–	60
no	6	13	2	21
total	90	91	2	183

Table 4: Confusions on FraCaS data (all sections)

adjectives, and comparatives is satisfying.

The confusion matrix shown in table 4 is instructive. By far the largest category of confusions comprise problems where we guess *unk* when the correct answer is *yes*. This reflects both the bias toward *yes* in the FraCaS data, and the system's tendency to predict *unk* (entailment relation $\#$) when confused: given the composition rules for entailment relations, the system can predict *yes* only if all atomic-level predictions are either $\sqsubset$ or $=$. On the other hand, there are a number of problems where we predict *yes* mistakenly. Several of these errors arise in a series of problems in §5 which concern operator adjectives such as *former*. The entailment model wrongly assumes that such modifiers, like any others, can safely be deleted in upward-monotone contexts, but in fact *former student* $\not\sqsubseteq$ *student*. If the feature set used by the entailment model were extended to represent occurrences of operator adjectives, and if appropriate examples were included in the training data, our accuracy in §5—and the average accuracy for the "applicable" sections—could easily be boosted over 80%.

5 Experiments with RTE data

Textual inference problems from the PASCAL RTE Challenge (Dagan et al., 2005) differ from FraCaS problems in several important ways. (See table 5 for examples.) Instead of textbook examples of semantic phenomena, RTE problems are more natural-seeming, with premises collected "in the wild" from newswire text. The premises are much longer, averaging 35 words (vs. 11 words for FraCaS). Also, the RTE task aims at a binary classification: the RTE *no* answer combines the *no* and *unk* answers in FraCaS.

Due to the character of RTE problems, we do not expect NatLog to be a good general-purpose solution to solving RTE problems. First, most RTE problems depend on forms of inference, such as paraphrase, temporal reasoning, or relation extraction, which NatLog is not designed to address. Second, in most RTE problems, the edit distance between premise and hypothesis is relatively large. More atomic edits means a greater chance that prediction errors made by the atomic entailment model will propagate, via entailment composition, to the system's final output. Rather, in applying NatLog to RTE, we hope to make reliable predictions on a subset of RTE problems, trading recall for precision. If we succeed, then we may be able to hybridize with a broad-coverage RTE system to obtain better results than either system individually—the same strategy that was adopted by (Bos and Markert, 2006) for their FOL-based system.

For this purpose, we have chosen to use the Stanford RTE system described in (de Marneffe et al., 2006). In applying NatLog to RTE problems, we use alignments from the Stanford system as input to our entailment model. A Stanford alignment is a map from hypothesis words to premise words. When we translate such alignments into the NatLog representation described in section 3, each pair of aligned words generates a *substitution* edit (or, if the words are identical, an *advance* edit). Unaligned premise words yield *deletion* edits, while unaligned hypothesis words yield *insertion* edits. Where possible, contiguous sequences of word-level edits are then collected into equivalent span edits. While the result of this translation method cannot be interpreted as a conventional edit script (there is no well-defined or-

ID	Premise(s)	Hypothesis	Answer
518	The French railway company SNCF is cooperating in the project.	The French railway company is called SNCF.	*yes*
601	NUCOR has pioneered a giant mini-mill in which steel is poured into continuous casting machines.	Nucor has pioneered the first mini-mill.	*no*

Table 5: Illustrative examples from the RTE3 test suite

RTE3 Development Set (800 problems)				
System	% yes	precision	recall	accuracy
Stanford	50.25	68.66	66.99	67.25
NatLog	18.00	**76.39**	26.70	58.00
Hybrid, bal.	50.00	69.75	67.72	68.25
Hybrid, opt.	55.13	69.16	**74.03**	**69.63**

RTE3 Test Set (800 problems)				
System	% yes	precision	recall	accuracy
Stanford	50.00	61.75	60.24	60.50
NatLog	23.88	**68.06**	31.71	57.38
Hybrid, bal.	50.00	64.50	62.93	63.25
Hybrid, opt.	54.13	63.74	**67.32**	**63.62**

Table 6: Performance on the RTE3 development and test sets. *% yes* indicates the proportion of *yes* predictions made by the system. Precision and recall are shown for the *yes* label.

dering of edits, and multiple edits can operate on the same input spans), we find that this poses no great impediment to subsequent processing by the entailment model.

Table 6 shows the performance of the NatLog system on RTE3 data. Relative to the Stanford RTE system, NatLog achieves high precision on its *yes* predictions—about 76% on the development set, and 68% on the test set—suggesting that hybridizing may be effective. For comparison, the FOL-based system reported in (Bos and Markert, 2006) attained a similarly high precision of 76% on RTE2 problems, but was able to make a positive prediction in only about 4% of cases. NatLog makes positive predictions far more often—at a rate of 18% on the development set, and 24% on the test set.

The Stanford RTE system makes *yes/no* predictions by thresholding a real-valued *inference score*. To construct a hybrid system, we adjust the Stanford inference scores by $+x$ or $-x$, depending on whether NatLog predicts *yes* or *no/unk*. We choose the value of x by optimizing development set accuracy, while adjusting the threshold to generate balanced predictions (that is, equal numbers of *yes* and *no* predictions). As an additional experiment, we fix x at this value and then adjust the threshold to optimize development set accuracy, resulting in an excess of *yes* predictions. (Since this optimization is based solely on development data, its use on test data is fully legitimate.) Results for these two cases are shown in table 6. The parameters tuned on development data were found to yield good performance on test data. The optimized hybrid system attained an absolute accuracy gain of 3.12% over the Stanford system, corresponding to an extra 25 problems answered correctly. This result is statistically significant ($p < 0.01$, McNemar's test, 2-tailed).

However, the gain cannot be attributed to NatLog's success in handling the kind of inferences about monotonicity which are the staple of natural logic. Indeed, such inferences are quite rare in the RTE data. Rather, NatLog seems to have gained primarily by being more precise. In some cases, this precision works against it: NatLog answers *no* to problem 518 (table 5) because it cannot account for the insertion of *called* in the hypothesis. On the other hand, it correctly rejects the hypothesis in problem 601 because it cannot account for the insertion of *first*, whereas the less-precise Stanford system was happy to allow it.

6 Related work

While the roots of natural logic can be traced back to Aristotle's syllogisms, the modern conception of natural logic began with George Lakoff, who proposed "a logic for natural language" which could "characterize all the valid inferences that can be made in natural language" (Lakoff, 1970). The study of natural logic was formalized by Johan van Benthem, who crucially connected it with categorial grammar (van Benthem, 1986), and later was brought to fruition by Victor Sánchez Valencia, who first gave a precise definition of a calculus of monotonicity (Sánchez Valencia, 1991). A small current of theoretical work has continued up to the present, for example (Zamansky et al., 2006).

There has been surprisingly little work on building computational models of natural logic. (Fyodorov et al., 2003) describes a Prolog implementation for a small fragment of English, based on a categorial grammar parser.[6] In an unpublished draft, (van Eijck, 2005) describes a preliminary implementation in Haskell.

Doing inference with representations close to natural language has also been advocated by Jerry Hobbs, as in (Hobbs, 1985).

To our knowledge, the FraCaS results reported here represent the first such evaluation. (Sukkarieh, 2003) describes applying a deductive system to some FraCaS inferences, but does not perform a complete evaluation or report quantitative results.

7 Conclusion

Our NatLog implementation of natural logic successfully handles a broad range of inferences involving monotonicity, as demonstrated on the FraCaS test suite. While a post-hoc analysis of performance on the RTE3 Challenge suggests that monotonicity-related inferences have limited applicability in RTE data, the greater precision of the NatLog system nevertheless significantly improved the performance of a hybrid RTE system. An area for future work is further consideration of what kinds of inference are prevalent and important in prominent computational linguistic applications.

Acknowledgements The authors wish to thank Marie-Catherine de Marneffe and the anonymous reviewers for their helpful comments on an earlier draft of this paper. This work was supported in part by ARDA's Advanced Question Answering for Intelligence (AQUAINT) Program.

References

Elena Akhmatova. 2005. Textual entailment resolution via atomic propositions. In *Proc. of the PASCAL RTE Challenge Workshop*.

Johan Bos and Katja Markert. 2006. When logical inference helps determining textual entailment (and when it doesn't). In *Proc. of the 2nd PASCAL RTE Challenge Workshop*.

Robin Cooper, Dick Crouch, Jan Van Eijck, Chris Fox, Johan Van Genabith, Jan Jaspars, Hans Kamp, David Milward, Manfred Pinkal, Massimo Poesio, and Steve Pulman. 1996. Using the framework. Technical Report LRE 62-051 D-16, The FraCaS Consortium.

Ido Dagan, Oren Glickman, and Bernardo Magnini. 2005. The PASCAL Recognising Textual Entailment Challenge. In *Proc. of the PASCAL RTE Challenge Workshop*.

Marie-Catherine de Marneffe, Bill MacCartney, Trond Grenager, Daniel Cer, Anna Rafferty, and Christopher D. Manning. 2006. Learning to distinguish valid textual entailments. In *Proc. of the 2nd PASCAL RTE Challenge Workshop*.

Abraham Fowler, Bob Hauser, Daniel Hodges, Ian Niles, Adrian Novischi, and Jens Stephan. 2005. Applying COGEX to recognize textual entailment. In *Proc. of the PASCAL RTE Challenge Workshop*.

Yaroslav Fyodorov, Yoad Winter, and Nissim Francez. 2003. Order-based inference in natural logic. *Logic Journal of the IGPL*, 11(4):385–416.

Andrew Hickl, John Williams, Jeremy Bensley, Kirk Roberts, Bryan Rink, and Ying Shi. 2006. Recognizing textual entailment with LCC's GROUNDHOG system. In *Proc. of the 2nd PASCAL RTE Challenge Workshop*.

Jerry R. Hobbs. 1985. Ontological promiscuity. In *Proc. of ACL-85*, pages 61–69.

Valentin Jijkoun and Maarten de Rijke. 2005. Recognizing textual entailment using lexical similarity. In *Proc. of the PASCAL RTE Challenge Workshop*.

Dan Klein and Christopher D. Manning. 2003. Accurate unlexicalized parsing. In *Proc. of ACL-03*.

George Lakoff. 1970. Linguistics and natural logic. *Synthese*, 22:151–271.

Roger Levy and Galen Andrew. 2006. Tregex and Tsurgeon: tools for querying and manipulating tree data structures. In *Proc. of LREC-06*.

Bill MacCartney, Trond Grenager, Marie-Catherine de Marneffe, Daniel Cer, and Christopher D. Manning. 2006. Learning to recognize features of valid textual entailments. In *Proc. of HLT-NAACL-06*.

Erwin Marsi and Emiel Krahmer. 2005. Classification of semantic relations by humans and machines. In *Proc. of the ACL 2005 Workshop on Empirical Modeling of Semantic Equivalence and Entailment*.

Lorenza Romano, Milen Kouylekov, Idan Szpektor, Ido Dagan, and Alberto Lavelli. 2006. Investigating a generic paraphrase-based approach for relation extraction. In *Proc. of EACL-06*.

Victor Sánchez Valencia. 1991. *Studies on Natural Logic and Categorial Grammar*. Ph.D. thesis, Univ. of Amsterdam.

Jana Z. Sukkarieh. 2003. An expressive efficient representation: Bridging a gap between NLP and KR. In *Proc. of the 7th Int'l Conf. on Knowledge-Based Intelligent Information and Engineering Systems*.

Johan van Benthem. 1986. *Essays in logical semantics*. Reidel, Dordrecht.

Jan van Eijck. 2005. Natural logic for natural language. *http://homepages.cwi.nl/~jve/papers/05/nlnl/NLNL.pdf*.

Anna Zamansky, Nissim Francez, and Yoad Winter. 2006. A 'natural logic' inference system using the Lambek calculus. *Journal of Logic, Language and Information*, 15:273–295.

[6]Available at *http://yeda.cs.technion.ac.il/~yaroslav/oc/*

Author Index